THE
BOOK OF REVELATION

the Smart Guide to the Bible™ series

BE SMART · BE INSPIRED ·™

Daymond R. Duck
Larry Richards, General Editor

THOMAS NELSON
Since 1798

NASHVILLE   DALLAS   MEXICO CITY   RIO DE JANEIRO   BEIJING

The Book of Revelation
The Smart Guide to the Bible™ Series
Copyright © 2006 by GRQ, Inc.

Published by Nelson Reference, a Division of Thomas Nelson, Inc., P.O. Box 141000, Nashville, Tennessee 37214.

Originally published by Starburst Publishers under the title *Revelation: God's Word for the Biblically-Inept*. Now revised and updated.

Scripture quotations are taken from The New King James Version® (NKJV), copyright © 1979, 1980, 1982, 1992, Thomas Nelson, Inc., Publishers.

To the best of its ability, GRQ, Inc., has strived to find the source of all material. If there has been an oversight, please contact us, and we will make any correction deemed necessary in future printings. We also declare that to the best of our knowledge all material (quoted or not) contained herein is accurate, and we shall not be held liable for the same.

General Editor: Larry Richards
Managing Editor: Lila Empson
Associate Editor: W. Mark Whitlock
Scripture Editor: Deborah Wiseman
Assistant Editor: Amy Clark
Design: Diane Whisner

ISBN 978-1-4185-0990-3
Printed in the United States of America
    11 12   15 14 13 12

Introduction

People could not know God's will for their lives without the Bible. God gave it to the world because he wants everyone to hear, read, and understand it. But those who seek to get acquainted with the heavenly message sometimes find it difficult. Its not always easy to understand the Divine voice. So *The Book of Revelation—The Smart Guide to the Bible*™ has been designed to help you. Our people recognize the authority of God and pray for this book to be a light for your soul.

To Gain Your Confidence

Welcome to *The Book of Revelation—The Smart Guide to the Bible*™. It is the first book in a new series that will take the Bible and make it fun and educational. This is not one of the traditional humdrum, boring Bible studies and commentaries you are used to seeing; its straightforward overview will change your outlook on the Bible.

The Book of Revelation—The Smart Guide to the Bible™ series is for those people who are not interested in all that complicated stuff. You can be sure that I have tried to take an educational approach, but much effort has gone into keeping things simple. The message is sacred, and not one word should be changed. But the message is also glorious and needs to be presented so people can receive all the knowledge and blessings God wants you to have.

Jesus promised a blessing to all those who read, hear, and keep those things written in Revelation. He also promised a curse on all those who add to or take away from it. I take that seriously, so I have undertaken this project with great care. To help explain things in Revelation, I will use the age-old Golden Rule of Interpretation, which states: When the plain sense of Scripture makes common sense, seek no other sense. . . . The Bible explains itself. You do not need to go anywhere else. That is why I have included other verses of Scripture from the Bible to explain difficult areas of Revelation.

Why Study Revelation?

REVELATION 1:1 *The Revelation of Jesus Christ, which God . . . (NKJV)*

Society is living in perilous times. The constant barrage of bad news has many people frightened and wondering about the future. Preachers are saying more prophecy is being fulfilled today than at any other time in history. Today, one out of every four Christian adults believe Jesus could return in their lifetime. Revelation is God's message to all who are concerned about the future. It reveals that the world will get better, but only after it goes through a series of terrible judgments.

Revelation reveals that God is the One who is really in control. It encourages faith and perseverance, warns against making certain mistakes, and tells how to gain eternal life.

Anyone who picks up this book might ask, "Why study Revelation?" Here are eight good reasons:

1. Revelation is the Word of God (the Bible).

2. Jesus told us to watch for signs of things to come.

3. Revelation is about Jesus.

4. Revelation reveals God's plan for the future.

5. A special blessing is promised to all those who read Revelation.

6. Revelation will change our lives.

7. Revelation will give us a concern for those who reject God and his Son, Jesus.

8. If prophecy is being fulfilled, people should want to know the details.

How to Study Revelation

As you study Revelation, keep in mind its three main divisions:

Part One is called **The Church Age** (chapters 1–3). We are now living in the Church Age, and it is almost over.

Part Two is called **From the Rapture to the Second Coming** (chapters 4–19). It will be a terrible time in which to live. Many prophetic signs indicate that it is drawing closer, so we need to learn what to watch for and what to do so it can be avoided.

Part Three is called **The Millennium and Beyond** (chapters 20–22). Some of the most precious verses in the Bible are found in these chapters. They are filled with inspiration and hope for the future.

Also keep in mind the four ways to interpret (explain) Revelation:

1. As a message to each one of us

2. As a message to the entire Church

3. As a message to seven specific churches

4. As a message of prophecy

Who Wrote Revelation?

John, one of the twelve disciples of Jesus, wrote Revelation under the guidance of its true author—the Holy Spirit, the third person of the Trinity. The word *trinity* is not found in the Bible, but it is used to explain the three different ways God reveals himself—as God the Father; his Son, Jesus; and the Holy Spirit. These are three different expressions of God, just as thoughts, spoken words, and written words are three different expressions of every person.

How Did We Get the Revelation We Have Today?

Revelation was originally written in the Greek language around AD 96. By AD 250, the entire Bible had been translated into what is known as Old Latin, but the first officially recognized Latin translation (the Vulgate) did not appear until AD 382. The first officially recognized English translation (the King James Bible) was circulated in AD 1611.

Revelation is the last book in the New Testament. It is divided into 404 verses, of which at least 265 contain quotes drawn from the Old Testament and many quotes from the New Testament. This does not mean one has to be a Bible expert to understand it, but it does mean that John had an excellent understanding of all the other books of the Bible. Therefore, it is good for all of us to have some knowledge of these books.

Symbols, Symbols, and More Symbols

Revelation is filled with symbols. John was in prison when he wrote this book, and some believe he used symbols to smuggle it to the outside world. They seem to believe that he had to convince the prison authorities these were the writings of a madman. Others believe God had John write with symbols to make us study the entire Bible to understand their meanings. Whatever the reason, the symbols make some people believe one needs a Ph.D. to understand Revelation. No one can deny the value of a good education, but people of all educational backgrounds do read it, even people who are not theologians, seminary professors, or pastors. They are just ordinary people who seem to love it and get a lot out of it. They learn about God, Jesus, the Church, and the future. I ask, "If they can do that, why can't everybody?" The answer is, "Everybody can if they want to."

So Many Different Viewpoints

Obviously, with so many symbols there are bound to be many different interpretations. I try, as much as possible, not to take sides and to explain each viewpoint. One of the biggest areas of discrepancy involves when the Church will go to heaven (aka the Rapture). I explain these, but take what is the most widely accepted viewpoint—pre-Tribulation—throughout the book.

Many are tempted to date the events found in Revelation. Don't do it! Many have tried and failed. Believe what the Bible says: "But of that day and hour no one knows, not even the angels of heaven, but My Father only" (Matthew 24:36 NKJV).

About the Author

Daymond is the best-selling author of *On the Brink, An Easy-to-Understand End-Time Bible Prophecy; The Book of Revelation—The Smart Guide to the Bible™* series; *The Book of Daniel—The Smart Guide to the Bible™* series; and *Prophecies of the Bible—The Smart Guide to the Bible™* series. He is the coauthor of *The End-Times Survival Handbook.* And he is a contributing author to *Forewarning—The Approaching Battle Between Good and Evil; Foreshadows of Wrath and Redemption; Piercing the Future—Prophecy and the New Millennium;* and *Prophecy at Ground Zero.*

Daymond worked his way through college and graduated from the University of Tennessee with a B.S. in agricultural engineering. In 1979, at the age of forty, he entered the ministry and became a bi-vocational pastor. He completed the five-year Course-of-Study Program at Emory University for United Methodist Pastors. He has twice served as honorary state chaplain for the Tennessee Rural Carriers, is a prophecy conference speaker, and is a member of the Pre-Trib Study Group in Arlington, Texas. Daymond and his wife, Rachel, make their home in Dyer, Tennessee. They have three children and five grandchildren.

About the General Editor

Dr. Larry Richards is a native of Michigan who now lives in Raleigh, North Carolina. He was converted while in the Navy in the 1950s. Larry has taught and written Sunday school curriculum for every age group, from nursery through adult. He has published more than two hundred books that have been translated into twenty-six languages. His wife, Sue, is also an author. They both enjoy teaching Bible studies as well as fishing and playing golf.

Understanding the Bible Is Easy with These Tools

To understand God's Word you need easy-to-use study tools right where you need them—at your fingertips. The Smart Guide to the Bible™ series puts valuable resources adjacent to the text to save you both time and effort.

Every page features handy sidebars filled with icons and helpful information: cross references for additional insights, definitions of key words and concepts, brief commentaries from experts on the topic, points to ponder, evidence of God at work, the big picture of how passages fit into the context of the entire Bible, practical tips for applying biblical truths to every area of your life, and plenty of maps, charts, and illustrations. A wrap-up of each passage, combined with study questions, concludes each chapter.

These helpful tools show you what to watch for. Look them over to become familiar with them, and then turn to Chapter 1 with complete confidence: You are about to increase your knowledge of God's Word!

Study Helps

The thought-bubble icon alerts you to commentary you might find particularly thought-provoking, challenging, or encouraging. You'll want to take a moment to reflect on it and consider the implications for your life.

Don't miss this point! The exclamation-point icon draws your attention to a key point in the text and emphasizes important biblical truths and facts.

death on the cross
Colossians 1:21–22

Many see Boaz as a type of Jesus Christ. To win back what we human beings lost through sin and spiritual death, Jesus had to become human (i.e., he had to become a true kinsman), and he had to be willing to pay the penalty for our sins. With his <u>death on the cross</u>, Jesus paid the penalty and won freedom and eternal life for us.

The additional Bible verses add scriptural support for the passage you just read and help you better understand the <u>underlined text</u>. (Think of it as an instant reference resource!)

How does what you just read apply to your life? The heart icon indicates that you're about to find out! These practical tips speak to your mind, heart, body, and soul, and offer clear guidelines for living a righteous and joy-filled life, establishing priorities, maintaining healthy relationships, persevering through challenges, and more.

This icon reveals how God is truly all-knowing and all-powerful. The hourglass icon points to a specific example of the prediction of an event or the fulfillment of a prediction. See how some of what God has said would come to pass already has!

What are some of the great things God has done? The traffic-sign icon shows you how God has used miracles, special acts, promises, and covenants throughout history to draw people to him.

Does the story or event you just read about appear elsewhere in the Gospels? The cross icon points you to those instances where the same story appears in other Gospel locations—further proof of the accuracy and truth of Jesus' life, death, and resurrection.

Since God created marriage, there's no better person to turn to for advice. The double-ring icon points out biblical insights and tips for strengthening your marriage.

The Bible is filled with wisdom about raising a godly family and enjoying your spiritual family in Christ. The family icon gives you ideas for building up your home and helping your family grow close and strong.

Isle of Patmos
a small island in the
Mediterranean Sea

something significant had occurred, he wrote down the substance of what he saw. This is the practice John followed when he recorded Revelation on the **Isle of Patmos.**

What does that word really mean, especially as it relates to this passage? Important, misunderstood, or infrequently used words are set in **bold type** in your text so you can immediately glance at the margin for definition. This valuable feature lets you better understand the meaning of the entire passage without having to stop to check other references.

the big picture

Joshua

Led by Joshua, the Israelites crossed the Jordan River and invaded Canaan (see Illustration #8). In a series of military campaigns the Israelites defeated several coalition armies raised by the inhabitants of Canaan. With organized resistance put down, Joshua divided the land among the twelve Israelite

How does what you read fit in with the greater biblical story? The highlighted big picture summarizes the passage under discussion.

what others say

David Breese

Nothing is clearer in the Word of God than the fact that God wants us to understand himself and his working in the lives of men.[5]

It can be helpful to know what others say on the topic, and the highlighted quotation introduces another voice in the discussion. This resource enables you to read other opinions and perspectives.

Maps, charts, and illustrations pictorially represent ancient artifacts and show where and how stories and events took place. They enable you to better understand important empires, learn your way around villages and temples, see where major battles occurred, and follow the journeys of God's people. You'll find these graphics let you do more than study God's Word—they let you *experience* it.

Chapters at a Glance

Part One
The Church Age

Revelation 1

Chapter Highlights:
• Read, Hear, and Keep
• Ruler of All Rulers
• Alpha and Omega
• Seven Lampstands
• Our High Priest
• He Holds the Keys

Let's Get Started

Since we will be studying Revelation, it is important to understand what a revelation is. The word **revelation** comes from the Greek word "*apokalupsis.*" It means "the uncovering, the unveiling, or the disclosing." Revelation is the disclosing of Jesus Christ. It can be taken two ways: as the revealing of the person of Jesus Christ, or as the revealing of what he intends to do starting with the "Church Age" and running through to the end of time.

The Church Age is that period of time that the "Church" is on earth. The Church consists of the followers of Jesus Christ, as opposed to a church that is a building where people meet to worship. The Church Age started fifty days after Jesus was raised from the dead on the Jewish holy day called <u>Pentecost</u> (the Feast of Weeks). It will end when the Church is **raptured**. Just as one week is divided into seven days, the Church Age is divided into seven periods (more on this later in chapter 1).

John, one of Christ's original twelve disciples, was selected by Jesus to record Revelation. Since he knew Jesus personally, John is often called the **apostle** <u>John</u>. He never boasted of that, but simply called himself "a **servant** of Jesus."

Pentecost
Exodus 34:22–23;
Acts 2:1–47

raptured
1 Corinthians 15:52

apostle John
Acts 1:21–26

revelation
an uncovering of
something hidden

raptured
the Church is taken
to heaven at Christ's
return

apostle
someone commis-
sioned by God to
represent Christ

servant
one who follows
Jesus

Don't Jump Ahead!

> **REVELATION 1:1** *The Revelation of Jesus Christ, which God gave Him to show His servants—things which must shortly take place. And He sent and signified it by His angel to His servant John,* (NKJV)

Most people who study Revelation have a tendency to rush to those hot-button topics like the mark of the Beast and the two witnesses that come later. They are skipping parts of the Bible that contain many great truths. Every verse in the Bible is important, and we should want to understand what each one of them has to say.

God gave the message of Revelation to his Son, Jesus. He wanted Jesus to pass it on to his servants, so Jesus gave it to an **angel**. The angel then gave it to John, who gave it to the Church.

God's purpose for giving this message was to let the Church know what was to come in the future. "Must" means it is absolutely certain that these events will take place, and "shortly" means they will begin in the near future. However, remember that God's definition of "shortly" is a lot different from our definition.

Who Wrote Revelation?

REVELATION 1:2 *who bore witness to the word of God, and to the testimony of Jesus Christ, to all things that he saw. (NKJV)*

John wrote it. It was his task to record what he saw, and what he saw was the word of God and the **testimony** of Jesus Christ. The things written in this book are the word of God, and they come from God through his Son, Jesus.

The book of Revelation has been called the Book of Sevens: seven churches, seven spirits, seven seal judgments, seven trumpet judgments, seven bowl judgments, seven thunders, seven blessings, seven "I am" statements of Jesus, and more. People often want to know why so many sevens (fifty-four in all). Many scholars call them evidence of divine inspiration and instruction.

Read, Hear, and Keep

REVELATION 1:3 *Blessed is he who reads and those who hear the words of this **prophecy**, and keep those things which are written in it; for the time is near. (NKJV)*

Revelation is more than a book of doctrine, reproof, correction, and instruction. It is also a book of prophecy. The fulfillment of this prophecy began on the first day of the Church Age (Pentecost). God did not have John write Revelation for it to be ignored. He had John write it to be read, heard (*hear*), and kept (*keep, take to heart*). Yet some people won't read it because they are either uninterested, scared, or find it difficult to understand. All God asks is simply for us to read Revelation.

The word "hear" could simply mean to listen to someone else read Revelation. But it probably means to recognize that Revelation is the word of God and needs to be **heard with one's heart**. The word "keep" requires obedient action to do what the Bible says. God promised a blessing to those who read, hear, and keep the Word of God. This means he will help us understand it.

Grace and Peace

> REVELATION 1:4 *John, to the seven churches which are in Asia: Grace to you and peace from Him who is and who was and who is to come, and from the seven Spirits who are before His throne, (NKJV)*

Revelation is for all believers, but here at the beginning is a section specifically addressed to seven particular churches. The greeting is "grace" and "peace," the common need of all people. Without the **grace of God**, we would perish. Without the **peace of God**, we would be unsure of our <u>salvation</u>. The source of grace and peace is the eternal God; the God who is, who was, and who is to come.

In addition to the peace of God, the Bible talks about peace between people and peace between nations. The world doesn't have to have wars, a tribulation period, and things like that. It can have peace between people and nations by accepting Jesus.

The Holy Spirit occupies a place before the **throne of God**. He has a <u>sevenfold nature</u>. This nature is made up of seven virtues, which are called the seven spirits.

The Sevenfold Nature of the Holy Spirit

The Seven Spirits	The Spirits Defined
The Spirit of the Lord	The nature of Jesus
The Spirit of wisdom	The ability to make the right decisions
The Spirit of understanding	The ability to understand everything
The Spirit of counsel	The ability to give sound advice
The Spirit of might	The power to do what God wants
The Spirit of knowledge	The ability to know beyond human comprehension
The Spirit of the fear of the Lord	The ability to respect God's will

go to

salvation
John 3:16;
Romans 10:9

sevenfold nature
Isaiah 11:2

heard with one's heart
freely believed and acted on

grace of God
the undeserved, saving work of God in the hearts of people

peace of God
the harmony God gives to our heart because of his grace

salvation
forgiveness and cleansing

throne of God
the place where God sits in heaven

Ruler of All Rulers

go to

kingdom there would
be no end
Luke 1:29–33

Word Made Flesh
the Word (Jesus) was
born in the flesh

sins
thoughts, acts, and
omissions contrary
to God's will

crucifixion
execution on a cross

REVELATION 1:5 *and from Jesus Christ, the faithful witness, the firstborn from the dead, and the ruler over the kings of the earth. To Him who loved us and washed us from our sins in His own blood,* (NKJV)

God intends to establish his kingdom here on earth, and Jesus is the chosen One who will rule over that kingdom. Even at his birth, an angel visited his mother, the virgin Mary, and told her she would have a son who would sit on a throne and of whose <u>kingdom there would be no end</u>. The promise that God would send his Son, Jesus, the first time to die on a cross was literally fulfilled. Therefore, many believe the promise that God will send his Son, Jesus, a second time to rule over all things will also be literally fulfilled.

Jesus is called

1. *The Faithful Witness*—Jesus was faithful in all the things God gave him to do. He was the **Word Made Flesh**. A faithful example of the very nature of the living God (Jesus).

2. *The Firstborn from the Dead*—Jesus was the first to die and be raised from the dead. He never died again. Others have been raised from the dead, but they eventually died again.

3. *The Ruler over the Kings of the Earth*—This is his position in the world. World rulers do not yet realize that Jesus is in charge, but he is. The day will come when he will physically reign over every power on earth.

We are also told that Jesus loves us. He loves us with an everlasting love; a love that never fails. And the proof of his love is in the fact that he removes our **sins** through the shedding of his own blood—his **crucifixion**.

> **what others say**
>
> **David Breese**
>
> We should never forget that we are what we are, and we are participants in the grand scenario of history, because Jesus Christ in his own blood has given forgiveness and cleansing.[1]

We Are Subjects?

REVELATION 1:6 *and has made us kings and priests to His God and Father, to Him be glory and dominion forever and ever. Amen. (NKJV)*

Jesus has made us a kingdom of priests, a <u>royal priesthood</u>. This is what he has done for us. Here is what we can do for him: We can give him **glory and dominion** throughout all eternity. Jesus is our King, and we are subjects in his kingdom. Because he has exalted us, we will **exalt** him.

Focus on This!

REVELATION 1:7 *Behold, He is coming with clouds, and every eye will see Him, even they who pierced Him. And all the tribes of the earth will mourn because of Him. Even so, Amen. (NKJV)*

<u>Jesus went away in the clouds</u>, and he is <u>coming back in the clouds</u>. The second coming of Jesus will not be a secret. Even those who rejected and crucified him will see him. Everyone will know who he is, and those who rejected him will mourn because they were so blind to the truth. Every generation would be wise to heed the clear teaching that Jesus is coming back.

Q. Why will the unbelievers mourn?

A. Because they rejected him.

The Beginning and the End

REVELATION 1:8 *"I am the **Alpha** and the **Omega**, the Beginning and the End," says the Lord, "who is and who was and who is to come, the Almighty." (NKJV)*

Jesus says he is the Alpha and the Omega, the Beginning and the End. He is everything that can be said about God from start to finish, from *A* to *Z*. He is the Creator of all things, and he will be the final judge of all things. He is the Lord of all.

In verse 4 of this chapter we noted that Jesus is the eternally existing God; the God who is, who was, and who is to come. In verse 8 he calls himself the same thing. He is equal to the almighty God, who has power over all things.

go to

royal priesthood
1 Peter 2:9

Jesus went away in the clouds
Acts 1:9

coming back in the clouds
Matthew 24:30

glory and dominion
honor Jesus and recognize his authority

exalt
honor Jesus

Alpha
the first letter of the Greek alphabet

Omega
the last letter of the Greek alphabet

something to ponder

Jesus Is the Eternal God

Who	When
Jesus is	The God of the present
Jesus was	The God of the past
Jesus is to come	The God of the future

go to

persecution
2 Timothy 3:12

Christian
a believer in Jesus
Christ

witness
what Jesus said
and did

winning crowns
rewards for doing
his will

what others say

Todd Strandberg and Terry James

Revelation, the book in the Bible that most specifically presents prophecies covering the future, is another word for "apocalypse" or "unveiling." So the Tribulation or Apocalypse is the revealing or unveiling of something. Actually it is the revealing of Jesus Christ in His full glory, majesty, and power when He returns to put an end to Armageddon.[2]

My Spiritual Brother

REVELATION 1:9 *I, John, both your brother and companion in the tribulation and kingdom and patience of Jesus Christ, was on the island that is called Patmos for the word of God and for the testimony of Jesus Christ. (NKJV)*

In verse 8, Jesus introduced himself. Now, John introduces himself. He is the **Christian**'s spiritual brother, a brother in Christ. He is also the Christian's companion, a companion in suffering for Christ's sake. All Christians are members of God's spiritual kingdom (the Church), a kingdom that teaches and requires patience.

John was on the Isle of Patmos, a small island in the Mediterranean Sea (see Illustration #1), where he was imprisoned by the Roman Emperor Domitian. That explains his suffering. What was his crime? Two things: (1) he would not deny the truth of the Bible, and (2) he would not deny the **witness** of Jesus Christ. John would rather be cast in prison and killed than reject Christ.

Becoming a servant of God will not keep a Christian out of trouble. We are not going to slide through life without problems. We are in the process of **winning crowns**. However, there are crosses to bear (persecution) before we receive them.

Why Should I Worship on Sunday?

REVELATION 1:10 *I was in the Spirit on the Lord's Day, and I heard behind me a loud voice, as of a trumpet,* (NKJV)

By the time John was in prison, Christians had adopted the practice of worshiping on Sunday. There are two reasons for this: (1) Jesus arose on Sunday, and (2) Pentecost falls on Sunday.

It was Sunday, the Lord's Day, and John was most likely praying when the Holy Spirit began to **take control of him**. While under the Holy Spirit's influence, John heard an unusual voice—a voice that sounded like a trumpet.

Christians will hear the <u>trumpet</u> of God when they are raised from the dead. And John heard a voice like a trumpet when he was called up into heaven. Also notice that even though John was in prison on a faraway island, Jesus still knew where he was.

Jesus Picked Seven

REVELATION 1:11 *saying, "I am the Alpha and the Omega, the First and the Last," and, "What you see, write in a book and send it to the seven churches which are in Asia: to Ephesus, to Smyrna, to Pergamos, to Thyatira, to Sardis, to Philadelphia, and to Laodicea."* (NKJV)

The voice told John to write in a book what he was about to see. That book is Revelation. By this time in history, there were probably thousands of churches in the world. Out of all of those churches, Jesus picked seven. He even identified them in a precise order.

Looking back on history, we now realize why Jesus picked these seven particular churches, and why he listed them in that order. Their good and bad qualities and the problems they faced are ideal for instructing all of God's people, and those same qualities and problems have turned out to be prophecies revealing the future history of the Church.

This fits what Jesus said when he called the Book of Revelation words of <u>prophecy</u>. In addition to other things, the seven letters to the seven churches are a prophetic outline of Church history. They reveal phases of stages in the life of the Church.

go to

persecution
2 Timothy 3:12

trumpet
1 Thessalonians 4:16;
Revelation 4:1

prophecy
Revelation 1:3; 20:7,
10, 18–19

take control of him
to have power over
him

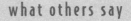

go to

high priest
Leviticus 8:7–9

Melchizedek
Hebrews 7:17–27

lampstands
stands made to hold
pots of burning oil

high priest
the spiritual head of
Old Testament Israel

**order of
Melchizedek**
the ultimate royal
priesthood

intercede
work or pray on our
behalf

Seven Golden Lampstands

REVELATION 1:12 *Then I turned to see the voice that spoke with me. And having turned I saw seven golden lampstands,* (NKJV)

Upon hearing the voice, John turned around to see the speaker, but the first thing he saw was seven golden **lampstands**. In verse 20, we will learn that these seven golden lampstands represent the seven churches. These seven churches represent seven different periods of the Church Age.

Our Great High Priest

REVELATION 1:13 *and in the midst of the seven lampstands One like the Son of Man, clothed with a garment down to the feet and girded about the chest with a golden band.* (NKJV)

Next, John saw where the voice came from. Someone who looked like the Son of Man was standing in the middle of the seven churches. He was wearing a long robe that went down to his feet with a golden sash around his chest.

What is the significance of this? Why this vision of Jesus standing in the middle of these seven churches dressed in the official attire of the **high priest**? Jesus said, "For where two or three are gathered together in My name, I am there in the midst of them" (Matthew 18:20 NKJV). This vision means that Jesus will stand in the midst of the Church throughout the Church Age. He is the Great High Priest who is always with his Church; a priest after the **order of Melchizedek**; a priest who is always able to **intercede** for us.

During the Millennium, the Jewish priests will serve Jesus and be subordinate to him. The priests will be after the order of Aaron, but Jesus will be after the order of Melchizedek. Jesus is from a superior priesthood.

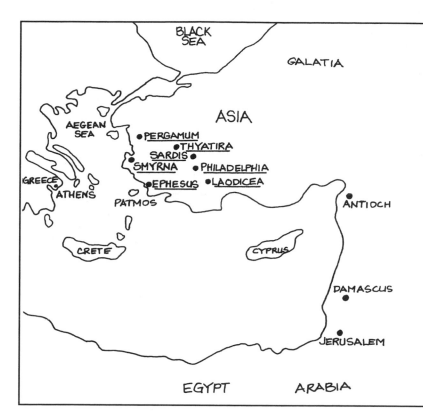

Illustration #1
The locations of the seven churches, which also represent the seven periods of the Church Age.

go to

his hair is like the hair of God
Daniel 7:9

Ancient of Days
a name for God

Hair As White As Snow

REVELATION 1:14 *His head and hair were white like wool, as white as snow, and His eyes like a flame of fire; (NKJV)*

When Jesus was crucified, his hair was probably a mess, so that the crown of thorns forced down on his head most likely created blood clots in his hair. Now <u>his hair is like the hair of God</u> in Daniel's vision of the **Ancient of Days**. It shines with the pure white brightness of heaven.

Illustration #2
The high priest of Israel dressed in official royal attire. The twelve stones in the breastplate represent the twelve tribes of Israel.

hooves of bronze
Micah 4:13

creation
Genesis 1:1–31

Rapture
Revelation 4:1–2

authority over all creation
Psalm 33:6–9

seven stars
Revelation 1:20

judge
determines our destiny and rewards

While out in the wilderness, Moses told the Hebrews, "The LORD your God is a consuming fire, a jealous God" (Deuteronomy 4:24 NKJV). The eyes of Jesus were burning like a blazing fire as he looked over the seven churches. Nothing escaped his penetrating gaze. He could see every good deed and every bad deed for generations to come.

Rise Up and Crush Your Enemies

REVELATION 1:15 *His feet were like fine brass, as if refined in a furnace, and His voice as the sound of many waters; (NKJV)*

In the Old Testament, God told the Hebrews to rise up and crush their enemies with <u>hooves of bronze</u>. This is a reminder that he will judge everyone. "We must all appear before the judgment seat of Christ" (2 Corinthians 5:10 NKJV).

His voice roared like the mighty waves of the ocean. It was the voice of the One who spoke everything into existence (<u>creation</u>), the voice of the One who will raise the dead (the <u>Rapture</u>), the powerful voice of the One who has <u>authority over all creation</u>.

- Jesus is our GOD (Revelation 1:8).
- He is our great HIGH PRIEST (Revelation 1:13).
- He is our **JUDGE** (Revelation 1:15).

what others say

Hal Lindsey

John was put in a kind of divine time machine, shot up to the twentieth (twenty-first) century and then brought back to the first century and told to write about what he had seen. He had to use phenomenal language to describe what he saw.[4]

Sharper Than Any Two-Edged Sword

REVELATION 1:16 *He had in His right hand seven stars, out of His mouth went a sharp two-edged sword, and His countenance was like the sun shining in its strength. (NKJV)*

Jesus tells us the <u>seven stars</u> are the seven angels of the seven churches. Whether these angels are divinely appointed spiritual leaders of the churches is much debated. Whatever they are, it is their responsibility to look after the churches. The fact that they are in the right hand of Jesus means they are his own precious, personal possession.

Scripture tells us the sharp two-edged sword represents the Bible. We read, "For the word of God is living and powerful, and sharper than any two-edged sword, piercing even to the division of soul and spirit, and of joints and marrow, and is a discerner of the thoughts and intents of the heart" (Hebrews 4:12 NKJV). Jesus will deal with his Church through his Word. The Bible is a very efficient sword, a sword that stabs and cuts both ways. We would be wise to heed what the Bible has to say. He will judge us by its standards.

The Shekinah Glory

Jesus is also known as the Sun of Righteousness and the Light of the World. Let there be no doubt, that when John looked upon Christ's face, he was seeing the **"shekinah glory."**

Nothing Before or After

REVELATION 1:17 *And when I saw Him, I fell at His feet as dead. But He laid His right hand on me, saying to me, "Do not be afraid; I am the First and the Last.* (NKJV)

What would you do if you met Jesus face-to-face? John collapsed. But Jesus did not leave him lying there. He placed his right hand upon him and said, "Do not be afraid; I am the First and the Last." There were none before Jesus, and there will be none after. Nothing came before him, and nothing will come after. There never was a time when he did not exist, and there never will be a time when he does not exist. He is from <u>everlasting to everlasting</u>.

everlasting to everlasting
Psalm 41:13

shekinah glory
glory brighter than
the noonday sun

what others say

David Breese

We are going to stand in the presence of one who occupies a throne, from which the heavens and the earth flee away, and we will see Jesus Christ, not now simply as the Person of Galilee in the old days, but as the God who presides over history.[5]

go to

rising from the dead
Acts 2:31–36

past tense—I was on
Revelation 1:9

past tense—I was in
Revelation 1:10

past tense—I turned
Revelation 1:12

past tense—I saw
Revelation 1:17

Hades
the place of the
dead (hell)

resurrection
refers to the dead
coming back to life

He Holds the Keys

REVELATION 1:18 *I am He who lives, and was dead, and behold, I am alive forevermore. Amen. And I have the keys of* **Hades** *and of Death.* (NKJV)

Jesus said about himself:

1. I am the living One.

2. I was dead.

3. I am alive forever and ever.

He has risen from the dead and will never die again. His crucifixion will not be repeated. He holds the keys, so he is in total control of death and hell. He conquered both by rising from the dead (**resurrection**) so John and any other Christian need not fear death or hell. He can raise us from the dead. He can deliver us from hell. Why are people so afraid of Revelation when it is such a book of comfort? After all, Jesus has removed the sting of death and hell for those who follow him.

Keys in the Book of Revelation

Key	Scripture
The keys of Hades and of Death	Revelation 1:18
The key of David	Revelation 3:7
The key to the bottomless pit	Revelation 9:1; 20:1

Past, Present, and Future

REVELATION 1:19 *Write the things which you have seen, and the things which are, and the things which will take place after this.* (NKJV)

What John had seen was not for his own personal knowledge. Jesus wanted it written down for all of God's people. What you have seen (chapter 1) refers to the events we have covered so far in this chapter. Notice that several of chapter 1's verses are written in the past tense. What is now (chapters 2–3) refers to the events of the present Church Age. They describe seven churches which actually existed when John had this vision, but they were selected for this revelation because they reveal aspects of the seven periods of the Church Age. What will take place later (chapters 4–22) refers to future events that will take place after the Church Age is over. They reveal what will happen during the **Tribulation Period** plus what will happen during the **Millennium** and beyond. That is why this book is divided into three sections: (1) the Church Age, (2) the period from the Rapture to the Second Coming, and (3) the Millennium and beyond (see Time Lines #1, #2, #3 in Appendix A).

It is wrong to divide the Bible by shifting events from one time period to another.

The events in Revelation must be kept in their proper time periods. John's vision in chapter 1 is of past events. They will not be repeated. The events in chapters 2–3 are present events. They do not have anything to do with future events found in chapters 4–22. The stage is now being set for these future events, but they will not be fulfilled until after the Church Age is over.

The Bible Interprets Itself

> REVELATION 1:20 *The mystery of the seven stars which you saw in My right hand, and the seven golden lampstands: The seven stars are the angels of the seven churches, and the seven lampstands which you saw are the seven churches."* (NKJV)

To avoid any misunderstanding, God often uses the Bible to interpret itself. Jesus clearly identified the seven stars in his right hand as the angels of the seven churches. Again, whether they are literal angels or great spiritual leaders is debatable, but they clearly have authority over their respective churches. The seven lampstands signify the seven churches. They also foretell the history of the Church from Pentecost to the Rapture.

A mystery is a hidden truth that has not been made known before. Until it is revealed, it is meaningless to the reader. Once it is revealed, it ceases to be a mystery and becomes a revelation.

Tribulation Period
seven years of God's wrath

Millennium
thousand-year reign of Christ on earth

Chapter Wrap-Up

- God promised a blessing to those who read, hear, and keep the Word of God. (Revelation 1:3)
- Christ is the Ruler of all rulers, and the day will come when he will reign over all the nations of the earth. (Revelation 1:5)
- Jesus is the Alpha and the Omega. He is everything from the beginning to the end. (Revelation 1:8)
- The seven lampstands symbolize seven churches and seven church periods. Each church represents one of the seven periods of the Church Age. (Revelation 1:12, 20)
- Jesus is the Great High Priest of the Church. He works on our behalf to reconcile our relationship with God that has been damaged by sin. (Revelation 1:13)
- Jesus holds the keys to death and hell since he conquered both through his death and resurrection. (Revelation 1:18)

Study Questions

1. How did Jesus make his message known to John?

2. Should we be afraid of Revelation?

3. Who will see Jesus when he returns?

4. What is the relevance of the seven churches today?

5. What is the importance of the high priest?

Chapter Highlights:
- Four Church Letters
- The Second Death
- Fire and Bronze
- Jezebel
- The Bright and Morning Star

Revelation 2

Let's Get Started

Now we are about to embark on the study of seven remarkable letters to seven specifically selected churches. In one sense, they are as ancient as the apostle John, but in another, they are as modern as today's computers. We could read them as personal messages to people who lived almost two thousand years ago, but we would be more correct to read them as personal messages to those living today. They were inspired by the Holy Spirit, and their message is of the utmost importance. We should keep in mind that these seven churches represent seven time periods giving us a panoramic view of church history running from Pentecost to the Rapture.

The Church Age

Author	Ephesus Period	Smyrna Period	Pergamos Period	Thyatira Period	Sardis Period	Philadelphia Period	Laodicea Period
Tim LaHaye[1]	AD 30 to AD 100	AD 100 to AD 312	AD 312 to AD 606	AD 606 to Trib. Per.	AD 1520 to Trib. Per.	AD 1750 to Trib. Per.	AD 1900 to Trib. Per.
Hal Lindsey[2]	AD 33 to AD 100	AD 100 to AD 312	AD 312 to AD 590	AD 590 to AD 1517	AD 1517 to AD 1750	AD 1750 to AD 1925	AD 1900 to Trib. Per.
J. Vernon McGee[3]	AD Pentecost to AD 100	AD 100 to AD 314	AD 314 to AD 590	AD 590 to AD 1000	AD 1517 to AD 1800	AD 1800 to Rapture	Does not say
Daymond R. Duck	AD Pentecost to AD 100	AD 100 to AD 312	AD 312 to AD 590	AD 590 to AD 1517	AD 1517 to AD 1750	AD 1750 to AD 1900	AD 1900 to Trib. Midpoint

I Will Never Leave You

REVELATION 2:1 "To the angel of the church of Ephesus write, 'These things says He who holds the seven stars in His right hand, who walks in the midst of the seven golden lampstands: (NKJV)

seven stars
Revelation 1:16, 20

seven golden lampstands
Revelation 1:12–13, 20

As we just saw in Chapter 1, the <u>seven stars</u> represent seven angels, and the <u>seven golden lampstands</u> represent seven churches. Since we are following the Golden Rule of Interpretation, we will say this letter was directed to the angel over the church in Ephesus, the same angel who presides over the Ephesus period of the Church Age.

Jesus told John to write this letter, and it is Jesus who holds the seven angels in his right hand and walks in the midst of the seven churches. Jesus is the One who controls the angels and the One who will never leave or abandon his Church. He is obviously a person of great power and love who has a message for the church in Ephesus and the Ephesus period of the Church Age.

what others say

David Breese

I would like, therefore, to suggest that the Bible may be telling us that your church, my church, has an angel.[4]

The Revelation of Jesus Christ

Past	Present		Future		
Chapter 1	Chapters 2–3 **Pentecost**	Chapters 4–6 **Rapture**	Chapters 7–19 **Tribulation Period**	Chapter 20 **Second Coming**	Chapters 21–22 **Satan Loosed**
	1. Ephesus Period 2. Smyrna Period 3. Pergamos Period 4. Thyatira period 5. Sardis Period 6. Philadelphia Period 7. Laodicea Period				
	7 Letters to 7 Churches	Church in Heaven			
	Church Age	Rise of Antichrist	Tribulation Period	Millennium	Ages to Come

The Eyes of God Are Everywhere

go to

eyes
Proverbs 15:3

REVELATION 2:2–3 *"I know your works, your labor, your patience, and that you cannot bear those who are evil. And you have tested those who say they are apostles and are not, and have found them liars; and you have persevered and have patience, and have labored for My name's sake and have not become weary. (NKJV)*

The penetrating <u>eyes</u> of Jesus are everywhere, beholding the evil and the good. He knows everything we do. He knew that the Ephesus church toiled with great difficulty, and he recognized their perseverance under trial. This church refused to tolerate evil men in their congregation who falsely claimed to have known and seen Jesus. These evil men were put on trial and found guilty of lying. If people are teaching or preaching false doctrines in the church, instead of leaving the church, the faithful should try to convert or replace them.

Jesus noted how the Ephesus church remained faithful, even though it was surrounded by immorality and pagan beliefs. This church stood firm against religious deception in the name of Jesus.

> **what others say**
>
> **Jack Van Impe**
>
> Major Christian denominations have been captured by those who reject the essential truth of the Bible, and the deity of Jesus Christ.[5]

Why are these problems important to the church?

1. So we can learn from them.

2. So we will not repeat them.

3. So we will be encouraged to work hard, remain faithful, and oppose evil.

Backsliders

REVELATION 2:4–5 *Nevertheless I have this against you, that you have left your first love. Remember therefore from where*

go to

loves the person,
but hates the sin
Amos 5:15;
John 15:12

backsliding
slipping back into sin

first love
original commitment
to Christ

in the flesh
with the human body

the spirit
the immaterial part
of man; the soul

false doctrines
beliefs contrary to
God's teachings

false practices
dishonest or
deceptive practices

you have fallen; repent and do the first works, or else I will come to you quickly and remove your lampstand from its place—unless you repent. (NKJV)

In spite of all the good things about the church in Ephesus, there was a problem. There was a decline in the people's relationship with Jesus because they had stopped loving him the way they once did.

Jesus asked them to recall the relationship they once had with him, to take inventory of their lives, and to turn from the things of the world and back to him. If they did not, he warned, they would lose their right to exist as a church. They must stop **backsliding** or they would die out. The choice was theirs.

Many mistakenly believe the early Christians of the Ephesus church period got on a spiritual mountaintop and stayed there. When the period began, the people's highest priority was Jesus. As time went on, they started backsliding. By the end of the period, they needed to get back to their **first love**. Believers should always be aware of the danger of drifting away from Jesus. Try to find more time for prayer and study, and do not slack off on your church attendance and service.

Love the Person, but Hate the Sin

REVELATION 2:6 *But this you have, that you hate the deeds of the Nicolaitans, which I also hate. (NKJV)*

Exactly who the Nicolaitans were, and what they did, is anyone's guess. Some say they were a cult that tried to create a ruling class of priests in the Ephesus church. Others say they taught that Christians could sin because what is done **in the flesh** does not affect **the spirit**. Still others say they taught that Christians needed to indulge in sin to understand it. Whoever they were, and whatever they did, the church in Ephesus hated it. And so did Jesus.

During the Ephesus period, many groups tried to introduce **false doctrines** and **false practices** into the Church. What they were doing was repulsive to Christians, and, more important, it was repulsive to Jesus.

Jesus didn't say he hated the Nicolaitans, but he did say he hated what they were doing. This is a classic example of New Testament teaching—Jesus <u>loves the person, but hates the sin</u>.

overcome
1 John 5:4

Garden of Eden
Genesis 3:3–22

> ## what others say
>
> **Ron Carlson and Ed Decker**
>
> Over the past 150 years the classical definition of a cult has referred to this first category as the pseudo-Christian cults. These are religious organizations or movements that claim to be Christian and claim to believe in the Bible. But instead of building their theology and teaching on God's Word, the Bible, they claim some "new revelation" or man-made teaching as superior to the Bible.[6]

overcome
overcoming sin through faith in Jesus

paradise
the heavenly abode

1. Sin is the transgression of the Law; breaking God's rules (1 John 3:4).

2. Sin is knowing to do good but not doing it (James 4:17).

3. Sin is anything that is not of faith; not trusting in God (Romans 14:23).

4. Sin is all unrighteousness; wickedness (1 John 5:17).

5. Sin is a disease of the soul; the inner part of man that lives forever (Psalm 41:4).

6. Sin is foolishly thinking we can ignore God (Proverbs 24:9).

Overcomers

> REVELATION 2:7 *He who has an ear, let him hear what the Spirit says to the churches. To him who overcomes I will give to eat from the tree of life, which is in the midst of the Paradise of God."' (NKJV)*

Although this letter was specifically addressed to the church in Ephesus, the last line is addressed to anyone who will listen. He has a blessing for those who **overcome**. After Adam and Eve sinned in the Garden of Eden, they were forbidden to eat the fruit of the tree of life. Apparently there was something on that tree that could cause a person who ate it to live forever. It amounted to a permanent cure for death. Jesus promises to give overcomers the opportunity to eat from that tree. It was located in the Garden of Eden, but now is located in **paradise**.

What does a backsliding church need to know? That Jesus walks in our midst, sees our sin, and knows that we have backslid.

Three steps to overcoming sin

apply it

1. Remember the height from which you have fallen (your first love).

2. Repent of your backsliding or falling away.

3. Restore the good deeds you did at first.

go to

the First and the Last
Revelation 1:8

nailed him to a cross
Matthew 27:35

rose from the dead
John 20:15–18

Great Persecution

REVELATION 2:8 *"And to the angel of the church in Smyrna write, 'These things says the First and the Last, who was dead, and came to life: (NKJV)*

The church in Smyrna was experiencing great persecution, so Jesus reminded them that he is <u>the First and the Last</u>, the Alpha and Omega. He is the One who created all things, and the One who will end all things.

Just like this church, Jesus was also persecuted. His enemies falsely accused him, beat him, spit on him, ripped out his beard, crowned him with thorns, and <u>nailed him to a cross</u>, where he died.

If the Antichrist or False Prophet kills you for refusing to take the Mark of the Beast, or if enemies or terrorists kill you, Jesus will raise you from the dead. Remain faithful. Don't be afraid.

What does a persecuted church need to know?

That Jesus always existed, that Jesus never ceased to exist, that Jesus died, that Jesus triumphed when he <u>rose from the dead</u>.

Laying Up Your Treasures in Heaven

REVELATION 2:9 *"I know your works, tribulation, and poverty (but you are rich); and I know the blasphemy of those who say they are Jews and are not, but are a synagogue of Satan. (NKJV)*

key point

We can be either rich in the temporary things of this world or rich in the permanent things of heaven—we can't have both.

Jesus knows what his Church is facing. He knows every prayer, every hymn, every gift, every Sunday school lesson, every sermon, every visit, every good thing, and every bad thing. He knew about the poverty of the Christians in Smyrna. He knew they were serving under the most difficult of circumstances. Their property was being seized and many had no source of personal income. Those of us who live today often think of poverty in terms of not having enough money to live comfortably. In a real sense, poverty is not having an acceptable relationship with God. In that sense, these Christians were rich. They were children of God and were destined for heaven. They were <u>laying up their treasures in heaven</u>. We can be rich in the temporary things of this world and poor in the permanent things of heaven, or we can be poor in the temporary things of this world and rich in the permanent things of heaven.

Jesus also knew about a group in Smyrna who falsely called themselves Jews. They even called their place of worship a **synagogue**, inferring that it was the synagogue of the Lord. But Jesus called it the synagogue of Satan. Even today some religious pretenders call themselves members of God's Church, but Jesus knows they really are members of Satan's church. It does not matter what we call ourselves because Jesus knows <u>his sheep</u>.

Today, there are Satan worshipers who call themselves the Church of Satan, Kabala cults who mix Bible teachings with gnosticism and numerology, New Agers who worship many gods and goddesses, Wiccans who are involved with the occult, and this is just the tip of the iceberg. It's sad that people try to bring these things into the Church, but people straying from sound doctrine will grow worse and worse as the end of the age approaches.

Do Not Be Afraid

> **REVELATION 2:10** *Do not fear any of those things which you are about to suffer. Indeed, the devil is about to throw some of you into prison, that you may be tested, and you will have tribulation ten days. Be faithful until death, and I will give you the crown of life. (NKJV)*

Jesus knew that Satan intended to attack these Christians, so he had a word of encouragement for them: "Do not fear those who kill the body but cannot kill the soul. But rather fear Him who is able to destroy both soul and body in hell" (Matthew 10:28 NKJV).

In a sense, there is <u>no real power</u> except that which comes from God. Satan may <u>test us</u>, but only because God allows it in order that we may be strengthened.

laying up their treasures in heaven
Matthew 6:19–21

his sheep
John 10:14

no real power
Romans 13:1

test us
Job 1–42

synagogue
a place where Jewish people worship

crown of life
a crown symbolizing
eternal life

stood fast
did not waver

Jesus told his people they would be persecuted for ten days. Exactly what these ten days mean is not certain, but history reveals that there were ten distinct periods of intense persecution during the Smyrna period. During this time, Satan let loose all the forces of hell in an effort to stamp out the fledgling Church. Christians were beaten, jailed, tortured, and killed, yet Jesus urged faithfulness. He even promised a **crown of life** to those who **stood fast**. Many did, even unto death.

Heavenly crowns for overcomers:

1. The Imperishable Crown (1 Corinthians 9:24–27).

2. The Crown of Rejoicing (1 Thessalonians 2:19–20).

3. The Crown of Life (James 1:12; Revelation 2:10).

4. The Crown of Righteousness (2 Timothy 4:8).

5. The Crown of Glory (1 Peter 5:2–4).

Ten periods of persecution known by their Roman emperors (dates are approximate):

1. *Nero (AD 64–68)*—burned Rome and blamed Christians; crucified and threw Christians into pits with wild animals; executed Paul and possibly Peter

2. *Domitian (AD 90–96)*—killed thousands in Rome; banished John to the Isle of Patmos

3. *Trajan (AD 104–117)*—outlawed Christianity; burned Ignatius at the stake

4. *Marcus Aurelius (AD 161–180)*—tortured and beheaded Christians

5. *Severus (AD 200–211)*—burned, crucified, and beheaded Christians

6. *Maximinius (AD 235–237)*—executed Christians

7. *Decius (AD 250–253)*—tried to wipe out Christianity and executed those he could find

8. *Valerian (AD 257–260)*—tried to wipe out Christianity; executed the Bishop of Carthage

9. *Aurelian (AD 270–275)*—persecuted Christians any way he could

10. *Diocletian (AD 303–312)*—burned the Scriptures

go to

second death
Revelation 20:14

lake of fire
Revelation 20:14–15

born twice
John 3:3

A Second Death?

REVELATION 2:11 *He who has an ear, let him hear what the Spirit says to the churches. He who overcomes shall not be hurt by the second death." (NKJV)*

Once again Jesus turns from addressing a specific church to addressing anyone who will listen. No other church or individual can do our listening for us.

We have already noted we can be overcomers by our faith in Jesus Christ. Now we learn that faith in Jesus is also rewarded with victory over the <u>second death</u>. The Bible teaches that there are two deaths: a first death and a second death. The first death is physical. The second death is spiritual. But do not think of death as the end of things. Think of it as a separation. The first death is a separation of the soul and spirit from the body. The second death is a separation of the soul and spirit from God. A person would be better off having physical death be the end of things than to die this second death—being cast into the <u>lake of fire</u> forever and having eternal separation from God.

The Bible also teaches that there are two births. The first is physical, and the second is spiritual, which is known as being born again. Birth is being "joined to," and death is being "separated from." When a person is born physically, that person's body is joined to a soul and spirit. When a person is born again, that person's soul and spirit are joined to God. Christians sometimes call this second birth "receiving Jesus" or "receiving the Holy Spirit."

If we are born just once, we will die twice, but if we are **born twice**, we will die just once.

born twice
born physically (first time) and spiritually (second time); the second time is also known as being born again

go to

two-edged sword
Revelation 1:16

heathen
an unsaved person

idolatry
worshiping false
gods

martyr
one who dies for
his beliefs

Compromise

REVELATION 2:12 *"And to the angel of the church in Pergamos write, 'These things says He who has the sharp two-edged sword:* (NKJV)

Compromise was the big problem for those under this angel's authority. It was caused by a merging of church and state. The church in Pergamos allied itself with the world.

Jesus identified himself as the One who has the sharp <u>two-edged sword</u>. We know from the last chapter that the sharp two-edged sword is the Word of God. Jesus reminds this church that he will deal with it through the Bible. It is a book that can create or destroy, heal or afflict, soothe or trouble. And it is always successful.

What does a compromising church need to know?

That Jesus wields a sword called the Word of God. Please be fore-warned!

Don't Back Off

REVELATION 2:13 *"I know your works, and where you dwell, where Satan's throne is. And you hold fast to My name, and did not deny My faith even in the days in which Antipas was My faithful martyr, who was killed among you, where Satan dwells.* (NKJV)

Jesus knows where his Church is. This particular church was located in a city run by **heathen** intellectuals—a city given over to **idolatry** and the temple worship of Athena, Caesar Augustus, Dionysus, Asklepios, Hadrian, and Zeus. Satan had a large power base there, and his rulers of darkness were a major force to be reckoned with.

Satan's power was strong, but the power of the Holy Spirit was stronger. These Christians refused to surrender. They didn't back off, and greater words could not be spoken of anyone than were spoken of Antipas. He was a "faithful **martyr**."

what others say

Ed Hindson

The ultimate crisis in education is spiritual and philosophical. Public universities sold their souls to secularism early in this century and have survived to reap the consequences. The void of spiritual values has led to the great ethical crises of our times. People just don't care what is right or wrong anymore. All they care about is themselves.[7]

Balaam

REVELATION 2:14–15 *But I have a few things against you, because you have there those who hold the doctrine of Balaam, who taught Balak to put a stumbling block before the children of Israel, to eat things sacrificed to idols, and to commit sexual immorality. Thus you also have those who hold the doctrine of the Nicolaitans, which thing I hate. (NKJV)*

Satan's vicious attack from outside the church was failing, but he had a growing danger brewing inside the church. Within its walls were two groups of people who called themselves Christians but did not measure up. Both groups were very liberal on their view of what sin is. One espoused the teachings of Balaam. The other espoused the teachings of the Nicolaitans.

To properly understand the teachings of Balaam, we have to go back to the Old Testament. Balaam, a prophet, took money from a king named Balak to pronounce a curse on Israel. When God stopped Balaam, Balaam told Balak to have women of his country intermarry with the Jews. These women could then tempt their Jewish husbands to sin against God. Balak used these women to entice the **children of Israel** into idolatry and **fornication**. There were those in Pergamos, and also during the Pergamos period, who were doing the same thing. They were liberal on sin and were enticing others to sin.

The teachings of the Nicolaitans were more complicated. As far as we know, they believed a person's spirit is inherently good and a person's flesh is inherently evil. They also believed that it did not matter what one did in the flesh because sin in the flesh had no effect on the spirit. In essence they were saying, "Live it up; immorality doesn't matter." That tickled some people's ears. They liked the idea of loose living, but Jesus was not pleased. He knew that "a little

go to

killed Balaam
Numbers 31:6–8

body of Christ
those who truly
believe in Jesus

lights in the world
examples of God's
love

**person of Jesus
Christ**
the Messiah called
Jesus

leaven leavens the whole lump" (1 Corinthians 5:6 NKJV). A little compromise would eventually corrupt a lot of people.

Our Spiritual Sword

REVELATION 2:16 *Repent, or else I will come to you quickly and will fight against them with the sword of My mouth. (NKJV)*

Jesus warned the church in Pergamos to stop following the Nicolaitans. In the Old Testament, we learn that the children of Israel eventually <u>killed Balaam</u> (along with King Balak and his nation) with a sword. Here in the New Testament, we learn that Jesus warns loose-living members of this church that he will fight them with a spiritual sword, the Bible, if they do not change their evil ways. The Bible is the effective weapon against sin in the Church because it confronts the sinner with his sin.

Our spiritual sword is the Bible, which:

1. Reveals all things that pertain to life and godliness (2 Peter 1:3).

2. Shines the light of God on our failures (John 3:20).

3. Reveals the true will of God (1 Thessalonians 4:3).

4. Convicts us of sin (John 8:7).

5. Reveals the love of God (John 3:16).

6. Reveals the judgment of God (Romans 14:10).

7. Calls for repentance (Acts 2:38).

what others say

J. Vernon McGee

What a mistake we make if we think that the Church has the authority to decide what is right and what is wrong. The true Church is made up of believers in Jesus Christ—what Scripture calls the **body of Christ**. They are to be **lights in the world**. And if we are going to be lights in this dark world, we need to be careful to identify with the **person of Jesus Christ** and to recognize, not the Church, but the Word of God as our authority.[8]

Manna from Heaven

REVELATION 2:17 *He who has an ear, let him hear what the Spirit says to the churches. To him who overcomes I will give some of the hidden manna to eat. And I will give him a white stone, and on the stone a new name written which no one knows except him who receives it."* (NKJV)

manna from heaven
Exodus 16

never hunger spiritually
John 6:35

The hidden manna takes us back to another Old Testament story. As the children of Israel were wandering in the wilderness, they ran short of food. They began to complain, so God fed them <u>manna from heaven</u>. When the manna fell, Moses told Aaron to collect a potful and hide it in the ark as a reminder to future generations that God had met their needs. Since we cannot see Jesus, he is our hidden manna. He promises that we will <u>never hunger spiritually</u> because he is always with us.

The white stone is a reference to the way votes were cast at the courts of justice in John's day. When a case was tried, the jurors voted by dropping stones into an urn: black for guilty or white for innocent. Jesus promises that overcomers will be found innocent when God judges all things. Because of the shed blood of Jesus, overcomers are set free from the penalty of sin.

The new name that no one knows has many interpretations, but the most common seems to be that overcomers will receive a white stone bearing a secret name of Jesus. It will symbolize that each one of us has a special, intimate relationship with him. We will know him by a very personal name that no one else knows. Think about it. We will be innocent, never hunger, and have a personal relationship with Jesus. Jesus promises to take care of his people and provide for their future. Overcomers will enter God's glory with many rewards from a Lord who loves each one of us.

Eyes of Fire and Feet of Fine Brass

REVELATION 2:18 *"And to the angel of the church in Thyatira write, 'These things says the Son of God, who has eyes like a flame of fire, and His feet like fine brass:* (NKJV)

Jesus is the Son of God, which reveals his relationship to God, the Father.

Jesus goes on to further identify himself as the One whose eyes are

go to

judgment seat
2 Corinthians 5:10

fruit of the Holy Spirit
Galatians 5:22–23

love is of God
1 John 4:7

It produces good deeds
James 2:17–18

adulterous nature
their willingness to sin

Great White Throne Judgment
the judgment of the unsaved

like a flame of fire. His fiery eyes depict his penetrating insight, his anger, and his attitude toward the **adulterous nature** of the church in Thyatira and its church period. His eyes are burning with strong displeasure as he looks upon the wickedness of this church.

Jesus describes himself as the One whose feet are like fine brass. This is a reminder that he will judge his Church. Those who bring evil into the Church in the name of Christianity are begging to be judged by the Son of God.

What does an adulterous church need to know?

That Jesus is the Son of God, that he sees everything, and that he will judge us.

We Are What We Do?

REVELATION 2:19 *"I know your works, love, service, faith, and your patience; and as for your works, the last are more than the first. (NKJV)*

The Bible teaches that all believers will appear before the judgment seat of Christ. This is not the **Great White Throne Judgment**, where only the lost will appear. It is the judgment seat of Christ, where heavenly crowns will be given. To be a righteous Judge, Jesus must know how we lived. Concerning this church, he knew their:

1. *Deeds.* We are what we do! Christians do the works of Christians. Those who do not do the works of Christians, are not Christians.

2. *Love.* When people turn to God they receive the Holy Spirit in their hearts. The first fruit of the Holy Spirit is love. Love is of God, and God's people will love.

3. *Service.* Service is a ministry. The purpose of the Church is not for entertainment, enhancing our image, or doctoring our sore toes. Its purpose is service to God.

4. *Faith.* Genuine faith is something that can be seen. It produces good deeds. It is how an unbelieving world sees Christ in us.

5. *Perseverance.* This is often called long-suffering in the Bible. It is the fourth fruit of the Holy Spirit. Many in this church endured under great pressure for long periods of time.

6. *Last works*. This church was doing more and more. That should be the goal of every church: to grow, to do more, to **reach more people**, and to increase in good works.

Jezebel

> REVELATION 2:20–21 *Nevertheless I have a few things against you, because you allow that woman Jezebel, who calls herself a prophetess, to teach and seduce My servants to commit sexual immorality and eat things sacrificed to idols. And I gave her time to repent of her sexual immorality, and she did not repent.* (NKJV)

Something Jesus did not like was the fact that this church was using a false teacher named Jezebel. History shows that she was a priestess at a pagan temple. She was also deeply involved in fortune-telling but was passing herself off as a prophetess of God. She was enticing God's people to **depart from the faith**. Instead of teaching them to be faithful, she was teaching them to commit fornication. Instead of teaching them to avoid idolatry, she was teaching them to eat food sacrificed to idols. Instead of leading them to Jesus, she was leading them astray.

This is a good example of what **inclusiveness** does. The church leaders in Thyatira thought their inclusiveness would bring in more people. They wanted to make more people comfortable at church, so they allowed Jezebel to tickle their ears with **heresies**.

Jesus was patient with Jezebel. He gave her plenty of time to repent, but those who are caught up in the **occult** find it difficult to change. Such was the case with Jezebel, who persisted in her sin.

Jesus gave the Thyatira church approximately one thousand years to turn around. This is why some call it the Devil's Millennium. Jesus held his peace while the Church cooperated with false teachers. Multitudes were led astray. Instead of repenting, some in charge of the Church often had the true servants of God killed.

Playing with Fire

> REVELATION 2:22 *Indeed I will cast her into a sickbed, and those who commit adultery with her into great tribulation, unless they repent of their deeds.* (NKJV)

reach more people
tell them the message of salvation

depart from the faith
leave one's beliefs

inclusiveness
the tendency to accept anyone into the church regardless of what they believe

heresies
false teachings

occult
Satanic practices

go to

wolves in sheep's
clothing
Matthew 7:15

This church is a forerunner to the harlot church in chapter 17. When we reach that chapter we will study events that will occur during the Tribulation Period, and learn that world leaders will turn on the harlot church and destroy it with a vengeance.

Jezebel was a spiritual harlot at Thyatira. Harlots are known for committing sins in bed, so Jesus warns this church that he will make a bed for Jezebel and her adulterous followers. He will put them in bed together and cast them into intense suffering. If a church wants to play with fire, Jesus will let it play with fire. If it does not repent, he will eventually let it die out and pay for its sins. False teachings should never be tolerated.

Not everyone in this church was bad. But there have always been people who get baptized and join the church without getting saved. When this happens, true believers should not follow them. If they make the mistake of following a false teacher, they should repent.

what others say

Hal Lindsey

Today some leaders of churches and "Christian" colleges who ought to know better are doing the same sort of thing. They invite noted fortune-tellers to speak in churches and classrooms to satisfy curiosity. These occultic mediums are Trojan horses (<u>wolves in sheep's clothing</u>) in the midst of God's camp. Only evil can come from listening to their poisonous doctrines.[9]

You Get What You Do

REVELATION 2:23 *I will kill her children with death, and all the churches shall know that I am He who searches the minds and hearts. And I will give to each one of you according to your works. (NKJV)*

Some would argue that Jezebel was entitled to her own beliefs, but her beliefs were passed on from generation to generation. Her children followed in her footsteps and also led others astray. The Bible says, "Therefore consider the goodness and severity of God" (Romans 11:22 NKJV). Everyone needs to keep in mind these two natures of God: (1) He is good, but (2) he will judge sin. He is good, but he will be no more tolerant of spiritual adultery in our day than he was in Jezebel's day. The offspring of Jezebel's teachings will suffer the same fate as Jezebel. They will suffer the second death and be cast into the lake of fire. Everyone will receive according to what they have done on earth.

When Jesus talks about being the One who searches hearts and minds, he is reminding us that he looks inside us to our innermost core. He looks to see what our real affections are. He looks at our emotions, desires, and thoughts. Nothing is hidden from him.

When Jesus talks about giving to everyone according to their deeds, he is talking about the coming judgment. Every person will be judged in the future. There will be degrees of reward in heaven and degrees of punishment in hell. Everyone will receive according to what they did on earth.

key point

Hold On

REVELATION 2:24–25 *Now to you I say, and to the rest in Thyatira, as many as do not have this doctrine, who have not known the depths of Satan, as they say, I will put on you no other burden. But hold fast what you have till I come.* (NKJV)

Jesus is talking to those in Thyatira who either rejected Jezebel's teachings or were unaware of her teachings. He promised not to place any other burdens upon them. They were already serving under difficult circumstances, so he would not ask anything more of them.

He did have some advice, though. Hold on to your love, faith, ministry, patience, and ever-increasing works. Hold on to these until I return. This is another reference to the Rapture. It is also another indication that there is some overlapping of the seven church periods. It tells us that there will be some people in every church period who have characteristics of other church periods.

Satan's attack on the church:

1. "I know the blasphemy of those who say they are Jews and are not, but are a synagogue of Satan" (Revelation 2:9 NKJV).

2. "You hold fast to My name, and did not deny My faith even in the days in which Antipas was My faithful maryr, who was killed among you, where Satan dwells" (Revelation 2:13 NKJV).

go to

works of Jesus
John 6:29

position of power
1 Corinthians 6:2

you will receive power
and authority
2 Timothy 2:12

he received power
and authority
Acts 1:8;
Revelation 20:4

Bright and Morning
Star
Revelation 22:16

exhortation
a plea to do
something

3. "Now to you I say, and to the rest in Thyatira, as many as do not have this doctrine, who have not known the depths of Satan, as they say, I will put on you no other burden" (Revelation 2:24 NKJV).

A Promise

REVELATION 2:26–28 *And he who overcomes, and keeps My works until the end, to him I will give power over the nations—*
'He shall rule them with a rod of iron;
They shall be dashed to pieces like the potter's vessels'—
as I also have received from My Father; and I will give him the morning star. (NKJV)

If you refuse to follow Jezebel's teachings, refuse to do her works, continue in the <u>works of Jesus</u>, and persist until your death or Christ's return, you will receive a <u>position of power</u> over the nations.

Be a faithful believer, and you will rule over nations with a strong, loving hand. You will break those who resist your authority like a potter breaks vessels of clay. <u>You will receive power and authority</u> from Jesus in the same way <u>he received power and authority</u> from God the Father.

The planet Venus is called the morning star because it is the brightest object in the sky just before the sun rises. It is sometimes a guide to navigators, who use it to determine their location on earth. The <u>Bright and Morning Star</u> is also one of the names of Jesus, so when he promises to give the morning star to the overcomer, the gift is himself. This is a promise that Jesus will indwell in the believer, that he will never leave the believer, and that he will guide the believer during the dark or difficult times of life.

What does an adulterous Church need to do?

The faithful need to remain faithful, and the adulterous need to overcome (get saved).

Faithful unto Death

REVELATION 2:29 *He who has an ear, let him hear what the Spirit says to the churches.'" (NKJV)*

We have already seen this same statement four times. The fact is, Jesus ends every letter with this same **exhortation**. It is a command for all to listen and pay attention to what is in these letters. History tells us that the followers of Jezebel did not listen, just as many churches today are not listening. Yet some in Thyatira were faithful unto death, just as some today will be faithful unto death.

Rapture
Revelation 4:1

Before the Tribulation Period begins, Jesus will remove his faithful from the earth. True believers will not suffer the terrible events found later in Revelation, but instead will be removed from this earth in what we know as the <u>Rapture</u>. In Revelation 13:9 we read, "If anyone has an ear, let him hear" (NKJV). The question is, why did Jesus leave out that last part about what the Spirit says to the churches? Why does he say seven times, "He who has an ear, let him hear what the Spirit says to the churches," and then suddenly shorten it by saying, "If anyone has an ear, let him hear"? Could it

be that the Church is no longer on earth? That's what I think.

Chapter Wrap-Up

- The first four church letters are addressed to: Ephesus, Smyrna, Pergamos, and Thyatira. Each letter explains the churches' problems and offers a solution.

- Those who conquer their sinful nature can overcome the second death. Through faith in Jesus Christ one can live forever with God. (Revelation 2:11)

- Christ is described as having eyes of fire and feet of fine brass. His eyes depict his ability to see everything that we do, and his feet refer to his position as judge over of all creation. (Revelation 2:18)

- Jezebel, a false priestess in Thyatira, was leading people away from God. God told this church to rid themselves of her or face punishment. (Revelation 2:20–23)

- When Christ promises to give the Bright and Morning Star to overcomers he is really promising the gift of himself to the believer. (Revelation 2:28)

Study Questions

1. What did God hold against the church in Ephesus?

2. What was the affliction of the church in Smyrna?

3. What was the good asset of the church in Pergamos?

4. Why was God upset with the church in Thyatira?

5. What message should Christians today get from these letters?

Revelation 3

Chapter Highlights:
- Three Church Letters
- Lamb's Book of Life
- Key-Holder
- Lukewarm
- Standing at the Door

Let's Get Started

Chapter 3 continues the seven letters to the seven churches in Asia Minor. We will now study the last three letters. Keep in mind the fact that these last letters are personal messages from Jesus to each one of us, and that they represent a prophetic view of Church history beginning around AD 1517 and running to the Tribulation Period midpoint. There are some great messages here for all who will heed what the Holy Spirit has to say.

A Pretend Church

> **REVELATION 3:1** *"And to the angel of the church in Sardis write, 'These things says He who has the seven Spirits of God and the seven stars: "I know your works, that you have a name that you are alive, but you are dead.* (NKJV)

As we have seen, the <u>seven spirits</u> of God refer to the sevenfold nature of the Holy Spirit. The <u>seven stars</u> are the seven angels of the seven churches. Jesus is the One who possesses and gives the **fullness of the Holy Spirit**, but his authority is greater than that. He also controls these angels. This is an awesome amount of power. It means the destiny of the Church is in his hands.

Jesus knew the works of these churches. Sardis is not like Thyatira. In Thyatira the last works were greater than the first, but in Sardis their works were decreasing. Jesus said Sardis had a reputation of being alive, but it was actually dead. It had become a church in name only, a pretend church, one that was just going through the motions.

It's unacceptable for a church to focus on ritual and ceremony instead of on worship and service. The idea is not to have a meeting, but to create and maintain a relationship. Either God is God, or he is not. If he is, it's dangerous to put on a show. If he isn't, it's foolish to pretend he exists. Everyone needs to get this right before they step out of this life.

seven spirits
Revelation 1:4

seven stars
Revelation 1:20

fullness of the Holy Spirit
Luke 1:15; 4:1; John 20:21–22

fullness of the Holy Spirit
the indwelling and empowering of the Holy Spirit

What does a dead or pretend church need to know?

That Jesus possesses the Holy Spirit, decides who will receive the Holy Spirit, and controls the angels who oversee the church.

Experts agree that the Sardis period began with what most historians call the **Reformation**. In 1517, a priest named Martin Luther nailed **Ninety-five Theses** to a Church door in Wittenberg, Germany. This ultimately led to a split in the Church and the birth of Protestantism. But after many good steps, the Reformation stalled, and spiritual lethargy took hold. The Church needed revival, but it chose to live off its reputation instead.

Time for a Spiritual Overhaul

REVELATION 3:2 *Be watchful, and strengthen the things which remain, that are ready to die, for I have not found your works perfect before God.* (NKJV)

Jesus told the church in Sardis to "wake up, and stay awake." He told them there were certain aspects of their faith and practice that were still alive, but they needed to be more serious about their worship, study, and ministry. He was calling on them to overhaul their relationship with God. The steps they had already taken were good, but they had not yet reached God's standards. It is not enough for a church to hold right doctrines or go through a ritual or form of worship. For a church to have a valid relationship with God, it must back up its doctrines and words with devotion and works. When the apostle John received Revelation, it was not for his own personal knowledge. He was told to write it down for others. When a church receives a great revelation from God, it needs to put that revelation into practice. If it doesn't, it will die out. This is where the Sardis church failed. It was just sitting around.

> ## what others say
>
> ### Todd Strandberg and Terry James
>
> After making Jesus the Lord of your life, you need to change the direction of your life. When on vacation, traveling in an unfamiliar place, people often make a wrong turn somewhere along the line. At some point, they realize they are lost. A spirited debate might ensue about which direction is the correct one. They have to then turn around and head in the right direction. So it is with the salvation process. Once you realize you have been heading in the wrong direction, the only option that makes sense is to turn right around and start heading in the right direction.[2]

Surprise!

REVELATION 3:3 *Remember therefore how you have received and heard; hold fast and repent. Therefore if you will not watch, I will come upon you as a thief, and you will not know what hour I will come upon you. (NKJV)*

Jesus wanted his followers to recall their better days; to reflect on what they had received and heard. They had received forgiveness of their sins, salvation, eternal life, and future rewards in heaven. They had heard the preaching of the true Word of God with its clear and correct teachings. Jesus wanted his followers to recognize that they had backslid and needed to return to his teachings.

History shows that on two separate occasions, when enemy armies had surrounded Sardis, her careless guards fell asleep. Each time, the opposing army slipped in and captured the embarrassed city. Jesus seems to be using this example to teach this church a great truth. If we do not return to worshiping, believing, and living the way we once did, we will not recognize the prophetic signs of his coming. The Rapture will catch unbelievers asleep, causing them to miss it. This is an important point.

Research shows that fewer than half the people who call themselves Christians attend church on a regular basis. Many who do attend do so for the wrong reason. Many others are either dozing or letting their minds wander when they should be focusing on worship and the Word of God. The church has a purpose. It needs to wake up and fulfill it before it's too late.

go to

Book of Life
Revelation 20:12–15

Lamb's Book of Life
Revelation 21:27

name blotted out
Exodus 32:33

what others say

Life Application Bible Commentary

Only a change of heart could save them from punishment. That would mean taking God's Word seriously and purposefully obeying it. If they refused to wake up and see what was happening to them, Christ would come like a thief, unexpectedly, as had the soldiers who had climbed the walls to capture the city. The soldiers had brought destruction; Christ would bring punishment, giving them what they deserved.[3]

Two Different Books of Life

REVELATION 3:4–5 *You have a few names even in Sardis who have not defiled their garments; and they shall walk with Me in white, for they are worthy. He who overcomes shall be clothed in white garments, and I will not blot out his name from the Book of Life; but I will confess his name before My Father and before His angels.* (NKJV)

Jesus knew all his people in this church by name. Not many people in Sardis were faithful, but he could identify the ones who were. He said they were the ones who had refused to defile their garments, the ones who refused to be dirtied or influenced by the sins of those around them. He promised that they would walk with him in robes of white. Why? Because they had sincerely accepted Jesus as their Savior and, by the power of the Holy Spirit, lived holy lives.

Jesus promised never to blot out their names from the Book of Life. Many people confuse the Book of Life with the Lamb's Book of Life, but they are completely different. The Book of Life is a list of all who are born once; every person who ever lived. The Lamb's Book of Life is a list of all who are born twice; in other words, all who truly accept Jesus. It is possible to have one's name blotted out of the Book of Life for sinning against God, for denying Jesus, and for taking away from the words in Revelation. But many believe it is impossible for a saved person's name to be blotted out of the Lamb's Book of Life.

Jesus also promised to acknowledge the names of the saved before God and his holy angels. Wouldn't it be great to hear your name called out in heaven? Jesus said, "Therefore whoever confesses Me before men, him I will also confess before My Father who is in heaven. But whoever denies Me before men, him I will also deny before My Father who is in heaven" (Matthew 10:32–33 NKJV).

Jesus promised:

1. They would walk with him in robes of white.

2. He would never blot out their names from the Book of Life.

3. He would acknowledge the names of the saved before God and his holy angels.

Hear with Your Ears

REVELATION 3:6 *He who has an ear, let him hear what the Spirit says to the churches.'" (NKJV)*

It is no accident that Jesus keeps talking about <u>hearing</u>. We cannot begin to understand how important this is. It is the Bible that teaches us to remember, repent, and be righteous. To live our lives with <u>glorification</u>, <u>justification</u>, and <u>sanctification</u>. We must overcome, hold fast, and live holy lives. The great truths that sparked the Reformation started with people hearing what the Bible had to say. From the Bible they learned about the total depravity of man, justification by faith, and the authority of the Bible. When we hear the Word, we receive life, light, and truth; we learn God's commandments, judgments, and promises; we get to know his heart, mind, and will; and we find comfort, peace, and strength.

"He who has an ear, let him hear. . . . " Hearing is of the utmost importance. It does us no good to spend years in church without change or without hearing. We should give careful consideration to what Jesus is saying. It would be a great tragedy to think we are saved only to discover that we have made a mistake. We would never eat from the tree of life, receive the crown of life, rule over nations, dwell in the presence of God, or share in Christ's throne. If your church is almost dead, if it seems like rigor mortis has set in, Jesus says, strengthen the things that remain.

The One True God

REVELATION 3:7 *"And to the angel of the church in Philadelphia write, 'These things says He who is holy, He who is true, "He who has the key of David, He who opens and no one shuts, and shuts and no one opens":* (NKJV)

go to

hearing
Revelation 1:3; 2:7, 11, 17, 29; 3:6

glorification
Romans 8:17–18

justification
Romans 5:16–18 KJV

sanctification
1 Thessalonians 4:3–4 KJV

Eliakim
Isaiah 22:20–25

holy
different or separate
from everyone and
everything

true
real or genuine

New Age
false religious
movement

evangelistic
declaring the Word
of God to the
unsaved

revival
renewed zeal
to obey God

Holy and **true** are attributes of God. He has the nature of deity. When put together, this means Jesus is the true God. He is not a false god like today's popular **New Age** gods such as Ishtar, Mother Earth, Gaia, Diana, and Sophia. He is the only real God.

"He who has the key of David" takes us back to the Old Testament. There was a priest named <u>Eliakim</u> who held the office of keyholder in King David's palace. His office gave him full authority to act on behalf of the king. If he unlocked a palace door, it remained unlocked. If he locked a palace door, it remained locked. Just like Eliakim, Jesus is the ultimate Keyholder. No matter what door it is, if Jesus opens it, no one can close it. If he closes it, no one can open it.

What does an evangelistic church need to know?

That Jesus is holy, the true God, the Keyholder, the One who opens and shuts doors, the One who controls all things.

God Plus One Is a Majority

REVELATION 3:8 *"I know your works. See, I have set before you an open door, and no one can shut it; for you have a little strength, have kept My word, and have not denied My name. (NKJV)*

The church in Philadelphia was more like what the Church should be than any of the other churches. It was a working, **evangelistic**, Bible-believing church.

Jesus is the One who opens and closes doors. We are totally dependent upon him. We cannot evangelize or expect God to send revival without Jesus. Satan cannot stop **revival** if Jesus is on our side. Jesus told this small church in Philadelphia that he knew they had little strength. All they needed was him behind them. God plus one faithful church member is a majority.

what others say

J. Edwin Orr

In the mid 1800s, people began to be converted at the rate of 10,000 a week in New York City. The movement spread throughout New England. Church bells would bring people to prayer at eight in the morning, twelve noon, and six in the evening. The revival went up the Hudson and down the Mohawk. Baptists had so many people to baptize, they couldn't get them into their churches. They went down to the river, cut a big square in the ice, and baptized them in cold water. In one year (1857), more than one million people were converted. The revival crossed the Atlantic, broke out in Northern Ireland, Scotland, Wales, England, South Africa, South India—anywhere there was an evangelical cause, there was revival—and its effect was felt for 40 years.[4]

This is badly needed today when so many people want to deny the name of Jesus by saying "Happy Holidays" instead of "Merry Christmas" and use "BCE" (Before the Common Era) instead of "BC" (Before Christ). Revival can't begin until people stop denying the name of Jesus and start humbling themselves in repentance and obedience.

The Synagogue of Satan

REVELATION 3:9 *Indeed I will make those of the synagogue of Satan, who say they are Jews and are not, but lie—indeed I will make them come and worship before your feet, and to know that I have loved you. (NKJV)*

There were those who wanted the church in Philadelphia to deny the name of Jesus. They refused to believe in Jesus or the gospel. They worshiped at a synagogue and said they were Jews, but Jesus called them impostors. He called their place of worship the synagogue of Satan.

Jesus assured the Philadelphia church that these pretenders would pay for their misdeeds. He said they would be forced to bow down and worship at their feet, acknowledging that Jesus is Lord of this church.

Antichrist
1 John 2:18

child of God
1 John 3:10

hour of trial
Revelation 17:12

This prophecy was fulfilled in Philadelphia when the Romans tried to wipe out the Jews. However, some also believe it is a prophecy that will be fulfilled during the Tribulation Period. Then, the Antichrist will turn against the Jews. Many will be killed, and a remnant will flee into the wilderness before they realize that Jesus is indeed the Messiah.

People are not always what they claim to be. Jesus told a group of Jews who said God was their Father, "You are of your father the devil" (John 8:44 NKJV). Even the apostle Paul said, "They are not all Israel who are of Israel" (Romans 9:6 NKJV). Many people fail to live up to their spiritual claims. That was true of the Jews in Philadelphia, and it is still true of the Church today. Not everyone who claims to be a child of God truly is.

An Hour of Trial

REVELATION 3:10 *Because you have kept My command to persevere, I also will keep you from the hour of trial which shall come upon the whole world, to test those who dwell on the earth.* (NKJV)

This church was following God's commandments in two ways: (1) it was working in the name of Jesus, and (2) it was patiently waiting for his return. Because of this, Jesus promised to keep these believers out of the hour of trial that would come in the future to test everyone. He will not permit this church or any who follow in their footsteps to go through the Tribulation Period. It will be a time of literal hell on earth, replete with famine, natural disasters, epidemic sickness, war, and murder.

It will be worse than the destruction of a 9.0 earthquake, an unprecedented tsunami with waves twenty feet high, the devastation of a Category 5 hurricane, and the carnage of multiple terrorist bombings with planes crashing into buildings. It will be disaster piled upon disaster, deadly persecution piled upon mockery and ridicule, diseases without cures, and it will come upon the whole world. Believers should rejoice that faithful church members won't have to go through that. Perhaps, this is why John began the next chapter with an example of the Rapture.

twinkling
1 Corinthians 15:52

reward
2 John 1:8

reward
a crown given to
Christians for their
faithful service

> ## what others say
>
> ### John Hagee
>
> The Rapture is the literal, physical "snatching away" of those who have placed their faith in Jesus Christ. The Rapture could come at any moment, and it will occur without warning. Every single member of the corporate body of Christ, the genuine believers, will be taken alive to meet him in the air (1 Thessalonians 4:17). Those who have suffered physical death will be resurrected with incorruptible, supernatural bodies.[6]

Five Reasons for the Rapture

Reason	Scripture
To resurrect deceased Christians	1 Thessalonians 4:13–18; 1 Corinthians 15:50–57
To protect the church from wrath	1 Thessalonians 1:10; 5:9; Romans 5:9
To judge Christians for rewards	2 Corinthians 5:10
To give Christians a glorified body like Jesus	Philippians 3:21; 1 John 3:2
To present the church to Jesus for marriage	Revelation 19:6–9

Twinkling of an Eye

> **REVELATION 3:11** *Behold, I am coming quickly! Hold fast what you have, that no one may take your crown. (NKJV)*

Some think Jesus was telling the Philadelphia church he would come soon. That is not the case. He was telling them that when he comes back, it will happen very fast. "For as the lightning comes from the east and flashes to the west, so also will the coming of the Son of Man be." (Matthew 24:27 NKJV). Both the Rapture and the Second Coming will take place in the twinkling of an eye.

Hold on to what you have—do not abandon your doctrines and deeds, keep believing the Bible, keep evangelizing, and keep sending out missionaries to tell the world about Jesus. So that no one will take your crown—let no one else have your **reward**. God's work will still be accomplished.

go to

name of God
Revelation 9:4

New Jerusalem
Revelation 21:9–22:6

name of Jesus
Revelation 22:4

what others say

Todd Strandberg and Terry James

Jesus Christ, who is the second member of the Holy Trinity, can't change. "Jesus Christ is the same yesterday, today, and forever" (Hebrews 13:8). Neither can His message: "Repent and be saved." This is the business to which every believer of every era of human history has been assigned. Christians are to concern themselves with God's business of living for Christ, and telling the Good News (the Gospel of Christ).[7]

A New Jerusalem

REVELATION 3:12–13 *He who overcomes, I will make him a pillar in the temple of My God, and he shall go out no more. I will write on him the name of My God and the name of the city of My God, the New Jerusalem, which comes down out of heaven from My God. And I will write on him My new name. He who has an ear, let him hear what the Spirit says to the churches."* (NKJV)

Jesus' promises for those who overcome:

- *I will make you a pillar in the temple of my God*—Jesus will make his followers strong, durable, and stable in the house of God.

- *He shall go out no more*—Jesus will make his followers secure. They will desire to stay forever, and no one will move them.

- *I will write on him*—Jesus will write three things upon the foreheads of his followers:

  1. the name of God to designate them as a child of God;

  2. the name of his eternal home which is New Jerusalem;

  3. and a new name of Jesus, signifying their personal relationship to the Lord of lords and King of kings. Those who overcome will belong to God. They will be citizens of the New Jerusalem and will have a special relationship with Jesus.

Once again, the entire Church is asked to pay attention to these things. The faithful will escape the terrible judgments, but the unfaithful will not unless they repent of their sins and fix their relationship with God. Writing the name of Jesus on the faithful may be where Satan gets the idea to inspire the False Prophet to write the name of the Antichrist on his followers. Satan is a copycat.

true
John 14:6

creation
John 1:3;
Colossians 1:16–17

The Great Amen

> REVELATION 3:14 *"And to the angel of the church of the Laodiceans write, 'These things says the Amen, the Faithful and True Witness, the Beginning of the creation of God:* (NKJV)

The Laodicean church period is the last period of the Church Age, and the last letter to the Church before the Rapture. We are living in the Laodicean church period today.

Jesus is the Amen, the Truth, the One we can trust. There is no greater person to believe in, no greater One to lean on.

Jesus is the faithful and <u>true</u> witness, the One who faithfully serves God. His deeds and words accurately testify to God.

Jesus is the ruler of God's <u>creation</u>, the One who is the source of all things. Some people theorize that the universe began as an explosion that took place billions of years ago. Some think we came into being through evolution. But Jesus says he created all things.

If you search the entire Bible, examine every leader of every religion, and scour every period of history, you will find that Jesus is the only perfect and truly righteous man who ever lived.

What does a lukewarm Church need to know?

That Jesus has the last word, won't change, is the Creator, and always tells the truth.

Hot, Cold, or Lukewarm?

> REVELATION 3:15–16 *"I know your works, that you are neither cold nor hot. I could wish you were cold or hot. So then, because you are lukewarm, and neither cold nor hot, I will vomit you out of My mouth.* (NKJV)

Church members in Laodicea were neither cold nor hot, but lukewarm. Any church or church member can find itself in one of these three states: cold, lukewarm, or hot. Cold signifies formal or without spiritual life, lukewarm means indifferent or straddling the fence, and hot expresses passionate or zealous.

go to

his kingdom
Matthew 6:33

treasure
Matthew 6:21

The church in Laodicea had become complacent. Its people were not being persecuted, but were comfortable, prospering, and self-satisfied. They were doing nothing to evangelize, grow, or glorify Jesus.

According to Jesus, this is the worst state of all. It would be easier to judge a cold or dead church and easier to bless a hot or spiritual church. But what do you do with an indifferent church that claims Christ's name? Jesus wished they would be hot or cold, but since they were neither, he would spit them out of his mouth.

How many people in your church are like this? Are you like this? The thought that people in this condition won't go to heaven is terrible. It demands serious self-evaluation and commitment.

> **what others say**
>
> **Warren W. Wiersbe**
>
> All the church's man-made programs can never bring life, any more than a circus can resurrect a corpse. The church was born when the Spirit of God descended on the Day of Pentecost (Acts 2), and its life comes from the Spirit. When the Spirit is grieved, the church begins to lose life and power. When sin is confessed and church members get right with God and with each other, then the Spirit infuses new life—revival![8]

All the Money in the World Won't Save Your Soul

REVELATION 3:17 *Because you say, 'I am rich, have become wealthy, and have need of nothing'—and do not know that you are wretched, miserable, poor, blind, and naked—(NKJV)*

This church did not have a realistic view of itself. It saw itself in one light, but Jesus saw it in another. It prided itself in its bank accounts, buildings, and members of high standing. It said we have money and material things, so why do we need anything else. Obviously, they had lost sight of Jesus and what it means to be in <u>his kingdom</u>.

It is not enough to build showy sanctuaries, great gymnasiums, and paved parking lots. Worldly <u>treasure</u> is not God's measuring stick. The church in Laodicea thought they were high on the social register, but Jesus said they were wretched. They thought they were happy, but Jesus said they were miserable. They thought they were rich, but Jesus said they were poor.

It is unfortunate, but many churches today are making the same mistake. They do not recognize the <u>writing on the wall</u>. Unfortunately, they will never know the <u>fullness of Jesus</u> if they don't wake up. God <u>did not spare the Jews</u> when they abandoned him, so he will not spare churches that do the same.

God's Furnace

go to

writing on the wall
Daniel 5

fullness of Jesus
Colossians 1:19; 2:9

did not spare the Jews
Romans 11:21–22

refine it
1 Peter 1:7

came into this world with nothing
1 Timothy 6:3–10

righteousness of Christ
the nature or qualities of Christ (his purity, love, kindness, etc.)

what others say

Hal Lindsey

There is this health and wealth gospel that is out today that is a flat out error . . . that's leading many astray . . . that says that God is going to make you rich, and if you are not, you are just not believing God.[9]

REVELATION 3:18 *I counsel you to buy from Me gold refined in the fire, that you may be rich; and white garments, that you may be clothed, that the shame of your nakedness may not be revealed; and anoint your eyes with eye salve, that you may see. (NKJV)*

Mined gold is placed into a red-hot furnace not to destroy it, but to purify it. The ore is melted, the impurities are drawn out, and the residue is left—pure gold. We are put into God's furnace of testing not to destroy our faith, but to <u>refine it</u>. Trials humble us, our sins are drawn out (through repentance), and the residue is left—an improved Christian.

If we really want to be rich, we must buy from Jesus, with a spiritual currency, a faith that grows stronger with every test. Without this spiritual currency, we are paupers. We <u>came into this world with nothing</u>, and apart from a faith in Jesus, we will leave this world with nothing.

This church was naked and had no covering for their sins. Jesus told them they should put on spiritual garments—white clothes—the **righteousness of Christ**. The finest earthly clothes cannot hide the tiniest sin from God's eyes. When we stand before the judgment throne, the only thing that will hide our spiritual nakedness is the righteousness of Jesus.

Nicodemus
John 3:1–21

discipline
Hebrews 12:5–8

free will
the ability to choose

Jesus said this church was blind and had no spiritual discernment. He desired that they seek him for the salve to cure their spiritual blindness. To <u>Nicodemus</u> he said, "Most assuredly, I say to you, unless one is born again, he cannot see the kingdom of God" (John 3:3 NKJV). The apostle Paul said, "But the natural man does not receive the things of the Spirit of God, for they are foolishness to him; nor can he know them, because they are spiritually discerned" (1 Corinthians 2:14 NKJV).

Open Your Heart

REVELATION 3:19–22 *As many as I love, I rebuke and chasten. Therefore be zealous and repent. Behold, I stand at the door and knock. If anyone hears My voice and opens the door, I will come in to him and dine with him, and he with Me. To him who overcomes I will grant to sit with Me on My throne, as I also overcame and sat down with My Father on His throne. He who has an ear, let him hear what the Spirit says to the churches."''* (NKJV)

The Lord will not allow anyone he loves to escape <u>discipline</u>. Even the harshest discipline is a sign of his love. It is done for two reasons: (1) to cause people to be honest about their sins, and (2) to bring them to repentance.

Jesus could have demanded that the church in Laodicea come to his door. He could have required them to knock, beg, cry, and plead for salvation, but instead, he was the One who knocked, begged, and pleaded. He gave them their own **free will** to accept or reject him. He did not force them to open the door.

Here lies the final promise to the overcomer: Just as Jesus overcame Satan by his life of obedience to God and his ultimate sacrifice on the cross, and just as he now sits in an exalted position on his Father's throne, the overcomer will sit on the throne of Jesus and reign with him. And for a seventh and last time, all are invited to hear what the Holy Spirit has to say to the churches.

Before Christians leave this chapter, be aware that individual church members, churches, and this present church period can be put into one of seven different categories: backsliding, persecuted, compromising, adulterous, pretend (or dead), evangelistic or lukewarm. Five out of the seven (more than 70 percent) are told to

key point

repent. Also notice that the dominant characteristic of this present church period is lukewarm (lost).

There is a famous painting by the artist Holman Hunt of Jesus standing at the door and knocking. People say when he painted it, he asked friends to come by and critique it. One friend told him he left out something very important, the door handle. Holman Hunt replied, "This door is a picture of the human heart, and the handle is on the inside."

Chapter Wrap-Up

- The last three church letters are to Sardis, Philadelphia, and Laodicea. Each letter explains further problems for the Church and offers solutions.

- Jesus promises to keep the names of overcomers in the Lamb's Book of Life, and he will acknowledge the believers' names before God. (Revelation 3:4–5)

- Christ holds the keys to our lives. What doors he opens for us cannot be shut, and those he shuts cannot be opened. (Revelation 3:7)

- For a Christian, the worst state to be in is lukewarm—neither on fire for the Lord nor ignorant of him. Indifference leads to Christ's anger. (Revelation 3:15–16)

- Jesus comes to us (our door) and knocks to be let in. Those who let him in will be allowed to eat (fellowship) with him. (Revelation 3:20)

Study Questions

1. What false reputation did the church at Sardis have?

2. Why was the church at Philadelphia so weak?

3. What was the admonition to the church at Laodicea?

4. Which letter probably applies to today's church?

5. How does one avoid being lukewarm?

Part Two
From the Rapture to the Second Coming

Revelation 4

Chapter Highlights:
- **Rapture**
- **God's Throne**
- **Approaching Storm**
- **Four Living Creatures**
- **Twenty-four Elders**

Let's Get Started

Here in chapter 4, we come to a major turning point. Chapters 1–3 revealed John's vision of Jesus and the Church Age. John's vision of Jesus is past. Most of the Church Age is past, but the little that remains will soon be over. Now every chapter beginning with chapter 4 reveals things to come in the future.

Antichrist
against the Christ

How God Divided the Book of Revelation

(As Found in Revelation 1:19)

"Write" the things which you have seen,	Past Things (Chapter 1)
And the things which are,	Present Things (Chapters 2–3)
And the things which will take place after this	Future Things (Chapters 4–22)

Revelation is one of the most sequence-oriented books in the Bible. We must understand this before going any further. Revelation 4:1 reveals the Rapture, Revelation 6:2 reveals the appearance of the **Antichrist**, and Revelation 6:17 reveals the beginning of the Tribulation Period.

Notice that this sequence of events indicates a period of time between Revelation 4:1 (the Rapture) and Revelation 6:17 (the Tribulation Period). The Bible does not tell us how long that period of time will be. We only know that the Antichrist must have enough time to rise to power in Europe, take over the world government, and negotiate a covenant to protect Israel (more on these events later). It is also important to note that there are three different theories regarding the sequence of these events. They are called:

Pre-Tribulation Rapture—The Church is raptured before the Tribulation Period:

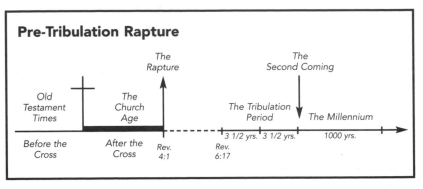

Mid-Tribulation Rapture—The Church is raptured during the Tribulation Period (at its midpoint):

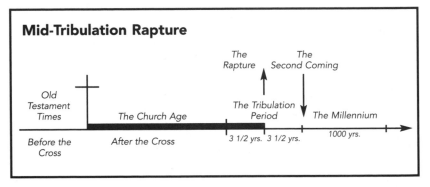

Post-Tribulation Rapture—The Church is raptured after the Tribulation Period:

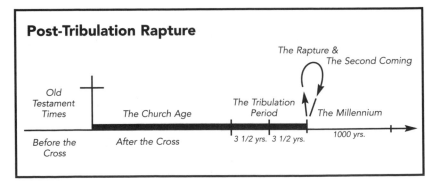

Ten Reasons to Believe in a Pre-Tribulation Rapture

1. The Bible never says the Church will go through the Tribulation Period.

2. The Church had no part in the first sixty-nine weeks of Daniel and it will have no part in the seventieth week (Daniel 9:24).

3. The Church is mentioned more than twenty times in the first three chapters of Revelation, but there is no mention of the Church between Revelation 4:1 and Revelation 19:1.

4. Jesus comes to meet his Church in the Rapture (1 Thessalonians 4:16–17). He comes with his Church in the Second Coming (1 Thessalonians 3:13). The Church goes up from the earth in the Rapture and it comes down to the earth in the Second Coming.

5. The Antichrist cannot be revealed until after the Rapture (2 Thessalonians 2:6–8). But if the Church goes through the Tribulation Period, the Church will know who the Antichrist is because he will head up the one-world government (Revelation 13:10); put a statue of himself in the rebuilt Temple (Matthew 24:15); demand that people take his Mark, name, or number (Revelation 13:15–17); kill the Two Witnesses (Revelation 11:7), and more.

6. No one can know the day or hour of the Second Coming (Matthew 24:36). But if the Church goes through the Tribulation Period, some will know the day because it will be seven years from the signing of the seven-year covenant (Daniel 9:24–27) and 1,260 days from the day the Antichrist defiles the Temple (Revelation 12:6).

7. The Church must go to heaven for the marriage of the Lamb (Revelation 19:7) before the Second Coming at the end of the Tribulation Period (Revelation 19:11–14).

8. The Antichrist will prevail against the saints during the Tribulation Period (Revelation 13:7), but the gates of hell won't prevail against the Church (Matthew 16:18).

9. The twenty-four elders (representatives of the Church) will be in heaven before the seven-sealed scroll is broken.

10. The Pre-Tribulation Rapture is more consistent with God's grace, love, and mercy.

what others say

The New King James Version Prophecy Bible

Sometime after the Rapture, a seven-year period will begin which is called the Tribulation. It is nowhere specified that the Tribulation will immediately follow the Rapture, so there may be some interval between the two events.[1]

David Hocking

We may be in heaven for many years until the Tribulation actually starts. The Rapture could happen many years ahead of that. From my perspective, the Rapture could happen tonight and it still may be 20 years until the Tribulation.[2]

go to

God creating
Genesis 1:1–2:3

Messianic
reference to the
expected delivery of
the Jews by the
Messiah

The 7,000-Year Theory of Mankind

For the most part, major news commentators do not believe what the Bible has to say, but they frequently find themselves describing current events as "disasters of biblical proportions." Today, there is a sense of change in the air with mounting anticipation about the Rapture and the Second Coming of Jesus Christ. **Messianic** expectations are rampant among Jews in Israel, predictions of the Rapture and the Second Coming are widespread among Christians, and doomsday prophecies are flourishing among cults. There has never been a better time to study the book of Revelation.

The 7,000-Year Theory is one of the oldest theories dating from the earliest days of the Church. It begins with God creating the heavens and the earth in six days and resting on the seventh. It rationalizes that God will deal with mankind for six days and rest on the seventh. It also assumes that all the days of the week are of equal length. Knowing three other Scripture verses will help in understanding: (1) 2 Peter 3:8 teaches one day with the Lord is as 1,000 years, (2) Hebrews 4:4–11 presents the Millennium as a day of rest, and (3) Revelation 20:1–9 gives us the idea of a 1,000-year Millennium. The theory states that God will deal with mankind for six of his days (6,000 of our years) and rest on the seventh day (the 1,000-year Millennium). According to the Jewish calendar, 3,760 years after Creation the Christian Era began (AD 1 on our calendar). That is almost four of God's days.

And to show just how important this is, some modern scholars say they can prove the Jewish calendar is off by 240 years. Use the Jewish figure of 3,760 years before the Christian Era, add 240 years of error, and you come up with exactly 4,000 years or four of God's days. Since its beginning, the Christian Era has lasted almost 2,000 years or two more of God's days. This means the seventh God-day is upon mankind (the Millennium). But before the Millennium occurs two things must take place—the Rapture and the Tribulation Period.

Come In

rapture
1 Thessalonians 4:16;
1 Corinthians 15:52

REVELATION 4:1 *After these things I looked, and behold, a door standing open in heaven. And the first voice which I heard was like a trumpet speaking with me, saying, "Come up here, and I will show you things which must take place after this." (NKJV)*

John first saw a door opening to heaven. He then heard a voice, that sounded like a trumpet, inviting him to come in and see the things that will take place after this (after the Church Age). John looked and heard. What we see with our own eyes and hear with our own ears is real to us, but what John saw was a world that the natural eye cannot see and the natural ear cannot hear. The voice John heard was like a trumpet. It was the same kind of voice the Bible says will <u>rapture</u> the Church. For that and other reasons, many prophecy experts believe John represents the whole Church, and his ascending into heaven is symbolic of the Rapture. When the Rapture occurs, the Church will ascend into heaven at the sound of a trumpet just as John did. Who can estimate the value of the grace of God? He will receive the Church into heaven, let her sing with angels, and let her watch the Tribulation Period from the balconies of heaven.

Confusion over whether or not there will be a Rapture does exist. One reason for this is that the word "rapture" is not in the Bible. This is correct, but only to a point. The word "rapture" is not in English translations of the Bible. It is an English version of a word that appears in Latin translations. Keep in mind that most of the New Testament was written in Greek, which was then translated into Latin and then to English. Saint Jerome completed most of the Latin translation in AD 405. His translation eventually was translated into the English Bible we know today. Several verses of the Bible in the Latin translation contain the word "rapere" or one of its derivations. It means "to be caught up, plucked up, or taken by force." Christians translate this Latin word to mean "Rapture." Christians will be both called up and caught up to heaven just as John was.

Notice that the voice said, "I will show you things which must take place after this." The word "must" should not be overlooked. It means the Old Testament prophecies, the predictions of Jesus, and the words of all the sacred writers have to be fulfilled. What else can be said? God said he will do certain things and he has to keep his Word. So don't ignore or dismiss the things written in the book of Revelation.

The Pre-Tribulation Rapture in the Old Testament

Dead raised, God's people hide, the Tribulation comes	Isaiah 26:19–21
God will hide his people in the time of trouble	Psalm 27:5
Seek the Lord and be hidden in the day of the Lord's anger	Zephaniah 2:3

what others say

Grant R. Jeffrey

The early Christian writer and poet Ephraem the Syrian (who lived from 306 to 373 A.D.) was a major theologian of the early Byzantine Eastern Church. Ephraem's fascinating teaching on the Antichrist has never been published in English until now. This critically important prophecy manuscript from the fourth century of the Church era reveals a literal method of interpretation and a teaching of the pre-millennial return of Christ. More importantly, Ephraem's text revealed a very clear statement about the pre-tribulation return of Christ to take his elect saints home to heaven to escape the coming Tribulation.[4]

Examples of the Rapture

Person	Scripture
Enoch	Genesis 5:24—Enoch went to heaven without first dying. Hebrews 11:5 NJKV—"By faith Enoch was taken away so that he did not see death."
Elijah	2 Kings 2:11—Elijah was walking on earth when he was suddenly taken up into heaven.
Jesus	Acts 1:9—Jesus was taken up into the clouds to heaven.
Philip	Acts 8:39—Philip was taken away but then reappeared in another location.
Paul	2 Corinthians 12:1–4—Paul was caught up into heaven, and then later returned to earth.
2 Witnesses	Revelation 11:3–12—After being killed, they will rise from the dead and ascend into heaven.

Notice that Enoch was Raptured before the flood; Elijah was Raptured between the flood and the cross; Jesus, Philip and Paul were Raptured in the Church Age; and the Two Witnesses will be Raptured in the Tribulation Period. All of these time periods have had a Rapture.

The Four Doors of Revelation

Name of Door	Purpose	Scripture
The Door of Opportunity	Evangelism and missionary activity	Revelation 3:8
The Door of One's Heart	Salvation	Revelation 3:20
The Door of Heaven	The Rapture	Revelation 4:1
The Door of Heaven	The Second Coming	Revelation 19:11

go to

glorified
Philippians 3:21

righteousness
Romans 8:10

cleansing
John 1:7

breastplate
Exodus 28:15–20

God promised Noah
Genesis 9: 8–17

glorified
transformed into a
resurrected body

In the Spirit

REVELATION 4:2 *Immediately I was in the Spirit; and behold, a throne set in heaven, and One sat on the throne.* (NKJV)

John saw the door, heard the voice, and suddenly he was in the Spirit. In the Spirit means his spirit left his body. It was changed by the Holy Spirit into a sort of spiritual rocket ship. His body could not enter heaven because it had not yet been **glorified**. However, his spirit could enter because of the righteousness of Christ and the cleansing or purifying of his sins.

Jasper and Sardius

REVELATION 4:3 *And He who sat there was like a jasper and a sardius stone in appearance; and there was a rainbow around the throne, in appearance like an emerald.* (NKJV)

The one on the throne, Jesus, had the appearance of white and red light flashing off two precious stones, jasper and sardius. These are the first and the last stones in the breastplate of the High Priest. They remind us that the One on the throne is our High Priest forever and ever. Jasper (the white flashing light) is opaque or translucent like a diamond and represents the purity or holiness of Jesus. Sardius (the red flashing light) is fiery red like the blood Jesus shed on the cross.

In the Old Testament God promised Noah he would never destroy the earth with a flood again. He placed a rainbow in the sky as a reminder of that promise. When the Church enters heaven, there will be a rainbow surrounding God's throne promising he will not destroy the earth during the Tribulation Period. The rainbow is a reminder that God is a God of grace, a God who keeps his promises. Where Jesus had the appearance of jasper and sardius, the throne has

go to

eternal life
1 John 5:11–12

dressed in white
Revelation 3:5

righteousness of
Christ
2 Corinthians 5:21

crowns
Revelation 2:10

the appearance of emerald green. Green is the color of life, the <u>eternal life</u> that comes from God as a result of the shed blood of Jesus and the grace of God.

Because human words cannot describe what John saw, he used symbols to help us understand. Notice how he used the following phrases to tell us everything about what he saw: "on the throne" (v. 2); "around the throne" (vv. 3, 4, 6); "from the throne" (v. 5); and "before the throne" (vv. 5–6). We will see these same things when the Church is raptured into heaven.

The Twenty-Four Elders

> REVELATION 4:4 *Around the throne were twenty-four thrones, and on the thrones I saw twenty-four elders sitting, clothed in white robes; and they had crowns of gold on their heads.* (NKJV)

On one occasion, the entire nation of Israel was represented by twenty-four special priests. Just as these priests represented all of Israel, twenty-four elders will one day represent all believers from Pentecost to the Rapture. They will surround the throne of God as representatives of a nation of kings and priests. They will stand in for all overcomers.

Just as these elders were <u>dressed in white</u>, in heaven we will all be clothed in white representing the <u>righteousness of Christ</u>. We will wear golden <u>crowns</u>—rewards for our earthly deeds. These elders will stand in for all those who love the Lord. It is very important to note that the Church will receive its robes and crowns, and it will begin its reign with Jesus in heaven before the Tribulation Period begins. There can be no doubt that God is showing us the pre-Tribulation Rapture.

A Storm Is Approaching

> REVELATION 4:5 *And from the throne proceeded lightnings, thunderings, and voices. Seven lamps of fire were burning before the throne, which are the seven Spirits of God.* (NKJV)

Think of the last time you saw lightning and heard thunder in the distance. You turn on the television and the weatherman says a storm is approaching. He obviously appears to be right. In the same way the lightning and thunder from the throne of God are also a signal that a storm is coming. God's patience with those on earth is wearing thin. The Tribulation Period is approaching.

We learned in Revelation 1:4 that the Holy Spirit has a sevenfold nature, and that the seven spirits of God are the seven virtues of the Holy Spirit. The Holy Spirit indwells believers, but he also occupies a place in the presence of God. He is everywhere.

A Glassy Sea

> REVELATION 4:6 *Before the throne there was a sea of glass, like crystal. And in the midst of the throne, and around the throne, were four living creatures full of eyes in front and in back.* (NKJV)

In front of the throne was something that was so calm that it looked like a beautiful, crystal, glassy sea. Prophecy experts suggest this sea of glass is (1) the Church because the sea is a biblical symbol for the masses of humanity, (2) the water of the Word, and (3) the water of baptism. Whatever it is, it indicates that all is calm in front of the throne of God. Nothing is present that could cause turbulence or unrest. The Church will be at peace with God when it goes before him.

Around the throne were four unusual creatures with many eyes in front and in back. These creatures are some type of angelic beings who possess characteristics of the **seraphim** and the **cherubim**. Their many eyes indicate they can see all that is happening in every direction. They could be the highest and greatest of all heavenly beings.

The Water of Baptism

Jesus was baptized with water and he told his disciples to baptize others in the same way. For that reason, the Church uses water baptism as an outward sign or symbol that a change has taken place in the believer's heart. Upon being baptized, a new believer is added to the list of members of his church. Water baptism by immersion symbolizes the death, burial, and resurrection of Jesus. Being put under water (immersed or buried in water) symbolizes the death and bur-

go to

sea is a biblical symbol
Revelation 17:15

water of the Word
Ephesians 5:26

four unusual creatures
Ezekiel 1:5–13,
19–20; 10:20

seraphim
Isaiah 6:1–3

**Jesus was baptized
with water**
Matthew 3:13–17

**he told his disciples to
baptize others**
Matthew 28:19–20

seraphim, cherubim
angels that guard
the throne of God

baptism of the Holy
Spirit
Acts 1:5; 2:16–17

cleansing work of God
Ezekiel 36:25–26

sprinkling of the blood
of Jesus
Hebrews 12:24

Lion of the tribe of
Judah
Revelation 5:5

King of the Jews
Matthew 2:2; 21:5;
27:11

Jesus came as a
servant
Mark 10:45

Son of Man
Luke 5:24; 6:5; 7:34

creator
John 1:3

ial of Jesus. Being brought up out of the water symbolizes his resurrection. When a new believer is baptized by immersion he is also announcing that his old self has died, his old ways have been buried, and he has been raised to live a new life in Christ.

Some churches pour water over the new believer as a form of baptism. This may symbolize the baptism of the Holy Spirit or the pouring out of the Holy Spirit. Other churches sprinkle water over the new believer. This symbolizes the cleansing work of God in our hearts and the sprinkling of the blood of Jesus. But it's very important to understand that water baptism won't save us. Many people get baptized with water without being saved. Everyone has to trust in Jesus and be baptized by the Holy Spirit into the body of Christ.

The Four Gospels

REVELATION 4:7 *The first living creature was like a lion, the second living creature like a calf, the third living creature had a face like a man, and the fourth living creature was like a flying eagle.* (NKJV)

The first angelic being is like a lion—Jesus is the Lion of the tribe of Judah. The lion is the king of beasts and Jesus is the King of kings. The apostle Matthew describes Jesus as the King of the Jews. The second angelic being is like a calf, or an ox—Jesus came as a servant. Just like the ox, a beast that carries its burden, Jesus carried our sins. The apostle Mark describes Jesus as a servant. The third angelic being is like a man—Jesus was human. The apostle Luke describes Jesus as the Son of Man. The fourth angelic being is like an eagle—Jesus is God. Just as the eagle rules the skies, Jesus rules the heavens and reigns over all things. The apostle John describes Jesus as the creator of all things. These four living creatures remind us of the qualities of Jesus that are found in the Four Gospels: Matthew (King of kings), Mark (servant), Luke (Son of Man), and John (Son of God).

The Four Living Creatures

Creature	Nature	Gospel Link to Jesus
Lion	King of beasts	The Gospel of Matthew calls Jesus the King of the Jews
Calf/Ox	Beast of burden	The Gospel of Mark calls Jesus a Servant
Man	Human	The Gospel of Luke calls Jesus the Son of Man
Eagle	Rules the skies	The Gospel of John calls Jesus God

Holy, Holy, Holy

REVELATION 4:8 *The four living creatures, each having six wings, were full of eyes around and within. And they do not rest day or night, saying:*
"Holy, holy, holy,
Lord God Almighty,
Who was and is and is to come!" (NKJV)

six wings
Isaiah 6:2

eyes of the Lord
2 Chronicles 16:9

never sleep
Psalm 121:4

**exalt the name
of Jesus**
Isaiah 24:14–15

**who was, and who is,
and who is to come**
Revelation 1:8

falling down
1 Corinthians 14:25

Their <u>six wings</u> are characteristic of the seraphim. Their eyes are like the <u>eyes of the Lord</u>: they are everywhere, beholding everything. Their stamina is like the stamina of the Lord: they never stop singing, and they <u>never sleep</u>. They are there to <u>exalt the name of Jesus</u>, the One <u>who was, and who is, and who is to come</u>.

Notice that they say, "Holy, holy, holy." Could it be that they are saying, "Holy is the God of the past, holy is the God of the present, and holy is the God of the future"? Or could it be that they are in the presence of the Trinity (Lord God Almighty) and they are saying, "Holy is the Father (Almighty), holy is the Son (Lord), and holy is the Spirit (God)"? Be sure of this: they surround the throne and they know the character of the One-in-Three they are worshiping.

falling down
drop on one's knees
or lie prostrate on
the ground

Glory, Honor, and Thanks

REVELATION 4:9 *Whenever the living creatures give glory and honor and thanks to Him who sits on the throne, who lives forever and ever, (NKJV)*

The purpose of the four living creatures is to worship and give glory, honor, and thanks to the One on the throne. In doing so, they acknowledge that he is eternal and almighty. But each time they glorify the Lord, something else happens.

Fall on Your Knees

REVELATION 4:10 *the twenty-four elders fall down before Him who sits on the throne and worship Him who lives forever and ever, and cast their crowns before the throne, saying: (NKJV)*

The twenty-four elders always follow the lead of the four living creatures. Whenever the four living creatures worship the one on the throne, the twenty-four elders also worship him by **falling down** and exalting him. This falling down is a deliberate act of humility.

go to

creator of all things
Isaiah 40:28

The elders remove their crowns and place them before the throne. Even these kings, high priests, and leaders recognize that he is their power and their source.

what others say

David Hocking

When they fall down before him (Revelation 4:10) they give recognition to his authority and position. It is a lesson to all believers; we need to submit to his authority as a daily principle in our lives. That's why it is a good thing to kneel when we pray to indicate our submission to the Lord.[5]

REVELATION 4:11
"You are worthy, O Lord,
To receive glory and honor and power;
For You created all things,
And by Your will they exist and were created." (NKJV)

This has been called the song of creation. The twenty-four elders proclaim his worthiness and acknowledge him as the creator of all things, the One who holds all things together. "By Your will" expresses the desire of Jesus to create all things. We may not understand a great deal about his marvelous creation, but we can understand that it was brought into existence because Jesus wanted it to exist. And it continues to exist because it is his will.

what others say

Bruce Wilkinson with David Kopp

When you and I stand in the presence of God—knowing and seeing who He is and all that He has done in His sovereign power to move us from birth to "that Day"—we will pour out our thanks and praise to Him, joyfully doing our best to shake the rafters of heaven.[6]

Chapter Wrap-Up

- When John goes to heaven in the spirit it is symbolic of the Rapture of the Church. (Revelation 4:1–2)

- God's throne is surrounded by a rainbow, the twenty-four elders, seven lamps, a sea of glass, and the four living creatures. (Revelation 4:2–6)

- The flashes of lightning, rumblings and peals of thunder coming from the throne of God are symbolic of the approaching storm known as the Tribulation Period. (Revelation 4:5)

- The four living creatures have six wings and are covered with eyes. Each creature resembles a different animal: lion, calf, man, and eagle. (Revelation 4:7–8)

- When the four living creatures glorify God, the twenty-four elders will lay their crowns before the throne and proclaim God's worthiness. (Revelation 4:9–11)

Study Questions

1. What did the trumpet voice say to John?

2. What stones describe the appearance of the One on the throne?

3. What will the twenty-four elders wear in heaven?

4. What do the blazing lamps before the throne represent?

5. Following the symbolic act of the twenty-four elders, what crowns should we lay before the throne?

Chapter Highlights:
• The Seven-Sealed Scroll
• The Lion of Judah
• Worship of the Lamb
• Praise from All
  Creatures

Revelation 5

Let's Get Started

Revelation is a book of symbols. Under the inspiration of the Holy Spirit, John recorded God's message using these symbols to make it easier for us to understand. Unfortunately, now we have the task of deciphering what is the meaning of these symbols. To do that we look to the Old Testament book of the prophet Jeremiah.

Jeremiah 32 explains the <u>law for redemption of land</u>. Its purpose was to help those in Israel who fell behind in their debts. Those who got behind lost their land but were not without hope.

They still had the right to buy their land back in the future. Even if they did not, or could not buy their land, after a prescribed period of time their heir or next of kin could buy it. In this way, their land remained in their family.

On one occasion, God told Jeremiah that his cousin would ask him to redeem his land. His cousin had fallen in debt, lost his land, and been sentenced to prison. It wasn't long before Jeremiah went to see his cousin in prison. There the cousin asked Jeremiah to buy his land and told him it was <u>his right to redeem</u> it and possess it. Understanding that it was God's law, Jeremiah bought the land.

Even this wasn't enough. Jeremiah had not yet met all of the requirements of the law. When his cousin lost the land, two scrolls (contracts) containing terms for redeeming the land were drafted. One scroll became a public record and was displayed unsealed for all to read. The other was rolled up and sealed with seven seals and placed in storage at the temple. It was brought out only when someone showed proof of their right to **redeem** the land.

After this redeemer presented the necessary proof of ownership, the temple priest would retrieve the seven-sealed scroll from storage. He would then unseal the scroll and read it. If everything was in order, the redeemer would receive all ownership to the land. When God created all things, he gave earth to man, but Adam sinned and lost it to Satan. However, Adam is still a **joint heir** with Jesus, an

go to

law for redemption of land
Leviticus 25:8–24;
Jeremiah 32:1–25

his right to redeem
Jeremiah 32:8

redeem
to buy back

joint heir
one who shares in the inheritance of others

go to

Kinsman Redeemer
Isaiah 63:16

qualifies to redeem
Romans 3:23–24;
1 Peter 1:18–19;
Ephesians 1:7;
1 John 2:2

the Flood
Genesis 6 and 7

Sodom and Gomorrah
Genesis 18:16;
19:29

adopted child of God. Jesus is a <u>Kinsman Redeemer</u> who can buy back the earth and mankind.

In chapter 5 the Church is now in heaven, and we are in that period of time between the Rapture and the Tribulation Period. The question before us is, who <u>qualifies to redeem</u> Adam's lost property?

---

what others say

Hal Lindsey

Sealing a scroll was a common and important practice in biblical times. The wills of both Emperor Vespasian and Caesar Augustus, for example, were secured with seven seals. For such a document, a scribe would procure a long roll of parchment and begin writing. After a period of writing he would stop, roll the parchment enough to cover his words, and seal the scroll at that point with wax. Then he would resume writing, stop again, roll the scroll, and add another seal. By the time he was finished, he would have sealed the scroll seven times. The scroll would be read a section at a time, after each seal was opened.[1]

Safely Out

REVELATION 5:1–2 *And I saw in the right hand of Him who sat on the throne a scroll written inside and on the back, sealed with seven seals. Then I saw a strong angel proclaiming with a loud voice, "Who is worthy to open the scroll and to loose its seals?"* (NKJV)

John is still in heaven and beside God's throne at the opening of chapter 5. He sees a scroll in God's right hand that is sealed seven times with writing on both sides. Whatever this scroll is, there is no doubt that it is important. Why would God reveal this scroll to his Church? Could it be that he has the destiny of all mankind in his hands? Could it be that he is in charge of all that happens on earth? We know that God did not allow the earth to be destroyed by <u>the Flood</u> until Noah and his family were safely in the ark. We also know that God would not allow <u>Sodom and Gomorrah</u> to be destroyed by fire and brimstone until Lot and his family were safely out of the city. Could it be that God will not allow this scroll to be opened until his church is safely in heaven?

Scrolls were made from strips of leather (animal skins) in John's day. They were very expensive and very valuable. In fact, they were so costly the Hebrew scribes often wrote on both sides to save money. This scroll in God's right hand has writing on both sides. It's a very valuable document.

John also saw a powerful angel. What made this angel appear to be so strong is not revealed, but he had the authority to speak in the presence of God. We do not know who this angel is, but because the name Gabriel means "strength of God," some believe he is indeed the **archangel** Gabriel. "Who is worthy to open the scroll and to loose its seals?" is a gripping question. Who could ever qualify as a redeemer for Adam and our fallen world?

The Root of David

REVELATION 5:3–5 *And no one in heaven or on the earth or under the earth was able to open the scroll, or to look at it. So I wept much, because no one was found worthy to open and read the scroll, or to look at it. But one of the elders said to me, "Do not weep. Behold, the Lion of the tribe of Judah, the Root of David, has prevailed to open the scroll and to loose its seven seals." (NKJV)*

No one in heaven or earth, either living or dead, will be able to open the scroll and look inside. Obviously John was heartbroken because he desired to know what the scroll contained. He had a great love for all mankind and had hoped the scroll would provide the answers to its problems, but that was not to be. The message of the scroll would have to wait.

Church members often hear Christians say there are no tears in heaven, but that's not wholly true. John wept much. And God can't wipe away tears in heaven unless there are tears in heaven. The tears of God's people will not cease to exist until the New Jerusalem comes out of heaven and God destroys death, sorrow, and crying (Revelation 21:4).

Suddenly, one of the twenty-four elders told John to stop crying. Someone worthy to open the scroll had been found. It is the Lion of the tribe of Judah, the Root of David. These two Old Testament names of God remind us of the first and second coming of Jesus.

Judah, one of the twelve sons of Israel (also called Jacob), was also the first leader of one of the twelve tribes of Israel. God promised

go to

Gabriel
Daniel 9:21,
Luke 1:19

Judah
Genesis 35:23–26

Israel
Genesis 32:28

twelve tribes
Genesis 49:28

archangel
a leader among
angels

go to

Messiah
Genesis 49:9–10;
2 Samuel 7

Lion of the tribe of Judah
Genesis 49:9

Root of David
Isaiah 11:1,
Revelation 22:16

not because we are righteous
Romans 3: 10, 23

John the Baptist
Matthew 3:1–17

led to slaughter
Isaiah 53:7

the <u>Messiah</u> would come from that tribe whose symbol was a lion. Jesus, a descendant of the tribe of Judah, is the Messiah—<u>the Lion of the tribe of Judah</u>. At the end of the Tribulation Period Jesus will return with the strength of a lion.

Jesus is also the <u>Root of David</u>. God promised David that one of his descendants would be the Messiah. Jesus is a fulfillment of that prophecy. His earthly mother was Mary, a descendant of David. Jesus came as a lamb the first time.

> **what others say**
>
> **Leon Morris**
>
> John *wept and wept* (his word means a noisy grief, a wailing), perhaps because he found it depressing that *no-one was found . . . worthy* for the task. More probably his distress was connected with the contents of the book. He had been promised that he would see things that would happen (4:1). Would he after all fail to see the revelation? Would God's purpose not be worked out?[2]

When we get to heaven, it will <u>not be because we are righteous</u> or because we are worthy redeemers, but because we have been redeemed by the grace of God.

Sacrifice the Lamb

REVELATION 5:6 *And I looked, and behold, in the midst of the throne and of the four living creatures, and in the midst of the elders, stood a Lamb as though it had been slain, having seven horns and seven eyes, which are the seven Spirits of God sent out into all the earth. (NKJV)*

When Jesus walked upon this earth, <u>John the Baptist</u> introduced him by saying, "Behold! The Lamb of God who takes away the sin of the world!" (John 1:29 NKJV). When the John of Revelation saw him in heaven, he described Jesus as a Lamb that looked as if it had been slain. Jesus is our sacrificial Lamb. The Old Testament prophet Isaiah foretold that he would be as a lamb <u>led to the slaughter</u>. Peter said Christians are redeemed "with the precious blood of Christ, as of a lamb without blemish and without spot" (1 Peter 1:19 NKJV).

Jesus looked like he had been killed, but he was not lying on an altar, in bed, or in a casket. He was standing in the center of the throne, surrounded by the four living creatures and twenty-four elders.

Seven is the number of perfection in the Bible, and horns are symbols of power. Seven horns means that Jesus had **omnipotent,** perfect power. He may have looked like a little lamb, but he had all the power of God. After being raised from the dead, Jesus said, "All authority has been given to Me in heaven and on earth" (Matthew 28:18 NKJV).

The seven eyes are defined as the seven spirits of God sent out to all the earth. He looked like he had been slain, but his eyes were not closed. He had the all-seeing **omniscient** vision of the Holy Spirit. He sees and knows all. He has perfect knowledge, understanding, and wisdom.

The seven virtues of the Holy Spirit are, the nature of Jesus, wisdom, understanding, counsel, might, knowledge, and respect for God's will. Jesus also possessed these same virtues—and the Holy Spirit continually spreads them over all the earth. Not everyone is willing to receive them, but they still are everywhere.

omnipotent
all powerful

omniscient
all knowing

From Lamb to Lion

> REVELATION 5:7–8 *Then He came and took the scroll out of the right hand of Him who sat on the throne. Now when He had taken the scroll, the four living creatures and the twenty-four elders fell down before the Lamb, each having a harp, and golden bowls full of incense, which are the prayers of the saints.* (NKJV)

Keep in mind that John was seeing those things that will take place after the Church is raptured. The Rapture is a very significant event because it marks a distinct change in the way Jesus deals with mankind. Up until now he has dealt with us as a lamb, but from this point on through the Tribulation Period, he will deal with those who are left behind as a lion.

This will be a great day. Paul mentioned it in the famous sermon he preached at Athens about the unknown God. He said, God "has appointed a day on which He will judge the world in righteousness by the Man whom He has ordained. He has given assurance of this to all by raising Him from the dead" (Acts 17:31 NKJV).

satanic trinity
consists of Satan, the
Antichrist, and the
False Prophet

Calvary
the site in Jerusalem
where Jesus died

transgressions
sins

John watched as Jesus took the scroll from the right hand of God. All of creation has waited almost six thousand years for this pivotal moment. Adam lost the title deed to earth for all mankind, but Jesus has proven himself a worthy redeemer and will get the deed back.

When Jesus took the scroll, the four living creatures and the twenty-four elders fell down and worshiped him each with a harp and a golden bowl. The harps are musical instruments that will accompany the singing in heaven. The golden bowls will contain the prayers of the saints. Who and what will we be praying for? We will be praying for our loved ones on earth who are being persecuted. We will pray for the defeat of the **satanic trinity**, and we will pray for the Second Coming and the subsequent reign of Jesus.

The Godhead is thought of as the Trinity. Father, Son, and Holy Spirit. Satan seems to try to duplicate that with his own trinity called the satanic trinity. Satan tries to replace God, the Antichrist tries to replace Christ, and the False Prophet tries to replace the Holy Spirit. Satan will indwell the Antichrist and False Prophet, so they will be pure evil. When the Antichrist supposedly dies and is resurrected some think he will come back to life because Satan has possessed his body.

A New Song

REVELATION 5:9–10 *And they sang a new song, saying:*
"You are worthy to take the scroll,
And to open its seals;
For You were slain,
And have redeemed us to God by Your blood
Out of every tribe and tongue and people and nation,
And have made us kings and priests to our God;
And we shall reign on the earth." (NKJV)

The four living creatures and the twenty-four elders sang a new song with a new form of praise. Their song speaks of what Jesus is to do, and what he has already done. It tells why Jesus is worthy to take the scroll and open the seals.

Jesus is worthy because he was slain on the cross at **Calvary**. The Old Testament prophet Isaiah said, "Surely He has borne our griefs and carried our sorrows; yet we esteemed Him stricken, smitten by God, and afflicted. But He was wounded for our **transgressions**,

He was bruised for our iniquities; the chastisement for our peace was upon Him, and by His stripes we are healed. All we like sheep have gone astray; we have turned, every one, to his own way; and the LORD has laid on Him the **iniquity** of us all" (Isaiah 53:4–6 NKJV).

Jesus is worthy because with his blood he purchased our sins. He paid the price of our redemption. "Knowing that you were not redeemed with corruptible things, like silver or gold, from your aimless conduct received by tradition from your fathers, but with the precious blood of Christ, as of a lamb without blemish and without spot" (1 Peter 1:18–19 NKJV). The blood of Jesus was precious. God said, "For the life of the flesh is in the blood, and I have given it to you upon the altar to make **atonement** for your souls" (Leviticus 17:11 NKJV). It was the blood of Jesus that made atonement for our sins.

Iniquity is a type of sin. It is a sin of commission, such as theft or murder. *Sin* is wrongdoing of any kind. It can be an act of omission (not doing something) or of commission (doing something).

Jesus is worthy because he is <u>no respecter</u> of persons. He died for the sins of all the world—every tribe and language and people and nation—because he <u>loves the world</u>.

Jesus is worthy because he made us a royal priesthood to serve and reign with him. He commissioned his Church to go and make <u>disciples</u> of all nations. And when he returns in his Second Coming at the end of the Tribulation Period, we will <u>reign with him</u> on earth for one thousand years (the Millennium).

go to

no respecter
Acts 10:34 KJV

loves the world
John 3:16

disciples
Matthew 28:19

reign with him
Revelation 20:6

ten thousand times ten thousand
Daniel 7:10

iniquity
sin

atonement
Jesus' crucifixion that restored our relationship with God

> ## what others say
>
> ### Leon Morris
>
> This particular song arises from the opening of the seals as its first words show. The Lamb's saving word has created a new situation and this elicits a new outburst of praise. No song meant for another situation quite fits this.[3]

<u>Worthy Is the Lamb</u>

REVELATION 5:11–12 *Then I looked, and I heard the voice of many angels around the throne, the living creatures, and the elders; and the number of them was <u>ten thousand times ten thousand</u>, and thousands of thousands, saying with a loud voice:*

Revelation 5   75

"Worthy is the Lamb who was slain
To receive power and riches and wisdom,
And strength and honor and glory and blessing!" (NKJV)

John looked and he saw a multitude of angels gathered around the living creatures, the twenty-four elders, and the throne of God. Then he heard them singing declaring the worthiness of God. Who is to receive:

- *Power*—the authority to do whatever he wants (forgive sins, give eternal life, and command angels)
- *Riches*—the wealth of God (everything belongs to him)
- *Wisdom*—the natural wisdom of God (his counsel, his understanding, and the ability to create, uphold, govern, judge, and redeem)
- *Strength*—the physical strength to do whatever he wants (perform miracles, conquer, create, destroy, cast into the lake of fire)
- *Honor*—rewards (the rewards of God and his people)
- *Glory*—the image of God (God's glory, God's magnificence, God's splendor, the royal dignity and the royal majesty)
- *Blessing*—worship, acknowledgment, and commendation

what others say

H. Grady Hardin, Joseph D. Quillian Jr., and James F. White

Victory is the basis of Christian worship. It is the victory of Almighty God through Jesus Christ. It is God's victory over our death and for our life; it is the triumph of his purpose to redeem his whole creation to willing responsiveness to him. It is a victory that was won in principle by the death and resurrection of Jesus Christ, and now is to be realized in full. Because it is victory, the whole telling forth (announcing, proclaiming) of what God has done, will do, and is doing through Jesus Christ is called the gospel—"good news."[4]

Every Creature

REVELATION 5:13–14 *And every creature which is in heaven and on the earth and under the earth and such as are in the sea, and all that are in them, I heard saying:*

"Blessing and honor and glory and power
Be to Him who sits on the throne,
And to the Lamb, forever and ever!"
Then the four living creatures said, "Amen!" And the twenty-
four elders fell down and worshiped Him who lives forever and
ever. (NKJV)

Father and the Son
Philippians 2:9–11

John heard every creature praise God and his Son, Jesus. Every creature in heaven, under the earth, and on the sea. Every creature that is alive or dead. Every creature who has been judged or will be judged. Every creature from the **days of Adam** to the Rapture will praise him.

The four living creatures responded to the praise by saying, "Amen!" signifying that they were in agreement with the praise of every other creature. They affirmed their praise and worship. Then the twenty-four elders responded by falling down and worshiping the Father and the Son. Praise and worship are due the <u>Father and the Son</u> throughout all eternity. Both were involved in the redemption of all things and both should be praised as long as anything exists.

days of Adam
beginning of Creation

what others say

Mal Couch

True worship always is directed toward God and extols His character and accomplishments and promises over our character, our accomplishments, and our promises. Colossians 2:18 and 2 Thessalonians 2:3–4 make it clear that there is such a thing as false worship as well, so Christians need to be discerning in this regard.[5]

Three Songs in Revelation Chapter 5

Who	Where	What
Four living creatures and twenty-four elders	Revelation 5:8–10	Jesus is worthy, died, redeemed multitudes, made us kings and priests, and we will reign on earth
Angels	Revelation 5:11–12	Jesus is worthy to receive power, riches, wisdom, strength, honor, glory, and blessing
Every creature everywhere	Revelation 5:13	Blessing, honor, glory, and power belong to God and Jesus forever

Chapter Wrap-Up

- God will hold a seven-sealed scroll in his right hand as an angel asks, "Who is worthy to open the scroll?" John will weep when no one steps forward. (Revelation 5:1–4)

- Jesus is the Lion of Judah, and he is the only One worthy to open the scroll. He is worthy because he was slain for the sins of the world. (Revelation 5:5–7)

- Once Jesus takes the scroll, the four living creatures and twenty-four elders will sing a new song; the angels will also join in proclaiming Christ's worthiness. (Revelation 5:8–12)

- When heaven is singing to Jesus, all creatures on earth and under the sea will also sing praise to him. (Revelation 5:13)

Study Questions

1. What is the implied significance of the scroll?

2. How are the two comings of Jesus symbolized in John's vision?

3. How does this chapter explain the seeming injustice of God's letting sin go unpunished?

4. Why is the Church a royal priesthood?

5. How do we know that Jesus was more than just a good man or a prophet?

Revelation 6

Chapter Highlights:
• The First Seal
• The Four Horsemen
• The Tribulation Saints
• The Great Earthquake

Let's Get Started

In chapter 6, the scene shifts from future events in heaven to future events on earth. We have looked at what will happen in heaven between the Rapture and the Tribulation Period. Now we turn our attention to what will happen on earth during this same period of time. There is much debate about how long this period will last, but three years is a good possibility.

seven feast days
Leviticus 23

The Seven Jewish Feast Days

God gave the Jews <u>seven feast days</u> to observe forever (see Time Line #4, Appendix A). It can be shown that

1. Jesus was crucified on Passover (the first feast day)

2. Jesus was in the grave on the Feast of Unleavened Bread (the second feast day)

3. Jesus arose from the dead on the Feast of Firstfruits (the third feast day)

4. the Church began on Pentecost (the fourth feast day)

5. there is reason to believe the Church will be raptured on the Feast of Trumpets (the fifth feast day)

6. there is reason to believe the Second Coming will occur and the Tribulation Period will end on the Day of Atonement (the sixth feast day)

7. there is reason to believe the Millennium will begin on the Feast of Tabernacles (the seventh feast day)

Interestingly enough, between the Feast of Trumpets (the Rapture) and the Day of Atonement (the Second Coming and the end of the Tribulation Period), there is a ten-day period called the "ten

Tribulation Period
Revelation 6:17

restrained
2 Thessalonians
2:6–8

days of awe," "the awesome days," or the "ten days of repentance." Since the seventieth week (or the <u>Tribulation Period</u>) corresponds to seven years (one day of the seventieth week = one year of the Tribulation Period), it is reasonable to assume that the ten days of awe will correspond to ten years. This period of time will give people, Gentiles and Jews, an opportunity to grieve, mourn, repent, and accept Jesus as Messiah before the Second Coming occurs and their fate is sealed forever. It will also allow three years for the Antichrist to come on the scene and rise to power before the Tribulation Period begins.

The Number Seven

During the Tribulation Period, Jesus will start to deal with the satanic trinity and man's rebellion on earth. His course of discipline will be directed from heaven, but the terrible events will take place on earth. The Holy Spirit has divided these events into three sets of seven: seven seal judgments, seven trumpet judgments, and seven bowl judgments. It would be easy to say that twenty-one judgments will occur, but that is not the case. The first six seals will be broken one at a time, and each seal will produce a judgment, for a total of six judgments. The seventh seal will not produce a seventh judgment. Instead, it will produce the seven trumpets. The first six trumpets each produce a judgment, for a total of six. But the seventh trumpet will produce seven bowls. When the seventh bowl is poured out, the Tribulation Period will come to an end.

A small number of prophecy experts suggest that these judgments will occur simultaneously. This can't be. The seven trumpets do not begin until the seventh seal is opened, and the seven bowls do not begin until the seventh trumpet is blown. Over the centuries people have always tried to figure out the Antichrist's identity, since he will probably be alive when the Church is raptured. But the problem with this is that he will be <u>restrained</u> and will not be revealed until the proper time. When the true Church is raptured, it will be time to start watching for the Antichrist. He will not stand out at first, so the best thing to look for will be a popular and powerful person. When he signs a seven-year treaty to protect Israel, his identity will be known.

The Seven Seals

Seal	Symbol	Result	Scripture
First	Rider on White Horse	Release the Antichrist	Revelation 6:1–2
Second	Rider on Red Horse	Removes Peace, Causes War	Revelation 6:3–4
Third	Rider on Black Horse	Economic Collapse and Famine	Revelation 6:5–6
Fourth	Rider on Pale Horse	Death of Unbelievers —1/4 of World	Revelation 6:7–8
Fifth	Souls Under the Altar	Persecution and Death of Believers	Revelation 6:9–11
Sixth	Great Earthquake	Cosmic Upheaval (Sun, Moon, etc.)	Revelation 6:12–14
Seventh	The 7 Trumpet Judgments	(See chart on the Seven Trumpets on page 110)	Revelation 8:1–2

It's important to note that Daniel indicates that the Tribulation Period will begin when the Antichrist confirms a seven-year covenant (Daniel 9:27). This indicates that the covenant will be worked out and signed by others first, and confirmed by the Antichrist later. Note that it will be a covenant with many. There have been several peace agreements between Israel and others (Camp David, Wye River, Oslo, etc.), but the Road Map is the first treaty to involve the whole world (the United Nations, the United States, Russia, and the EU). Society can't get a greater "many" than this. Notice that it involves the EU from which the Antichrist will ascend.

Furthermore, some skeptics say the Bible mentions a spirit of antichrist, but not a person called the Antichrist. The fact is, the Bible refers to Jesus by many different names: Son of God, Lamb of God, Savior, Christ, etc., and it's the same way with the Antichrist. He is called the Man of Sin, the Little Horn, the Beast Out of the Sea, the King of Fierce Countenance, the Lawless One, the Prince That Shall Come, and much more. Jesus called him the Abomination of Desolation in Matthew 24:15. Jesus didn't say the Antichrist is a person, but he said the Antichrist will stand in the holy place, and other verses say he will sit in the Temple, sign a covenant, and demand to be worshiped. The Bible doesn't always say Satan, but everyone knows what it means when it says Lucifer, Devil, or Old Serpent. So everyone should know what it means when it says Man of Sin, etc.

<u>Like a Tiny Snowball Rolling Down a Hill</u>

REVELATION 6:1 Now I saw when the Lamb opened one of the seals; and I heard one of the four living creatures saying with a voice like thunder, "Come and see." (NKJV)

The terrible judgments will not begin like a nuclear explosion, but rather like a tiny snowball rolling down a long hill. They will not appear that bad at first, but they will gain strength and momentum with each roll. Things will eventually get out of control and become so bad that mankind would destroy the earth were it not for the second coming of Jesus.

Notice who opens the seals. Jesus! He is in charge of the judgments and their timing. He once said, "For the Father judges no one, but has committed all judgment to the Son, that all should honor the Son just as they honor the Father" (John 5:22–23 NKJV). When he opens the first seal, one of the four living creatures will speak in a voice like thunder.

In each of the first four seals, a horse and rider are released by one of the four living creatures of chapter 4. Each horse is waiting in its stall ready to charge, as if in a race, when the command is given. They will not, however, all race out at once. Each horse must wait for its command, and its command will be given by a different living creature when Jesus breaks a seal. When all four living creatures have commanded their horses to come forth, all four horses will have been released. Each living creature summons its horse by speaking just three words—*Come and see*. This is consistent with what Paul taught. The Antichrist is being restrained and cannot come forth until the restrainer (Church and Holy Spirit) is taken out of the way (2 Thessalonians 2:6–8). Jesus won't break the seal and this first living creature won't say "Come" until the Church is removed.

As long as <u>Noah</u> was on the earth, God did not send the Flood, but when Noah entered the ark, God did send the Flood and judged the world. As long as Lot and his family were in <u>Sodom and Gomorrah</u>, God did not send fire and brimstone to destroy the cities. But likewise, when Lot and his family were safely out of Sodom and Gomorrah, God did not hesitate to judge these cities. Today, as long as the Church is in the world, God will not send these terrible judgments. But as soon as the Church is taken to heaven, God will not hesitate to pour out his wrath. This is the grace of God.

Noah
Genesis 6, 7

Sodom and Gomorrah
Genesis 18:16–19:29

gift
Revelation 13:2, 4–5, 14–15

A White Horse

REVELATION 6:2 *And I looked, and behold, a white horse. He who sat on it had a bow; and a crown was given to him, and he went out conquering and to conquer. (NKJV)*

Chapter 19 also speaks of a rider on a white horse—Jesus. For this reason, a few experts suggest that this rider will also be Jesus. But most experts disagree, believing this rider to be none other than the counterfeit Christ, or Antichrist.

A very small minority of individuals say this rider on a white horse is an unidentified nation. But the Rider in chapter 19 is Jesus, and he's followed by armies of other riders (angels, church, Tribulation Saints), not some unknown nation. Consistency says this rider will be a person.

He will come forth with a bow. A bow was an effective weapon in John's day; a symbol of military power. However, nothing is said about arrows, so many think this rider will come forth as a man of peace.

Crowns were worn by heads of state. Those who wore them usually earned or inherited the right to wear their crown. But this man will receive his crown as a <u>gift</u>, meaning he will not earn or inherit it.

The world will be looking for such a ruler who can put an end to nuclear weapons, environmental and economic problems, poverty, terrorism, etc. He will go forth as a conqueror bent on conquest, thereby abandoning his peace program in an attempt to dominate the world. But his use of force to attain his goal of world domination will be a disaster, resulting in the persecution and death of all

go to

peace treaties
Daniel 9:27

prophets of Israel
2 Chronicles
36:15–16

those who oppose him. The earth will have a charismatic leader negotiating <u>peace treaties</u> that are a fake.

When Jesus made his triumphal entry into Jerusalem as a man of peace, he did not ride in on a conqueror's white horse, but on a donkey. When he returns as a conqueror at the end of the Tribulation Period, he will ride on a white horse. Notice that the Antichrist does not ride in on a donkey of peace like Jesus did at his first coming, but rather on a horse in conquest like Jesus when he returns at his second coming.

Be aware that most prophetic writers believe the Antichrist will rise to power in Europe (the Revived Roman Empire of Daniel 9:24–27). This makes the founding of the European Union very significant. And it's most interesting that the nations in this union have organized and equipped a new army they call an "Army of Peace."

what others say

David Reagan

This is the Antichrist riding on a white horse as an imitator of Jesus who will return at the end of the Tribulation, also riding on a white horse (Revelation 19:11). He goes forth to conquer the world. Jesus does not conquer by war. Jesus conquers by the power of the Word of God. So this is definitely the Antichrist.[2]

John Hagee

In the surge of advocates for peace, voices of dissent will be shouted down or ignored. The peace process will cease to become a political action; it will become a spiritual mandate for a nation. Based on the words of the <u>prophets of Israel</u>, I believe this peace process will lead to the most devastating war Israel has ever known.[3]

Notice the Spirit World

Evil	Good
Abaddon attacks with demon locusts (Revelation 9:1–12)	Angels seal 144,000 (Revelation 7:1–3)
Satan attacks Israel (Revelation 12:13)	Jesus breaks the seven seals (Revelation 6:1–8:1)
Evil spirits set up Armageddon (Revelation 16:13–14)	Jesus at Armageddon (Revelation 19:11–21)
Antichrist comes from bottomless pit (Revelation 17:8)	Angel binds Satan (Revelation 20:1–2)
Satan deceives the nations (Revelation 20:7–10)	God sends Holy City (Revelation 21:1–2)

A Fiery Red Horse

go to

attack Israel
Ezekiel 38–39

against his brother
Ezekiel 38:21–23

REVELATION 6:3–4 *When He opened the second seal, I heard the second living creature saying, "Come and see." Another horse, fiery red, went out. And it was granted to the one who sat on it to take peace from the earth, and that people should kill one another; and there was given to him a great sword. (NKJV)*

The Antichrist will barely have his peace program off the ground when Jesus breaks the second seal. This time it will be the second living creature who speaks the command, *Come and see.*

A fiery red horse will go forth, and its rider will have an unusual power. He will take peace from the earth and cause men to slay one another. This rider will charge forth with a great sword in his hand, signifying that he will go forth with many powerful weapons of war.

Some experts associate this rider on a red horse with Communism. The prophet Ezekiel foretells the rise of a dictator from the far north (possibly Russia) who will go forth to <u>attack Israel</u> in the last days. He will advance with a great army carrying swords and riding horses, but will meet defeat when many of his own troops slay each other because God will turn each man <u>against his brother</u> so that God's glory may be shown.

People have trouble believing Jesus will break the seal to remove peace from the earth. But it's more difficult to believe he will sit idly by while the Antichrist establishes a satanic one-world religion that kills Christians and Jews. It's an act of grace because world peace without Jesus is worthless if everyone on earth is about to wind up in hell.

what others say

Dave Hunt

Jerusalem would not be a problem if Israel itself and the nations of the world would acknowledge that the one true God "is the God of Israel" and would submit to His plans for His chosen people. Instead, world political and religious leaders continue to defy God, determined to force their agenda upon Israel. That policy can only lead ultimately to Armageddon and God's judgment upon this world—and it will.[4]

The Prince of Peace — The Prince of War

The Antichrist will be a false prince of peace. God will show the world he is a fake by causing his phony peace programs to fail. Jesus is the true Prince of Peace. When world leaders reject him, they reject the only solution to their problems. Then the world will be plunged into "wars and rumors of wars" (Matthew 24:6 NKJV). It has always had this, but at some point, the frequency and intensity will greatly increase. In fact, it's by the grace of God that war is being restrained to a degree today. But when Jesus breaks this second seal and the living creature says *Come and see*, war will escalate.

A Black Horse

> **REVELATION 6:5–6** *When He opened the third seal, I heard the third living creature say, "Come and see." So I looked, and behold, a black horse, and he who sat on it had a pair of scales in his hand. And I heard a voice in the midst of the four living creatures saying, "A quart of wheat for a denarius, and three quarts of barley for a denarius; and do not harm the oil and the wine." (NKJV)*

Peace without the Prince of Peace is no peace. The end result can only be war. War will rule the whole world after the Rapture. The wars of foolish and deceitful men will kill farmers, destroy land and crops, and cause the collapse of social, physical, and political structures. These wicked men will destroy, confiscate, and hoard food supplies, causing despair, misery, poverty, and death.

When Jesus opens the third seal, the third living creature will give the same command as the first two, *Come and see*. This horse will be black, the color of grief and mourning. Its rider will hold a pair of scales that symbolize economic disaster and famine. The scales will be used to weigh food, which will sell for a ridiculously high price. A small quart of wheat will cost the equivalent of a day's wages, but many will not be able to survive on this, so they will be forced to buy barley, a cheaper food that is usually fed to animals. Three quarts of barley will still cost the equivalent of a day's wages, so no money will be left for clothes, housing, or automobiles. In spite of all this, the rich will still be able to afford luxury items such as oil and wine.

Jesus is the <u>Bread of Life</u>, but the Antichrist will be a false bread of life. The Antichrist will prove to be a fake when his food programs result in famine.

Bread of Life
John 6:31–35

Ultimately, the nations will pay for their growing budget deficits, increased consumer debt, explosion of bankruptcies, and international business corruption. And if this doesn't trigger it, there's the ever-growing threat of terrorists overthrowing the governments of oil-producing nations; the oft-predicted problem of oil production peaking out; the real possibility of terrorists or natural disasters destroying oil refineries and nuclear power plants; the determined efforts of Islamic terrorists and Islamic nations who support them to replace or disrupt global financial systems; the food needs of an exploding population with more and more people teetering dangerously close to starvation; the overwhelming expense of the "wars and rumors of wars," and the tendency of sinful people to take advantage of disasters and charge several times the normal price for essentials such as food, water, fuel, lumber, and medicine. The picture is gloomy, but Christians can be thankful that this coming economic collapse is restrained by our loving God until after the Rapture.

what others say

Grant R. Jeffrey

A nation cannot continue to borrow forever, going deeper and deeper in debt each year. Finally, they "hit the wall" and economic collapse or hyper-inflation is the only remaining option.[6]

Ed Hindson

Despite the initial success of global economic unity, a worldwide economic disaster will occur, increasing the need for further global economic controls, including a personalized insignia.[7]

A Pale Horse

REVELATION 6:7–8 *When He opened the fourth seal, I heard the voice of the fourth living creature saying, "Come and see." So I looked, and behold, a pale horse. And the name of him who sat on it was Death, and Hades followed with him. And power was given to them over a fourth of the earth, to kill with sword, with hunger, with death, and by the beasts of the earth.* (NKJV)

The world will have a false peace, then war, and then economic collapse and famine. Things will grow progressively worse. This obviously contradicts those who say things will get better and better, or those who teach that the Church will eventually bring in a perfect society. The Bible says, "In the last days perilous times will come . . . [and] evil men and impostors will grow worse and worse, deceiving and being deceived" (2 Timothy 3:1, 13 NKJV).

This writer preached the funeral of a man who survived Hurricane Katrina. His food, water, and other essentials started running out, so he left the area and drove several hundred miles to his parents' home. Shortly after he arrived, he was killed in an automobile accident. Other victims of that same hurricane were evacuated to Houston, Texas. About one month later, Hurricane Rita came along, and they had to be evacuated from there. It happened again three or four weeks later. People moved to shelters when Hurricane Wilma was bearing down on Florida. But one of the shelters suffered damage, and they had to be relocated. That's the way the Tribulation Period will be. "It will be as though a man fled from a lion, and a bear met him! Or as though he went into the house, leaned his hand on the wall, and a serpent bit him!" (Amos 5:19 NKJV).

When Jesus opens the fourth seal, it will be the fourth living creature's turn to command a horse by saying, *Come and see*. This horse will surge forth, creating an eerie sight because of its pale color. In the Greek translation of the Bible, the word used for pale is "*chloros*," meaning pale green like chlorophyll. This horse is the color of spoiled meat and rotting flesh. His rider and the creature following him are personified by Death and Hades. This rider won't be looking for the saved who have been raptured or the few who have accepted Jesus during the Tribulation Period. Instead, he will be hunting the great mass of people who are destined for an eternity in hell. Sadly, this horse and rider will go forth to harvest the souls of unbelievers to fuel the fires of hell.

Notice the progression: The rider on the white horse will be only partially armed. He will have a bow but no arrows. The rider on the red horse will carry a single large sword. The rider on the black horse will have two weapons—economic collapse and famine. This rider will have four weapons—a sword, famine, plagues, and wild animals. Things will get worse and worse, not better.

The sword signifies continuing war and bloodshed; famine signifies starvation; plague signifies diseases; and wild beasts signify the animals of the earth. This last weapon will be a strong signal to the "politically correct" who worship Mother Nature and value the lives of animals over unborn babies' lives. God will show the world that it's wrong to worship Mother Nature. Hungry animals will turn on the unbelieving world and add to the death and **eternal damnation** of more than one billion people.

Today there are troubling signs of plagues sweeping the earth. Experts are sounding alarms that stockpiles of biological weapons are more than enough to destroy the world many times over. Some believe they will become the terrorist weapons of choice in the future. One U.N. report reads, "The al-Qaeda terror network is determined to use chemical and biological weapons and is restrained only by the technical difficulties of doing so." The world does not have enough facilities to produce vaccines. For some diseases there are no known vaccines or insufficient quantities of vaccines. Overpopulation and increased travel make it impossible to localize epidemics. Fleeing refugees will spread deadly diseases. Medical facilities will be overwhelmed, and some will be destroyed. It's a growing challenge that the United Nations seems powerless to change.

what others say

Billy Graham

It is not God's intent that any should perish, but when people defiantly refuse God's plan, the consequence of this disobedience is death. The rider on the pale horse is only taking his due.[8]

Hal Lindsey

It staggers the imagination to realize that one-fourth of the world's population will be destroyed within a matter of days

go to

death
Matthew 24:9

> . . . When I think about this awful judgment that awaits the Christ-rejecting world, it gives no satisfaction to my heart; it fires me up to get out the message that God has provided an alternative in Jesus.[9]

Tribulation Saints

REVELATION 6:9 *When He opened the fifth seal, I saw under the altar the souls of those who had been slain for the word of God and for the testimony which they held. (NKJV)*

Following the Rapture, multitudes will accept Jesus. They are usually called the Tribulation Saints. World leaders will say these Christians are a threat to world government, world peace, world religion, and the environment. Therefore they must be dealt with. Followers of the New Age Movement teach that the earth must go through a cleansing in order to proceed to perfection. This cleansing they envision will include the <u>death</u> of all who turn to Jesus. The opening of the fifth seal switches attention from the deaths of unbelievers to the deaths of believers; from the pit of Hades to under the altar in heaven. The four living creatures will summon no more horses. The last three seals will be different from the first four.

Jesus obviously will not forget his people, because he showed John the souls of these slain believers gathered in a special place. They will have died because of the Word of God and because of the testimony they maintain. Many of these will be from families of Christians who left in the Rapture. Others will be Jews who realize the mistake they made in not accepting Jesus. Some will have heard the Word of God for the first time. Others will finally come to grips with their sin and turn to Jesus, who said, "Do not fear those who kill the body but cannot kill the soul. But rather fear Him who is able to destroy both soul and body in hell" (Matthew 10:28 NKJV). These believers will realize that the Antichrist can do nothing worse than kill the body, for God will raise them from the dead. They will choose to die one death (physical), rather than two (physical and spiritual).

Glorified Bodies

REVELATION 6:10 *And they cried with a loud voice, saying, "How long, O Lord, holy and true, until You judge and avenge our blood on those who dwell on the earth?" (NKJV)*

glorified bodies
new bodies believers
receive in heaven

The souls of the Tribulation Saints are under the altar crying out, instead of rejoicing and praising God around the throne with the rest of the Church. Unlike those who received their **glorified bodies** in the Rapture, these saints will have to wait until later for theirs. Because of this they will be fully conscious and able to rationalize the persecution, torture, and murder they have endured. They will have a sense of justice and want to be raised, vindicated, and given glorified bodies.

They will cry out with a loud voice reminiscent of Psalm 94:1–3: "O Lord God, to whom vengeance belongs—O God, to whom vengeance belongs, shine forth! Rise up, O Judge of the earth; render punishment to the proud. Lord, how long will the wicked, how long will the wicked triumph?" (NKJV). They will utter the prayer Jesus prayed, "Father, forgive them, for they do not know what they do" (Luke 23:34 NKJV). They will appeal to God's sovereign nature and to his sense of justice and fairness when they ask to be avenged. Some people have trouble with the idea that saints in heaven will cry out for vengeance against those who sin on earth. They suggest that these martyred souls are asking God to move against those who rejected his Word and their testimonies about Jesus, and to quickly establish his kingdom on earth (Revelation 6:9).

what others say

Hal Lindsey

It's a sobering fact that if people will not give their hearts to Christ now, while it is still easy and small cost is involved, when the Tribulation judgment sets in, although they can still be saved, it will be "so as by fire" (1 Corinthians 3:15 KJV).[10]

Be Patient

REVELATION 6:11 *Then a white robe was given to each of them; and it was said to them that they should rest a little while longer, until both the number of their fellow servants and their brethren, who would be killed as they were, was completed. (NKJV)*

These martyrs will not be rebuked for asking to be vindicated. They will receive white robes signifying the righteousness of Jesus. Some experts suggest these robes may indicate some type of intermediate body, but whatever the case, we know that the martyrs will be able to hear, understand, and converse, because Jesus tells them to be patient. Their condition seems to be similar to that of the rich man and Lazarus whom Jesus talked about (Luke 16:19–31).

The Tribulation Saints will be told to wait until other believers are killed, indicating Jesus has a specific plan for the rest of the world.

what others say

Billy Graham

We learn two important facts from this mysterious moment. First, there will be a point at the end of time when God will judge the inhabitants of the earth. Second, before that moment can come, other men and women equally dedicated to God and his kingdom will be martyred for the Word of God and for the testimony they maintain. Are you prepared for the risk such words describe?[11]

David Jeremiah with C. C. Carlson

As I write this, I long for everyone to give their hearts to Christ now, when it is comparatively easy to be a Christian. During the Tribulation, the fate of believers will be worse than what happened in the Nazi concentration camps during World War II.[12]

Definitely Not a Harvest Moon

REVELATION 6:12 *I looked when He opened the sixth seal, and behold, there was a great earthquake; and the sun became black as sackcloth of hair, and the moon became like blood. (NKJV)*

When Jesus opens the sixth seal, the whole earth will shake. John calls this shaking "a great earthquake," but the description sounds more like a nuclear explosion. It may be a great earthquake triggered by one or more nuclear explosions. Whatever it is, it will be massive. The whole earth will go into convulsions, and the appearances of the sun and the moon will be changed.

While the earth is going through tremendous vibrations, the sun will be darkened as if almost black, and the moon will turn blood-red. It could be that one or more nuclear explosions will take place, causing the earth to shake violently and spew tons of debris into the atmosphere. The resulting atmospheric pollution will cause darkness to cover the land and the moon to appear red. The 1980 eruption of Mount St. Helens and the 2001 collapse of the World Trade

Center Towers are vivid reminders that darkness can cover the land in the brightest part of the day.

Today the Middle East is brimming with weapons of mass destruction. There are unsubstantiated reports that now both Israel and Iran have the nuclear bomb. Couple this with unfulfilled prophecy, and we can understand why the prophet Isaiah said <u>Damascus</u> will be turned into a ruinous heap, and the mountains of Lebanon will be on fire. The prophet Ezekiel said <u>Egypt</u> will turn to utter waste and desolation for forty years. It is easy to see the possible results of atomic or nuclear weapons.

The prophet Joel said, "The sun shall be turned into darkness, and the moon into blood, before the coming of the great and awesome **day of the LORD**" (Joel 2:31 NKJV). According to Ezekiel, the sword will come upon Egypt when the day of the Lord is near.

Damascus
Isaiah 17:1

Egypt
Ezekiel 29:9–12;
30:3–6

day of the LORD
another name for the Tribulation Period

what others say

Warren W. Wiersbe

God made clear to these martyrs that their sacrifice was an appointment, not an accident; and that others would join them. Even in the death of His people, God is in control (Ps. 116:15); so there is nothing to fear.[13]

Star Wars

REVELATION 6:13 *And the stars of heaven fell to the earth, as a fig tree drops its late figs when it is shaken by a mighty wind.* (NKJV)

The Golden Rule of Interpretation states, "When the plain sense of Scripture makes common sense, seek no other sense." This, however, is one of those instances where the plain sense does not seem to fit because most stars are bigger than the earth. No star could fall to the earth as late figs drop from a fig tree without decimating the planet.

Since the word "stars" in the Greek translation could also be translated "meteors," this could indicate a meteor shower. It could also mean a missile attack. During the Persian Gulf War, nights were filled with cruise missiles and laser-guided smart bombs. One can easily see how someone living almost two thousand years ago would describe scenes like this as falling stars. Whatever these are—stars,

sky actually rolls up
Isaiah 34:1–10

meteors, or missiles—they will fall to earth in abundance like over-ripe figs dropping from a fig tree in a mighty wind.

A Giant Tidal Wave

REVELATION 6:14 *Then the sky receded as a scroll when it is rolled up, and every mountain and island was moved out of its place.* (NKJV)

This seems to be another indication of a coming nuclear war. During a nuclear blast the wind is rapidly pushed out (displaced) for several miles, creating a vacuum at the center of the blast site. Suddenly, this wind, like a giant tidal wave, rushes violently back into the vacuum. The sky actually rolls up on itself. This explosion will be so great it will cause every mountain and island on earth to move.

Skeptics say God will never allow these things to happen. They say it's impossible to move mountains and islands. But the world will long remember that 9.0 earthquake in the Indian Ocean on December 26, 2004, that scientists said packed the energy of a million atomic bombs. It caused a tsunami with waves thirty feet high traveling at 500 miles per hour. The waves struck ten nations, killed more than one hundred thousand people, injured more than one-half million, and left millions homeless. Islands were moved from their original locations. One report said the Island of Sumatra, an island of about 30 million people and mountains 12,000 feet high, moved one hundred feet to the southwest. Another report said the earth wobbled in its orbit and time stopped for three microseconds. It reminds us of the sun standing still for almost a day (Joshua 10:12–13) and later moving backward ten degrees (2 Kings 20:9–11) in Old Testament times. And it reminds us that the Bible predicts a time when "the earth shall reel to and fro like a drunkard, and shall totter like a hut" (Isaiah 24:20 NKJV). Don't say God won't let it happen. Be thankful for the grace that's holding it back until his Church is out of here.

what others say

Billy Graham

Pope John Paul II has stated, "Our future on this planet, exposed as it is to nuclear annihilation, depends on one single factor: humanity must make a moral about-face."[14]

go to

panic
Isaiah 24:1–13

call
Acts 4:12

Run for Your Life

REVELATION 6:15 *And the kings of the earth, the great men, the rich men, the commanders, the mighty men, every slave and every free man, hid themselves in the caves and in the rocks of the mountains,* (NKJV)

But it will be worse than when people fled the winds and floods of hurricanes early this century to sleep on bridges, gymnasium floors, and in sports complexes until they could be evacuated to remote places in other areas of the United States. There will be worldwide panic. Regardless of one's status in life, all people will try to hide. Multitudes will leave everything behind and rush into caves and bomb shelters. Multitudes will flee the cities to hide in the mountains. Kings and princes will flee their palaces. Great generals and mighty men will turn and run in fear for their lives. People of every class will flee and hide. Survival will be man's only concern. And the basic necessities of life will be scarce.

Nothing Will Escape

REVELATION 6:16 *and said to the mountains and rocks, "Fall on us and hide us from the face of Him who sits on the throne and from the wrath of the Lamb!* (NKJV)

Will these panic-stricken people call on Jesus? No! They will call on Mother Nature. They will call on the rocks and mountains to fall on them, because they will want to hide from the face and wrath of God.

Read Zephaniah (handwritten)

go to

day of wrath
Zephaniah 1:14–16

Daniel
Daniel 9:20–27

literally fulfilled
happened as
predicted

Time is a brand new mercy, blessing each day. (handwritten)

Multitudes will finally admit the existence of God. They will even admit that it is possible to anger Jesus, but they will not turn to him. Instead, they will try to hide, but to no avail since nothing can escape the sight of God.

A Day of Wrath

REVELATION 6:17 *For the great day of His wrath has come, and who is able to stand?" (NKJV)*

3½ wk (handwritten)

The <u>day of wrath</u> is another name for the <u>Tribulation Period</u>. The multitudes will recognize the beginning of that day when the sixth seal is opened. Sadly, we read nothing about people repenting and accepting Jesus—only the realization that the dreaded Tribulation Period has come. And there is the question: "Who is able to stand?" The answer is in Revelation 6:18.

what others say

Craig S. Keener

God's time is not always our time, but even if we do not live to see the fulfillment of all our prayers, we can die in hope that God will bring about the things he has promised. After the saints' cries, God judges the world (6:12–17); despite the arrogant fantasies of God's enemies (Proverbs 18:11), human power will provide no refuge in that day when the true King executes justice on the entire social order from Caesar on down (6:15).[17]

A Tribulation Yet to Come

1. In <u>Daniel</u>'s 70-Weeks Prophecy, the first sixty-nine weeks of Daniel's prophecy are the period of time (69 weeks x 7 years/week = 483 years) between the decree for the captive Jews in Babylon to return to Israel to restore and rebuild Jerusalem, and the triumphal entry of Jesus into Jerusalem. Since these first sixty-nine weeks of Daniel's prophecy were **literally fulfilled**, we can only assume that the seventieth week (the last week of seven years) will also be literally fulfilled.

2. Some people do not understand why prophecy teachers say there is a gap between the first sixty-nine weeks of Daniel's prophecy and

the seventieth week (the Church Age—the period between the triumphal entry of Jesus into Jerusalem and the Tribulation Period). A careful study of the prophecy reveals that Jesus would be killed, and Jerusalem and the temple would be destroyed after the sixty-ninth week. That happened in AD 70 when the Romans overran Israel, burned Jerusalem, tore down the temple, and killed five million Jews. Part of the prophecy has been fulfilled. But a careful study also reveals that the seventieth week will not begin until the Antichrist signs a seven-year covenant to protect Israel, that he will break that covenant and stop all animal sacrifices. For this to happen, Israel had to be restored as a nation (which happened in 1948), and the temple must be rebuilt (which has yet to happen). Part of the prophecy is yet to come.

go to

future events
Matthew 24:15

3. Some believe the Church will succeed in establishing the kingdom of God on earth without the world going through the Tribulation Period. But the angel Gabriel told Daniel the Jews would go through the entire seventy weeks before the kingdom of righteousness is brought in. Since the earth has never experienced some of the things prophesied for that time, it must go through them before the kingdom of God can be established.

4. Some people believe that the seventieth week of Daniel had been fulfilled by the time Jesus arrived, but Jesus spoke of these things as <u>future events</u>, not events of the past.

Eight Reasons for the Tribulation Period

Reason	Scripture	*Read these*
To fulfill prophecy	Daniel 9:24	
To defeat Satan, the Antichrist, and the False Prophet	Revelation 19–20	
To uphold Jerusalem's cause and punish those who mistreat the Jews	Isaiah 34:8	
To punish Israel for sinning	Micah 7:9	
To embarrass the Jews and cause them to accept Jesus as their Messiah	Zechariah 13:8–9	
To punish those who claim Israel's land	Ezekiel 36:1–38	
To punish the inhabitants of the earth for sin	Isaiah 24:1–6; 26:20–21	
To cause the inhabitants of the earth to seek righteousness	Isaiah 26:9	

Chapter Wrap-Up

- The judgments of the Tribulation Period begin when Christ opens the first of the seven seals. (Revelation 6:1)
- The four horsemen will bring about the Antichrist, war, economic ruin, famine, and death. (Revelation 6:2–8)
- During the Tribulation Period people will still turn to Christ and be killed for their faith. These people will be known as the Tribulation Saints, and they will ask to be avenged. (Revelation 6:9–10)
- An earthquake will rack the earth, affecting the sun, moon, sky, land, and sea. (Revelation 6:12–14)
- Following the sixth seal, fear will grip everyone on earth as they try to hide from the wrath of God. (Revelation 6:15–17)

Study Questions

1. What weapon did the rider on the white horse carry?

2. What power was given to the rider on the red horse?

3. How much will a quart of wheat cost during the Tribulation Period?

4. What was the name of the rider on the pale horse and who was following him?

Baby can be burned, Saul can be saved.

Chapter Highlights:
• The Mark of God
• The 144,000
• A Great Multitude
• A Great Worship Service
• Never Again!

Revelation 7

Let's Get Started

Today Christians are spreading the Word of God throughout the world by shortwave radio, television, and the Internet. The Bible has been translated into more than half of the known languages in the world, and it will be available in every language of every nation in just a few short years. The world has repeatedly heard the message of salvation, and yet following the Rapture, there will be multitudes who have rejected the Bible and its message.

Jesus said, "And this gospel of the kingdom will be preached in all the world as a witness to all the nations, and then the end will come" (Matthew 24:14 NKJV). Everyone will hear his message and have the opportunity to accept salvation before they die or take the mark of the Beast. God's judgments will fall like mighty bombs dropping to the earth, but his glorious grace will still emerge.

mark of the Beast
Revelation 13:17

Hold Back the Wind

REVELATION 7:1 *After these things I saw four angels standing at the four corners of the earth, holding the four winds of the earth, that the wind should not blow on the earth, on the sea, or on any tree.* (NKJV)

After the first six seals are opened, four angels will stand at the earth's four corners to prevent any wind from blowing. This does not mean the earth will become square. It is simply a symbolic expression meaning the angels will be standing at the four points of the compass: north, south, east, and west. They will control the winds of the earth. Without these angels, the airborne plagues from the previous seals would spread around the world.

The Bible clearly teaches that God controls all things. He controls the good winds and the bad: the trade winds, the hurricanes, the tornadoes, and everything else. "Whatever the LORD pleases He does, in heaven and in earth, in the seas and in all deep places. He causes the vapors to ascend from the ends of the earth; He makes lightning for the rain; He brings the wind out of His treasuries" (Psalm 135:6–7 NKJV). He does it for a reason. "Praise the LORD from the earth, you great sea creatures and all the depths; fire and hail, snow and clouds; stormy wind, fulfilling His word" (Psalm 148:7–8 NKJV).

The Angel from the East

REVELATION 7:2 *Then I saw another angel ascending from the east, having the seal of the living God. And he cried with a loud voice to the four angels to whom it was granted to harm the earth and the sea,* (NKJV)

Christians have always believed in angels. It would be impossible to believe the Bible without believing in angels. They play a prominent role in God's plan for mankind. This is especially true of the stories about Jesus and the judgments of Revelation.

Angels are divided into different categories or ranks. Some rank higher than others, and some serve Satan and not God. We do not know who this angel from the east is, but we do know that he will have authority over the other four angels. The four angels will have the power to harm the earth and sea, but just before they unleash their great power, the angel from the east will intercede with a loud voice and stop them. He will have the seal of the living God in his hand, and it will be used to mark a group of special messengers.

go to

sealed
Ephesians 1:13

God has been marking
Ezekiel 9:4;
Genesis 4:15

The Mark of God

REVELATION 7:3 *saying, "Do not harm the earth, the sea, or the trees till we have sealed the servants of our God on their foreheads." (NKJV)*

The four angels will be commanded to hold back their destructive forces until God's servants can be <u>sealed</u>. Nothing will happen to the land, sea, or trees until these special messengers are protected.

The Bible does not say what this seal will be. We are told only that these believers will be protected by some type of mark. Since the beginning of creation <u>God has been marking</u> his people. God's mark will be placed on their foreheads. It will be an actual mark that will show others that these are God's people.

666 / Mark of the Beast

144,000

REVELATION 7:4–8 *And I heard the number of those who were sealed. One hundred and forty-four thousand of all the tribes of the children of Israel were sealed: of the tribe of Judah twelve thousand were sealed; of the tribe of Reuben twelve thousand were sealed; of the tribe of Gad twelve thousand were sealed; of the tribe of Asher twelve thousand were sealed; of the tribe of Naphtali twelve thousand were sealed; of the tribe of Manasseh twelve thousand were sealed; of the tribe of Simeon twelve thousand were sealed; of the tribe of Levi twelve thousand were*

go to

Dan
Judges 18:30; 1
Kings 12:28–30

Ephraim
Hosea 4:17

False Prophet
Genesis 49:17

tribe of priests
Deuteronomy
10:8–9

tribe of Joseph
Numbers 13:11;
36:5

sealed; of the tribe of Issachar twelve thousand were sealed; of the tribe of Zebulun twelve thousand were sealed; of the tribe of Joseph twelve thousand were sealed; of the tribe of Benjamin twelve thousand were sealed. (NKJV)

God will seal 144,000 of his servants, but they will not come from the Church or any particular denomination. Instead, all 144,000 will come from the twelve tribes of Israel—the Jews. The list of tribes is unusual in that two of the original twelve tribes of Israel—Dan and Ephraim—will be left out. Most experts believe these two tribes will be skipped because they were both guilty of idolatry, thus disqualifying them as special servants of God. Some even believe the False Prophet mentioned in chapter 5 will come from the tribe of Dan.

The tribes of Levi and Joseph will be added to make the twelve marked tribes of the Tribulation Period. As the tribe of priests, Levi was not counted among the original twelve tribes of Israel. The tribe of Joseph was also not one of the original twelve. Joseph was Ephraim's father, and it looks like he will replace his idolatrous son.

For years, some commentators talked about ten missing tribes and said Israel no longer has twelve tribes, but they don't say much about this today. Israeli researchers are using DNA to identify the tribe some Jews belong to. Jews from every tribe have been found. Researchers can't determine which tribe every Jew is from because of centuries of intermarriage, but they can determine which tribe roughly one-third of the Jews are from.

And don't overlook the grace of God here. He will call these Jews and supernaturally protect them from the Antichrist and his followers for the primary purpose of winning multitudes to Jesus.

Even though these verses are clear and straightforward, some people still want to spiritualize them. The Jehovah's Witnesses, for example, believe this refers to 144,000 of their members. However, the verse clearly states that the 144,000 will come from the twelve tribes of Israel, which excludes all Gentiles. It is best to ignore the mental gymnastics and accept the literal interpretation.

key point

turn away from
the faith
Matthew 24:9–14

entered the city of
Jerusalem
John 12:12–13

what others say

David Reagan

What would God have to do to convince us that He is speaking about 144,000 Jews? He says they are Jews. Specifically, He calls them, "the sons of Israel" (Rev. 7:4). He even enumerates them by their tribes, stating that 12,000 will come from each tribe. Does He need to put a flashing neon sign in the sky that says, "I'm talking about Jews!"?[5]

Listen to the Gospel

REVELATION 7:9 *After these things I looked, and behold, a great multitude which no one could number, of all nations, tribes, peoples, and tongues, standing before the throne and before the Lamb, clothed with white robes, with palm branches in their hands,* (NKJV)

Once God has sealed his 144,000, the whole world will hear his message. Multitudes will believe and be saved. The Antichrist and his False Prophet will be furious and try to stop the revival by forcing new believers to turn away from the faith. They will deny people food and medicine. Executions will be frequent and numerous. The number of **martyrs** will be more than any man can count.

These martyrs will be given white robes, symbolizing the righteousness of Jesus. They will also receive palm branches, symbolizing their triumphal entry into heaven. You may remember Jesus was also given palm branches when he entered the city of Jerusalem before his death. The martyrs will stand in the presence of Jesus before the throne of God.

Here the Scriptures give an important clue as to what deceased believers are like before they are raised from the dead. Even though these saints haven't yet been raised, they are not ghosts or vapors. They have some type of materiality or substance. John could see them. He could tell they come from different nationalities and races. He could hear them speak. They wore robes. And they had hands that could hold palm branches. Even though the soul and spirit of a Christian leave their body, people will still be able to identify them. This is further evidence that the believer's knowledge will be greatly improved in heaven.

One Choice

go to

way to heaven
Ephesians 4:5

Saints
those who are
truly saved

REVELATION 7:10 *and crying out with a loud voice, saying, "Salvation belongs to our God who sits on the throne, and to the Lamb!" (NKJV)*

This is a great worship service of victory and rejoicing whose central theme is salvation. The glory of salvation that belongs to God and his Son, Jesus. God is the author of salvation and has narrowed the <u>way to heaven</u> down to one—the Lamb of God.

> **what others say**
>
> **Dave Hunt**
>
> Moses wrote, "So teach us to number our days [that is, to realize how quickly they come to an end], that we may apply our hearts unto wisdom" (Psalm 90:12). The implication is clear that something lies beyond the grave for which we ought to make plans.[6]

Worship Before the Throne

REVELATION 7:11 *All the angels stood around the throne and the elders and the four living creatures, and fell on their faces before the throne and worshiped God, (NKJV)*

This may well be the greatest worship service ever. When this multitude of Tribulation **Saints** stand before the throne praising and glorifying the Father and the Son, all the angels of heaven will join in; followed by the twenty-four elders and four living creatures.

Notice all the different groups: the Tribulation Saints, the twenty-four elders (representing the Church), the angels, and the four living creatures. Everyone in heaven will participate in this service.

Sevenfold Worship

REVELATION 7:12 *saying:*
"Amen! Blessing and glory and wisdom,
Thanksgiving and honor and power and might,
Be to our God forever and ever.
Amen." (NKJV)

"Amen" indicates that the angels will agree with the Tribulation Saints. Salvation belongs to God and his Son, and they deserve the credit for getting this great multitude to heaven. Then the angels will break forth with a sevenfold declaration of worship: blessing, glory, wisdom, thanks, honor, power, and might all belong to God forever and ever.

blood of the Lamb
blood of Jesus

> **what others say**
>
> **Leon Morris**
>
> This concerns *all the angels*. They were standing round the throne and therefore round the elders and the living ones. But at the cry of the redeemed they prostrated themselves and worshipped. They first said *Amen*, which is their assent to the cry of the multitude. It also shows that this act of worship is called into existence by the angels' joy at God's saving act.[7]

Two Questions

REVELATION 7:13 *Then one of the elders answered, saying to me, "Who are these arrayed in white robes, and where did they come from?"* (NKJV)

One of the twenty-four elders will ask two questions: Who are they, and where did they come from? He already knows the answer, but he will ask them anyway to make sure everyone else does.

> **what others say**
>
> **Tim LaHaye**
>
> These "Tribulation Saints" constitute a distinctive category, just as the Church and Israel or Old Testament Saints form a special company. Each group has its own relationship to Christ, depending on the period of time in which these individuals were converted. That these are believers is unquestionable in view of the fact that they have washed their robes and made them white in the **blood of the Lamb** (Revelation 7:14).[8]

The Blood of the Lamb

[go to]

shed blood of the Lamb
Ephesians 1:7;
Hebrews 9:22

face-to-face with Jesus
2 Corinthians 5:8

protected by God
1 John 5:18;
Psalm 121

REVELATION 7:14 *And I said to him, "Sir, you know." So he said to me, "These are the ones who come out of the great tribulation, and washed their robes and made them white in the blood of the Lamb. (NKJV)*

This great multitude before the throne of God will come out of the Tribulation Period. They will be saved people; people clothed in the righteousness of Jesus; people who trusted in the <u>shed blood of the Lamb</u>.

Some say the Church will convert the world, but Daniel talked about a time when the Antichrist will dominate the saints (Daniel 7:25), Jesus talked about a time of tribulation when the saints will be killed (Matthew 24:9, 21–22), Paul talked about a time when the Antichrist will oppose everyone who worships God (2 Thessalonians 2:3–4), and here John confirms what they said.

The elder's answer tells us what the 144,000 will be preaching. They will preach the blood of the Lamb. The fact that these 144,000 are Israelites will not alter their message.

When most prophecy experts talk about the "Great Tribulation," they are talking about the last three and one-half years of the seven-year period. But in this verse, the term refers to all those who have come out of the entire seven-year Tribulation Period.

Suddenly

REVELATION 7:15 *Therefore they are before the throne of God, and serve Him day and night in His temple. And He who sits on the throne will dwell among them. (NKJV)*

This is a very special promise. On earth, the saved will not be safe anywhere. They will either starve, die of disease, or be murdered. There will be no way to escape the clutches of the Antichrist. Suddenly, they will find themselves in the throne room of God, <u>face-to-face with Jesus</u>, surrounded by angels, clothed in white robes, and <u>protected by God</u>.

A Covering of Protection

REVELATION 7:16 *They shall neither hunger anymore nor thirst anymore; the sun shall not strike them, nor any heat;* (NKJV)

The Tribulation Saints will face hunger, thirst, death from starvation and poisoned water, burning by the blazing sun, and suffocation by scorching heat. Once they arrive in heaven, though, it will never happen again. They will be in the <u>fortress</u>, a refuge of the almighty God. It is a place of constant protection that cannot be breached. God promises in heaven we will never suffer again. This is God's promise.

fortress
Psalms 91:1–16;
46:1–11

tree of life
Revelation 2:7

> ## what others say
>
> ### Jack Van Impe
>
> The World Watch Institute recently reported that carbon emissions, deforestation, and soil erosion are worsening. Birds are disappearing. Destructive insects are developing resistance to pesticides. The seas are producing fewer harvests of edible fish. Grain stocks are down. Tropical rain forests are dwindling.[9]
>
> ### Jack Hayford
>
> Our blessed hope in Christ's return resounds throughout the millennia of church history; all Christians have looked expectantly to His coming: "Even so come, Lord Jesus!" (Revelation 22:20).[10]

No More Tears

REVELATION 7:17 *for the Lamb who is in the midst of the throne will shepherd them and lead them to living fountains of waters. And God will wipe away every tear from their eyes." (NKJV)*

The Lamb, who stands in the midst of the throne of God, will preserve the Tribulation Saints. He will feed the saints from the <u>tree of life</u> and let them drink from fountains of living water.

This also tells us the saints are destined for a great deal of weeping before they depart this earth. They will face incredibly harsh living conditions, terrorizing circumstances, and the loss of loved ones. Their tears will have reason to fall, but when they get to heaven, God will wipe them away.

Chapter Wrap-Up

- An angel will place the mark of God on the foreheads of God's servants so that his judgments do not harm them. (Revelation 7:2–3)

- God is not finished with Israel. He will seal 144,000 of them with his mark of protection; 12,000 will come from each of the twelve tribes of Israel. (Revelation 7:4–8)

- During the Tribulation multitudes will be killed on earth. These martyrs will find themselves in heaven standing before Jesus. (Revelation 7:9)

- A Great Worship Service will start in heaven when the Tribulation Saints, followed by the rest of heaven's inhabitants, start worshiping God for being the author of salvation. (Revelation 7:10–11)

- God promises that the martyrs will never again endure the hardships they suffered on earth, and he promises to wipe their tears away. (Revelation 7:15–17)

Study Questions

1. What will the first four angels do? Why are they doing it?

2. What will the 144,000 preach? Why is their message so important?

3. What seven things do the angels say belong to God? Why do they belong to him?

4. What is the difference between the twenty-four elders and the Tribulation Saints?

5. Will God let people die for their faith?

Revelation 8

Let's Get Started

Chapter 6 described the opening of the first six seals, but it ended before reaching the seventh seal. Chapter 7 covered the sealing of the 144,000 but, likewise, failed to mention the seventh seal. It is not until chapter 8 that we learn about this final seal. The opening of the seventh seal reveals the appearance of seven angels with seven trumpets (see Time Line #2, Appendix A).

Note the pattern being established. The seven seals were broken down into two sets: the four horsemen followed by three additional judgments. Likewise, the seven trumpets will be broken down into two sets: four judgments called "one-third" judgments followed by three judgments called "woes." After one-half hour of silence in heaven, these judgments will take place on the earth.

The Seventh Seal

REVELATION 8:1 *When He opened the seventh seal, there was silence in heaven for about half an hour. (NKJV)*

When this seal is broken, the scroll will be completely open. Nothing will remain to restrain the carrying out of the remaining judgments. Before they can begin, though, there will be silence in heaven for about a half hour.

The flashes of lightning, rumblings, and peals of thunder coming from the throne of God will cease. The four living creatures will cease their talk about the holiness of God. The twenty-four elders will suspend their declarations about the **worthiness** of the Lamb. The heavenly hosts will stop their singing, and the Tribulation Saints will cease their praise. An eerie, foreboding silence will move across heaven. Everyone will wait in anticipation of what is to come next. Will people be given time to repent? Will God destroy the earth? Something will be on the horizon—something of tremendous importance.

worthiness
the merit or qualifications of Jesus to open the seals

Seven Archangels

go to

Time of Jacob's Trouble
Jeremiah 30:7

Seventieth Week of Daniel
Daniel 9:24–27

Lord's Vengeance
Isaiah 34:8

Michael
Daniel 10:13

Gabriel
Luke 1:19

REVELATION 8:2 *And I saw the seven angels who stand before God, and to them were given seven trumpets.* (NKJV)

The Tribulation Period carries many names: the Time of Jacob's Trouble, the Seventieth Week of Daniel, and the Day of the Lord's Vengeance. The prophet Zephaniah gives it seven different names, and it is significant to notice that the last one is "a day of trumpet and alarm" (Zephaniah 1:14–16 NKJV).

Out of all the angels in heaven, only seven particular angels constantly stand in the presence of God. They are most commonly known as archangels, but some call them the Angels of the Presence. The 1611 King James Version of the Bible identifies only two, Michael and Gabriel, but the Apocrypha—noncanonical books that are usually omitted from Protestant Bibles—identifies the other five as Uriel, Raphael, Raguel, Remiel, and Sariel. These seven archangels, who make announcements of great significance, will each be handed a trumpet on this day of trumpet and battle cry.

Notice that these are angels that receive the trumpets in heaven as they stand before the throne of God and Jesus. God will judge the earth, but not without purpose. Society can't expect God to ignore

> ## what others say
>
> ### William Barclay
>
> That they were called the angels of the presence means two things. First, it means that they enjoyed a special honour. In an oriental court it was only the most favoured courtiers who had the right at all times to the presence of the king. To be a courtier or a counsellor of the presence was a very special honour. Second, there was more than honour here. Although to be in the presence of the king meant special honour, even more it meant immediate readiness to be dispatched on service.[1]

the persecution and death of the saints on earth. Society can't expect him to be unoffended by the blasphemy of the Antichrist and the False Prophet. Society can't expect him to delay his answer to the prayers of the righteous forever. Paul said it is a righteous thing for God to repay those who harm his people (2 Thessalonians 1:6–8).

Illustration #3
Golden Altar—Made by King Solomon for God's temple. Symbolizes the altar of God, where an angel will mix incense with the prayers of the Tribulation Saints.

An Eighth Angel?

REVELATION 8:3 *Then another angel, having a golden censer, came and stood at the altar. He was given much incense, that he should offer it with the prayers of all the saints upon the golden altar which was before the throne. (NKJV)*

go to

golden altar
Exodus 30:1–8

golden censer
2 Chronicles 4:22

frankincense
Matthew 2:11

burned
Exodus 30:7–10, 34–38

died for sin
1 Peter 2:24

Even though this eighth angel is not identified, some experts believe he is Jesus. He could be Jesus, but he is probably just another powerful angel. We do know this angel holds a special position of service before the <u>golden altar</u> of God.

This <u>golden censer</u> is similar to the one used in the Old Testament Jewish temple. It contained charcoal that was burned under a layer of incense. When the hot charcoal warmed the layer of incense, a sweet fragrance was produced. This fragrance or aroma may be that of the spice <u>frankincense</u>, one of the gifts the wise men gave to the baby Jesus. Frankincense was also one of the spices <u>burned</u> in the censer at the Jewish temple. Its fragrance reminds God of his Son, who came and <u>died for the sins</u> of the world.

1. The Redeemed - stand before God's throne
2. Redemption - divine transaction
3. Bema Seat.
God is present - he is in their midst
Confession
belief
obey
Sanctified - set apart for God's use

Illustration #4
Golden Censer—Similar to the censer used in the Old Testament Jewish temple for burning incense.

go to

incense to mix with
the prayers
Psalm 141:2

hear the prayers, and
prepare an answer
James 5:16

The eighth angel will come with a golden censer and stand before the altar of God. He will be given a great quantity of <u>incense to mix with the prayers</u> of the saints. Then he will place the censer on the golden altar before the throne of God.

No Other Choice

> REVELATION 8:4 *And the smoke of the incense, with the prayers of the saints, ascended before God from the angel's hand. (NKJV)*

Revelation 8:3 told us that the eighth angel will be given the prayers of all the saints. We may never know what all those requests may be, but Revelation 6:10 identifies one of them as a prayer of the Tribulation Saints: "How long, O Lord, holy and true, until You judge and avenge our blood on those who dwell on the earth?" (NKJV). Judgment is not God's first choice, but patience is. He is patient and will hold off his judgment longer than any man. Nevertheless, when all options fail, his judgment will fall.

The angel will take the censer containing the hot incense and the prayers of the saints, and wave it around, causing the smoke to drift toward the throne of God. The almighty God will smell the incense, <u>hear the prayers, and prepare an answer</u>.

Answered Prayers

> REVELATION 8:5 *Then the angel took the censer, filled it with fire from the altar, and threw it to the earth. And there were noises, thunderings, lightnings, and an earthquake. (NKJV)*

When the incense and all the prayers of the saints have been consumed in the censer, the angel will take the empty censer, go back to the altar, fill it with fire, and hurl it down on the earth. The prayers will go up to God, and the answers will come down to earth. God will avenge the death of the Tribulation Saints with fiery trials on earth.

Try to visualize this great scene. The Antichrist and False Prophet will rise to power, leading the inhabitants of the earth to worship Satan, while, at the same time, God's people will be hunted down, persecuted, and killed. These martyred saints will arrive in heaven praying to be avenged. At first, they will be told to wait until the number of saved is increased, but then, after a brief time, God will hear their prayers and respond by having his angel hurl the burning censer (possibly in the form of a meteor) to earth. This will be a clear statement of God's wrath. It will be followed by loud thunderclaps, flashes of lightning, and an earthquake. The earnest prayers of God's hurting people will finally reach into his wrath and cause a response that will be felt by the <u>whole earth</u>.

whole earth
Psalm 82:8

seventh plague
Exodus 9:18–2

Sodom
Genesis 18:16–19:29

futurist
a person who uses data, science, and technology to try to predict future events

> ### what others say
>
> **Jack Van Impe**
>
> **Futurist** Gordon-Michael Scallion, editor of *Earth Changes* Report, has been suggesting for months that a frightening global killer earthquake pattern is emerging. He is predicting that a series of magnitude 10.0 quakes will rip up America's West Coast in the next few years.[2]

Thus It Begins

REVELATION 8:6 *So the seven angels who had the seven trumpets prepared themselves to sound.* (NKJV)

Once the burning censer has hit the earth, the archangels will prepare to sound their trumpets. The prayers of the saints will be heard, and the whole world will be ripe for judgment. God's wrath will be kindled to unleash the next set of judgments, and the archangels will prepare to sound the alarm.

Destruction of the Earth

REVELATION 8:7 *The first angel sounded: And hail and fire followed, mingled with blood, and they were thrown to the earth. And a third of the trees were burned up, and all green grass was burned up.* (NKJV)

Some Bible experts will not accept a literal fulfillment of this verse. However, prophecy experts have little difficulty believing this will happen. The <u>seventh plague</u> on Egypt in the days of Moses was a rain of grievous hail mixed with fire that smote the cattle, herbs, and trees. It was a plague directed against Egypt's false goddess, Isis. God also rained hail, fire, and brimstone on <u>Sodom</u> and Gomorrah. There is no reason to believe he will not do it again. The result of

hail, fire, and blood
Joel 2:30

<u>hail, fire, and blood</u> being hurled down upon one-third of the earth in a furious storm is almost unimaginable. Not only will it cause immediate and indescribable destruction, it will also bring many other terrible consequences. Much of the lumber needed to build houses will be gone, along with much of the grain used for food. The entire balance of nature will be upset, and the loss of life will be horrendous.

Still, to not recognize the grace of God would be a mistake, for along with his great wrath that will burn one-third of the earth, there will flow an ocean of love to allow two-thirds of the earth more time.

The Seven Trumpets

Trumpet	Symbol	Result	Verse
First	Hail, fire, blood	1/3 plants burned	Revelation 8:7
Second	Like burning mountain	1/3 sea, ships, fish affected	Revelation 8:8–9
Third	Burning star Wormwood	1/3 fresh water polluted (death)	Revelation 8:10–11
Fourth	Heavenly bodies struck	1/3 sun, moon, stars darkened	Revelation 8:12
Fifth	1st woe—Satan opens pit	Demon-possessed locusts released	Revelation 9:1–12
Sixth	2nd woe—4 fallen angels	Fire, smoke, brimstone (1/3 die)	Revelation 9:13–21
Seventh	3rd woe—7 bowls	(see chart on the Seven Bowls on page 229)	Revelation 11:15–12:12

what others say

Hal Lindsey

With this massive loss of vegetation will come soil erosion, floods, and mudslides. Air pollution will be immense; the smoke of the fire will fill the atmosphere, and the remaining vegetation will be unable to adequately absorb the hydrocarbons from automobiles and industry. Ecology will be thrown chaotically out of balance.[3]

waters into blood
Exodus 7:14–25

Jack Van Impe

Comet Shoemaker-Levy 9's impact on Jupiter grabbed the attention of the entire world. Was it a sign? Enormous explosions, hundreds of times more powerful than all the earth's nuclear warheads, made people realize just how vulnerable our planet is to a similar occurrence.[4]

If God opposed the false goddess Isis, would he not oppose any other false god or goddess?

Destruction of the Sea

REVELATION 8:8–9 *Then the second angel sounded: And something like a great mountain burning with fire was thrown into the sea, and a third of the sea became blood. And a third of the living creatures in the sea died, and a third of the ships were destroyed.* (NKJV)

The first trumpet will signal judgment upon the earth. This trumpet will signal judgment upon the sea. It reminds us of the first plague on Egypt in the days of Moses, which turned the <u>waters into blood</u>. It was a plague directed against Egypt's false goddess Hika that killed the fish and frogs, and made the water unfit for consumption.

Pay close attention to the wording in this verse. It does not say a burning mountain will be thrown into the sea. It says something *like* a great burning mountain will be thrown into the sea. Some think it will be a nuclear missile. Others think it will be a burning meteor. Whatever it is, it will be big, blazing, and cause the sea to turn into blood. It will kill one-third of sea life and destroy one-third of the ships. Those who depend upon the sea for jobs, food, defense, or cargo transport will suffer. As a result of this "mountain" hitting the sea, it is likely that everything close to the sea will probably be damaged or destroyed by a great tidal wave.

Wormwood

REVELATION 8:10–11 *Then the third angel sounded: And a great star fell from heaven, burning like a torch, and it fell on*

Wormwood
Deuteronomy 29:18;
Lamentations 3:15

Wormwood
a bitter, intoxicating,
and poisonous herb

a third of the rivers and on the springs of water. The name of the star is Wormwood. A third of the waters became wormwood, and many men died from the water, because it was made bitter. (NKJV)

Some believe this star blazing like a torch will be a meteor. Others suggest a nuclear missile. While they hold different opinions about what it is, they usually agree about what it will do.

A great blazing object containing some type of pollutant or poisonous substance will fall out of the sky. It will be named after a bitter herb called **Wormwood** in the Bible. It will contaminate one-third of earth's fresh water supply, causing many people to die from drinking the tainted water. Although the Bible does not say, it is reasonable to assume that many others will die from thirst. With one-third of the fresh water tainted, most people will be unable to obtain drinkable water before extreme thirst sets in. Adults will survive without water for about three days, while the sick and infants will have fewer.

Why? In the days of Jeremiah, God said, "I will feed them with wormwood, and make them drink the water of gall; for from the prophets of Jerusalem profaneness has gone out into all the land" (Jeremiah 23:15 NKJV). The prophets of Jerusalem should have been decrying evil by giving out the pure water of the Word, but they were catering to the morally corrupt by giving out the poisoned water of false doctrines. Hence, God judged them.

> **what others say**
>
> **David Hocking**
>
> This tragic judgment, affecting the water supply of the world and bringing about the death of many, is a consequence upon those who refuse to submit to God's authority in their lives. We all need water; it is basic to human survival. One can only imagine what sort of additional tragedies will occur because of the terrible pollution caused by this third trumpet judgment.[5]

Lights Out

REVELATION 8:12 *Then the fourth angel sounded: And a third of the sun was struck, a third of the moon, and a third of the stars, so that a third of them were darkened. A third of the day did not shine, and likewise the night.* (NKJV)

The fourth trumpet judgment will affect the heavenly bodies: the sun, the moon, and the stars. Pagan religions worship these objects. Astrologers, fortune-tellers, and witches rely on them to predict the future. A few bizarre interpretations of this judgment exist, but the generally accepted meaning is that the light of the sun, the moon, and the stars will be diminished by one-third. We can be sure that smoke from the burning of one-third of the earth will block out a lot of the light from the sun, the moon, and the stars. Nuclear winter brought on by smoke, dirt, and debris being hurled into the atmosphere is also a possibility.

How long this will continue is not said, but there is no question that a reduction of the earth's sunlight will affect the weather, crops, and all of life in general. Major winter storms will sweep the earth, causing multitudes to freeze to death.

what others say

The World Book Encyclopedia

Nuclear winter refers to the deadly worldwide environmental effects that could result from a major nuclear war. Such a war could bring on nuclear winter by causing disastrous changes in the earth's atmosphere and climate.

Nuclear winter could begin to develop from city fires created by the extreme heat of nuclear explosions. Large amounts of smoke from these fires could spread and cover at least half the earth's surface. The smoke could prevent most sunlight from reaching the ground. Temperatures could drop substantially, and rainfall could be reduced. These conditions might last for several months or years. With greatly reduced sunlight, less rain, and lower temperatures, farming could stop, and worldwide famine could result.[6]

Trumpet Woes

REVELATION 8:13 *And I looked, and I heard an angel flying through the midst of heaven, saying with a loud voice, "Woe, woe, woe to the inhabitants of the earth, because of the remaining blasts of the trumpet of the three angels who are about to sound!"* (NKJV)

Balaam's donkey
Numbers 22:21–30

Who or what is this angel? Some say it will be the Raptured Church. Others say it will be an eagle. One thing is for sure: If God could make Balaam's donkey talk, he can make an eagle talk.

This angel will fly through the air pronouncing three woes upon the inhabitants of the earth. These three woes correspond to the last three trumpets. Some even call them the "trumpet woes." It is hard to imagine, but these woes will be worse than any judgment previously mentioned.

what others say

J. H. Melton

Long was the old world left to drive its crimes, jeer at Noah's odd notions, and fling defiance into the face of God; but presently the earth broke down beneath their feet, and their lifeless bodies dashed upon each other amid the waves of an ocean world. The trampled law will assert its rightful honour, and Christ will not endure the smiting, taunts, and wrongs of Pilate's hall forever. And when these trumpets once give out their clangour, the vibrations will run through the universe, and everything created for human blessedness shall turn into a source of disaster and trouble to them that know not God and obey not the Gospel of Christ.[7]

Chapter Wrap-Up

- Silence fills heaven for a half hour upon the opening of the seventh seal. (Revelation 8:1)

- The aroma coming from the incense mixed with the prayers of the saints will elicit a response from God when an angel takes the Golden Censer filled with fire and hurls it to earth. (Revelation 8:3–5)

- The first four trumpet judgments will burn a third of the earth, turn a third of the seas to blood, pollute a third of all drinkable water, and diminish a third of the light from heavenly bodies. (Revelation 8:7–12)

- After the first four trumpets have sounded an angel will fly through the air proclaiming three woes upon the earth. These woes correspond to the last three trumpet blasts. (Revelation 8:13)

Study Questions

1. What is the reason for the heavenly silence?

2. The fragrance of the incense reminds God of what?

3. Why would God call for an earthquake?

4. What is the correlation between the plagues of Egypt, Sodom and Gomorrah, and the judgment of thirds?

Revelation 9

Chapter Highlights:
- Opening the Abyss
- Demon-Possessed Locusts
- Four Bound Angels
- 200 Million Troops
- Unrepentant Hearts

Let's Get Started

Interpreting the symbols in the book of Revelation is one reason why it's considered one of the most difficult books in the Bible. Readers have to seek John's explanation of the symbols or search other books of the Bible for explanations that seem to fit. But John offers few explanations for what is recorded in chapter 9, and a search of the other books is not very helpful. It's difficult to believe, and kind of scary, but some of what has traditionally been considered symbolic may not be symbolic after all. People will be dealing with the subterranean world, so it's entirely possible that some of the hellish characteristics of these creatures are literal. In that case, no explanations are needed, and the judgments may be more fearsome than once thought.

Now it's time to read about the fifth and sixth trumpet judgments that correspond to the first and second "trumpet woes." But keep in mind that John said the seven stars in chapter 1 were symbols of angels.

Come Blow That Trumpet, Gabriel

REVELATION 9:1 *Then the fifth angel sounded: And I saw a star fallen from heaven to the earth. To him was given the key to the bottomless pit.* (NKJV)

This is not a literal star. This is not even a star that will fall, but one that has already fallen—Satan. Revelation 9:2 refers to this star as a "he." The prophet Isaiah said, "How you are fallen from heaven, O Lucifer, son of the morning! How you are cut down to the ground" (Isaiah 14:12 NKJV). Satan will be cast down indeed. He will be given the key to his **subterranean** home called the **bottomless pit**. The bottomless pit, or Abyss, is a place of torment where the worst of his demonic spirits are held and from where the Antichrist will come forth.

Some people think Jesus was referring to the bottomless pit when he said, "For as Jonah was three days and three nights in the belly of

Abyss
Luke 8:30–31

subterranean
beneath the earth's surface

bottomless pit
a deep pit where demons are kept

Revelation 9 ———————————————— 121

the great fish, so will the Son of Man be three days and three nights in the heart of the earth" (Matthew 12:40 NKJV).

Darkness over the Earth

REVELATION 9:2 *And he opened the bottomless pit, and smoke arose out of the pit like the smoke of a great furnace. So the sun and the air were darkened because of the smoke of the pit. (NKJV)*

Satan will descend and open the bottomless pit. When he does, a thick black smoke will rush out, covering the earth in darkness. The sky will be blackened, and the sun will be obscured.

Following the terrorist attacks on the World Trade Center towers in New York City in 2001, the burning buildings collapsed. Gasping for breath, people ran away through the smoke and debris. In a similar manner, the open Abyss will spew forth pollutants like a gigantic furnace or volcano and make breathing difficult and convulsive.

Locusts Will Come

REVELATION 9:3 *Then out of the smoke locusts came upon the earth. And to them was given power, as the scorpions of the earth have power. (NKJV)*

Locusts will come out of the smoke, but not locusts as we know them. They will not be the short-horned grasshoppers that have plagued people around the world. Instead, they will be demon-possessed and have horrible features—part animal and part human.

These locusts will be like scorpions. They will have stingers to stab and poison their victims. Victims rarely die from the sting of a scorpion, but often turn black and blue and go into convulsions. The pain is unbearable. What could be worse than millions of demon-possessed locusts dive-bombing us like mosquitoes?

go to

cast them into a herd of pigs
Luke 8:26–33

seal of God
Ephesians 4:30;
2 Corinthians
1:21–22

Gerasenes
descendants of the
Jewish tribe Gad

> **what others say**
>
> **The World Book Encyclopedia**
>
> Many locusts can make a sound by rubbing their ridged hind legs on their front wings. This causes the wings to vibrate, which makes the noise. . . . Plagues of crop-destroying locusts have been known since ancient times. One swarm by the Red Sea was believed to cover an area of 2,000 square miles. . . . Swarms of migrating locusts are sometimes so large they shut out the sunlight. They interfere with railroad trains, airplanes, and make automobile travel dangerous.[3]

Jesus once visited the **Gerasenes**, where he encountered a demon-possessed man living among the tombs. The demons begged Jesus not to cast them into the Abyss, so he <u>cast them into a herd of pigs</u> instead. The demons would rather be cast into the pigs than cast into the Abyss.

Demon-Possessed Locusts

REVELATION 9:4 *They were commanded not to harm the grass of the earth, or any green thing, or any tree, but only those men who do not have the seal of God on their foreheads. (NKJV)*

As intelligent as these demon-possessed locusts will most likely be, it's ironic that they will still be under God's control. They will harm only those who do not have the <u>seal of God</u> on their foreheads (the 144,000 Jews).

The evil empire of the subterranean world will have to obey, and even though God will be angry with the wickedness on earth, he will still demonstrate his mercy and grace.

Even though locusts eat plants, God commands these locusts not to harm the grass, plants, or trees. We may wonder why, but can only speculate how locusts would not eat their most staple foods. Perhaps it will be because the earth may be in such ecological chaos that any further damage by locusts would destroy it altogether. If the grass, plants, and trees were gone, the earth could no longer produce oxygen, and if there were no oxygen, God's people would not survive during the Millennium.

A Scorpion's Sting

REVELATION 9:5 *And they were not given authority to kill them, but to torment them for five months. Their torment was like the torment of a scorpion when it strikes a man.* (NKJV)

These locusts will not kill but only torture for a period not to exceed five months. They will be the masters of suffering by inflicting pain similar to a scorpion's sting.

God could let them kill, but he sometimes uses suffering to bring people to salvation through Jesus. God could let the torture last for more than five months, but his grace will restrain it.

what others say

David Hocking

While a scorpion sting is usually not fatal (although children often die from such a sting), it is painful. The venom affects the veins and nervous system. Normally the pain and discomfort last for several days. This plague lasts for five months.[4]

Begging to Die

REVELATION 9:6 *In those days men will seek death and will not find it; they will desire to die, and death will flee from them.* (NKJV)

During these five months of the Tribulation Period, people will hurt so much they will want to die. Their nervous systems will become infected, parts of their bodies will swell and hurt, and other parts will fail to function altogether. Some will suffer seizures and convulsions, and others will lose consciousness. Many will take medicines that fail to provide relief. Because of this torture, many will try to commit suicide, but God will not let them find death to end their suffering. They will be wise to accept Jesus. Some things are worse than death.

A Grasshopper? No, a Locust

REVELATION 9:7–10 *The shape of the locusts was like horses prepared for battle. On their heads were crowns of something like gold, and their faces were like the faces of men. They had hair like women's hair, and their teeth were like lions' teeth. And they had breastplates like breastplates of iron, and the sound of their wings was like the sound of chariots with many horses running into battle. They had tails like scorpions, and there were stings in their tails. Their power was to hurt men five months. (NKJV)*

How would you describe a locust? I'm sure you wouldn't say it has a body shaped like a horse, hair like that of a woman, and two eyes like a man, but that's what John saw.

The word "like" appears eight times in these verses. Obviously, John is using comparisons and symbolic language to describe what these demon-possessed locusts will look like.

They will have bodies shaped like a horse prepared for battle. Something similar to a crown of gold will adorn their heads, and their faces will resemble that of a human. Their manes will be long like a woman's hair, and their teeth will be small and sharp like a lion's. They will have tails like a scorpion's, and their wings will sound like an army of chariots. Does the sound of a mosquito bother you? Hope you never hear the sound of one of these frightening monsters.

go to

unnatural
Proverbs 30:27

Abaddon
destruction

Apollyon
destroyer

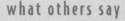

what others say

Oliver B. Greene

In Italy and some other foreign countries locusts are called "little horses" and some of them resemble a horse.[6]

John F. Walvoord

Demons and angels can take on appearances other than human, and the description of the locusts who stung like scorpions does not fit any category of man or beast.[7]

A Demon Army

REVELATION 9:11 *And they had as king over them the angel of the bottomless pit, whose name in Hebrew is Abaddon, but in Greek he has the name Apollyon.* (NKJV)

This <u>unnatural</u> army of locusts will be under the direction of an angelic king. Some say this angelic king will be Satan, but it seems more likely he will be one of Satan's powerful assistants. Satan will not be one of the demons confined in the Abyss. He is the Fallen Star who opens the pit to let this angelic king and his ungodly army loose.

This must be one of Satan's top henchmen. His Hebrew name will be **Abaddon**, meaning "destruction," and his Greek name **Apollyon**, meaning "destroyer." Since his name is given in both Hebrew and Greek, he will probably be permitted to attack both Jew and Gentile alike. His name is given twice, so it is a double warning of his destructive powers.

what others say

Jim Combs

This may be a fallen "principality" (Ephesians 6:12) and not Satan himself, but rather a high-ranking fallen angel, a follower of Satan in his original rebellion (Isaiah 14:12–14).[8]

J. H. Melton

Most Bible students underestimate the power of the devil. To do so is a grievous error. The misery Satan has wrought in God's creation and in mankind should be reason enough to recognize his power and mind.[9]

One Down and Two to Go

REVELATION 9:12 *One woe is past. Behold, still two more woes are coming after these things.* (NKJV)

This verse is further proof that Revelation is sequence-oriented. The trumpet woes will not overlap. They will come in sequence. It is obvious why the angel called them woes—tormented people, losing their minds and begging to die.

The Sixth Trumpet Angel

REVELATION 9:13 *Then the sixth angel sounded: And I heard a voice from the four horns of the golden altar which is before God,* (NKJV)

This is the altar of chapter 8. It is where the angel mixes the incense with the prayers of the Tribulation Saints. The mixture rises to God and kindles his wrath. Then the sixth angel will stand up and sound his trumpet, and a voice will be heard coming from the horns of the altar that will speak for the martyred saints.

The horns of the golden altar refer to horns like animal horns that were extensions or spires that were placed at the <u>four corners</u> of the altar of burnt offerings. Sometimes sacrificial animals were tied to the horns, and there are even two instances of men <u>grabbing hold of the horns</u> when they thought they were going to be killed. They hoped to receive mercy. This idea probably originated when Abraham prepared to offer his only begotten son, Isaac, as a sacrifice. After God stopped him, Abraham turned and saw a ram caught in a thicket by its horns (Genesis 22:13). The ram was offered as a substitute for Isaac. The entire story pictures God's mercy by sending his only begotten Son, Jesus, to die on the cross as a substitute for the sins of the world.

The Great River

REVELATION 9:14 *saying to the sixth angel who had the trumpet, "Release the four angels who are bound at the great river Euphrates."* (NKJV)

The <u>Euphrates River</u> first appears in Genesis. It was close to the Garden of Eden where Adam sinned and <u>Cain murdered Abel</u>. It is

go to

four corners
Exodus 27:1–2

grabbing hold of the horns
1 Kings 1:49–50;
2:28–34

Euphrates River
Genesis 2:14

Cain murdered Abel
Genesis 4:8

Tower of Babel
Genesis 11:1–9

where the Flood began, where the <u>Tower of Babel</u> stood, where Babylon was built, and where world government and world religion began. It has long been associated with astrology, idolatry, demon worship, witchcraft, and other sordid sins.

This demonic place was the scene of several battles in America's War on Terrorism. Islamic militants committed gruesome murders, torturing and beheading several people in the area. Some victims were found chained to a wall and starving to death.

Who are these four angels? The fact that they are bound indicates that they are four more fallen angels. Why they fell and are bound we are not told, but they appear to be powerful cohorts of Satan who may have had a part in the many sins committed along the Euphrates. In any case, the voice coming from the golden altar will tell the sixth angel to release these four angels.

Four Fallen Angels

REVELATION 9:15 *So the four angels, who had been prepared for the hour and day and month and year, were released to kill a third of mankind.* (NKJV)

These four fallen angels will be restrained and kept ready for the precise month, day, and year of God's choosing. God's precise timing for the seven-year Tribulation Period is laid out to the exact hour, minute, and second.

Some people say all prophecy has been fulfilled. When the Rapture occurs, the earth will lose multitudes of its citizens. When the fourth seal is opened, one-fourth of those who remain on earth—perhaps one and one-half billion people—will die. When these four angels are released, the earth will lose one-third of what's left. This is why Jesus said, "Unless those days were shortened, no flesh would be saved" (Matthew 24:22 NKJV). Since society has not witnessed such speedy and cataclysmic loss of life, it is safe to say Revelation has not yet been fulfilled.

An Army of Two Hundred Million

REVELATION 9:16 *Now the number of the army of the horsemen was two hundred million; I heard the number of them.* (NKJV)

This army of mounted troops must be a future army since it numbers more than the entire population of the earth in John's day. It is significant to note that today only two nations have the capability of fielding a two-hundred-million-man army—China and India.

China seems to be the most likely nation because her oil reserves are almost gone, her gasoline requirements are increasing seven times as fast as the United States', she is relying more and more on oil from the Middle East, and she is using the strength of her growing economy to build, equip, and restructure her military so her troops can be moved around the world. Also, Iran has asked China to intervene in the Middle East to stop "Israel's crimes."

India has the second largest population in the world, but, at this time, she doesn't have the troops. Her regular armed forces number fewer than half of China's. And her reserves and militias are much smaller. She could only do this if she made up the difference by adding allies.

The leaders of this army will be seduced by the four angels that will be released from the Euphrates River. God will allow these evil angels to convince the army's leaders to go on the rampage and kill a third of mankind. However, without God's permission, these angels would still be bound at the great river.

John "heard the number." It's doubtful that he could count that high. But someone in heaven told him how large this great army will be.

Like Fire-Breathing Dragons

REVELATION 9:17 *And thus I saw the horses in the vision: those who sat on them had breastplates of fiery red, hyacinth blue, and sulfur yellow; and the heads of the horses were like the heads of lions; and out of their mouths came fire, smoke, and brimstone.* (NKJV)

This great force will have two hundred million mounted troops. These troops and their horses (possibly machines) will have breastplates that will be fiery red, hyacinth blue, and sulfur yellow. The heads of these horses will resemble the heads of lions, and out of their mouths will come fire, smoke, and brimstone (possibly explosions, projectiles, or missiles).

It is interesting to note that China's flag is red and yellow; that many of China's army wear dark blue uniforms; that China is commonly called the yellow peril; and that fire-breathing dragons with large heads are a favorite Chinese symbol.

what others say

Tim LaHaye

Thanks to American capitalists who have invested heavily in developing this backward nation merely to gain incredible profits, China, which otherwise would never have been able to compete economically on the world scene, is experiencing its first real growth in hundreds of years. If allowed to go unchecked, those investors, or their grandchildren, will live to regret such profit-motive investments without demanding internal social reforms that would have granted basic freedoms to the Chinese people.[11]

Where Is the Antichrist?

REVELATION 9:18 *By these three plagues a third of mankind was killed—by the fire and the smoke and the brimstone which came out of their mouths.* (NKJV)

He promised world peace? But in reality, without the Prince of Peace, there will be no peace. When Jesus broke the second seal peace was removed from the earth (Revelation 6:3–4). The Antichrist will not be allowed to succeed. This army of two hundred million will do what the demon-possessed locusts couldn't do—kill, until a third of mankind is gone.

But even here the goodness of God is apparent. Except for God's restraining influence, men would destroy the whole world.

> **what others say**
>
> **Life Application Bible Commentary**
>
> This sort of destruction had fallen on the evil cities of Sodom and Gomorrah (see Genesis 19:24). Sulfur, or brimstone, was found near regions with volcanic activity and, in the Bible, it represents the wrath of God (see 14:10; Isaiah 30:33; 34:9).[12]

What Are They?

REVELATION 9:19 *For their power is in their mouth and in their tails; for their tails are like serpents, having heads; and with them they do harm.* (NKJV)

What these will be is anyone's guess. Some believe they are horses as we know them. Others think they are demon monstrosities, and still others think they are tanks, helicopters, or some type of future weapon. If they are not human, why are they called an army of horsemen, why are they mounted on horses, and organized like a cavalry, and why are they involved in human warfare? On the other hand, if they are human, how do readers explain the heads and tails on their horses? Interpreters can only speculate on what they really are, and they say they are future, unlike anything the world would recognize today, and they will be deadly.

The First Two Sins

REVELATION 9:20 *But the rest of mankind, who were not killed by these plagues, did not repent of the works of their hands, that they should not worship demons, and idols of gold, silver, brass, stone, and wood, which can neither see nor hear nor walk.* (NKJV)

"The rest of mankind" refers to a worldwide problem: something that will require God's attention. Those remaining on earth at this time will persist in their sins, refusing to repent, and continuing to reject Jesus. Two of the six sins that will be prominent during the Tribulation Period are demon worship (satanism) and idolatry. The Satanic Bible will be widely read, and the Church of Satan will fill its pews. Goddess worship and witchcraft will be the rage of the politically correct. Statues and images of the Antichrist will be common, and multitudes will bow before them. These nations will soon learn what happens to those who <u>forget God</u>.

Four More Sins

REVELATION 9:21 *And they did not repent of their murders or their sorceries or their sexual immorality or their thefts.* (NKJV)

Four more sins of the Tribulation Period are murder, sorceries, sexual immorality, and theft. It is apparent that unbelievers will be determined to trample on the laws of God and refuse to repent.

Depraved men and women will kill God's children without fear of punishment. Abortion, euthanasia, gang warfare, and terrorism will probably go unabated. This will contribute to the slaughter of believers seen in the fifth seal (Revelation 6:9–11). Drug abuse, astrology, fortune-telling, signs and omens, and theft will be worldwide. The world will move from an over-tolerance of perversion and sexual immorality to a blatant promotion of these sins. "Evil men and impostors will grow worse and worse" (2 Timothy 3:13 NKJV).

Most expositors fail to recognize that the problem in Sodom was not a few homosexuals. It was the public acceptance of that sin by the "old and young, all the people from every quarter" (Genesis 19:4 NKJV). For four thousand years, God has tolerated this sin, but only from a small percent of society, and there has been a stigma attached to it.

Today, society has turned a corner by re-creating Sodom with multitudes of gays who are often allowed to marry, adopt children, and be ordained as preachers. It's a dramatic change from the pits of hell, and Satan knows it will bring him lots of fuel for his fire. Theft is always bad, but the chaos, violence, rioting, and looting that occurred when hurricanes struck the United States and Mexico early this century are indications of fearful things to come.

Baal
Hosea 9:10

go to

what others say

John Hagee

Instead of seeking God's wisdom, the "New Age" religions search for spiritual answers from alien beings, fortune tellers, and demons. Environmental pagans are now worshiping Mother Earth. Increasingly they call on Gaia, the ancient earth goddess who is only a recycled version of <u>Baal</u>, the pagan god of biblical history.[15]

Grant R. Jeffrey

Modern criminologists, sociologists, and liberal politicians claim that the crime wave is caused by society, poverty, and poor career opportunities. This premise underlies the appalling short prison sentences handed out to violent criminals. Rather than demanding that individuals take responsibility for their choices and actions, criminal behavior is blamed on social problems.[16]

Jack Van Impe

Moral chaos in America is tearing apart the fabric of our society—with no end in sight. Drug addiction, physical, emotional, and sexual abuse are becoming enemies in America, and throughout the world—West and East. Crime, riots, unemployment, poverty, illiteracy, mental illness, illegitimacy, and other social problems are also on the rampage.[17]

Chapter Wrap-Up

- When the fifth trumpet is sounded Satan will be given the key to the bottomless pit. The sun and sky will be darkened from the smoke pouring out of the pit. (Revelation 9:1–2)

- Demon-possessed locusts will come out of the bottomless pit to torment mankind for five months. The pain from the locusts will be so bad that men will seek death, but God will not let them find it. (Revelation 9:3–6)

- After the sixth trumpet is sounded the four angels that have been bound at the Euphrates will be released to kill a third of mankind. (Revelation 9:13–15)

- An army of two hundred million mounted troops will kill a third of mankind through the three plagues of fire, smoke, and sulfur that will come out of their horses' mouths. (Revelation 9:16–19)

- Those who are not killed by these plagues will still refuse to repent of their sins. Instead, they will cling to their idols and demon worship. (Revelation 9:20–21)

Study Questions

1. For what purpose would God allow an invasion of demon-possessed locusts?

2. What will be the human characteristics of the demon-possessed locusts?

3. What is the meaning and the significance of the locust king's Hebrew and Greek names?

4. Who asked for the release of the four angels at the river Euphrates?

5. What are some of the Tribulation Period sins?

Revelation 10

Chapter Highlights:
- A Mighty Angel
- No More Delay!
- Be a Doer
- Eat the Book
- A Commission

Let's Get Started

Chapter 6 provided information about the first six seal judgments, but not the seventh. There was an interruption in chapter 7 to seal the 144,000 and to provide information about the multitudes they will win to Jesus.

Chapter 8 ended the interruption with the opening of the seventh seal, which described the first four trumpet judgments but not the last three. Chapter 9 kept things going with the next two trumpet judgments, but not the seventh. So it seems that it should be time to read about the seventh trumpet judgment. But chapter 10 is another interruption.

This time there is an interruption so John can receive a message from a mighty angel who will present him with a little book. The angel won't tell John what the seventh trumpet judgment is, but he will tell John what it will do. The results are recorded in chapters 11 and 12.

He Will Wear a Cloud

> REVELATION 10:1 *I saw still another mighty angel coming down from heaven, clothed with a cloud. And a rainbow was on his head, his face was like the sun, and his feet like pillars of fire.* (NKJV)

John saw a mighty angel in Revelation 5:2. Now we read that he saw another mighty angel. We do not know the identity of this angel, but we do know that he will have great authority. He will be allowed to stand in the presence of God and will speak for God. He will probably be an archangel who will come down from heaven wearing some unusual garments.

First, this mighty angel will be clothed in a cloud. In the Bible, clouds have been associated with at least two things: the presence of

go to

Mount Sinai in a cloud
Exodus 19:9–11

pillar of cloud
Exodus 13:21

ascended to heaven in a cloud
Acts 1:8–11

return in the clouds
Matthew 24:30

rainbow
Genesis 9:11–16

around the throne
Revelation 4:3

face shone
Exodus 34:29–33

Isle of Patmos
Revelation 1:9–16

ascended
going up from the earth into heaven

God and the return of Jesus. God came down to <u>Mount Sinai in a cloud</u> and led the Israelites with a <u>pillar of cloud</u>; Jesus **ascended** <u>to heaven in a cloud</u> and will <u>return in the clouds</u>. This mighty angel's clothing could be a reminder that he will be a messenger from God, or it could also be a reminder that Jesus will be returning soon.

Second, this mighty angel will either wear a "hat" that looks like a rainbow or he will have a rainbow circling his head. The <u>rainbow</u> is a reminder that God promised to never destroy the world with a flood again. He even placed a rainbow <u>around his throne</u> as a reminder. We can only speculate about the rainbow on the mighty angel's head, but it probably will symbolize that God is a God of grace, a God who keeps his promises, a God who will not let the world destroy itself, and a God whose Son is coming back.

Third, this mighty angel's face will shine like the sun. When Moses came down from Mount Sinai with the Ten Commandments, his <u>face shone</u> from being in the presence of God. When John saw Jesus on the <u>Isle of Patmos</u>, Christ's face shone like the sun. The shekinah glory of God on this mighty angel's face will indicate he has been in the presence of God.

Fourth, this mighty angel's legs will be as pillars of fire. When John saw Jesus on the Isle of Patmos, his feet were like fine brass—a symbol of judgment. This angel's fiery legs will represent God's plan to take control of the earth through divine judgment.

what others say

David Hocking

In the book of Revelation, angels are angels, not symbols of events, things, places, or persons.[1]

John F. Walvoord

The angel here also is said to come down from heaven, and there is no Scripture that indicates that Christ would return to the earth during the Great Tribulation prior to His second coming.[2]

God is a God of grace.
God will keep his promises.
God will not let the world destroy itself.
God's Son, Jesus, is coming back.

earth is the Lord's
Psalm 24:1

seven thunders is a symbol for the voice of God
Psalm 29:3;
Job 37:5

In the Name of My King

REVELATION 10:2 *He had a little book open in his hand. And he set his right foot on the sea and his left foot on the land,* *(NKJV)*

The mighty angel will carry a small open book in his hand. While he is holding it, he will plant his right foot on the sea and his left foot on dry land. This is a symbolic gesture that has been played out in the movies many times. The main character sails to some new island or far-off country. When he arrives he leaves his ship, gets into a row-boat, and his sailors row him to land. Then he steps out of the row-boat onto dry land, and claims that island or country in the name of his ruler. The same is true of this angel. He will have one foot on the sea and one foot on the land as he stakes a claim in the name of his King because <u>the earth is the Lord's</u>.

This could also be a direct message to the False Prophet, who will come up out of the earth (Revelation 13:11), and the Antichrist, who will come up out of the sea (Revelation 13:1): Do not harm the earth and sea. They belong to God.

He Speaks with Thunder

REVELATION 10:3 *and cried with a loud voice, as when a lion roars. When he cried out, seven thunders uttered their voices.* *(NKJV)*

The voice of this mighty angel will be as when a lion roars. He is not the Lion of the Tribe of Judah, as some say, but his voice will be as the voice of Jesus when he is angry. He will speak as Jesus would speak, and what he will say will be the same as Jesus said it.

At the same time he speaks, a voice in heaven will roar like the seven thunders. The <u>seven thunders is a symbol for the voice of God</u>. He will make a strong statement after this angel speaks.

go to

God's wrath
Job 26:14

Craig S. Keener

The image of thunder is appropriate. Ancients widely understood that the supreme God ruled thunder, and in some traditions thunder could sound like God's voice (cf. John 12:29).[3]

David Jeremiah with C. C. Carlson

This is like a seven-gun salute in the skies.[4]

Seal It Up

REVELATION 10:4 *Now when the seven thunders uttered their voices, I was about to write; but I heard a voice from heaven saying to me, "Seal up the things which the seven thunders uttered, and do not write them." (NKJV)*

God will make an emphatic remark in his voice of seven thunders that even John will be able to hear and understand because he will start to write it down. No one knows why John was prevented from recording this mysterious message, but he heard and knows much more than he was allowed to reveal. And people don't have to know everything to trust God or be saved. Just remember that thunder is also a symbol of <u>God's wrath</u>, and that what he utters will probably be followed up with divine judgment.

Tim LaHaye

Since the Apostle John was commanded by the voice to seal up their utterances, it is foolish to conjecture any further.[5]

Oliver B. Greene

Already set before us are blood, tears, famine, heartache, and heartbreak; killing, misery, hail, fire, burning mountains, demon monstrosities, men begging to die and unable to do so. Surely what John was forbidden to write must have been beyond human imagination and understanding.[6]

The Time to Act Is Now!

REVELATION 10:5–6 *The angel whom I saw standing on the sea and on the land raised up his hand to heaven and swore by Him who lives forever and ever, who created heaven and the things that are in it, the earth and the things that are in it, and the sea and the things that are in it, that there should be delay no longer. (NKJV)*

Just as a witness raises his right hand to take the oath to tell the whole truth in a courtroom, this angel will also raise his hand toward heaven to swear to tell God's truth. His oath will emphasize the fact that he has the authority and power of God behind him.

The Tribulation Saints asked in Revelation 6:10–11: "How long, O Lord, holy and true, until You judge and avenge our blood on those who dwell on the earth?" (NKJV). Then each of them was given a white robe, and told to delay a little longer, until the number of their fellow servants and brothers who were to be killed was completed.

Here the mighty angel will say its time to stop the delay. When the time comes for the seventh angel to sound the seventh trumpet (When the time comes for the third "trumpet woe," which will release the 7 bowl judgments), God will complete his plan.

It will be the answer the martyred Tribulation Saints have been waiting for. God will no longer delay his vengeance for their persecution and death. To the believers on earth who have been running, hiding, and waiting, these words will mean they will no longer have to wait for God to move against the wicked. And to the unbelievers on earth, they will mean God is now going to fulfill his wrath with no more delay.

This message should be a word of consolation to the saved and a word of terror to the lost. In a moment, the awesome, final judgments of God will start falling, and nothing will stop them.

what others say

Jim Combs

I submit that the mighty angel is announcing that time as we know it, measured time from the dawn of history, is about to change radically, that a process involving 3 1/2 more years will now commence, consummating in the ultimate establishment of the millennial reign and the final judgments of Israel, the nations and unbelievers.[7]

go to

prophets predicted
Jeremiah 51:25;
Isaiah 13:19–20

**mystery of
lawlessness**
2 Thessalonians 2:7

N. W. Hutchings

At Nineveh God changed His mind when Nineveh repented. However, we read in the last two verses of chapter nine that men on earth were determined not to repent. Therefore, God is justified in completing the judgments for the last half of the Tribulation. There would be no further delay in ending man's inhumanity to man and lifting nature from the curse of sin.[8]

David Hocking

Although at times we wonder if God knows or cares about what is taking place on earth, the Bible assures us that he does.[9]

God's Mystery Accomplished

REVELATION 10:7 *but in the days of the sounding of the seventh angel, when he is about to sound, the mystery of God would be finished, as He declared to His servants the prophets.* (NKJV)

Jesus has now opened all seven seals, and six of the angels have sounded their trumpets. The last trumpet will bring the seven bowl judgments. But before the seventh angel blows his trumpet, a voice from heaven will declare, the mystery of God will be accomplished, just as he announced to his servants the prophets. One of God's great secrets will unfold during the seventh trumpet judgment exactly as the prophets predicted.

The Bible identifies several mysteries. One of them is called the mystery of iniquity or the mystery of lawlessness. It is a mystery why God allowed Satan to cause the fall of mankind, a mystery why he allowed sin to do so much damage in the world, a mystery why he will allow his people to be persecuted and martyred in the Tribulation Period, and a mystery why he will allow the Antichrist and the False Prophet to reign. All of these mysteries will finally be answered when we reach heaven.

Seven Bible Mysteries

Mystery	Scripture
The mystery of the Rapture	1 Corinthians 15:51
The mystery of Israel's blindness	Romans 11:25
The mystery of God's wisdom	1 Corinthians 2:7

Seven Bible Mysteries (cont'd)

Mystery	Scripture
The mystery of Christ and the Church	Ephesians 5:31–32
The mystery of Christ in us	Colossians 1:26–27
The mystery of the kingdom of heaven	Matthew 13
The mystery of godliness	1 Timothy 3:16

go to

hearer/doer
James 1:22

go and preach
Mark 16:14–20

Be a Doer of the Word

REVELATION 10:8 *Then the voice which I heard from heaven spoke to me again and said, "Go, take the little book which is open in the hand of the angel who stands on the sea and on the earth." (NKJV)*

Now John must be more than just a <u>hearer</u>, he must also be a <u>doer</u>. The same voice of the seven thunders tells John to go and take the open book out of the mighty angel's hand. The same is true for all believers. Serving God requires doing, not just hearing. The Word of God should be like a cavalry bugle blowing for an attack—sparking believers to action.

> **what others say**
>
> **The Preacher's Outline and Sermon Bible**
>
> The Word of God is never just handed to us: it is never forced upon us. If we are to receive its message, we have to go over to the book shelf, table, or drawer and take it and study it.[10]

Eat the Book?

REVELATION 10:9 *So I went to the angel and said to him, "Give me the little book." And he said to me, "Take and eat it; and it will make your stomach bitter, but it will be as sweet as honey in your mouth." (NKJV)*

Whether John will move from heaven to earth or whether he will already be on earth is a matter of debate, but he will go to the mighty angel and request the little book. This is a form of receiving a commission or special task from God. John was switched from being a spectator of these amazing things to being a participant in them. God does that with all of his people. Before Jesus ascended to heaven he instructed his disciples to <u>go and preach</u> the gospel to everyone. Christians are not saved to be waited on; they are saved to serve.

go to

ate the words of God
Jeremiah 15:16

ate a scroll
Ezekiel 3:1–15

received into the heart
Ezekiel 3:10

be doers of the law
Romans 2:13

taste sweet
Psalm 119:103

The angel tells John to take the book and eat it. This may sound off-the-wall, but it's not new to the Bible. Jeremiah <u>ate the words of God</u>. Ezekiel <u>ate a scroll</u> from God. The implied idea is that the Word of God must be <u>received into the heart</u> (not left outside one's body). The Bible will profit us little unless it becomes part of us, so it must be brought inside of one's self and assimilated. We need to read the Bible, and then <u>be doers of the law</u>. We need to read the Bible, and then obey its instructions.

Jesus said, "It is written, 'Man shall not live by bread alone, but by every word that proceeds from the mouth of God'" (Matthew 4:4 NKJV). There is a higher life, a life of the spirit and soul that must be nourished with spiritual food, which comes from hearing, believing, and abiding by the Word of God.

The instruction to eat the little book will come with a warning that the Word of God will <u>taste sweet</u> but will turn sour once digested. Learning the Word of God with its plans and mysteries can be enjoyable and exciting, but understanding the reality of its judgments is sickening. Isn't it sweet to know that Satan will soon be bound and chained, but bitter to contemplate what people will go through beforehand? Isn't it sweet to know that final victory is assured, but bitter to contemplate the plagues, pain, loss of life, and eternal destiny of the lost? It was pleasant for John to receive the message from God, but painful for him to contemplate the steps toward fulfillment.

what others say

John P. Newport

Even the message of forgiveness is preceded by the realization of guilt and judgment. What is important to note is that John is commissioned to tell the whole world the twofold message, the whole truth—it is bitter and sweet. Only the false prophet proclaims the sweet and is silent about the bitter elements of the divine Word.[11]

David Hocking

Perhaps the full impact of what John experienced is a reminder to all who proclaim God's wonderful Word and speak of his coming judgment and wrath. We must speak it with a measure of sorrow and bitterness. A broken heart is a prerequisite to the proclamation of God's judgment and wrath.[12]

Get the Word

REVELATION 10:10 *Then I took the little book out of the angel's hand and ate it, and it was as sweet as honey in my mouth. But when I had eaten it, my stomach became bitter. (NKJV)*

Ezekiel
Ezekiel 2:1–9

Jeremiah
Jeremiah 1:3–19

John did what he was instructed to do. He took the little book and ate it. It tasted good at first, but later it was sickening. But there's more to this verse.

True prophets hear the voice of God just as John did. What did John do? He got the Word of God (took it from the angel). This is the only place to find a prophetic message. Go and get the Word of God. Digest it. Here is a test. If everything comes up roses, you have eaten the wrong thing. True prophets prophesy because God loves the lost. He cares about what will happen to them.

When the prophet <u>Ezekiel</u> was called, he was told to stand on his feet while God spoke to him. Then the Spirit raised him up and spoke to him. He told Ezekiel, "I am sending you to the children of Israel, to a rebellious nation that has rebelled against Me; they and their fathers have transgressed against Me to this very day. For they are impudent and stubborn children . . . As for them, whether they hear or whether they refuse—for they are a rebellious house—yet they will know that a prophet has been among them" (Ezekiel 2:3–5 NKJV). Ezekiel was told to speak God's words whether the people listened or not.

When the prophet <u>Jeremiah</u> was called, he was told God had appointed him to be a prophet before he was born. Jeremiah did not want the assignment and said he was too young. But God told him he would tell Jeremiah what to say. Even though Jeremiah was only about twenty, he still obeyed.

For Them to Read

REVELATION 10:11 *And he said to me, "You must prophesy again about many peoples, nations, tongues, and kings." (NKJV)*

When John was told to eat the book, he was also given a commission from God. He was told to prophesy about many peoples, nations, tongues, and kings. This was his great privilege, his great calling, and his great responsibility.

John was not told to deliver the message *to* many peoples, nations, tongues, and kings but *about* many peoples, nations, tongues, and kings. This is what John does in the remaining chapters of Revelation. During the Tribulation Period, many peoples, nations, tongues, and kings will open these last chapters and read what John had to say about them.

Chapter Wrap-Up

- Another mighty angel will come down from heaven adorned in strange garments and holding a little scroll. He will claim the land and sea for God. (Revelation 10:1–2)

- The angel standing on the sea and land will raise his hand and declare that there will be no more delay for the judgment of earth. (Revelation 10:5–6)

- John will be told to take the book from the angel, which signifies a Christian's duty to act upon God's Word and not just listen to it. (Revelation 10:8)

- When John eats the book, it will taste sweet at first but will turn his stomach sour. This exemplifies that learning God's Word can be exciting, but understanding the realities of the judgments is sickening. (Revelation 10:9)

- God assigned John the task of prophesying about many peoples, nations, tongues, and kings. (Revelation 10:11)

Study Questions

1. What will the glow on the mighty angel's face indicate?

2. Who has the voice of seven thunders?

3. What are some of the mysteries that will not be answered until we reach heaven?

4. What are the two commissions God gave to all Christians through John?

Revelation 11

Chapter Highlights:
- Two Witnesses
- The Antichrist Retaliates
- A Severe Earthquake
- The Seventh Trumpet
- God's Heavenly Temple

REVELATION 11:1 *Then I was given a reed like a measuring rod. And the angel stood, saying, "Rise and measure the temple of God, the altar, and those who worship there.* (NKJV)

Let's Get Started

At the close of chapter 10, John was commissioned to prophesy about many peoples, nations, tongues, and kings. He starts fulfilling it in chapter 11. Facts are given about people, a nation, and a tongue in the events about Israel and the Tribulation Temple. Facts are given about many peoples, nations, and tongues in the events about the Gentiles. Included is information about the United Nations and the Antichrist. Details are provided about two particular people called the Two Witnesses. More is given about the King who rules over all things: Jesus or God. Then, there is the reaction of the nations and the residents of heaven.

what others say

Thomas Ice and Timothy Demy

The Bible speaks of four temples in Jerusalem. The first two temples, Solomon's and Herod's, have already been built and destroyed. The final two temples, the tribulation temple and the millennial temple, are yet to be built and are spoken of in great detail in biblical prophecy.[1]

J. Randall Price

It is necessary to distinguish in the context of the Old Testament whether the future Tribulation or millennial temple is in view. The tribulation temple will be built by unbelieving Jews and desecrated by the Antichrist (Dan. 9:27; cf. 11:36–45). The millennial temple will be built by Messiah (Zech. 6:12–13) and redeemed Jews, and as a particular sign of restoration, assisted by representatives from Gentile nations (Zech. 6:15; Hag. 2:7; cf. Isa. 60:10). It will be distinguished from the tribulation temple as the restoration temple by a return of the Shekinah Glory of God (Ezekiel 43:1–7; cf. Ezekiel 10:4, 18–19; 11:22–23) and by Gentile worship (Isaiah 60:6; Zephaniah 3:10; Zechariah 2:11; 8:22; 14:16–19).[2]

go to

gather against
Jerusalem
Zechariah 12:1–3;
14:1–3

break the nations in
pieces
Jeremiah 51:19–23

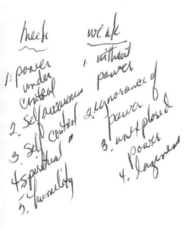

Another point needs to be examined—a very important one. In Revelation 10:6 we learned that God will start to finalize his wrath upon the world—there will be no more delays. It is extremely significant that when God begins to close out the age, he will focus his attention on Israel and the temple. In connection with this, it is good to recall Old Testament prophecies. From these we learn:

1. Israel will become the storm center of the world during the Tribulation Period. Zechariah 12 and 14 reveal some of God's judgments upon Israel and her enemies. We read that God will make Jerusalem a cup that will send all the nations reeling. In Zechariah's time, drinking from a cup was a metaphor similar to the expression "Take your medicine." In this case, the nations opposing Jerusalem will be sent reeling when they drink the concoction in Jerusalem's cup.

The nations of the earth will <u>gather against Jerusalem</u>. She will be captured and half of her Jews will flee into exile. Remember: Anyone who harms Israel will actually be harming themselves. They will be reaping what they sow because they will be setting themselves against God. This struggle over Jerusalem and the Temple will trigger the Second Coming and the Battle of Armageddon. Israel is God's weapon of battle and he will use her to <u>break the nations in pieces</u>.

This struggle is already underway. Israel has made Jerusalem its capital. The Palestinian Authority says Jerusalem will be the capital of their new Palestinian state. The Catholic Church has asked that it be designated an international city. The Arab League and most of the international community supports the Palestinian Authority. And the United States seems to switch sides from time to time. All of this is a thorn in the flesh for the United Nations, and there is a great desire to move against the Jews. When they do, they will bring destruction down on themselves.

2. The Jews want to rebuild the Temple, the heart and soul of their religion. They want it rebuilt on the same site as their two Old Testament Temples (Solomon's and Herod's). They have already prepared site preparation plans, architectural building plans, the cornerstones, the priestly garments, the instruments of music, the vessels and implements for animal sacrifices, the ephod, the menorah, and much more. They have collected money to re-build it, have requested permission to offer sacrifices and cleanse the Temple Mount, and some want to pre-fabricate the Temple, disassemble it and store it so it can be re-assembled in four to six weeks once they receive permission to start construction.

3. **The Palestinians want to keep this same site for their existing al-Aqsa Mosque and Dome of the Rock Mosque.** They believe they will incur the wrath of Allah if they give it up. They say moving or tearing one or both of these religious buildings down will trigger World War III.

The Middle East conflict is really a struggle between two religions—Judaism and Islam. It raises the question, "Whose god is God, and who worships the true God?" Neither side dares to give in because the reputations of both their god and their religion are at stake. The Antichrist will work out a temporary peace, the Tribulation Temple will be rebuilt, but Jerusalem and the Tribulation Temple will be in the line of fire until the Second Coming of Jesus.

Notice the above sequence of events. Since Jewish religious leaders have declared that the Messiah is the only one who can build the Temple, it will probably be built after they wrongly accept the Antichrist as their Messiah. But it must be built before the Tribulation Period midpoint because that's when the Antichrist will defile it. So it seems clear that the Temple will probably be rebuilt during the first half of the Tribulation Period.

One more point. If the Muslims could stop the Jews from rebuilding the Temple on the Temple Mount, they would. Thus, it seems reasonable to expect the Jews to take control of the Temple Mount, and for world leaders to designate it as an international site to be shared by everyone.

Islam - religion of deception
The first coming (Messiah) the Word Incarnate "the Way"
What's meaning "People of the Book" Israel contains fertile Crescent
Antichrist will defile Temple (sacrifice a pig)

Illustration #5
Layout of the
Temple—When the
Temple is rebuilt the
Jews will rule the
inner Temple, but
the Gentiles will rule
the outer court.

Temple
2 Chronicles 3:1

rebuilt
Daniel 9:27

altar of gold
2 Chronicles 4:19

bronze altar
1 Kings 8:64

atonement for sin
Leviticus 1:4

sins
Hebrews 10:4

shadow
Hebrews 10:1

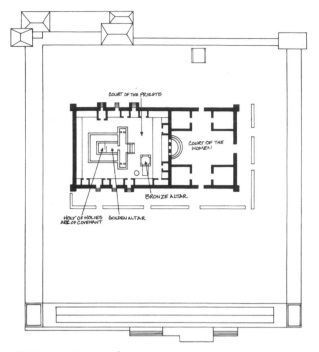

<u>None Were Found</u>

John was given a reed and told to measure the Tribulation Temple, measure the altar, and count the worshipers. This is significant because in the last days, the Temple and one of its two original altars will be rebuilt. The altar that will be rebuilt was called the <u>altar of gold</u> (see Illustration #3), or the altar of incense. It was located inside the Temple. The altar that will not be rebuilt was called the <u>bronze altar</u>. It will not be rebuilt because, as <u>Revelation 11</u>:2 says, it was located outside in the outer court. The Gentiles will rule the outer court.

God will evaluate (count) the worshipers to see how many people at the Tribulation Temple are truly worshiping Jesus. He will find none. The Jews will rebuild the temple so they can reestablish their old way of worship—sacrificial worship. In the Old Testament, God accepted animal sacrifices as a temporary <u>atonement for sin</u>. The New Testament, however, teaches that those animal sacrifices did not permanently take away the <u>sins</u> of people. These sacrifices were inadequate to truly remove the sins of the people, which is why they had to offer the same sacrifices repeated endlessly year after year (Hebrews 10:1). The reason God had the Jews sacrifice those animals was because it was a <u>shadow</u> of the things to come. It reminded the people of their sins and pointed them to the time when the Messiah would come to permanently take away their sins through his death on the cross.

Because animal sacrifice only brought temporary forgiveness, another method was needed for making atonement for sin. A permanent method was required. Christ's sacrifice on the cross is this permanent solution. His death so thoroughly pleased God that it will never need to be repeated. In fact, no other sacrifices will ever be needed again.

Animal sacrifices are no longer acceptable because the death of Jesus is the only sacrifice that God will accept. Jesus even spoke about this when he said, "I am the way, the truth, and the life. No one comes to the Father except through Me" (John 14:6 NKJV). It is only through Christ's offering of himself for our sins that we can gain everlasting life. During the Tribulation Period, when the Jews rebuild the Temple and resume animal sacrifices, their sacrifices will not be accepted, which is why God will not find any worshipers in his Temple.

go to

permanent solution
Hebrews 9:12; 10:12

only sacrifice
John 3:36;
Acts 4:12

everlasting life
John 3:16   *1 John 1:9*

James 1:27
Religious activity
enmity against God

Jesus gave us the right
to pray for forgiveness
Zechariah 3:12

> ## what others say
>
> ### Arnold G. Fruchtenbaum
>
> All these passages speak of the third Jewish Temple, namely the Tribulation Temple. But for now, suffice it to say that the Jewish Temple will be rebuilt and will begin to function again, for these verses view the Jewish Temple as having been rebuilt and functioning. All these verses also presuppose Jewish control of the Temple Compound, and that presupposes Jewish control of the Old City of Jerusalem.[3]
>
> ### Hal Lindsey
>
> I believe this very problem (the violent reaction of the Arabs to a Jewish Temple being rebuilt) may be the reason for the "strong covenant" which the Prophet Daniel says the Jewish people will make with the Roman Antichrist. In return for certain concessions from the Jews, he will guarantee protection for them so that they can rebuild their Temple and reinstate animal sacrifice. The religious Jews will push for this and accept the False Prophet as the Messiah because he helps to secure the rebuilding of the Temple.[4]

Priests and Levites believe they cannot make a mistake while offering animal sacrifices. They also believe the only way to prevent this from happening is to train on real animals. So priests are actually sac-

Olivet
Matthew 24–25

defile
2 Thessalonians 2:4

Olivet Discourse
Jesus' sermon concerning the end of the age and destruction of Jerusalem

Holy Place
the large room just inside the door of the temple building

Holy of Holies
innermost sanctuary of the temple; housed the ark of the covenant

Dome of the Rock
a Muslim shrine on the Temple Mount

rificing animals at Jewish Bible Colleges on the Temple Mount in preparation for the rebuilding of the Temple.

According to Numbers 19, the blood of a red heifer, without spot or blemish, must be sprinkled on the Temple Mount before the Temple can be rebuilt and before God will accept a service there. The Romans destroyed the herd of red heifers when they destroyed Jerusalem and Herod's Temple in AD 70. Then, for almost nineteen hundred years, there were no red heifers. But the herd has been reestablished, and machine gun–carrying Jews guard the animals day and night to prevent anything from happening to them. All the animals have been closely examined, and some have been found to qualify for sacrifice.

1. Daniel implied that the Temple will be rebuilt and in use by the middle of the Tribulation Period.

2. Jesus authenticated Daniel's prophecy in his **Olivet** Discourse.

3. Paul verified that the Temple will be rebuilt when he said the Antichrist will defile it.

Temples in the Bible

Temple	Building Schedule
Solomon's Temple	First temple in Jerusalem
Zerubbabel's Temple	Second temple in Jerusalem; later remodeled and called Herod's Temple
Tribulation Temple	Will be built before the Tribulation Period midpoint
Millennial Temple	Will be built after the Second Coming of Jesus
New Jerusalem	Will come down out of heaven to the New Earth

Note: Christians are a Temple of the Holy Spirit. There is also a heavenly Temple.

What About the Wall?

> **REVELATION 11:2** *But leave out the court which is outside the temple, and do not measure it, for it has been given to the Gentiles. And they will tread the holy city underfoot for forty-two months. (NKJV)*

John was told not to measure the outer court of the temple. This may signify that only the **Holy Place** and the **Holy of Holies** will be rebuilt. Some architects and prophecy experts say these could be rebuilt without disturbing the **Dome of the Rock** or the al-Aqsa

Mosque. Such an arrangement would allow the various religions to share the **Temple Mount**. Sharing that religious sight or sharing sovereignty over it could mean there may not be a wall around the outer court. Without the outer court wall, the Jews and **Muslims** would be able to share the Temple Mount.

John is told not to measure the outer court because it has been given to the Gentiles (see Illustration #5). They will trample on the holy city for forty-two months. This coincides with what Jesus taught. Gentiles will control Jerusalem and the Temple during the last three and one-half years of the Tribulation Period.

Temple Mount
the hill where all of the Jewish temples have been built

Muslim
one who practices the religion of Mohammed, which is called Islam

what others say

Charles H. Dyer

In a remarkable article in *Biblical Archaeology Review* Asher Kaufman argues that the ancient Holy of Holies was not located over the Dome of the Rock. Instead, he suggests that the Holy of Holies stood approximately a hundred yards farther north on the Temple Mount. . . . No major archaeologist in Israel finds Kaufman's views convincing, but the point here is not to argue whether Kaufman's views are correct. Many Orthodox Jews are poring over every scrap of data, trying to find where the Temple stood. If they conclude that Kaufman's position fits the evidence, then they will build the Temple where he suggested.[5]

John F. Walvoord

This brief summary of the end time of approximately three-and-a-half years is confirmed by other Scriptures. The beginning of the three-and-a-half years of the Great Tribulation will feature the abolishment of the daily sacrifices and the setting up of an abomination in the temple (Daniel 7:25; 9:27; Revelation 11:2–3). The time in view will be the Great Tribulation, the last three-and-a-half years leading up to the second coming of Christ.[6]

There are fifty-six Islamic nations (about 1.3 billion people), of which twenty-one are Arab nations (about 300 million people). The Islamic religion is a rapidly growing religion that is often controlled by militants who want to impose their beliefs on the rest of the world. Their three main goals are to:

1. Drive all Westerners out of the Middle East

2. Exterminate the Jews

3. Establish a one-world Islamic government and religion

Militants believe all Muslims are soldiers in Allah's army who must fight, or if they don't fight, they must give financial support to those who do. They believe all non-Muslims are their enemy, all non-Muslims must be forced to submit to Islam; all territory that has ever been under Islamic rule must be kept or brought back under Islamic rule forever; when Muslims become the majority in a country they must control the government; the Jews are only temporary residents of Jerusalem and Israel; there can be a temporary peace of up to ten years between Islam and others but no permanent peace; there can be no concessions to non-Muslims; all concessions by non-Muslims are signs of weakness and an indication that Muslims are winning, Muslims can sign a temporary peace treaty and break it if doing so advances the cause of Islam, and Muslims are in a holy war until Judgment Day.

Muslims believe Christians and Jews have distorted the Scriptures (they believe the Bible is full of errors); as Allah's messenger Mohammed corrected the distortions and gave Islam the Koran; Mohammed's teachings supersede those of Jesus and all others; Islam is the only true religion and is destined to replace all other religions; Muslims must do more good works than bad or die a martyr's death to be saved (salvation by works); and all Jews are cursed. The more radical members don't believe in a civil society. They quickly deny basic freedoms such as human rights, civil rights, and women's rights, and they readily justify the killing of innocent men, women, and children to promote their cause.

- Muslims worship the moon god of Mecca called Allah.
- Muslims say Allah is not love, but Christians say Jehovah is love.
- Muslims say Allah is not a Father, but Christians call Jehovah Father.
- Muslims say Allah cannot be known in a personal way, but Christians say Jehovah can be known personally.
- Muslims say Allah made a covenant with Abraham to give the Promised Land to Ishmael's descendants, but Christians and Jews say Jehovah made a covenant with Abraham to give the Promised Land to Isaac and his descendants.

- Muslims say Jesus was created from the dust like Adam, but Christians say Jesus was virgin born.

- Muslims say Jesus was a messenger of God, but Christians say Jesus is the Son of God.

- Muslims say Judas Iscariot died on the cross, but Christians say Jesus died on the cross.

- Muslims say their sins can be forgiven, but they have to kill an infidel (non-Muslim).

- Muslims believe in a Messiah called the Mahdi, but Christians say the Messiah is Jesus.

- Muslims say the Messiah will be a descendant of Mohammed, but Christians and Jews say the Messiah will be a descendant of King David.

- Muslims say the Messiah will reign on earth for seven years and die, but Christians say he will reign on earth for one thousand years and never die.

- Muslims say the Messiah will conquer Israel, but most Christians and Jews say he will rescue Israel.

- Muslims believe in a great war at the end of the age called the Mother of All Battles, but Christians call it the Battle of Armageddon, and Jews call it the Battle of All Battles.

Those who say all people worship the same God need to get their head out of the sand.

Jerusalem is considered the Holy City by Christians, Jews, and Muslims. Among other things, Christians consider it holy because Jesus was crucified there, Jews consider it holy because their temple was located their, and Muslims consider it holy because they believe Mohammed ascended into heaven there.

Muslims worship on Friday, Jews worship on Saturday, and Christians worship on Sunday. One proposal being given serious consideration is for these three groups to share the Temple Mount with each group worshiping on a different day. But Christians need to be aware that militant Muslims (Friday people) chant, "After we get rid of the Saturday people (Jews), we will get rid of the Sunday people (Christians)."

Two Witnesses

go to

Mosaic Law
Exodus 20:1–17

two witnesses
Deuteronomy 17:6;
19:15

Elijah
2 Kings 2:1

sackcloth
Isaiah 20:2;
Joel 1:13

mourning
Genesis 37:34;
Esther 4:1–4

John the Baptist
John 1:29–36; 5:33

Mosaic Law
the Ten
Commandments

sackcloth
a coarse cloth worn
as a sign of
mourning

REVELATION 11:3 *And I will give power to my two witnesses, and they will prophesy one thousand two hundred and sixty days, clothed in sackcloth." (NKJV)*

In the Old Testament the **Mosaic Law** required <u>two witnesses</u> to validate matters pertaining to Jewish religion. In the same way, God will send two witnesses to prophesy and validate the world's sin and blasphemy during the Tribulation Period.

The identities of these witnesses are unknown, but most experts agree that one of them will be Elijah. The main reason for this agreement is a verse found in the Old Testament: "I will send you Elijah the prophet before the coming of the great and dreadful day of the LORD" (Malachi 4:5 NKJV). Currently, <u>Elijah</u> is in heaven, but he will return to earth before the Tribulation Period.

Elijah and the second witness will stay and prophesy for 1,260 days or three and one-half years. Experts agree that this will be the first three and one-half years of the Tribulation Period.

The two witnesses will wear sackcloth. This type of attire undoubtedly seems strange to us but can be explained with help from the Old Testament. Old Testament prophets wore **sackcloth** when they were ministering to people who were deeply involved in sin. Sackcloth, however, is also worn as a garment of <u>mourning</u>. Most likely the Jews of the Tribulation Period will be grieving over their sins and their relationship with God.

Most people want to know who the two witnesses will be. Some say Elijah and Enoch. Others say Elijah and <u>John the Baptist</u>. Still others suggest Elijah and Moses. I believe they will be Jews, but no one knows for sure. It may possibly be that God does not tell us because it is not important.

Today, leaders of a Jewish group called the Temple Mount and Land of Israel Faithful put on sackcloth and ashes on Jewish feast days and parade to the Temple Mount to worship. The Jewish Sanhedrin has been brought back into existence, and these religious scholars believe Elijah will soon appear before their group to announce the identity of the Messiah. They believe the Holy One will be a descendant of King David, so they are using DNA to identify people who might qualify. They are also working to change

Israel's political system from a ruling Prime Minister to a king. But many prophecy experts find this troubling because they fear the Sanhedrin will create their own hand-picked Elijah and mistakenly identify the Antichrist as their messiah and king. Jesus said, "I have come in My Father's name, and you do not receive Me; if another comes in his own name, him you will receive" (John 5:43 NKJV).

Oil and Light

REVELATION 11:4 *These are the two olive trees and the two lampstands standing before the God of the earth. (NKJV)*

Each witness is represented by one olive tree and one lampstand. It takes two symbols to represent one person.

To understand this passage, we need to know what these symbols mean. The answer to the olive trees is found in Zechariah 4:2–6—two olive trees stand by a lampstand and provide oil to the lampstand. This oil represents the Holy Spirit. The two witnesses will be olive trees because they will be filled with the Holy Spirit.

Zechariah 4:11–14 explains what the lampstands represent—the lampstands hold pots of burning oil that provide light. The two witnesses will be lampstands because they will provide light to a dark world.

Now, combine the two symbols. Each witness will be one olive tree filled with the Holy Spirit and one lampstand giving off the light of God. They will be two witnesses, filled with the Holy Spirit, counteracting the forces of darkness in the world.

This continues to show the grace of God during the Tribulation Period. He will go to great lengths to reach out to the lost, to offer them blessings, and to be their God.

They Speak with Fire

plagues
afflictions or calamities that are sometimes viewed as an act of God

REVELATION 11:5 *And if anyone wants to harm them, fire proceeds from their mouth and devours their enemies. And if anyone wants to harm them, he must be killed in this manner.* *(NKJV)*

God told Jeremiah, "I will make My words in your mouth fire, and this people wood, and it shall devour them" (Jeremiah 5:14 NKJV). Those who reject the Word of God will be like wood when it is consumed by fire.

The two witnesses will be invincible. They will have the supernatural power of the Word of God in their mouths. When their enemies try to harm them, they will merely speak to consume their enemies.

I Don't Want to Be Here

REVELATION 11:6 *These have power to shut heaven, so that no rain falls in the days of their prophecy; and they have power over waters to turn them to blood, and to strike the earth with all plagues, as often as they desire.* *(NKJV)*

These two men will have unlimited power. They will be able to stop the rain from falling, turn water to blood, and smite the earth with many different kinds of **plagues**. Without rain for three and a half years, the ground will be cracked and dry like old leather, and the dust will be ankle-deep. When the waters turn to blood, they will be unfit to drink, and uninhabitable for fish. There is no telling what the other plagues will do, but one thing is for sure, this will not be the same planet we know today.

what others say

John Hagee

The seven seas of the earth will be turned into blood. Every river (and) stream will become as blood. Every basin in your home will run with hot and cold blood. This plague will produce mind-numbing thirst from which there will be no relief.[8]

David Jeremiah with C. C. Carlson

(The two witnesses) will tell men to their faces about their human wickedness; they will stab hearts with warnings of future judgments, even worse than the past. The hatred this pair arouses will be intense.[9]

The Beasts

> **REVELATION 11:7** *When they finish their testimony, the beast that ascends out of the bottomless pit will make war against them, overcome them, and kill them. (NKJV)*

Antichrist
Revelation 13:1

False Prophet
Revelation 13:11

days of Isaiah
Isaiah 1:1–10

beasts
in Revelation beasts
are persons who are
full of evil

The two witnesses will be supernaturally protected. Nothing will harm them. However, when they have finished their assignment of providing light to a dark and evil world, they will be killed. Revelation mentions two **beasts**: the <u>Antichrist</u> and the <u>False Prophet</u>. The Antichrist will hate the two witnesses. He will fail to cope with their condemnation of his world government, religion, social principles, and economic system, and will be infuriated when he hears them preaching about Jesus. He will be jealous of their number of converts, so he will throw all the power of his satanic government into an attack against them. The witnesses will be overpowered and killed.

what others say

The Preacher's Outline and Sermon Bible

Scripture never really uses the term *antichrist* to refer to the great "man of lawlessness" who is to appear in the end time. It does refer to false teachers as *antichrists* (1 John 2:22). However, down through the centuries, believers have always referred to the coming "man of lawlessness" as the *antichrist*. Why? Because he is to stand so opposed to Christ and fiercely persecute believers. He will be the very embodiment of evil against Christ and against the followers of Christ.[10]

Not Even a Burial Plot

> **REVELATION 11:8** *And their dead bodies will lie in the street of the great city which spiritually is called Sodom and Egypt, where also our Lord was crucified. (NKJV)*

Several cities are called "great cities" in the Bible. This great city, however, is clearly identified as the city where the Lord was crucified, which can only be Jerusalem.

In the <u>days of Isaiah</u>, Jerusalem was a wicked place. Things were so bad that Isaiah compared Jerusalem to the cities of Sodom and Gomorrah. That was strong language, considering God destroyed those cities with fire and brimstone.

go to

days of Ezekiel
Ezekiel 16:1–62

calf
Exodus 32

not what God wanted
Isaiah 1:11–17

In the <u>days of Ezekiel</u>, Jerusalem played the harlot and chased after idols and false gods. God said they acquired their adulterous and idolatrous ways in Egypt. Remember the golden <u>calf</u> the Israelites built on their way from Egypt to the Promised Land.

In Christ's day, Jerusalem was full of sin again. The leaders falsely accused him; tried him; and had him beaten and crucified. They offered daily sacrifices at the temple that were <u>not what God wanted</u>.

Jerusalem will be full of sin again in the Tribulation Period. It will become even more sinful after the temple is rebuilt. Worship of the Antichrist will flourish, while worship of Jesus will be condemned. God's two witnesses will be killed in Jerusalem, and no one will bother to bury them.

Seen by the Whole World

REVELATION 11:9 *Then those from the peoples, tribes, tongues, and nations will see their dead bodies three-and-a-half days, and not allow their dead bodies to be put into graves. (NKJV)*

In Bible times, because of heat and sanitation, people were often buried within twenty-four hours. Some were buried in caves or tombs, making it possible for friends and relatives to go back and anoint the body over the next few days. Some were buried with a bell tied around their finger that would ring if they moved (saved by the bell). Family often waited a minimum of three days before declaring someone dead. This may be why Jesus waited until the fourth day to raise his friend Lazarus (John 11:17). After three days, Lazarus was officially dead, and no one would question it. The dead bodies of the Two Witnesses will lie in the street three and a half days. By Jewish standards they will be officially dead. No one will accept their remains. Multitudes from every people, tribe, and nation will see their corpses and refuse them burial.

what others say

John Hagee

Prophecy states that the whole world will, at the same time, be able to see the two witnesses in the streets of Jerusalem. My father's generation could not explain that. How could the whole world see two dead men, lying in the streets of Jerusalem at one time? It was a mystery. Then came television, followed by international satellites, the Internet, and wireless communication.[11]

wise men
Matthew 2:1–12

Anti-Christmas

> REVELATION 11:10 *And those who dwell on the earth will rejoice over them, make merry, and send gifts to one another, because these two prophets tormented those who dwell on the earth.* (NKJV)

When Jesus was born, <u>wise men</u> traveled from the East to see him. When they arrived, they fell down and worshiped him with great joy, and presented him with extravagant gifts. We, too, celebrate the birth of Jesus by worshiping him and exchanging gifts at Christmas.

When the bodies of the two witnesses are lying in the street, the inhabitants of the earth will gloat. They will be proud of their Antichrist, proud they are following him, and proud of his great power because no one else could harm the two witnesses. They will praise his victory, worship him, and exchange gifts. The celebration will be like an Antichrist Christmas. Call it the first "Anti-Christmas." Some people just refuse to understand that God is going to win.

Let There Be Life

> REVELATION 11:11 *Now after the three-and-a-half days the breath of life from God entered them, and they stood on their feet, and great fear fell on those who saw them.* (NKJV)

This incredible scene is beyond human comprehension: The two witnesses will be killed. Television cameras (or something similar) will broadcast pictures of their bodies lying in the street around the world. No one will move them. The cameras will remain focused on the corpses while the whole world begins to celebrate. Food will probably be scarce, but parties will abound. Festivities will continue for three days or more. Then God will suddenly step in. He will do what he did when he created Adam (Genesis 2:7). He will breathe life into the two witnesses, causing them to move. The partying will stop; the revelry will end. The whole world will watch in terror as the two witnesses stand to their feet.

Jesus ascended
Acts 1:9

many did not believe
Matthew 28:12–13;
1 Corinthians 15:12

J. Vernon McGee

While the world is celebrating in jubilation the death of these witnesses and while the television cameras are focused upon them, the witnesses will stand on their feet. All of the networks will regret that they had their cameras pointed to (the witnesses), because (the networks) will not really want to give the news as it is.[12]

Believe What You See

REVELATION 11:12 *And they heard a loud voice from heaven saying to them, "Come up here." And they ascended to heaven in a cloud, and their enemies saw them.* (NKJV)

Following the death, burial, and resurrection of Jesus, skeptics tried to explain away his resurrection by blaming his disciples for carrying out an elaborate hoax. However, the world will not be able to claim a hoax when the two witnesses rise from the dead and disappear into heaven. Everyone will know they died because their bodies will lie in the street for three and a half days. Everyone will also know the witnesses were raised from the dead when they stand up.

Then, while some are wondering what to do, a great voice from heaven will call the two witnesses to heaven. None of their enemies will be able to harm them as they disappear into heaven in a cloud. They will only be able to look on in amazement.

When Jesus ascended into heaven, many did not believe. When the Church is raptured, the world will not believe. Excuses will abound to save people from the harsh reality of the truth. But when the two witnesses ascend to heaven, many will change their mind about Jesus and the Rapture.

To those who will struggle to survive the persecution of the Antichrist during the last half of the Tribulation Period, this is a message of hope. Remain faithful. If the Antichrist kills you, God will raise you from the dead. He will tell you what he told John (Revelation 4:1) and what he will tell the two witnesses, "Come up here."

Finally Some Will Believe

REVELATION 11:13 *In the same hour there was a great earthquake, and a tenth of the city fell. In the earthquake seven thou-*

160 ———————————— The Smart Guide to the Bible ————————————

sand people were killed, and the rest were afraid and gave glory to the God of heaven. (NKJV)

When the two witnesses stand to their feet, panic will spread around the world. Then as people are wondering what will happen next, the two witnesses will ascend to heaven. They will still be staring at the sky when the ground will begin to shake. Ten percent of the buildings in Jerusalem will collapse, killing seven thousand people. The fear of God will enter the hearts of the survivors. Many will change their minds about the two witnesses, praise the God of heaven, and begin a Jewish revival. Notice how good can come from things like earthquakes and death. God can use apparent disasters to bring about change. In this case, multitudes of Jews will see a great miracle and start praising God just before the Antichrist desecrates the Temple.

> **what others say**
>
> **Message of the Christian Jew**
>
> Over ninety major earthquakes have taken place in Israel in the last 2,000 years, with an average of 27 years between each. In the last 100 years, over 1,000 earthquakes of all measurable intensities have been recorded. Scientists predict another major earthquake in Israel but they are not prepared to say whether it will be next week, or next century. Complete buildings, including the Dome of the Rock in 1546, and even whole cities (Safed in 1837) were totally destroyed in past centuries.[13]

- When Jesus died, the earth shook (Matthew 27:51–52).
- When Jesus arose, there was a violent earthquake (Matthew 28:2).

Strike Two!

REVELATION 11:14 *The second woe is past. Behold, the third woe is coming quickly. (NKJV)*

This earthquake in Jerusalem will mark the end of the second woe or the sixth trumpet. The seventh trumpet will sound soon and bring the third woe.

The Seventh Trumpet

authority
Psalm 2:9;
Revelation 2:27;
12:5

evil
Psalm 37:9–17

twenty-four elders
Revelation 4:4–5

REVELATION 11:15 Then the seventh angel sounded: And there were loud voices in heaven, saying, "The kingdoms of this world have become the kingdoms of our Lord and of His Christ, and He shall reign forever and ever!" (NKJV)

When the seventh trumpet sounds there will be a heavenly declaration that God and his Son, Jesus, will be taking over. The apostle Paul talked about this when he said, "Then comes the end, when He [Jesus] delivers the kingdom to God the Father, when He puts an end to all rule and all authority and power" (1 Corinthians 15:24 NKJV). But remember that the sounding of this seventh trumpet unleashes the seven bowl judgments. They are one and the same so the world will still have a way to go.

Satan is the head of those rulers, authorities, and powers. They are organized and influence the nations to do evil. However, before the Tribulation Period ends, God and his Son will do away with them. God will take over and transform this world into a better place.

Fall on Your Knees

REVELATION 11:16–17 And the twenty-four elders who sat before God on their thrones fell on their faces and worshiped God, saying:
"We give You thanks, O Lord God Almighty,
The One who is and who was and who is to come,
Because You have taken Your great power and reigned.
(NKJV)

The announcement that God and Jesus will be taking over will cause a tremendous reaction in heaven. The Church will fall down on their faces and worship God. They will thank him because he is alive and will be exercising his great power by starting his earthly reign.

From this point on Satan's days will be drawing quickly to a close. Jesus will begin to exercise the authority over nations that became his when he died on the cross. He will go forth to conquer the forces of evil and usher in the Millennium.

The twenty-four elders represent the Church from Pentecost to the Rapture.

The Time Has Come

before the Judgment Seat of Christ
Romans 14:10;
2 Corinthians 5:10

temple
Hebrews 8:1–5

Moses
Exodus 25–27

REVELATION 11:18
> The nations were angry, and Your wrath has come,
> And the time of the dead, that they should be judged,
> And that You should reward Your servants the prophets and
> the saints,
> And those who fear Your name, small and great,
> And should destroy those who destroy the earth." (NKJV)

Satan will know his day will soon end, so he will stir the anger of the nations. At the same time he does that, God's wrath will burn brighter, which will put Satan and Jesus on a collision course.

Satan will unite the nations against Jesus. The ensuing conflict is referred to as the **Battle of Armageddon**.

Battle of Armageddon
the last and greatest war before the Millennium

Everyone is accountable to God. No one will escape his judgment. Even the dead will be judged. But the righteous will be rewarded before the Judgment Seat of Christ for reverencing the name of Jesus, and the wicked will be destroyed for their unrepented sin.

The Wrath of God in the Book of Revelation

Description	Scripture
The wrath of the Lamb	Revelation 6:16
The great day of His wrath	Revelation 6:17
Your wrath has come	Revelation 11:18
The wrath of God	Revelation 15:1
The bowls of the wrath of God	Revelation 16:1
The wine of the fierceness of His wrath	Revelation 16:19
The fierceness and wrath of Almighty God	Revelation 19:15

Mercy

REVELATION 11:19 *Then the temple of God was opened in heaven, and the ark of His covenant was seen in His temple. And there were lightnings, noises, thunderings, an earthquake, and great hail.* (NKJV)

Following the heavenly worship service (described in the three preceding verses), when the elders declare that Satan will stir the nations against God's people, God will open his heavenly temple. He has a temple similar to the tabernacle Moses constructed in the wilderness.

go to

ark of the covenant
Exodus 25:10–22

mercy seat
Leviticus 16:15

God's heavenly temple houses the <u>ark of the covenant</u>. The <u>mercy seat</u> rests on top of the ark, where the blood of sacrificial goats was sprinkled for the sins of God's people. The ark, with its mercy seat, will be a reminder that God has always shown mercy to his people.

Satan will stir the nations against Israel. The lightning, noises, thunder, earthquakes, and hailstorms will be signs of God's wrath to come, but God will show mercy by protecting Israel.

Most people do not understand the consequences of all the earthquakes that will take place during the Tribulation Period. Most of these quakes will be stronger than the 7.6 tremor that shook Pakistan in 2005. In addition to the multiple thousands that were killed and millions that were left homeless, it was estimated that more than one thousand hospitals were totally destroyed. Perhaps this helps explain why pestilence will. kill so many during the Tribulation Period. It will be next to impossible to find well-equipped medical facilities.

The ark of the covenant (see Illustration #6) was a rectangular-shaped box made of acacia wood and overlaid with gold. It had two rings on each side so that staves could be inserted to carry it. It had a gold lid on top called the mercy seat. On the gold lid were two cherubim with their wings spread over the mercy seat and looking down at the box, which contained the earthly presence of God. The ark was kept in the Holy of Holies inside the temple. The high priest would go in there, pour blood of sacrificial animals on the mercy seat as an atonement for sin, and God would communicate with him. The ark was a symbol of God's presence with his people, his protection of them, his mercy, and his forgiveness.

Illustration #6
Ark of the Covenant—Was kept in the Holy of Holies and was a symbol of God's presence on earth. The heavenly temple also has an ark of the covenant with a mercy seat representing God's mercy for his people.

Chapter Wrap-Up

- God will empower his two witnesses to prophesy for 1,260 days during which time they will be able to smite the earth with plagues and consume their enemies with fire. (Revelation 11:3–6)

- After prophesying for 1,260 days, the two witnesses will be killed by the Antichrist in Jerusalem. Their bodies will lie in the street while unbelievers celebrate. (Revelation 11:7–10)

- Three and a half days after the witnesses are killed, God will resurrect them, call them home to heaven, and destroy a tenth of Jerusalem with an earthquake. (Revelation 11:11–13)

- A heavenly declaration proclaiming that Jesus will soon start his earthly reign will follow the seventh trumpet blast. (Revelation 11:15)

- God will open his heavenly temple, revealing the ark of the covenant, which serves as a reminder that he has always shown Israel mercy. (Revelation 11:19)

Study Questions

1. Why will God tell John not to measure the outer court of the temple?

2. What symbols will be used to represent the two witnesses? What do they symbolize?

3. Why will God figuratively refer to Jerusalem as Sodom and Egypt?

4. What will cause the world to rejoice during the Tribulation Period?

5. What are the similar patterns of events God uses to prove his authority?

<table>
<tr><td>

Revelation 12

</td><td>

Chapter Highlights:
- **The Woman**
- **A Red Dragon**
- **War in Heaven**
- **Satan's Army**
- **Earth's Mouth**

</td></tr>
</table>

Let's Get Started

At the close of chapter 10, we learned that John was told to prophesy about many peoples, nations, tongues, and kings. Chapter 11 began this prophecy, which now continues into chapter 12. Here we will learn more about Israel, Jesus, Satan, the archangel Michael, and the inhabitants of the earth.

Most bad things that happen do so because the world is caught up in a great spiritual struggle between good and evil, which is sometimes called the Conflict of the Ages. It's a spiritual struggle between God and Satan that will intensify on earth at the end of the age. Jesus clearly taught that it will be worse than anything that's happened on earth before. This great spiritual struggle involves a woman (Israel), a dragon (Satan), a child (Jesus), and the remainder of the woman's offspring (Christians).

dreams
Genesis 37:9–11

Joseph
Genesis 30:22–24;
37:3–4

sign
a symbol for something else

> **what others say**
>
> ### Jim Combs
>
> The reader's attention is focused on the dragon's efforts to thwart the birth of the "manchild," Jesus, who is to rule all nations with a rod of iron (see Psalm 2:7–9 and Revelation 19:15).[1]

The First Great Sign from Heaven

> **REVELATION 12:1** *Now a great sign appeared in heaven: a woman clothed with the sun, with the moon under her feet, and on her head a garland of twelve stars.* (NKJV)

The symbols in this first **sign** take us back to the Old Testament to one of the <u>dreams</u> of <u>Joseph</u>. Joseph's father, a man named Jacob, interpreted the dream like this: the sun represented himself (Jacob, whose name was later changed to Israel), the moon represented his wife (whose name was Rachel), and the crown of twelve stars represented their twelve children (the twelve tribes of Israel). This family was the beginning of the nation of Israel.

Notice that the three symbols in Joseph's dream (the sun, the moon, and the twelve stars) are all associated with this woman in chapter 12. She is clothed with the sun (a symbol of Israel), has the moon (a symbol of Rachel) under her feet, and has a crown of twelve stars (a symbol of the twelve tribes of Israel) on her head. This woman represents the nation of Israel at its beginning.

what others say

Harper's Bible Dictionary

Historians see in Jacob, who was renamed "Israel" after his experience wrestling with an angel (Genesis 32:28; 35:10), the personification of the national Israel.[2]

Charles H. Dyer

In the Apostle John's vision the woman clothed with the sun, the moon, and the twelve stars represents the nation of Israel.[3]

A Nation in Travail

REVELATION 12:2 *Then being with child, she cried out in labor and in pain to give birth.* (NKJV)

Verse 5 of this chapter tells us that Israel is pregnant with a male child, who will rule all the nations. Her pregnancy is a reference to her condition just before the birth of Jesus. John says she cried out in pain as she was about to give birth.

Before Christ's birth, Israel was a captive nation to the Roman Empire. She had to submit to Roman leaders, pay Roman taxes, and obey Roman laws. She was a nation in **travail**.

what others say

N. W. Hutchings

In the Old Testament it was prophesied that the Messiah would be born of a virgin; what town He would be born in; what tribe He would come from; how He would grow from a child to manhood; that He would make the blind to see, the dumb to speak, the deaf to hear, and the lame to walk; how and why He would die; and that He would be raised from the grave. Yet, Israel never knew or recognized Him as the Christ.[4]

The Second Great Sign from Heaven

REVELATION 12:3 *And another sign appeared in heaven: behold, a great, fiery red dragon having seven heads and ten horns, and seven diadems on his heads. (NKJV)*

go to

killed
John 8:44

heads
Revelation 17:10

horns
Revelation 17:12

three
Daniel 7:8, 24

The first sign in heaven was a sun-clothed woman (the nation of Israel). The second sign in heaven is an enormous red dragon (Satan), which is explained further in Revelation 12:9. He is enormous because of his great power; red, since he has <u>killed</u> multitudes; and a dragon due to his fierce nature.

This fierce, powerful, murderous dragon will appear in heaven with seven <u>heads</u> (symbols of world governments), ten <u>horns</u> (symbols of powerful kings), and seven crowns (symbols of the seven divisions controlled by the ten powerful kings).

The dragon will have seven heads symbolizing the seven Gentile world governments that Satan has led since the beginning of creation. It will also have ten horns, symbolizing the ten kings that will reign with him during the entire Tribulation Period. The Bible teaches that these ten kings will rise to power, and that the Antichrist will come on the scene in a unified Europe (the European Union). The Antichrist will subdue <u>three</u> of those ten kings so that their power will ultimately be concentrated into seven crowns (or seven divisions) of the last world government. This must not be taken lightly. A one-world government empowered and controlled by Satan is a terrible thought. Some say it will make what Adolf Hitler did during WWII look like a Sunday picnic.

A good example of how this could happen is a proposal that came before the U.N. It called for the nations to surrender their sovereignty to the U.N., divide the world into ten regions, increase the number of permanent members on the U.N. Security Council to ten, and put one permanent member over each region. This is the kind of thing Christians need to watch.

The seven heads are seven Gentile world governments (Revelation 17:9–10). Five were past in John's day, the sixth was in power (Rome), and the seventh is the future kingdom of Antichrist:

1. Assyria

2. Egypt

3. Babylon

angels
Daniel 8:10;
2 Peter 2:4;
Jude 1:6

Jesus
Matthew 2:13–18

4. Medes and Persia

5. Greece

6. Rome

7. United Nations (It will go through three phases or stages at the end of the age)

Phase I—World divided into 10 regions with 10 leaders called kings (10 horns with 10 crowns)

Phase II—Antichrist takes over 3 regions (leaves 10 kings or horns, but only 7 regions or 7 crowns)

Phase III—Antichrist takes over whole world (He controls 10 kings and 7 crowns or regions)—this will be the kingdom with toes of Iron + Clay (EU + Others) on the statue in Nebuchadnezzar's dream (Daniel 2)

Note: The ten horns are ten future kings or leaders that will rule with the Antichrist at the end of the age (Revelation 17:12).

> **what others say**
>
> **Kerby Anderson**
>
> The term "new world order" has been used by leading establishment media and think tanks for decades. These groups advocate a world government, a merging of national entities into an international organization that centralizes political, economic, and cultural spheres into a global network.[5]

Falling Stars

REVELATION 12:4 *His tail drew a third of the stars of heaven and threw them to the earth. And the dragon stood before the woman who was ready to give birth, to devour her Child as soon as it was born.* (NKJV)

Stars are symbols of angels. The fact that Satan swept a third of the stars out of the sky means that he caused one-third of the <u>angels</u> to fall. Satan's mutiny was a tremendous rebellion involving millions of angels.

Satan has tried to destroy Jesus (or at least Jesus' mission of dying on the cross) many times while Jesus was on earth:

1. Satan waited for the birth of <u>Jesus</u> because he wanted to destroy <u>Jesus</u>. When Jesus was born, he stirred the wrath of Herod, king of Judea, to have all the male babies in and around Bethlehem killed. God, however, sent an angel to warn Jesus' earthly father, Joseph, to take Mary and flee with Jesus to Egypt.

2. At the beginning of Christ's ministry, Satan offered Jesus the <u>kingdoms</u> of the world if he would bow down and worship Satan.

3. Later, when Jesus told his disciples he would die, Peter disagreed and Jesus answered, "Get behind Me, Satan!" (Matthew 16:23 NKJV). Satan was working through Peter to tempt Jesus to bypass the cross.

4. Before Jesus was crucified, he went to the <u>Mount of Olives</u> to pray. There Satan came against him with such power that God sent an angel to strengthen him. Jesus was put under such agony and temptation that he sweat drops of blood, but he still prevailed.

5. When Jesus was hanging on the cross the chief priests, scribes, and elders mocked him, saying, "Let Him now come down from the cross, and we will believe Him. He trusted in God; let Him deliver Him now if He will have Him" (Matthew 27:42–43 NKJV). Satan was doing everything he could to keep Jesus from dying on the cross.

6. Satan even used the thieves who were crucified with Jesus. In the same way (with insults and taunting), the robbers who were crucified with him also heaped insults on him (Matthew 27:44).

go to

kingdoms
Matthew 4:8–9

Mount of Olives
Luke 22:39–46

---

what others say

Charles H. Dyer

Satan tried to short-circuit God's plans for the earth by eliminating God's Messiah.[6]

Snatched Up

REVELATION 12:5 *She bore a male Child who was to rule all nations with a rod of iron. And her Child was caught up to God and His throne.* (NKJV)

[handwritten margin notes:] Job 38–7 Rev 120– 9:1 Ezekial 15:1:24 Exodus 15: Rev 12:5

[handwritten notes:] Satan tried to destroy line of David (Father) Use Jesus as a High priest Priest

go to

Anointed
Psalm 2:2–9

Lord of lords
Revelation 19:15–16

ascension
Acts 1:9

resurrection
Luke 23:26–24:12

defiled
Matthew 24:15

flee
Matthew 24:16

iron scepter
a rod or staff that a
ruler carries to
demonstrate his
authority

The woman will give birth to a son who will rule all the nations with an **iron scepter**. The second psalm identifies the One who will do this as God's <u>Anointed</u> (Jesus). Chapter 19 calls him the King of kings and <u>Lord of lords</u>.

"Her [Israel's] Child was caught up to God" is a reference to the <u>ascension</u> of Jesus. He ascended to heaven following his death and <u>resurrection</u>.

Notice that Jesus will not rule the nations with love but with a rod of iron. The world is full of people who are in rebellion against God because they follow false teachings or religions (e.g., atheists, communists, Muslims). However, when Christ returns he will crush these rebellions with an iron rod.

Notice also that this woman is the mother of the Child (Israel the nation that gave birth to Jesus) and not the bride of the Child (not the bride of Christ). Some expositors wrongly say this woman is the bride (Church).

what others say

John P. Newport

This is John's vivid way of asserting the victory of God's anointed Messiah over every satanic effort to destroy Him. The messianic child comes, finishes His mission, is delivered from the dragon, and is enthroned in heaven.[7]

John saw a Lamb (Jesus), looking as if it had been slain, standing in the center of God's throne (Revelation 5:6).

Flee Away

REVELATION 12:6 *Then the woman fled into the wilderness, where she has a place prepared by God, that they should feed her there one thousand two hundred and sixty days. (NKJV)*

We are now at the midpoint of the seven-year Tribulation Period; 1,260 days (three and one-half years) have passed. Now there are 1,260 more days before Christ's second coming.

Jesus taught that the temple would be <u>defiled</u> by an image of the Antichrist at the Tribulation Period midpoint. He told those who live in Judea to <u>flee</u> to the mountains when that happens.

172 ———————————————— **The Smart Guide to the Bible** ————————————————

Where will they go? The woman (Israel) will flee into the desert to a place prepared for her by God. Most prophecy experts believe the Jews will flee to a mountainous area in the Jordan desert called Petra. It is an abandoned city that was carved into the rocks of the mountains centuries ago. It has only one entrance, so the Jews will be able to hide in those caves and barricade themselves in for protection. They will hide there for 1,260 days (three and one-half years), the last half of the Tribulation Period.

The ancient city of Petra (see Illustration #7) lies in a mountainous area about twenty miles south of the Dead Sea in the country of Jordan. These white and red sandstone mountains are simply a great volcanic crater where the Edomites lived about 500 BC. These people carved temples, houses, and businesses directly out of the rock face. The name Petra means "the rock," and the city is often called the "Rose Red City" because of its red stone buildings and the red cliffs they are cut out of. The city was long deserted and is still difficult to reach because of the narrow passages that serve as the only entrances. Due to the narrow passages, it would be easy for a small force to defend the city against a larger army.

Illustration #7
Petra—Was hidden at the end of a mile-long, one-thousand-foot-deep gorge. As you entered the city, through this corridor, you could see the columns of rose-red sandstone cut into the cliff.

Charge!

go to

Michael
Daniel 12:1

REVELATION 12:7 *And war broke out in heaven: Michael and his angels fought with the dragon; and the dragon and his angels fought,* (NKJV)

As soon as Israel flees, a great war will erupt in heaven. God's angels will be led by the archangel <u>Michael</u> in the fight against Satan and his angels. It will be a fierce spiritual battle, since the last thing Satan wants is to be cast out of heaven again.

> **what others say**
>
> **Charles H. Dyer**
>
> These spiritual beings fall into two classes—angels and demons. Angels are those beings who, after their creation, remained true to God. Demons are spirit beings who were created perfect but who chose to rebel against their Creator.[8]

Some of Satan's names:

- the tempter (Matthew 4:3 NKJV)
- the evil one (Matthew 6:13 NKJV)
- the ruler of the demons (Matthew 9:34 NKJV)
- the father of lies (John 8:44 NKJV)
- the ruler of this world (John 12:31 NKJV)
- the prince of the power of the air (Ephesians 2:2 NKJV)
- the god of this age (2 Corinthians 4:4 NKJV)

Banished Forever

REVELATION 12:8 *but they did not prevail, nor was a place found for them in heaven any longer.* (NKJV)

People often ask, when will Satan be cast out of heaven? There's little doubt that it was in the past, probably long before God created Adam and Eve, that Satan lost his exalted position and was cast out of heaven due to pride. But even though this happened, it's clear that he currently holds a lesser position with temporary access to God in heaven as the accuser of the bretheren. At the middle of the Tribulation Period, Satan and his angels will start a war in heaven and fight to no avail, this time losing their place in heaven forever.

And it will get worse because after three and one-half more years, he will be cast into the bottomless pit (Revelation 20:2–3), and then after the Millennium, he will be cast into the lake of fire and brimstone (Revelation 20:10).

Bittersweet

> REVELATION 12:9 *So the great dragon was cast out, that serpent of old, called the Devil and Satan, who deceives the whole world; he was cast to the earth, and his angels were cast out with him.* (NKJV)

There is no mistaking that the great dragon is Satan. He is also called that old serpent and the devil. This verse is bittersweet: Bitter because Satan and his demon angels will be thrown down to earth. Sweet because Satan and his angels will lose the war in heaven.

In the next chapter it will become obvious that Satan is the power behind world government. He will dominate it and be the object of its affection. But it won't last long.

what others say

John Hagee

Not powerful enough to prevail in heaven, Satan lashes out on the earth against everything God holds dear.[9]

Satan has always persecuted God's people. He especially hates the Jews because Jesus was a Jew. He and his demons will come to the earth with great wrath, but God will have Israel flee into the mountainous desert before they arrive.

Examples of Persecution of Jews:

- The Holocaust.
- Special taxes were imposed on Jews by Europeans during the Middle Ages.
- They were placed in ghettos during the Middle Ages in Europe.
- They were driven out of Spain in 1492.
- In the 1800s, Poland and Russia killed them in massacres called pogroms.

Advocate with the Father
1 John 2:1

confess
Matthew 10:32

For the Defense

> REVELATION 12:10 *Then I heard a loud voice saying in heaven, "Now salvation, and strength, and the kingdom of our God, and the power of His Christ have come, for the accuser of our brethren, who accused them before our God day and night, has been cast down. (NKJV)*

When Satan is cast out, heaven will rejoice because: (1) our salvation will be complete and Satan will be banished from our presence forever; (2) all power will belong to Jesus, and there will be no more evil (Satan) in heaven; (3) the kingdom of God will come to earth; and (4) Jesus will finally exercise the authority over earth that he won at the cross.

Today, Satan is the accuser of believers. He parades before the throne of God day and night, pointing out the sins of God's people. Jesus, too, is there—our <u>Advocate with the Father</u>. But his defense will end when Satan is cast out of heaven. Satan will never accuse us again.

We Have the Power

> REVELATION 12:11 *And they overcame him by the blood of the Lamb and by the word of their testimony, and they did not love their lives to the death. (NKJV)*

Believers will have the power to overcome Satan during the Tribulation Period by (1) trusting in the blood of the Lamb, because through the blood, atonement was made for our sins; (2) testifying to our faith, because if we acknowledge Jesus before men, he will <u>confess</u> us before God; and (3) not fearing death, because a physical death is far better than being cast into hell.

---

what others say

J. Ramsey Michaels

The voice in heaven makes clear from the start that God's people will not fall victim to his deceit.[10]

The Seventh Trumpet—The Third Woe

> REVELATION 12:12 *Therefore rejoice, O heavens, and you who dwell in them! Woe to the inhabitants of the earth and the sea!*

For the devil has come down to you, having great wrath, because he knows that he has a short time." (NKJV)

flee
Matthew 24:17–22

Heaven will celebrate its great triumph after Satan and his angels have been cast out. But watch out, earth and sea. Satan and his demons are on their way filled with fury, knowing that their days are numbered.

When Satan is cast out of heaven, Jesus will exercise his authority over the earth. He will declare that the kingdom of God will come to earth. Because of this, Satan will do all the damage he can with the time he has left.

He will make the earth a bloodbath and slaughter millions of Tribulation saints and Jews. Daniel called it "a time of trouble, such as never was" (Daniel 12:1 NKJV). Praise God, the Church will be delivered "from the wrath to come" (1 Thessalonians 1:10 NKJV).

Flee

REVELATION 12:13 *Now when the dragon saw that he had been cast to the earth, he persecuted the woman who gave birth to the male Child. (NKJV)*

Israel will <u>flee</u> when Satan is cast down to the earth, because his rage will burn against the nation of Israel for bringing forth Jesus. The quicker the Jews escape, the better.

Jesus told them to flee when they see the Antichrist defile the Temple at the Tribulation Period midpoint. He told them not to take anything out of their house, not to try to get extra clothes, that it would be dangerous for pregnant or nursing women, and they should pray it doesn't happen on the Sabbath (Matthew 24:15–20). Delaying will cost some their life.

Satan tried to destroy Israel and Jesus many times to prevent the First Coming and the Cross. He is trying to do it today to prevent the Second Coming and the Jews from serving him during the Millennium. He doesn't want to be bound and chained for a thousand years. But there's not a chance in the world that he will succeed.

The Wings of an Eagle

go to

eagles' wings
Exodus 19:4

escaped
Deuteronomy
32:11–12

bread and quail
Exodus 16:13–15

water
Exodus 15:22–27;
17:1–7

wear out
Deuteronomy 29:5

REVELATION 12:14 *But the woman was given two wings of a great eagle, that she might fly into the wilderness to her place, where she is nourished for a time and times and half a time, from the presence of the serpent. (NKJV)*

Israel will escape Satan's grasp on the wings of a great eagle. Some believe the United States is the wings of a great eagle. They believe she will rapidly airlift the Jews to safety. This is probably not the case.

By letting Scripture be our guide, we learn that God says he brought Israel out of Egypt on eagles' wings. The Jews interpret this to mean they escaped by the grace of God because they could not deliver themselves. This is most likely the way it will happen during the Tribulation Period. God will intervene to help them escape.

Notice that Israel will flee to the place prepared for her. God knows everything. He knows what Satan will try to do to Israel during the Tribulation Period, so he has already devised an escape route to safety. God will prepare this place of safety, so it will be ready when needed.

When Israel arrives, God will take care of her. He will supernaturally provide food, water, clothing, protection, and anything else she needs. It will be like it was during the days of Moses when they were wandering in the wilderness. God fed them bread and quail, provided water, and did not allow their clothes or sandals to wear out.

This will go on for three and one-half years. It is the meaning of "a time, times and half a time." God will sustain this remnant of Israel in her special place for the entire second half of the Tribulation Period.

Organization (UNESCO) has invested millions in excavation and improvement projects.[11]

David Reagan

What the chapter in effect says is that the Tribulation is the consummation of a cosmic battle between God and Satan that has been going on in the supernatural world since the revolt of man in the Garden of Eden. It reminds us that Satan tried to stop the first coming of the Messiah, just as he is now trying to prevent His second coming.[12]

A Faithful God

A woman can forget her nursing child, but God will not forget Israel	Isaiah 49:14–16
If the sun, moon, and stars stop shining, and the ocean waves stop moving, and someone measures heaven, God will forget Israel	Jeremiah 31:31–37
God has not cast away Israel	Romans 11:1–2
God's gifts to Israel (covenants, land, etc.) and his promise to save them are irrevocable	Romans 11:26–29

what others say

Charles Halff

Even in Bible times, you will remember, efforts to eliminate the Jew failed:

- The King of Egypt could not diminish the Jew (Exodus 1:9–12).
- The waters of the Red Sea could not drown him (Exodus 14:13–31).
- The gallows of Haman could not hang him (Esther 5:14; 7:10).
- The great fish could not digest him (John 1:17; 2:10).
- The fiery furnace could not burn him (Daniel 3:16–28).
- The lions of Babylon could not devour him (Daniel 6:3–28).
- Balaam could not curse him (Numbers 23:7–8).
- The nations of the world could not assimilate him (Esther 3:8; Exodus 33:12–16).
- The dictators of the nations cannot annihilate him (Isaiah 14:1–5; Zechariah 8:22–25).[13]

Like a Flood

floodwaters
Jeremiah 46:7–8;
46:13–47:3

Assyria
Isaiah 8:7–8

REVELATION 12:15 *So the serpent spewed water out of his mouth like a flood after the woman, that he might cause her to be carried away by the flood.* (NKJV)

In the Old Testament, God used the floodwaters of a river as a symbol to represent an attack by the King of Assyria on Judah. The floodwaters represented enemy troops pouring into the tiny nation.

This verse uses that same type of symbolism. When Satan sees Israel fleeing into the wilderness, he will probably speak through the Antichrist or his False Prophet, using their mouths to incite an attack on the terrified Jewish people. It will be his intent to pour many troops into the wilderness, and drown the woman (Israel) with an overwhelming force.

Into the Pit

REVELATION 12:16 *But the earth helped the woman, and the earth opened its mouth and swallowed up the flood which the dragon had spewed out of his mouth.* (NKJV)

God will intervene. A supernatural catastrophe will befall Satan's pursuing army. The earth opening its mouth probably symbolizes another great earthquake with the earth splitting open. Satan's troops will suddenly drop into the pit.

This is why the Jews should not go back after anything when they see the Antichrist defile the temple. Instead, they should escape the enemy troops and stay ahead of the great earthquake.

Pick Your Target

REVELATION 12:17 *And the dragon was enraged with the woman, and he went to make war with the rest of her offspring, who keep the commandments of God and have the testimony of Jesus Christ.* (NKJV)

The escape of Israel will infuriate Satan. Since he failed to wipe out Israel, he will pick another target—those who obey God's commandments and hold to the testimony of Jesus.

Notice two things:

1. We have now started reading about things that will happen during the second half of the Tribulation Period, and

2. There will be Gentile believers on earth at that time. Israel's offspring is a reference to Gentile believers. Satan will go on a rampage against God's people in the second half of the Tribulation Period. He will do everything he can to destroy the elect.

Chapter Wrap-Up

- Israel, represented as a woman clothed with the sun, is the first sign in heaven. She is pregnant with a child. (Revelation 12:1–2)

- A great red dragon, symbolic of Satan, is the second sign in heaven. He will cause a third of the angels to fall to earth due to rebellion. (Revelation 12:3–4)

- Satan will war against God in heaven, but God's angel will overpower him, expel him, and throw him to earth. (Revelation 12:7–9)

- After Satan's heavenly defeat, he will try to attack God's people on earth, so he will send an army to drown them. (Revelation 12:15)

- The earth, however, will help God's people by swallowing these troops in an earthquake. (Revelation 12:16–17)

Study Questions

1. What are the two signs in heaven and what do they represent?

2. What is the meaning of the number 1,260, and what will happen now?

3. Who is the angel that will cast Satan out of heaven?

4. Where will Satan go when he is cast out of heaven? Why will he be so angry?

5. What powers do believers have for overcoming Satan?

Revelation 13

Chapter Highlights:
- **False Prophet**
- **Image of the Beast**
- **Mark of the Beast**
- **Antichrist**
- **A Fatal Wound**

Let's Get Started

At the close of chapter 10, John was told to eat the little book and to prophesy about many peoples, nations, tongues, and kings. In chapter 11 John wrote about the rebuilding of the Tribulation Temple, the two witnesses, and the impact they will have on the world. In chapter 12 he wrote about Satan being cast out of heaven, and how it will affect Israel and the other believers in the world. Now in chapter 13 John will tell us about the two powerhouses of the Tribulation Period—the Antichrist (the political powerhouse) and the False Prophet (the religious powerhouse). These two end-time dictators will merge church and state. The results will be disastrous.

The world's most influential leaders keep talking about a New World Order. Winston Churchill said, "The purpose of the New World Order is to bring the world into a world government." Leaders have now created the World Bank, the World Health Organization, the World Trade Organization, two world courts (the International Criminal Court, and the International Court of Justice) and more. The United Nations wants a world constitution, a world currency, a world income tax, a world military more powerful than any military on earth, a global identification number, and a global ethic, which is another way of saying a one-world religion. In fact, some world leaders aren't honest about this, so they use such terms as "global management," the "rule of world law," "collective sovereignty," "global sovereignty," and "collective security." These buzz words mean one-world government.

Deception is common. People are often told that globalism means nothing more than global corporations, global standards, and global trade. It means these things, but it also means global cooperation to deal with hunger and poverty, to protect the environment, to protect natural resources, and to settle disputes. This growing monster is clearly transforming itself into a one-world government. Its earthly leader will someday be the Antichrist.

Many world leaders are desperate for world peace. But they believe it's impossible to have world peace without peace among the religions. And they believe to have peace among the religions, the world needs religious standards that everyone must abide by with no one being allowed to say their way is the only way. Secularists call this the "global ethic." Prophecy students call this the "coming one-world religion." Its earthly leader will someday be the False Prophet.

dragon
Revelation 12:9

Antichrist
1 John 2:18

sea
Revelation 17:15;
Isaiah 57:20

horns
Revelation 17:12

**seven world
governments**
Daniel 7:24;
Revelation 17:10

seven hills
Revelation 17:9–10

seven heads
Revelation 12:3;
17:3

The Beast from the Sea

REVELATION 13:1 *Then I stood on the sand of the sea. And I saw a beast rising up out of the sea, having seven heads and ten horns, and on his horns ten crowns, and on his heads a blasphemous name.* (NKJV)

The <u>dragon</u>, Satan, will stand on the shore of the masses of humanity in the last days. The Beast, the <u>Antichrist</u>, will rise up out of this <u>sea</u> of wickedness that will reign when the Church is gone. The ten <u>horns</u> are ten rulers who will reign with the Antichrist during the Tribulation Period. The seven heads have a double meaning: (1) they are <u>seven world governments</u>, and (2) they are <u>seven hills</u> where the world religion will be located for a short time during the Tribulation Period. The ten crowns are the ten divisions of the last world government. It will be divided into ten divisions, with each division having its own ruler and set of false religions.

blasphemous
showing contempt
for God

According to the Bible, mankind will go through <u>seven heads</u>—the heads of seven world kingdoms or seven world governments. Each of the seven heads will have a **blasphemous** name, because all seven world governments and their corresponding false religions will be noted for their wickedness. The seventh head (seventh world government) will be run by the Antichrist. His world government will be subdivided into ten crowns (ten major divisions), with each division having its own wicked ruler.

The prophet Daniel teaches that the Antichrist will come up among the ten horns and uproot three of them (Daniel 7:7–8, 23–25). There is some debate as to whether the Antichrist is one of the ten or whether he is an eleventh person who arises while the ten are in power. I personally do not think he is one of the ten. I think he rises while they are in power. He takes over the power of one, then a second, a third, and finally the remaining seven give him their power. He is then the head of the world government, which started with ten divisions and was whittled down to seven.

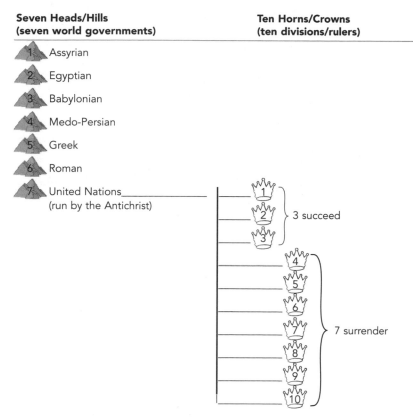

Seven Heads/Hills
(seven world governments)

1. Assyrian
2. Egyptian
3. Babylonian
4. Medo-Persian
5. Greek
6. Roman
7. United Nations
   (run by the Antichrist)

Ten Horns/Crowns
(ten divisions/rulers)

1
2 } 3 succeed
3

4
5
6
7 } 7 surrender
8
9
10

The seven heads are seven mountains (kingdoms). Five have fallen; one is; the other has not yet come (see Revelation 17:9–10). The ten horns will receive authority with the Antichrist (see Revelation 17:12). The Antichrist will subdue three kings (see Daniel 7:24). Then all ten will submit to the Antichrist (see Revelation 17:13).

what others say

Jack Van Impe

In man's search for international leadership, there has always been the drive to find the one who is destined to hold it all together. Are people today really ready to accept a "devil" as the new CEO of world affairs?[1]

Grant R. Jeffrey

The Ten Regions (Divisions) of the New World Government:

Region 1   Canada and the United States of America
Region 2   European Union—Western Europe Region
Region 3   Japan

Region 4	Australia, New Zealand, South Africa, Pacific Islands
Region 5	Eastern Europe
Region 6	Latin America—Mexico and Central and South America
Region 7	North Africa and Middle East (Moslems)
Region 8	Central Africa
Region 9	South and Southeast Asia
Region 10	Central Asia[2]

Mal Couch

To say that he [the Antichrist] emerges from the depths may simply mean that his wicked motivations are inspired from the pits of Satan. Other passages of Scripture show him to be an evil and rational earthly being and not simply a demonic creature. When he arrives upon the world scene, he may become the most powerful and most loathsome human being to reside on earth. He acts as the devil's arch tool for the physical and spiritual destruction of humanity.[3]

I wish I could say what happens to America, but I would only be speculating. All that can be said is that Europe is going to replace America as the dominant power in the world.

Three Groups

REVELATION 13:2 *Now the beast which I saw was like a leopard, his feet were like the feet of a bear, and his mouth like the mouth of a lion. The dragon gave him his power, his throne, and great authority. (NKJV)*

The word "beast" can represent either the Antichrist or his world government. In this verse, it represents his world government. This government will begin as a mixture of three groups of nations.

The Antichrist will have complete control of these groups at the beginning of his reign. He and the group known as the leopard will act as one body on all critical issues (Israel, Jesus, believers, etc.). He and the bear group will stand for the same things, while the lion group will **parrot** the Antichrist. The Antichrist's final world government will begin as a composite world government. At the start, three groups of nations will give the Antichrist his strongest support, but eventually his control will encompass the whole world.

In my opinion the interpretation of this beast is as follows:

1. *"Like a leopard"* refers to a future Arab coalition. The Antichrist and a group of Arab nations will act as one body. Leopards are native to Africa, and have been used at various times as a symbol of African nationality.

2. *"Feet . . . like the feet of a bear"* refers to Russia and her allies. The Antichrist will be supported by what is left of the Russian Empire (the Russian Bear) following the first Russian <u>invasion</u> of Israel.

3. *"Mouth like the mouth of a lion"* refers to England and those nations established out of England. The symbol of England is the lion. The Antichrist, England, and those nations coming out of England will speak with the same voice. They will parrot or mimic one another.

His power, office, and authority will come from Satan. Jesus was the incarnation of God in the world. The Antichrist will be the **incarnation** of <u>Satan</u>. Whoever he is and whatever he does comes from the pits of hell.

invasion
Ezekiel 38–39

Satan
2 Thessalonians 2:9–10

incarnation
the Antichrist will become Satan in the flesh

.

what others say

Mark Hitchcock

Scripture reveals eight attributes or characteristics of the Antichrist's personality:

1. He will be an intellectual genius (Daniel 8:23).

2. He will be an oratorical genius (Daniel 11:36).

3. He will be a political genius (Revelation 17:11–12).

4. He will be a commercial genius (Daniel 11:43; Revelation 13:16–17).

5. He will be a military genius (Revelation 6:2; 13:2).

6. He will be a religious genius (2 Thessalonians 2:4; Revelation 13:8).

7. He will be a Gentile (Revelation 13:1).

8. He will emerge from a reunited Roman Empire (Daniel 7:8; 9:26).[4]

William S. McBirnie

Is Satan cruel? The Antichrist will be cruel. Is Satan a liar? The Antichrist will be a liar. Is Satan treacherous, blood thirsty, contemptuous, unreliable? The Antichrist will be all that. That's why I'm urging you to go in the Rapture. Don't be on this earth after we Christians leave.[5]

go to

wounded head
Revelation 13:12

sword
Revelation 13:14

Up from the Dead

REVELATION 13:3 *And I saw one of his heads as if it had been mortally wounded, and his deadly wound was healed. And all the world marveled and followed the beast. (NKJV)*

Remember that the heads represent seven world governments. Also understand that the Bible speaks of the Antichrist and his world government interchangeably. The Antichrist will be given so much power that he will be the world government and the world government will be the Antichrist.

This verse tells us that one of the seven heads will seem to have a fatal wound. Other verses of Scripture tell us which head it is and how it will be wounded. The <u>wounded head</u> will be the Antichrist. He will appear to be fatally wounded with a <u>sword</u>. But something amazing will happen. His seemingly fatal wound will be healed. It will appear that he has been killed with a sword and miraculously raised from the dead. Obviously, this is another attempt to copy Jesus and make the world believe the Antichrist can do anything Christ can do.

> **what others say**
>
> **J. Dwight Pentecost**
>
> The Scriptures reveal that men are brought out of the grave by the voice of the Son of God (John 5:28–29). Satan does not have the power to give life. Since Christ alone has the power of resurrection, Satan could not bring one back to life. The wicked are not resurrected until the Great White Throne (Revelation 20:11–15). If a wicked one were resurrected at this point it would set aside God's divinely ordained program of resurrection.[6]

How Can They Be So Blind?

REVELATION 13:4 *So they worshiped the dragon who gave authority to the beast; and they worshiped the beast, saying, "Who is like the beast? Who is able to make war with him?" (NKJV)*

This will be a pivotal moment for Satan and his Antichrist. Every unbeliever in the world will be amazed. They will believe they have a new superhero. They will be encouraged to exalt him even higher, to follow him even more. At this point, they will be willing to go to war with him, to walk through fire with him, to do whatever he bids.

Satan has always wanted to be <u>worshiped</u>. His pride has been the root of all his problems and what caused his removal from heaven in the beginning. This resurrection of the Antichrist will boost Satan's stock and make satanic worship the worldwide rage. It will dominate the one-world religion. Such blasphemy is hard to imagine, but the **occult** will be in charge of this blind and corrupt world.

The Antichrist will also desire to be worshiped. Satan will have no problem with that since the Antichrist will receive his power from Satan. Those who worship the Antichrist will actually be worshiping Satan.

This adoration will lead to the questions: "Who is like the Antichrist?" and "Who can defeat him?" They will recall his meteoric rise to power, his great victories in other wars, his overwhelming personality, and of course, his miraculous healing. They will believe this man is invincible. Even the rulers of the other divisions of the world will be impressed and will turn their <u>authority</u> over to him.

Why won't they recall his failures: the way he handled the famine and pestilence, the world disintegrating before their very eyes, all the immorality in the world, and things like that? Because he will be a master deceiver with persuasive powers from the pits of hell.

Halfway There

> **REVELATION 13:5** *And he was given a mouth speaking great things and blasphemies, and he was given authority to continue for forty-two months.* (NKJV)

The search for a charismatic world leader will be over. This man will know it all, and his heart will be filled with pride. He will boast of his great achievements, power, and world government. He will make long, spellbinding speeches filled with passion and the vilest of <u>blasphemies</u>.

The Tribulation Period will last seven years being divided into two, three-and-a-half-year periods. When this miraculous healing occurs, the end of the Tribulation Period will be exactly forty-two months away. It will take place about the time the Antichrist sits in the temple and <u>declares that he is God</u>. It will also be about the time he sets up the abomination of desolation at the Tribulation Temple (Daniel

worshiped
Isaiah 14:13–14

authority
Revelation 17:13

blasphemies
Daniel 7:8, 11, 20, 25

declares that he is God
2 Thessalonians 2:4

occult
anything dealing with the mystic arts like satanism, black magic, witchcraft, etc.

anti-Semitic
prejudice or hostility
against the Jews

9:27). And it's when Jesus said the Jews should flee into the mountains (Matthew 24:15–16).

This is the same time that Daniel said the Antichrist will bring an end to the sacrifice and offering (Daniel 9:27). Bringing an end to these acts of worship presupposes the rebuilding of the Temple and the resumption of the animal sacrifices, which are two of the main goals of the modern Jewish Sanhedrin.

> ## what others say
>
> ### Jack Van Impe
> Revelation 13:5–7 makes it even clearer that war with the saints will be rampant, and that power will be given to those who oppose the Church.[7]

Notice the words "gave," "given," and "granted" in chapter 13. Everything the Antichrist does is given or granted to him.

VERSE 2	gave . . . his power . . . his throne
VERSE 4	gave authority
VERSE 5	given a mouth
VERSE 14	granted to do
VERSE 15	granted power

Watch Out If You're for God

REVELATION 13:6 *Then he opened his mouth in blasphemy against God, to blaspheme His name, His tabernacle, and those who dwell in heaven. (NKJV)*

Four kinds of blasphemy that will come from the Antichrist: (1) He will blaspheme God. (2) He will blaspheme the name of God. (3) He will blaspheme the tabernacle of God (the Church), and (4) He will blaspheme those who live in heaven. He will be anti-God, anti-Church, **anti-Semitic**, anti-anything that has to do with God the Father. The mere mention of things like Jesus, the Cross, and redemption will send him into a rage.

Bow Down or Die

REVELATION 13:7 *It was granted to him to make war with the saints and to overcome them. And authority was given him over every tribe, tongue, and nation.* (NKJV)

The Tribulation Saints will face the most intense persecution the world has ever known. In the short-term, their future will be bleak, but in the long-term, their future will be bright.

Satan will give the Antichrist power to conquer all who turn to God. He will go forth with a vengeance to wipe out all Christians. Multitudes will be slaughtered in his effort to establish a one-world satanic religion. No place on earth will be safe. The Antichrist will extend his domain to include every tribe, every tongue, and every nation on earth. Everyone must submit to him or be killed. This will be one-world government and religious persecution at its very worst.

what others say

David Jeremiah with C. C. Carlson

When we talk about the judgment of God upon our sinful, unbelieving world, we may not be popular, but lives will be saved for eternity. . . . As I write this, I long for everyone to give their hearts to Christ now, when it is comparatively easy to be a Christian.[8]

Agusta Harting

Cults proclaim a false gospel. One short definition of a cult from a Christian viewpoint is this: A cult is a group of people centered around a leader (or leaders) who teaches a false gospel.[9]

A parallel of the Antichrist can be found in the book of Daniel 3:1–30:

As the head of a world kingdom, King Nebuchadnezzar was like the Antichrist in at least two ways: (1) he was given authority over every tribe, people, language, and nation, and (2) he built a great image and ordered people to worship it. People from all over the world obeyed the command except for three Jews—Shadrach, Meshach, and Abed-Nego. Nebuchadnezzar was furious and ordered them thrown into a fiery furnace unless they changed their mind. They did not know whether or not God would deliver them

go to

cannot be separated
Romans 8:35–39

and they preferred death over worshiping the image so they refused again. The angry king had them cast into the blazing furnace, but God protected them and they came out unharmed.

One Willing to Die for the Godly, the Other Willing to Kill the Godly

REVELATION 13:8 *All who dwell on the earth will worship him, whose names have not been written in the Book of Life of the Lamb slain from the foundation of the world. (NKJV)*

It is difficult to imagine a world filled with Satan worshipers, but that is the way it will be. The only ones who will not worship the Antichrist will be those whose names have been written in the Book of Life. This is one of the few bright spots in this chapter. There are some who <u>cannot be separated</u> from the love of Jesus. Satan can rage, but God is still in control.

Satan's rage is why students of Bible prophecy are so opposed to the merging of the religions. "All who dwell on the earth" means one-world religion. Satan wants to exclude Jesus so multitudes will go to hell.

The Book of Life belongs to the Lamb that was slain. He is omniscient (all-knowing). He knows who will worship the Antichrist and who will not. He has already entered the names of those who will not fall in his book. Before the world was created, he planned to die for them. What a difference between the Christ and the Antichrist— one willing to die for the godly, the other willing to kill the godly.

---

what others say

Ed Hindson

Secularism is giving way to New Age mysticism as the do-it-yourself religion of our times. The end result will be the watering down of religious beliefs so that they are more palatable to the general public.[10]

Tim LaHaye

A man's name is written in the Lamb's Book of Life because he chooses to ask God to place it there. Jesus Christ offers men eternal life if they will receive him—if they will invite him into their life.[11]

Open Your Ears and HEAR!

REVELATION 13:9 *If anyone has an ear, let him hear. (NKJV)*

Everyone has ears and everyone should <u>listen</u> to the things from our all-knowing God. No one has to go through the Tribulation Period. God loves everyone. He is warning everyone. Will anyone commit his/her life to Jesus before it is too late to leave in the Rapture?

At the end of each of the seven letters to the seven Churches John said, "He who has an ear, let him hear what the Spirit says to the churches." The omission of "what the Spirit says to the churches" in this verse is an indication that the churches are not on earth during the Tribulation Period. The absence of the churches indicates a pre-Trib Rapture.

Believe, Trust, and Look

REVELATION 13:10 *He who leads into captivity shall go into captivity; he who kills with the sword must be killed with the sword. Here is the patience and the faith of the saints. (NKJV)*

In my opinion, there is a double meaning here. If a Tribulation Saint kills someone, even in self-defense, he will be killed in a similar manner. If an unbeliever kills a Tribulation Saint, he will be killed in a similar manner. Sin will have its own reward. This is the way it was in Old Testament days. It is commonly called an <u>eye for an eye</u> and a tooth for a tooth. The New Testament says it like this: "Whatever a man sows, that he will also reap" (Galatians 6:7 NKJV). If you sow corn, you get corn, and if you sow wheat you get wheat. During the Tribulation Period, if you kill, you will be killed.

This will require patience and faith. It will be the only way to stand up under the terrible persecution of the Tribulation Period. <u>Believe</u> in God, <u>trust</u> in the Lord, and <u>look</u> to the time when you will live again. Leave revenge to the Almighty.

The world seems to be going in a circle. In the Old Testament a person who killed someone was put to death. That worked quite well in Israel for several hundred years. It taught people to value human life, and there were few murders. America was founded on tough Bible-based laws and there were relatively few violent crimes, but

listen
Romans 10:17

eye for an eye
Leviticus 24:17–22

believe
1 Peter 1:21

trust
Proverbs 3:5

look
2 Corinthians 4:18

things have changed in this century. Now murderers usually serve less than seven years, with the average sentence being about twenty months. This leniency will not last, though, because God is going to do what society will not—kill those who kill others.

sea
Revelation 17:15;
Isaiah 57:20

earth
Psalm 25:13

Lamb of God
John 1:29

The Beast from the Earth

> **REVELATION 13:11** *Then I saw another beast coming up out of the earth, and he had two horns like a lamb and spoke like a dragon. (NKJV)*

John saw a second beast (the False Prophet). The first beast will come out of the sea, but this beast will come from the earth. The <u>sea</u> is a symbol of the masses of humanity, while the <u>earth</u> is a symbol of the land of Israel.

It is important to remember that the focus of the world will be mainly upon two places during the Tribulation. One pivotal location point will be the revived Roman Empire (see Revelation 6; 17; 18) with its one-world government. The other will be the land of Israel with its Jewish religion, temple, 144,000 sealed Jews, and two witnesses.

The first beast will have ten horns. The second will have two. Lambs do not have horns, so except for his two horns, the second beast will look like a lamb. This suggests that he will try to imitate the <u>Lamb of God</u>, but he will be a wolf in sheep's clothing. The first beast will get his power from the dragon. The second will speak like a dragon. He will do a lot of talking about loving, accepting, diversity, gender equality, etc. He will condemn racism, sexism, poverty, and all forms of discrimination. Underneath, though, he will be a slithering monster.

Last Days False Prophets

Will deceive many	Matthew 24:11
Will show great signs and wonders	Matthew 24:24
Will twist Bible teachings, misquote the Bible and deny Jesus	2 Peter 2:1

what others say

Thomas Ice and Timothy Demy

The Antichrist and the False Prophet are two separate individuals who will work toward a common, deceptive goal. Their roles and relationship will be that which was common in the ancient world between a ruler (Antichrist) and the high priest (False Prophet) of the national religion (religion often facilitates political rule).[12]

Words Sweeter Than Honey

REVELATION 13:12 *And he exercises all the authority of the first beast in his presence, and causes the earth and those who dwell in it to worship the first beast, whose deadly wound was healed.* (NKJV)

The second beast, the False Prophet, will hold as much authority as the first beast, the Antichrist. He will be the third member of the satanic trinity, but he will not use his great authority to exalt himself. He will use it to exalt the Antichrist.

His deeds will betray his sweet-sounding words. Instead of loving and accepting everyone, he will try to change everyone's beliefs. He will attempt to merge religion and politics by promoting a world religion and world government. He will order everyone to worship the Antichrist and will not hesitate to use force.

"Whose deadly wound was healed" refers back to Revelation 13:3. It reveals that the False Prophet will claim to be a healer and miracle worker. He will be what Jesus said: "For false christs and false prophets will rise and show great signs and wonders to deceive, if possible, even the elect" (Matthew 24:24 NKJV).

what others say

Mark Hitchcock

The false prophet is the satanic counterfeit of the Holy Spirit. And just as the ministry of the Holy Spirit is to give glory to Christ and to point people to him in trust and worship, the chief ministry of the false prophet will be to glorify the Antichrist and to lead people to trust and worship him.[13]

The Image of the Beast—How Vain Can We Get?

REVELATION 13:13–14 *He performs great signs, so that he even makes fire come down from heaven on the earth in the sight of men. And he deceives those who dwell on the earth by those signs*

turned into a serpent
Exodus 7:11–12

Satan sent fire
Job 1:16

which he was granted to do in the sight of the beast, telling those who dwell on the earth to make an image to the beast who was wounded by the sword and lived. (NKJV)

In the Old Testament book of Genesis, God had Moses cast his rod down before Pharaoh and it <u>turned into a serpent</u>. Then Pharaoh's magicians did the same thing with their rods. And in the book of Job, <u>Satan sent fire</u> from heaven to destroy Job's sheep, and the people thought it was the work of God. Satan can perform what appear to be miraculous signs and wonders. The apostle Paul tells us, "The coming of the lawless one is according to the working of Satan, with all power, signs, and lying wonders, and with all unrighteous deception among those who perish" (2 Thessalonians 2:9–10 NKJV).

One of the most impressive signs the False Prophet will perform is that of causing fire to fall from heaven before a great multitude. This in itself will not prove he is from God, but yet many will believe he is. He will order his followers to honor the Antichrist by setting up an image or a statue of the first beast. They will gladly do what he commands. When they do, emphasis will be placed on the Antichrist's wound and what appears to be a miraculous healing and resurrection.

It Speaks

REVELATION 13:15 *He was granted power to give breath to the image of the beast, that the image of the beast should both speak and cause as many as would not worship the image of the beast to be killed. (NKJV)*

The False Prophet will be given the power to impart breath to the image of the Antichrist. When he does, the image will appear to come to life. This will be a reminder that the Antichrist was once dead but is alive again. How the False Prophet will accomplish this is a matter of speculation, but there is no doubt that it will be an incredible event; one that will catch the world's attention.

After the image begins breathing, it will also speak. Whether that will be an act of ventriloquism, demonic possession, computers, or something else is left unsaid, but nevertheless, we know that it will be a convincing performance.

The image will proclaim that all who refuse to worship it will die. Jesus warned of this kind of persecution when he said, "Then they will deliver you up to tribulation and kill you, and you will be hated by all nations for My name's sake" (Matthew 24:9 NKJV). Paul warned us about it too when he said, "But know this, that in the last days perilous times will come" (2 Timothy 3:1 NKJV).

The False Prophet sure doesn't sound like the lamb he first appeared as. He now sounds more like a satanically inspired roaring lion. That's why he's called the False Prophet. He is a religious pretender who will not hesitate to break God's laws. The False Prophet will be responsible for the unwarranted deaths of multitudes of Christians even though God said, "You shall not murder" (Exodus 20:13 NKJV). God also said, "You shall have no other gods before Me. You shall not make for yourself a carved image—any likeness of anything that is in heaven above, or that is in the earth beneath, or that is in the water under the earth; you shall not bow down to them nor serve them" (Exodus 20:3–5 NKJV). Instead of putting the Bible into practice, the False Prophet will make every attempt possible to set it aside.

The Mark of the Beast

REVELATION 13:16–17 *He causes all, both small and great, rich and poor, free and slave, to receive a mark on their right hand or on their foreheads, and that no one may buy or sell except one who has the mark or the name of the beast, or the number of his name. (NKJV)*

Illustration #8
Phylacteries—These were strapped to the forehead and left arm for morning prayer. These small leather boxes contained folded slips of parchment with four passages from the Bible, including the Ten Commandments.

go to

Cain
Genesis 4:15

phylacteries
Deuteronomy 6:6–8

foreheads
Revelation 14:1

Holy Spirit
Ephesians 4:30

mark
Leviticus 19:28

In addition to building the image of the Beast, the False Prophet will also mandate that everyone be given a mark known as the mark of the Beast. People will be allowed to select one of two different places for the mark: the right hand or the forehead. When Cain slew Abel, God put a mark on <u>Cain</u> to protect him. Since the days of Moses, pious Jews have worn small leather pouches called <u>phylacteries</u> on their left hands and on straps tied around their foreheads. The phylacteries (see Illustration #8) contain small pieces of parchment with important passages of Scripture written on them. When they wear them, they are symbolically placing the Word of God on their hands (with the arm bent it is over the heart) and on their foreheads (in front of their minds).

In Revelation 7:2–4, we read about an angel of God that will mark 144,000 Jews on their foreheads. In chapter 14, we will see that they have the name of the Father on their <u>foreheads</u>. Just as Christians are sealed by the <u>Holy Spirit</u>, so will the False Prophet seal his servants. No one will be exempt. Laws will be enacted to identify and punish those who do not support the world government. To have food and medicine will be a privilege. Those who cooperate will receive these privileges. Those who refuse will be denied.

Taking the <u>mark</u> will be like buying a license to transact business. Merchants will need it to sell their goods. Those who want to visit a doctor or a specialist will need it to get treatment. Control over the necessities of life amounts to control over people. With these in his grasp, the False Prophet will force people to worship the image of the Beast. In this way, he will merge church and state.

Many prophecy experts see the ultimate result of the mark of the Beast as a "cashless society." Today the governments of the world want to eliminate coins and paper money so all transactions can be tracked electronically. In this way computers will have the ability to track all buying and selling.

The mark of the Beast is not my number, your number, or the number of anyone that can be identified at this time. It's not my driver's license number, Social Security number, National ID number, or anything like that. It's not a different number for different people. It's the same mark, name, or number for everyone. It's the mark, name, or number of the Antichrist.

Those who take the mark are accepting the Antichrist as God. They are choosing the Beast over Jesus and refusing God's offer of salvation, mercy, forgiveness, and love. This will be the end of their opportunities to be saved (Revelation 14:9–11). Everything that's needed in the form of chips and systems to enforce the mark is now available. Also, newer and more powerful chips, scanners, and computers are on the horizon.

In 2005, as a response to Islamic terrorism, the United States Senate passed the Real ID Act that forces states to transform driver's license numbers into National ID numbers and send information to a national database to be linked to databases in other countries. This will supposedly help nations track terrorists, criminals, missing persons, and those who are buying and selling weapons, explosives, airline tickets, and more.

One company is producing Radio Frequency Identification (RFID) tags that are now going on (or in) almost everything made. Large corporations and trade organizations are pushing to have these tags standardized all over the world so that any one tag can be read by every scanner on earth. They are also pushing for a standardized bar code and think they have found it in the European Article Numbering Code (EANC). It's more than interesting to students of Bible prophecy that these groups have selected the code used by the group of nations that will produce the Antichrist. The person who pays for an item with a check, credit card, thumb scan, or eye scan will forever have their name and all kinds of information linked to that item.

Chips were placed in the bodies of many of those who died in the Southeast Asian tsunami. This was repeated with many of the victims killed by hurricanes that struck the United States a few months later. Chips have already been inserted in living persons in several countries including at least one high-profile former politician in the United States.

And some international financial experts are saying the coming one-world government will have its own one-world currency. The global government will force people to use it by making it illegal to buy and sell in any currency except the one-world currency. And every transaction will include one's National (global) ID number.

Biometric Payment (Bio-Pay) systems are gaining wider acceptance and use. These systems use fingerprint and eye-scan technology to debit purchases from their customers' bank accounts. They offer great protection against identity theft and relieve the customer from carrying checks and credit cards. Businesses receive their money immediately with the added advantage of not getting stuck with bad checks.

> ## what others say
>
> ### Jack Van Impe
>
> Could information embedded in tiny biochips be the personal end-time ID code we are warned of in the Bible? Scripture tells us that in the future, a one-world system of government will require every person to receive a "mark" in his or her right hand or in their foreheads. Without this "Mark of the Beast," no one will be permitted to buy or sell. In years past, few could envision such a system in operation. The technology simply did not exist. But today, with what amounts to virtually daily breakthroughs in biometric technology, these advances now make such a system not only viable, but plausible.[16]
>
> ### Mark Hitchcock
>
> The mark of the beast is simply a vehicle to force people to declare their allegiance—to the Antichrist or Jesus Christ. All people will be polarized into two camps. It will be impossible to take a position of neutrality or indecision. Scripture is very clear that those who do not receive the mark will be killed (Revelation 20:4).[17]

These things are not the mark of the Beast, but they are a giant step in that direction because they establish a system to track the buying and selling of certain items. In the future, the push of a computer button will provide a list of those who take the mark and those who don't.

Reasons for the Mark:

1. To counterfeit the mark God will give to the 144,000 Jews
2. To extend favors to those who support the world government
3. To identify and eliminate opposition to the world government
4. To track and control commerce
5. To force people to stop worshiping God
6. To force people to worship the Antichrist
7. To permanently tie people to the kingdom of the Antichrist

Do not put <u>marks</u> on your body. Those who take the mark will face the <u>wrath of God</u>.

marks
Leviticus 19:28

wrath of God
Revelation 14:9–10

covenant
Daniel 9:27

Antichrist
Daniel 9:26

after the Rapture
2 Thessalonians 2:1–8

wisdom
the right use of knowledge

666—Not That Number Again

REVELATION 13:18 *Here is wisdom. Let him who has understanding calculate the number of the beast, for it is the number of a man: His number is 666. (NKJV)*

The first thing we need to note is that this verse calls for wisdom. Many are so caught up trying to figure out who the Antichrist is that they lose all sight of using any **wisdom**. The Antichrist could not exist until after Israel became a nation because he will sign a <u>covenant</u> with them, so obviously those who believed he was Hitler or Mussolini overlooked this important detail. In my opinion, the Antichrist will rise to power in Europe because Daniel told of the destruction of Jerusalem by the Romans and said the <u>Antichrist</u> will come out of those people. This is why he cannot be an American. Those who identified the American secretary of state Henry Kissinger overlooked this. The Antichrist will not be revealed until <u>after the Rapture</u>. Those who think they can identify him now are overlooking this. People eventually will be able to identify him in the future, but wisdom will be needed. All pieces of the puzzle will have to fall together.

This verse tells us that those with insight who will want to identify the Antichrist after the Rapture can calculate his number. It is the

sixth day
Genesis 1:27–31

seventh day
Genesis 2:2

eighth day
Mark 16:9

modern world
the world we live in

ancient world
the people in Israel
at the time of Christ

alphanumeric
letters that have a
numerical value

number of a man, and it equals 666. Two things are important here: how to calculate the number, and why it is 666.

To calculate the number, one needs to know that things have changed since John wrote Revelation. The **modern world** has two sets of symbols—the alphabet and numbers. We use two systems. A letter is a letter, and a number is a number. But the **ancient world** did not do this; they used a single set of symbols to represent both letters and numbers. Such a system is called an "**alphanumeric** system." Every number is a letter, and every letter is a number.

In an alphanumeric system, every word has a numeric value, every sentence has a numeric value, every paragraph has a numeric value, etc. The same is true of every name. Every name has a numeric value. For example, let A = 100, B = 101, C = 102, etc. Here is another example, 6 is the number of man, so let A = 1 x 6 or 6, B = 2 x 6 or 12, C = 3 x 6 or 18, etc.

This is how to calculate the number of the name of Antichrist. It will be 666 in somebody's alphanumeric system (Hebrew, Greek, computer, etc.). Many scientists are now studying the mathematical structure of the Bible with computers. All of them are finding remarkable mathematical patterns. It is quite possible that someone will unlock this mystery with a computer by the time the Antichrist arrives.

what others say

John Hagee

This information about how to identify the Antichrist is of no practical value to the Church since we will be watching from the balconies of heaven by the time he is revealed.

This cryptic puzzle is not intended to point a finger at some unknown person. It is, however, intended to confirm to the world someone already suspected as being the Antichrist. And in the idolatry of the end time, "the number of a man" is fully developed and the result is 666.[18]

Concerning why the Antichrist's name will equal 666 is another matter of speculation. The most common answer centers around the fact that 6 is the number of man, 7 is the number of God, and 8 is the number of Jesus; man was created on the <u>sixth day</u>, the Creator rested on the <u>seventh day</u>, and the Redeemer of creation rose on the <u>eighth day</u>. These numbers in their triplicate are 666, 777, and 888.

Chapter Wrap-Up

- The dragon will give his power and authority to the Antichrist, so the world will be deceived and worship the dragon. (Revelation 13:1–4)

- The Antichrist will receive what appears to be a fatal wound that will be healed. The world will marvel at this "miracle" and follow him. (Revelation 13:3–4)

- The False Prophet will perform miracles to deceive the earth's inhabitants into worshiping the Antichrist. (Revelation 13:11–13)

- The False Prophet will have the people erect an image of the Antichrist and worship it. Anyone who doesn't will be killed. (Revelation 13:14–15)

- Everyone who wishes to buy or sell will be forced to take the mark of the Beast. This mark is a man's number, 666. (Revelation 13:16–18)

Study Questions

1. Will people be saved during the Tribulation Period?

2. What part will miracles play in this?

3. What two spiritual things will the saints need to endure in the Tribulation Period? Why?

4. Is the mark your social security number, credit card number, or driver's license number?

Chapter 14

Chapter Highlights:
- **Sealed by the Lamb**
- **The Gospel Preached**
- **The Fall of Babylon**
- **An Angelic Warning**
- **Harvests of the Earth**

Let's Get Started

This chapter continues to discuss peoples, nations, languages, and kings that will exist during the Tribulation Period. We will learn more about the 144,000 Jewish evangelists, the Tribulation Saints, the city of Jerusalem, and those who take the mark of the Beast. We will also learn about Armageddon and Babylon.

foreheads
Revelation 7:3

preserve
Proverbs 2:8

Preserve and Protect

> **REVELATION 14:1** *Then I looked, and behold, a Lamb standing on Mount Zion, and with Him one hundred and forty-four thousand, having His Father's name written on their <u>foreheads</u>.* **(NKJV)**

After having the rise of the Antichrist and the False Prophet revealed to him, John now sees Jesus standing on Mount Zion in Jerusalem, with his 144,000 Jewish evangelists gathered around him. These 144,000 are those believers who will have the name of Jesus' Father written on their foreheads.

God is showing the world a great miracle. Jesus will seal the 144,000 Jewish evangelists between the opening of the sixth and seventh seals. The seventh seal will produce the seven trumpet judgments. During the seven trumpet judgments, one-third of the earth and trees will burn up, one-third of the sea will turn to blood, one-third of all ships will be destroyed, one-third of the fresh water will be polluted, and one-third of the light of the sun and moon will be diminished. The Antichrist will kill multitudes, try to eliminate most of the Jews, and try to stop the preaching of the 144,000, but not even one of these Jewish evangelists will die. They will not even be afraid to hold a worship service in the middle of the city. The name of God written on their foreheads will <u>preserve</u> and protect them from every judgment and all the diabolical attacks of the Antichrist and his followers.

go to

Antichrist
Revelation 13:16–17

Jebusites
2 Samuel 5:6–7

Jerusalem
1 Chronicles 11:4–8

Christians are sealed with the Holy Spirit as soon as they accept Jesus as their Savior. This sealing means that believers belong to God, and it is a guarantee that they will be protected throughout eternity. Christians may die a physical death, but not even one will perish. The followers of the Antichrist and False Prophet will have the mark, name, or number of the <u>Antichrist</u> on their head, but it will be worthless when they stand before Jesus at the judgment. Every one of them will perish.

Mount Zion was the name of an ancient fortified hill controlled by the <u>Jebusites</u>. King David captured the hill and took up residence in the fortress at the top. He then built a city around the fortress, which was called by two names: (1) the city of David, and (2) <u>Jerusalem</u>. Today, some refer to the hill as the Temple Mount and to Jerusalem as the political and religious capital of Israel. In the future, they will refer to the hill as the site of the Millennial Temple, and they will refer to the city as the City of God, City of Righteousness, City of Truth, city that God loves, city where God reigns, and more.

what others say

The Preacher's Outline and Sermon Bible

The Lord Jesus Christ is going to be victorious over the world. He is going to triumph over evil and bring righteousness and godliness to earth. The kingdom of God will reign upon earth. How do we know this for sure? Because the Scripture reveals it to us. This is the purpose of this great chapter: to show us that the victory of the Lord Jesus Christ over this world and its ungodliness is assured.[1]

Jim Combs

In this chapter, verse one, the Lamb is the Leader. In verse four the Lamb is the Redeemer. In verse ten the Lamb is the Judge.[2]

Robert H. Mounce

In chapter 7 we learned that the servants of God were sealed on the forehead to protect them from the coming judgments (vv. 2–4). In chapter 13 we discovered another kind of mark— the mark of the beast (v. 16). Without this mark on the right hand or forehead, no one would be able to buy or sell (v. 17; cf. also 14:11; 16:2; 19:20). In each case the "mark" is the name of the one to whom ultimate loyalty is given (13:17;

14:1). The 144,000 on Mount Zion bear the name of God; the unbelieving world carries the name (or its number) of the Satanic beast. The destiny of every person is determined by the mark that person bears. When judgment comes there will be no room for ambiguity; people will have by their "mark" declared their master.[3]

Heavenly Harps

REVELATION 14:2 *And I heard a voice from heaven, like the voice of many waters, and like the voice of loud thunder. And I heard the sound of harpists playing their harps. (NKJV)*

Singing will be heard in heaven for the 144,000 who stand unhurt on Mount Zion. They alone have survived the disasters of the Antichrist and False Prophet.

The singing will be (1) "like the voice of many waters"—the great sea or multitudes of people, Revelation 17:15; (2) "like the voice of loud thunder"—the voice of God or the seven thunders, Revelation 10:3; and (3) "harps"—calming and soothing.

You Would Have Had to Have Been There

REVELATION 14:3 *They sang as it were a new song before the throne, before the four living creatures, and the elders; and no one could learn that song except the hundred and forty-four thousand who were redeemed from the earth. (NKJV)*

The heavenly multitude will sing a new song before the throne of God, the four living creatures, and the twenty-four elders. No one will understand their song except the 144,000.

Often we sing songs without really understanding what the writer went through or is trying to convey. We would have needed to be there to understand what inspired them. The next two verses will give us an idea of the demands placed on the 144,000 that enabled them to understand this new song.

Notice that the 144,000 "were redeemed from the earth." These will be Jews who have accepted Jesus as the Messiah. They will be recipients of the grace of God having been purchased by the blood of Jesus and set free from the penalty of their sins.

Ed Hindson

Chapter 7 refers to them as the "bond-servants of our God" (7:3), and this passage calls them the "purchased" (14:3–4). They are never specifically called "witnesses"—the claims of the Jehovah's Witnesses notwithstanding.[4]

True to the End

REVELATION 14:4 *These are the ones who were not defiled with women, for they are virgins. These are the ones who follow the Lamb wherever He goes. These were redeemed from among men, being firstfruits to God and to the Lamb.* (NKJV)

This is a controversial verse. Some say the 144,000 will be **celibate**, while others claim they either will not break their marriage vows or will remain unmarried. Still others believe they will not commit **spiritual fornication** by worshiping idols and teaching false doctrines. It is difficult to say who is right, but we can be sure of two things: (1) during the Tribulation Period, it will be difficult for these men to be married and be good husbands and fathers, and (2) they will remain pure in spite of living in a world filled with immorality and spiritual fornication.

"The ones who follow the Lamb wherever He goes" means they will abide in his presence. They will not stray from the will or teachings of Jesus. "These were redeemed from among men" means they have been bought with the blood of Jesus. "Being firstfruits to God and to the Lamb" means they will be the first Jews saved during the Tribulation Period with more fruit to follow.

Tim LaHaye

The Bible does not teach celibacy; in fact, no hint of it is found in Scripture. The Bible everywhere advocates that Christians be holy and virtuous, undefiled by the world. Misuse of sex has always been one of man's greatest problems; infidelity and immorality one of man's greatest temptations.[5]

Faithful and True

REVELATION 14:5 *And in their mouth was found no deceit, for they are without fault before the throne of God.* (NKJV)

Truthfulness will also characterize the 144,000. They will have nothing to do with the lies of the Antichrist, or the counterfeit doctrines of the False Prophet. They will be faithful to God and clothed in the righteousness of Christ.

angel
Galatians 1:8–9

Characteristics of the 144,000

Characteristic	Reason
They stand with Jesus on Mount Zion	They are victorious with Jesus
They are marked on their foreheads	They have the names of Jesus' Father
They understand the heavenly new song	They understand because of their trials
They kept themselves pure	They avoid immorality and idolatry
They follow the Lamb wherever he goes	They abide in his presence
They are purchased from among men	They are bought with the blood of Jesus
They are offered as firstfruits to God and the Lamb	They are the first Jews saved during the Tribulation
No deceit was found in their mouths	They are faithful and true

Proclaim the Gospel

REVELATION 14:6 *Then I saw another angel flying in the midst of heaven, having the everlasting gospel to preach to those who dwell on the earth to every nation, tribe, tongue, and people—* (NKJV)

This is the first of several angels that appear in this chapter. Just when Satan, the Antichrist, and the False Prophet think they are about to take over the world, God will send angels to keep his plan on track.

Today, the Church is responsible for the proclamation of the gospel. But that will change after the Rapture. Jesus said, "And this gospel of the kingdom will be preached in all the world as a witness to all the nations, and then the end will come" (Matthew 24:14 NKJV). Because the Church will be in heaven, God will use the 144,000 Jews, the two witnesses, and even an <u>angel</u> to spread his message. He will go to great lengths to give the world one last chance to be saved.

What gospel will the angel preach? The fact that it is called the "everlasting gospel" is indication that it is identical to the gospel the Church preached. Some try to separate the gospel into different categories: the gospel of grace, the gospel of the kingdom, the gospel

go to

fear God
Psalms 111:10;
147:11

birthplace
Isaiah 47:9–13

possession
Luke 8:26–36

maddening
a symbol of evil
spirits or demon
possession

of judgment, the everlasting gospel, Paul's gospel, etc. But all of these are part of the same gospel.

Death or Life—That Is the Choice

REVELATION 14:7 *saying with a loud voice, "Fear God and give glory to Him, for the hour of His judgment has come; and worship Him who made heaven and earth, the sea and springs of water." (NKJV)*

People will have two choices: (1) believe the Antichrist, believe his lie, and worship him, or (2) fear God alone and give him all the glory. Choosing to follow the Antichrist can only lead to spiritual death, but choosing to follow God will surely lead to spiritual life.

What does it mean to fear God? Satan would have us believe it means to be afraid of God, but that is incorrect. To fear God means to have a holy respect for him, believe he exists, and believe he reigns and will judge all mankind. This kind of fear is the beginning of wisdom, and it pleases God.

Babylon the Harlot

REVELATION 14:8 *And another angel followed, saying, "Babylon is fallen, is fallen, that great city, because she has made all nations drink of the wine of the wrath of her fornication." (NKJV)*

Babylon is known as the city of Satan because of its long history of idolatry, astrology, witchcraft, and other occult practices. It is the birthplace of many false doctrines and religions such as goddess worship.

In Acts 2:13 the new believers of Christ were accused of being drunk on new wine, but they were actually being filled with the Holy Spirit. In that chapter wine is a symbol of the Holy Spirit. In this chapter, "the wine of the wrath of her fornication" is a reference to demon possession. Making the nations drink this **maddening** wine is a reference to Babylon's forcing her satanic-inspired false religion on the world.

The ancient city died out many centuries ago, but during the 1980s and 1990s Saddam Hussein poured hundreds of millions of dollars into rebuilding it. The rebuilt city will become a great center of religion and trade during the Tribulation Period. The False Prophet will locate the headquarters of his false religion there.

In verses 6 and 7, we learned that God will send the first angel of chapter 14 to proclaim the gospel to all people. That angel will also proclaim the arrival of God's judgment. Then a second angel will declare the fall of Babylon. This is a judgment the Old Testament <u>prophets</u> predicted, and it must come to pass. Babylon's fascination with the occult and her spread of a **one-world harlot religion** will bring a world-class fall.

The word "fallen" is repeated twice to mean two separate falls or judgments. The false religious system will fall first when the Antichrist turns on it just after the midpoint of the Tribulation Period. The rebuilt city of Babylon will fall again when it is burned to the ground in one hour near the end of the Tribulation Period (more on this later in chapter 17).

prophets
Isaiah 13:4–6, 19–20; Jeremiah 51:7, 25–26

one-world harlot religion
the set of religious and social values of the Antichrist and False Prophet

what others say

The Preacher's Outline and Sermon Bible

Is not a one-world government and religion a good thing? Will not the dream of men for a one-world government and religion bring the "kingdom of utopia" to earth? This verse says that Babylon will be destroyed for one reason: she will make all nations drink of the wine of her fornication.[6]

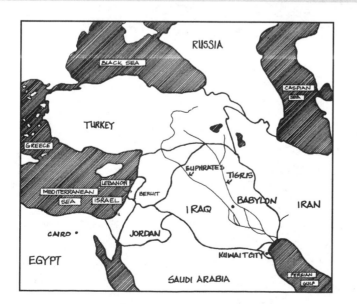

Illustration #9
Babylon—Modern-day map of the Middle East showing location of the city of Babylon and the Tigris and Euphrates Rivers.

Do Not Take the Mark

REVELATION 14:9 *Then a third angel followed them, saying with a loud voice, "If anyone worships the beast and his image, and receives his mark on his forehead or on his hand, (NKJV)*

A third angel will fly through the air with a third announcement. This announcement will concern those who worship the Antichrist, worship his image, and take his mark. The first angel will preach the gospel and plead with people to worship God. The second angel will announce the fall of Babylon. This angel will warn people not to worship the Antichrist or take the mark of the Beast.

Tormented by Fire

REVELATION 14:10 *he himself shall also drink of the **wine of the wrath of God**, which is poured out full strength into the **cup of His indignation**. He shall be tormented with fire and brimstone in the presence of the holy angels and in the presence of the Lamb. (NKJV)*

This is one of those "you will reap what you sow" verses. Babylon will make all the nations "drink of the wine of the wrath of God." Those who drink her wine will then be made to drink the wine of God's wrath, which will be unimaginable torment with burning sulfur. We know that burning sulfur increases the temperature of a fire, and therefore, in this case, would raise the level of suffering. Everyone should heed this warning. Following the Antichrist and worshiping him will stir the wrath of God.

Part of the awfulness of this will be their suffering in the presence of the holy angels, who warned them, and their suffering in the presence of the Lamb, who died for the sins of the world. It will be bad enough to suffer, but it will be worse to suffer in front of those who tried to prevent it and were spurned.

No End to It

REVELATION 14:11 *And the smoke of their torment ascends forever and ever; and they have no rest day or night, who worship the beast and his image, and whoever receives the mark of his name."* (NKJV)

The smoke will roll up like a stinking sulfuric cloud. Anyone who worships the Beast, his image, or who receives the mark will never rest.

Remain Faithful

REVELATION 14:12 *Here is the patience of the saints; here are those who keep the commandments of God and the faith of Jesus.* (NKJV)

go to

remain faithful
Matthew 24:13;
Luke 21:19

die
2 Timothy 2:11–12

follow
Matthew 6:20

clouds
Daniel 7:13

harvest
the gathering of the
wicked nations for
judgment

God has decreed that the Tribulation Period will come and the Antichrist will be given power over the world for seven years. When the Antichrist goes on his rampage, there will not be much that believers can do. God cannot go back on his Word. His prophecies must be fulfilled. Believers will have to endure, keep his commandments, and remain faithful.

A Blessing to Die

REVELATION 14:13 *Then I heard a voice from heaven saying to me, "Write: 'Blessed are the dead who die in the Lord from now on.'" "Yes," says the Spirit, "that they may rest from their labors, and their works follow them." (NKJV)*

This is a message of assurance and hope to those who will be trying to endure the trials of the Tribulation Period. God does not want believers to be afraid to die. It is a blessing to die in the Lord, but still, most of us do not want to die before our time.

A time will come during the Tribulation when it will be better for the saved to die than to live. They will leave their grief and torment behind, enter heaven, and rest in the presence of God where their deeds will follow them. This, obviously, is far better than taking the mark and suffering eternal damnation in hell.

what others say

John Hagee

Some Christians and Jews who are unable to flee to the Jordanian wilderness will be sheltered from the genocide by caring individuals (Matthew 25:31–46). Others will be captured and put to death, and these saints will receive a special blessing from God for their courageous devotion to him in the midst of horrific persecution and torture.[11]

The Harvest

REVELATION 14:14 *Then I looked, and behold, a white cloud, and on the cloud sat One like the Son of Man, having on His head a golden crown, and in His hand a sharp sickle. (NKJV)*

A day is coming when Jesus will take a seat in the clouds. He will wear a golden crown and hold a sharp sickle. The crown will identify him as a king, and the sickle will signify a coming **harvest**.

The Scriptures teach that Jesus will come back in the clouds as the King of kings and Lord of lords. He said, "The harvest is the end of the age, and the reapers are the angels. Therefore as the tares are gathered and burned in the fire, so it will be at the end of this age. The Son of Man will send out His angels, and they will gather out of His kingdom all things that offend, and those who practice lawlessness, and will cast them into the furnace of fire. There will be wailing and gnashing of teeth" (Matthew 13:39–42 NKJV). It will be a terrible day for the lost because not only will it be their last day on earth, but their destiny will be sealed for eternity as well.

<table>
<tr><td></td><td align="right">what others say</td></tr>
</table>

what others say

David Hocking

Jesus was called "the Son of Man" throughout the Gospels. It was the title he most often used for himself. It is a reminder that our coming Judge is one who knows what we are like. His humanity gives him valid credentials for judging mankind. John 5:27 (NKJV) says the Father "has given Him authority to execute judgment also, because He is the Son of Man."[12]

Not Too Soon

REVELATION 14:15 *And another angel came out of the temple, crying with a loud voice to Him who sat on the cloud, "Thrust in Your sickle and reap, for the time has come for You to reap, for the harvest of the earth is ripe."* (NKJV)

As Jesus appears in the clouds, an angel will come forth from the heavenly temple. He will urge Jesus to take his sickle and reap because the time of judgment has arrived and the harvest is ready. The Greek word for "ripe," *xeraino*, means "totally ripe, rotten, or withered." "The harvest of the earth is ripe" shows us that God will withhold his judgment until the last minute. When his judgment falls, the Church will have been raptured, most of the Tribulation Saints and Jews will have been killed, and the world will be totally corrupt. No one will be able to truthfully claim that Jesus acted too soon.

In fact, the Tribulation Saints have already asked God how long he would wait to judge and avenge their blood, and he told them to wait a little longer (Revelation 6:10–11). He will wait, but when the end of the Tribulation Period starts drawing near the time will come to wait no more.

Swoosh

sickle
Joel 3:13–14

everlasting fire
Matthew 25:41

True Vine
John 15:1

REVELATION 14:16 *So He who sat on the cloud thrust in His sickle on the earth, and the earth was reaped. (NKJV)*

Jesus will swing his sharp <u>sickle</u> over the earth. Many of the remaining unbelievers will be filled with terror and try to run and hide. Others will beg, cry, and plead, but it will be too late. They will have wasted their last chance, and he will take multitudes and cast them into the <u>everlasting fire</u> (Lake of Fire).

Mercy, Not Another Angel

REVELATION 14:17 *Then another angel came out of the temple which is in heaven, he also having a sharp sickle. (NKJV)*

This angel will come directly from the presence of God with a sharp sickle just like the one Jesus will have.

And Yet Another Angel

REVELATION 14:18 *And another angel came out from the altar, who had power over fire, and he cried with a loud cry to him who had the sharp sickle, saying, "Thrust in your sharp sickle and gather the clusters of the vine of the earth, for her grapes are fully ripe." (NKJV)*

Yet another angel will come forth—this time from the altar in the heavenly temple. We read about this altar before in Revelation 8:3. It is where the Tribulation Saints call upon God to avenge their blood. Now this angel will urge the angel with the sharp sickle (the angel in v. 5) to gather the clusters of grapes from the earth's vine, because its grapes are ripe. Since Jesus is the <u>True Vine</u>, it is likely that the earth's vine is a reference to the Antichrist. The clusters of grapes will be the fruit of the earth's vine or those nations that follow the Antichrist.

This indicates two things: (1) God will eventually answer the prayers of the Tribulation Saints who cried out for revenge, and (2) the wickedness of the earth will be great. God does not always answer prayers right away, but he will not let them go unanswered forever. Neither will he let wicked nations or individuals deny him forever.

The Three Harvests of Revelation 14

Harvest	Scripture
The harvest of firstfruits—the 144,000	Revelation 14:4
The harvest by Jesus—unbelievers	Revelation 14:14–16
The harvest of the angel—unbelievers	Revelation 14:18–20

Note: Not many unbelievers will survive, but those who do will be removed from the earth at the end of the Tribulation Period (Matthew 13:41–43, 49–50).

wrath to come
1 Thessalonians 1:10

wrath
1 Thessalonians 5:9

Cast Them Out

REVELATION 14:19 *So the angel thrust his sickle into the earth and gathered the vine of the earth, and threw it into the great winepress of the wrath of God. (NKJV)*

The fifth angel will use his great sickle to gather the wicked nations of the earth. He will then cast them into the winepress of God's wrath. This is a symbol to help us understand what is going to happen. When farmers go into their vineyards to harvest the grapes, they cast them into the winepress and squeeze the juice out of them. In this process the grapes are practically destroyed. The same thing will happen to the wicked when this angel harvests the earth. They will be like a grape being squashed in a winepress.

one thousand six hundred furlongs
about 200 miles

> **what others say**
>
> **J. R. Church**
>
> I believe that Christians will not be forced to endure the wrath of God's judgment. We will be raptured to meet our Lord in the air at some point prior to the beginning of that dreadful time.[13]

Two reasons why many believe the Church will be raptured before the Tribulation Period are that Jesus will rescue us from the <u>wrath to come</u>, and that God did not appoint us to <u>wrath</u>.

As High As a Horse's Bridle

REVELATION 14:20 *And the winepress was trampled outside the city, and blood came out of the winepress, up to the horses' bridles, for **one thousand six hundred furlongs**. (NKJV)*

go to

God's wrath
Isaiah 34:1–8

brass
Revelation 1:15

horses' bridles
about four feet high

valley of Megiddo
the valley where
the Battle of
Armageddon
will be fought

This is a reference to the Battle of Armageddon. The ripe grapes (wicked nations) will be trampled in the winepress of <u>God's wrath</u>. People will be crushed by the fine <u>brass</u> feet of Jesus like small grapes under the weight of a large man.

Since the blood will rise as high as the **horses' bridles** for approximately 200 miles, we know that millions will die. Before it happens, though, God will preach the gospel through the 144,000 Jews, the two witnesses, and his angel (the first angel of chapter 14). He will also send an angel (the third angel of chapter 14) to warn those who follow the Antichrist. He will give the world many chances to repent before he destroys it.

Muslims believe in the Battle of Armageddon, but they call it the Mother of All Battles. The name comes from the Koran which, among other things, is a twisted version of the Bible. It teaches that Allah will help Islam win this great battle. This is partly why religious fanatics are pushing the War on Terrorism. Some misguided Islamic militants actually believe they can trigger the Battle of Armageddon and win. It's doubtful that many, if any, will survive long enough to be involved, but if they do, they will get the great war they want, but the awful outcome will be more terrifying than anything they could have imagined.

what others say

Hal Lindsey

Apparently this whole valley [**valley of Megiddo**, or Armageddon, see Illustration #10 on page 239] will be filled with war materials, animals, bodies of men, and blood.[14]

When John saw Jesus, Christ's feet were like fine brass, as if refined in a furnace.

what others say

Homer Ritchie, Omer Ritchie, and Lonnie Shipman

Imagine looking to the Eastern sky and seeing the King of all Kings, the King of Glory and the King of the Universe coming with flaming fires of judgment. At that moment, those who have denied His name, have followed the Antichrist and taken his evil mark (666) will realize that Jesus is the true God and Savior of this world. They will see Him whom they have pierced and wail in fear under His wrath.[15]

Chapter Wrap-Up

- The 144,000 will stand with Jesus on Mount Zion and sing a new song since they will be redeemed from the earth and offered as firstfruits. These are also the ones who kept themselves pure during the Tribulation. (Revelation 14:1–5)

- An angel will fly through the air proclaiming the gospel to all the earth's inhabitants and warning them that the hour of God's judgment is near. (Revelation 14:6–7)

- A second angel will follow the first and proclaim the fall of Babylon because she caused the nations of the earth to sin. (Revelation 14:8)

- A third angel will follow the first two and warn the people of earth to not worship the Antichrist or receive his mark. Those who do follow the Antichrist will suffer God's fury forever. (Revelation 14:9–12)

- Two harvests of the earth will occur. The first one will be by Christ and the second by an angel who will throw his harvest into the winepress of God's wrath. (Revelation 14:14–20)

Study Questions

1. What sounds did John hear in heaven and what do they mean?

2. What is significant about "dying in the Lord"?

3. Who will send harvesters to the earth during the Tribulation Period, who will do the harvesting, and what will they harvest?

4. What does "the winepress was trampled" imply?

Revelation 15

Chapter Highlights:
- **Third Great Sign**
- **Second Glassy Sea**
- **Song of the Lamb**
- **Under the Law**
- **Seven Angels with Seven Plagues**

Let's Get Started

Chapter 15 is the shortest chapter in Revelation. Most scholars believe it should be combined with the next chapter because it is the introduction to the seven bowl judgments of chapter 16. It predicts what will go on in heaven just before the final judgments fall.

go to

crystal
Revelation 4:6

sea
Revelation 17:15

The Third Great Sign from Heaven

> REVELATION 15:1 *Then I saw another sign in heaven, great and marvelous: seven angels having the seven last plagues, for in them the wrath of God is complete. (NKJV)*

This will be the third of three great signs in heaven: first, the sun-clothed woman (Israel); second, the great red dragon (Satan); now, seven angels with seven last plagues. This sign will be great and marvelous because of its terrible nature and amazing result. It will bring on the full wrath of God, which will cause the fall of Satan and his devilish crew.

These plagues can be called "last plagues" because they will be God's final warnings to an unrepentant world. When these plagues are over, all of those who have not made a decision to side with God through Jesus will stand before the judgment of unbelievers and perish.

The Second Glassy Sea

> REVELATION 15:2 *And I saw something like a sea of glass mingled with fire, and those who have the victory over the beast, over his image and over his mark and over the number of his name, standing on the sea of glass, having harps of God. (NKJV)*

This will be the second glassy sea to appear in heaven. The first glassy sea will be as clear as <u>crystal</u>. This one will be mixed with fire. The <u>sea</u> symbolizes the masses of humanity, and the fire represents judgment.

victory
1 Corinthians
15:55–57

gain
Philippians 1:21

Moses
Exodus 15:1–19

The Tribulation Saints will come up out of the sea of humanity. They will have been in a fiery persecution. They are those who had been victorious over the Beast and his image and over the number of his name. They will not be deceived by the Antichrist or his False Prophet. They will be tracked down and ordered to take the mark of the Beast but will refuse. For their refusal they will face retaliation in the form of torture and death. <u>Victory</u>, however, will still be theirs because they will lose their earthly life but will <u>gain</u> an eternal one.

When they reach heaven God will give them harps. Their earthly trials will have caused a lot of crying, but when they get to heaven they will sing and play.

what others say

Robert H. Mounce

These who stand on the crystal pavement are those who have emerged victorious. They have not abandoned their faith nor succumbed to the threats of Antichrist. They are the overcomers to whom the seven letters hold out promise of eating of the tree of life (2:7), protection from the second death (2:11), hidden manna (2:17), authority over the nations (2:26), white garments (3:5), the honor of becoming a pillar in the temple of God (3:12), and the privilege of sitting with Christ on his throne (3:21). Little wonder that they break out in song.[1]

Hal Lindsey

Real victory is not found in seeking to avoid conflicts and living a don't-rock-the-boat kind of life. The cemetery is full of people who fit that category. The kind of triumph these martyrs of the Tribulation will experience will be deliverance through fire, not out of it.[2]

The Song of the Lamb

REVELATION 15:3 *They sing the song of Moses, the servant of God, and the song of the Lamb, saying:*
"Great and marvelous are Your works,
Lord God Almighty!
Just and true are Your ways,
O King of the saints! (NKJV)

The Tribulation Saints will sing two songs: (1) the song of Moses, and (2) the song of the Lamb. The song of <u>Moses</u> is found in the Old Testament. It celebrates the victory God gave Israel when he brought her out of Egypt. Pharaoh's army chased after the Hebrews to recapture them, but his troops were drowned in the Red Sea.

The song of the Lamb is found in this verse. It celebrates God's reign and victory over all the nations. The deeds of Jesus are great and marvelous because he died for the sins of the world and will defeat Satan. The ways of Jesus are just and true. He is never unjust, never untruthful. His judgments are righteous. His words are accurate and reliable. Jesus is the King of the ages. He is the eternal King. The One who has reigned, is reigning, and always will reign.

> **what others say**
>
> **J. R. Church**
>
> Just prior to the seven vial judgments, the saints in heaven will sing the song of Moses. They await the victory. Soon, Satan will be bound and the Messianic kingdom will be established.[3]

Fear and Glory

REVELATION 15:4

> *Who shall not fear You, O Lord, and glorify Your name?*
> *For You alone are holy.*
> *For all nations shall come and worship before You,*
> *For Your judgments have been manifested." (NKJV)*

Today, few people speak of having a reverential fear of the Lord or of giving glory to him. We seem to think there is something wrong with these. However, these are of the utmost importance now and in heaven for three reasons:

1. Jesus should be feared and glorified because he alone is holy. He is the only One to live by all of God's standards, the only One worthy of our worship, the only One who never sinned. He has been hallowed or set apart for God's special purpose: an atonement for our sin.

2. Jesus should be feared and glorified because he will be worshiped by all nations. The day will come when he will deal with the godless leaders of this world. He will do away with them, and every nation will worship him.

3. Jesus should be feared and glorified because his righteous acts will be revealed. The terrible judgments of the Tribulation Period will

Ten Commandments
Exodus 20:2–17

be righteous acts of Jesus. He will deal with those who do not accept his mercy.

what others say

Peter and Paul Lalonde

According to opinion polls, an overwhelming majority of North Americans believe they will spend eternity in heaven (about 93 to 95 percent). Yet it is obvious from the moral decay and decadence in the West that such a majority do not have the love of Christ in their hearts.[4]

Under the Law

REVELATION 15:5 *After these things I looked, and behold, the temple of the tabernacle of the testimony in heaven was opened. (NKJV)*

The temple in heaven will be opened. Then the Holy of Holies (see Illustration #5, page 148) inside the Temple will be opened, followed by the ark of the covenant (see Illustration #6, page 164) inside the Holy of Holies. The ark of the covenant contains the Ten Commandments, which are sometimes called the Law or the Testimony.

Those who reject the grace and mercy God offers through the death, burial, and resurrection of his Son will be judged under the Law (the Ten Commandments). In rejecting what God offers, they also reject Jesus. Many, including the Jews, do not realize this most important point. By rejecting Jesus, they reject God, and leave themselves open to be judged under the Law of Moses in the Old Testament.

The Law of Moses was given to reveal sin not to take sin away. Sin can only be taken away by the Lamb of God (Jesus).

Seven Angels with Seven Plagues

REVELATION 15:6 *And out of the temple came the seven angels having the seven plagues, clothed in pure bright linen, and having their chests girded with golden bands. (NKJV)*

Seven angels will come out of the Temple. They will be dressed in pure bright linen signifying their righteousness. They will wear golden bands around their chests (see Illustration #2, page 11) signifying their royal priesthood.

These seven angels will move away from the Temple and the **mercy seat**. They are royal and powerful priests preparing to pour out the wrath of God. Those on earth will receive judgment without mercy. Because they have flouted God, followed the Antichrist, took the mark, worshiped his image, and rejected Jesus, they will face the full <u>fury</u> of God.

fury
Hebrews 10:31

Day of Atonement
Leviticus 16:14–15

creatures
Revelation 6:1–8

mercy seat
the gold lid on the
ark of the covenant

The Seven Angels of God's Wrath

> **REVELATION 15:7** *Then one of the four living creatures gave to the seven angels seven golden bowls full of the wrath of God who lives forever and ever. (NKJV)*

One of the four living creatures will hand the seven angels seven bowls filled with the wrath of God. Some Bible translations call these bowls "vials," but that does not do justice to the meaning of this verse. When a vial is turned upside down the liquid bubbles out slowly, but when a bowl is upset the liquid is suddenly dumped out. That is the picture we have here. God's wrath will be suddenly dumped out on the inhabitants of earth.

In the Old Testament, once a year on the <u>Day of Atonement</u>, the high priest would take a bowl of blood from a sacrificial animal into the Holy of Holies and dump it on the mercy seat over the ark of the covenant. God had him do that to offer atonement for the sins of the people. Since the Antichrist and his followers will not accept the blood of Jesus as an atonement for their sins, these priestly angels will be given bowls filled with God's wrath instead of the blood of Jesus. And instead of dumping the bowls on the mercy seat, they will dump them on the earth.

First, the four living <u>creatures</u> summon the four horsemen. Now the four living creatures summon the seven angels of God's wrath.

what others say

Jim Combs

Man never gets away with sin and rebellion. In the final stages of the Tribulation, these "seven last plagues" are poured out on a Christ-rejecting world, run amok after Satan and the false religious worship that focuses on the image of the beast.[5]

No More!

smoke
Isaiah 6:4

REVELATION 15:8 *The temple was filled with <u>smoke</u> from the glory of God and from His power, and no one was able to enter the temple till the seven plagues of the seven angels were completed. (NKJV)*

Things just keep getting worse for those who reject God. When the priestly angels leave the temple, it will be filled with smoke from the glory and power of God. No one will be able to go back in or enter the Holy of Holies. No one can change their mind and pour blood on the mercy seat. There will be no more mercy, no more delays, and no more opportunities to repent until the seven plagues have passed.

This is a warning to those on earth who won't listen to the pleas of God made through his messengers—the 144,000 Jews, the two witnesses, the angel, and others. At some point in the Tribulation Period, God will say, "It's over. The destiny of those who keep rejecting my Son is sealed forever." He will pour out his wrath, keep people away from the mercy seat, and refuse to hear the pleas of those crying out for one more chance.

Chapter Wrap-Up

- The third great sign John will see will be seven angels carrying the seven last plagues, which will complete God's wrath. (Revelation 15:1)

- Standing beside the sea of glass mixed with fire will be those who will be victorious over the Antichrist. They will receive harps and sing about the deeds of Christ. (Revelation 15:2–4)

- Those who overcome the Antichrist will sing the song of the Lamb. They will sing about: his marvelous deeds, his just and true ways, and his holiness. (Revelation 15:3–4)

- Anyone who rejects Christ and his gift of eternal life will be judged according to the Law of Moses (the Ten Commandments). (Revelation 15:5)

- When the heavenly temple opens, the seven angels with the seven last plagues will come out of it. Once the angels leave the temple smoke from God's glory will fill the temple, preventing anyone from seeking mercy and obtaining one last chance. (Revelation 15:5–8)

Study Questions

1. How are the actions of angels in this chapter contrary to our concept of angels?

2. Is God unjust or unrighteous for sending the Tribulation Period?

3. What is meant when the Bible says, "You alone are holy"?

4. What will the golden bowls contain?

5. Why will smoke fill the temple?

Revelation 16

Chapter Highlights:
- Seven Bowls of Wrath
- Just and True
- Euphrates River
- Armageddon
- A Great Earthquake

Let's Get Started

We put the introduction to this chapter behind us when we studied chapter 15. Now we move on to see what will happen when the seven bowls of God's wrath are poured out on a sinful world. The severity of these judgments indicates the extent of God's wrath toward those who steadfastly refuse to acknowledge him. The severity also indicates the extent of God's love by showing how far he will go to get unbelievers to repent. He loves the wicked and wants them to change before he has to remove them from the earth to set up his kingdom of righteousness.

That's right! It will be like it was in the days of Noah when the wicked were removed from the earth by the Flood, and the righteous (Noah and his family) trusted God and survived. Every lost person will be removed from the earth when Jesus returns at the Second Coming. The saved will repopulate the earth during the Millennium.

The Seven Bowls

Bowl	Result	Scripture
First	Foul and loathsome sores on the followers of the Antichrist	Revelation 16:2
Second	Sea turns to blood and kills every living creature in it	Revelation 16:3
Third	Rivers and springs turn to blood to avenge saints and prophets	Revelation 16:4–7
Fourth	Sun scorches people; they blaspheme God and refuse to repent	Revelation 16:8–9
Fifth	Dark over land of Antichrist, great pain, sores, no repentance	Revelation 16:10–11
Sixth	Euphrates River dries up; armies gathered for Armageddon	Revelation 16:12–14
Seventh	Greatest earthquake, islands moved, mountains disappear, hail	Revelation 16:17–21

go to

sixth plague
Exodus 9:8–12

Seven Bowls

REVELATION 16:1 *Then I heard a loud voice from the temple saying to the seven angels, "Go and pour out the bowls of the wrath of God on the earth." (NKJV)*

In chapter 15 we read that the heavenly temple will be filled with smoke so that no man will be able to enter in. However, the Father, Son, and Holy Spirit will already be inside, which is where this voice originates. Remember that God has committed all judgment to Jesus, which means Jesus will order the seven angels to go and pour out the seven bowls of God's wrath on the earth. Each angel will be given a portion of God's wrath.

> **what others say**
>
> **Peter and Paul Lalonde**
>
> Armageddon is coming. . . . Who in their right mind would choose to fight with the Antichrist against God? Yet millions are making such a decision each day when they reject so great a salvation as that offered by God through his Son, Jesus Christ. For this is the heart of what Armageddon is all about. It is the world saying, "We will not bow our knee to anyone. We are too proud. We are too mighty. We are too important."[1]

The False Physician

REVELATION 16:2 *So the first went and poured out his bowl upon the earth, and a foul and loathsome sore came upon the men who had the mark of the beast and those who worshiped his image. (NKJV)*

The first bowl judgment will cause foul and loathsome sores. Some Bible commentators say these sores will have a very offensive odor. Only those who take the mark of the Beast or worship his image will be afflicted. When the Antichrist is unable to heal his own people, the world will know he is a false physician.

This plague will be similar to the <u>sixth plague</u> in Egypt when Moses was trying to have the Hebrews set free. At that time, God afflicted the Egyptian people with tumors, festering sores, and itching skin. The whole land, all the Egyptians, and even the animals were affected.

go to

> **what others say**
>
> ### J. R. Church
>
> In the end-time there will be several worldwide epidemics raging out of control.[2]
>
> ### Life Application Bible Commentary
>
> The outpouring of these bowls occurred in rapid succession, one right after the other, but the effects of each seem to have lingered. For example, the *malignant sores* that people get here still affect them during the fifth plague (16:10-11), along with the sunburns they received during the fourth plague.[3]

Seas of Blood

REVELATION 16:3 *Then the second angel poured out his bowl on the sea, and it became blood as of a dead man; and every living creature in the sea died.* (NKJV)

The second bowl judgment will be worse than the second trumpet judgment. It will pollute the sea by turning it into blood and killing everything in it. In the second trumpet judgment, one-third of the sea creatures were killed. One can easily imagine the repercussions of such a horrible event.

> **what others say**
>
> ### Henry M. Morris
>
> When men who know of the true existence of God refuse to glorify Him as God and are not thankful for the great gifts of His creation (Romans 1:20), God will finally give them up (Romans 1:24), so that even the creation itself turns against them.[4]
>
> ### John F. Walvoord
>
> In reference to the sea, it is possible that it may be limited to the Mediterranean, but the same word would be used if the entire world were involved.[5]

Rivers of Blood

REVELATION 16:4 *Then the third angel poured out his bowl on the rivers and springs of water, and they became blood.* (NKJV)

first plague
Exodus 7:17–25

wind
Revelation 7:1

justice
Psalm 89:14

eternal existence
Deuteronomy 33:27

holy nature
Psalm 99:4–5

The third bowl judgment will be worse than the third trumpet judgment. This plague will be similar to the first plague in Egypt. Back then, God turned all the waters of Egypt into blood. The fish died, the water smelled, and the people could not drink it. This plague will be far worse because all the earth's water will be polluted, causing worldwide suffering and death.

The Water Angel

REVELATION 16:5 *And I heard the angel of the waters saying:*
"You are righteous, O Lord,
The One who is and who was and who is to be,
Because You have judged these things. (NKJV)

We probably do not realize the important role angels play in managing God's creation. We have already encountered the four wind angels, those angels in charge of holding back the earth's wind. Now we learn that God has a water angel in charge of the earth's water. Were it not for these angels, man would not have survived as long as he has.

The angel in charge of earth's waters will look at this judgment and declare it to be a judgment deserved. He will express the justice of God, the eternal existence of God, and the holy nature of God.

A Round of Blood, Please

REVELATION 16:6
For they have shed the blood of saints and prophets,
And You have given them blood to drink.
For it is their just due." (NKJV)

The bloody waters will be God's response to the shedding of the blood of the Tribulation Saints and the Old Testament prophets. The Old Testament plainly says, "You shall not murder" (Exodus 20:13 NKJV), and Jesus clearly said, "All who take the sword will perish by the sword" (Matthew 26:52 NKJV). It is a hard truth, but these unbelievers will get what they have coming to them. It is bad enough to ignore the Bible, but it is even worse to turn one's back on the mercy of God at the same time. Those who shed blood will be forced to drink it.

Just and True

REVELATION 16:7 *And I heard another from the altar saying, "Even so, Lord God Almighty, true and righteous are Your judgments." (NKJV)*

The Antichrist and his followers will shed the blood of saints all over the world. God will eventually respond by turning their drinking water into blood. When he does, the martyred Tribulation Saints will declare that God's judgments are just and true.

A Hot Time in the Old Town

REVELATION 16:8 *Then the fourth angel poured out his bowl on the sun, and power was given to him to scorch men with fire. (NKJV)*

The fourth bowl judgment will cause the sun to scorch people with fire. According to the prophet Malachi, a day is coming when the earth will burn like an <u>oven</u>. Many evildoers will be reduced to ashes.

Multitudes will want to take a cold shower and wash their painful sores, but they will only be able to shower in blood. Those involved in the blood bath of Christians will experience the wrath of God by bathing in blood or not bathing at all. Neither option is good.

Still Cursing

REVELATION 16:9 *And men were scorched with great heat, and they blasphemed the name of God who has power over these plagues; and they did not repent and give Him glory.* (NKJV)

The strong heat of the sun will bear down on them with a vengeance. They will sweat and thirst but will have nothing to drink except blood. They will get sunburned on top of the painful sores caused by the first bowl judgment. Blisters, sunstroke, and extreme thirst will be like God's punishment to the unbelievers.

These afflictions will cause them to finally admit that God exists, and that he controls these plagues. But even with that in mind, they will still not fall on their sunburned faces and sore knees to ask for mercy. Instead, they will curse his name.

Darkness over All the Land

REVELATION 16:10 *Then the fifth angel poured out his bowl on the throne of the beast, and his kingdom became full of darkness; and they gnawed their tongues because of the pain.* (NKJV)

The fifth bowl judgment will mark a turning point. God will begin to focus his attention on one of his biggest adversaries on earth—the Antichrist. This beast will love spiritual darkness so he will get physical darkness. It will cover the planet. People will not be able to see the stars or moon or even the sun.

This darkness will be similar to the darkness that covered the land of <u>Egypt</u> when Moses was trying to free the Hebrews. The last time darkness covered the earth was when Jesus hung on the <u>cross</u>. The next time it will happen will be to fulfill several Old Testament <u>prophecies</u>.

People will become anxious and nervous. They will begin to ponder their future. Some will have misgivings about taking the mark of the Beast and following the Antichrist. Others may be tormented by insanity and chew their tongues in agony.

1. It was so dark in Egypt the people could not see one another, and they were afraid to move from the place they were in for three days.

2. When Jesus, who is the Light of the World (John 8:12), died, God plunged the world into darkness for three hours. Because the world cannot survive without light, many preachers understand this to mean that the world cannot survive without Jesus.

3. The prophet Joel says the Tribulation Period darkness will be unlike anything the world has ever experienced. The agony and fear will be indescribable.

It Ain't My Fault

REVELATION 16:11 *They blasphemed the God of heaven because of their pains and their sores, and did not repent of their deeds.* (NKJV)

God is great and good. He is the God of heaven. He deserves praise and exaltation, but these people will curse and **blaspheme** everything he is and does. Men will not repent but will blame God for their afflictions. They will not blame themselves for their sins or admit that these judgments are fair retribution for their wrongdoing. Instead of repentance, they will choose continued blasphemy. And, in spite of their misgivings, they will continue to follow the Antichrist and his False Prophet.

go to

Egypt
Exodus 10:21–22

cross
Matthew 27:45

prophecies
Isaiah 60:2;
Joel 2:1–2, 31

blaspheme
cursing, or directing false accusations against God

The Way Is Clear

go to

two hundred million
Revelation 9:14–16

> **REVELATION 16:12** *Then the sixth angel poured out his bowl on the great river Euphrates, and its water was dried up, so that the way of the kings from the east might be prepared. (NKJV)*

The Euphrates River (see Illustration #9, page 211) is mentioned more than twenty-five times in the Bible and is often referred to as the "great river." Nevertheless, this great river will dry up during the Tribulation Period. Why? Because it is a barrier that divides East from West. It prevents the kings of the East from moving their great army into the West (the Middle East).

When the sixth angel pours out his bowl, the river will dry up, the barrier will be gone, and the kings of the East will be able to move their two-hundred-million-man horde against Israel in the Battle of Armageddon. Notice the word "kings" is plural. This will likely be an alliance of Eastern nations.

No one knows exactly who the Kings of the East are, but experts think they will include China, North Korea, and perhaps India, Japan, and others. China alone has more that 200 million men of military age (Revelation 9:16), and the number increases by more than 10 million each year. In less than a generation, her oil wells will be dry, and she is investing heavily in the Middle East, building ships and vehicles to transport her troops, upgrading her weapons and communications systems, and threatening her neighbors not to help the United States if she gets into a war with America. This great battle will probably start early in the last half of the Tribulation Period and cover large portions of the earth, but it will wind up in the Middle East with the nations coming together to attack Israel.

what others say

J. Dwight Pentecost

It has been held commonly that the battle of Armageddon is an isolated event transpiring just prior to the second advent of Christ to the earth. The extent of this great movement in which God deals with "the kings of the earth and of the whole world" will not be seen unless it is realized that the "battle of that great day of God Almighty" (Revelation 16:14) is not an isolated battle, but rather a campaign that extends over the last half of the tribulation period.[10]

A Frog in Your Throat

> **REVELATION 16:13** *And I saw three unclean spirits like frogs coming out of the mouth of the dragon, out of the mouth of the beast, and out of the mouth of the false prophet.* (NKJV)

Ahab
1 Kings 22:20–37

second plague
Exodus 8:1–15

In the Old Testament, God was looking for someone to lure the wicked king <u>Ahab</u> into a death trap. An evil spirit stepped forward and volunteered to be a lying spirit in the mouths of Ahab's false prophets. God said that would work and sent the lying spirit forth. Shortly after that, Ahab asked his prophets if he should battle the Arameans at Ramoth Gilead. His prophets, influenced by the lying spirit, said he would win. Instead, he was killed.

John tells us that three evil spirits will come forward during the Tribulation Period: one from the mouth of Satan, one from the mouth of the Antichrist, and one from the mouth of the False Prophet. This verse is where we get the term "False Prophet."

We can only speculate about the froglike appearance of these demons. We know that the Egyptians worshiped Heka, a frog-headed goddess. She is one of the oldest goddesses who was said to have demonic powers. The <u>second plague</u> on Egypt during the days of Moses was a plague of frogs. We know, too, that frogs are connected with the occult. Witches are often portrayed with frogs and use them in their spells. Frogs breed in mire and muck and are a symbol of uncleanness.

There are other Scriptures on this subject. For example, the apostle Paul said, "The Spirit [Holy Spirit] expressly says that in latter times some will depart from the faith, giving heed to deceiving spirits and doctrines of demons" (1 Timothy 4:1 NKJV). Demons are real and will be very busy during the Tribulation Period. This provides insight as to why militant Muslims believe they can trigger the Battle of Armageddon and win.

A Death Trap

> **REVELATION 16:14** *For they are spirits of demons, performing signs, which go out to the kings of the earth and of the whole world, to gather them to the battle of that great day of God Almighty.* (NKJV)

Jesus was talking about the last days when he said, "For false christs and false prophets will rise and show great signs and wonders to deceive, if possible, even the elect. See, I have told you beforehand" (Matthew 24:24–25 NKJV). The apostle Paul said the Antichrist will come with the work of Satan displayed in all kinds of "power, signs, and lying wonders" (2 Thessalonians 2:9 NKJV). When the sixth bowl is poured out, spirits of demons will use miraculous signs to lure the leaders of the world and their God-defying troops into that death trap called the great day of God Almighty or the Battle of Armageddon.

what others say

David Hocking

When miraculous signs are performed, many people believe God is behind them. The Bible teaches otherwise. While it is possible that God is performing the signs, it is also possible they are being done through the power of Satan or demons.[11]

Why God Will Allow the Battle of Armageddon

Reason	Scripture
To do to nations what they do to Israel	Obadiah 1:15
People will be scattered for scattering the Jews	Joel 3:2
People will lose their land for seizing Jewish land	Jeremiah 12:14–17
People will be plundered for plundering Israel	Zechariah 2:8–9
Because people refuse to repent and give God glory	Revelation 16:9
Because people live wickedly and ignore the Second Coming	Revelation 16:15

A Thief in the Night

REVELATION 16:15 *"Behold, I am coming as a thief. Blessed is he who watches, and keeps his garments, lest he walk naked and they see his shame." (NKJV)*

It is Jesus who says, "I am coming as a thief." People do not usually expect thieves, or they would prepare for them. This means the coming of Jesus will be a surprise, but what is Christ talking about? It cannot be the Rapture, because by this time that will have already occurred. And who will be surprised? It cannot be the Church, because they went in the Rapture. This is a reference to the coming of Jesus at the end of the Tribulation Period. The unclean spirits will

238 **The Smart Guide to the Bible**

gather the armies of the world at Armageddon, and only then will Jesus return and catch them by surprise.

"Blessed is he who watches, and keeps his garments" is an encouragement for people to remain faithful. These garments (clothes) are the righteousness of Christ. Those who refuse the mark of the Beast will be blessed when Jesus returns, but those who take it will be exposed.

Armageddon

REVELATION 16:16 *And they gathered them together to the place called in Hebrew, Armageddon. (NKJV)*

This is the only time the word "Armageddon" can be found in the Bible. "Armageddon" is Hebrew and is the name of a place in northern Israel (see Illustration #10). When translated, the word means "Mount of Megiddo." The Mount of Megiddo is a large hill just west of the Jordan River, in the Plain of Esdralon (sometimes called the Valley of Jehoshaphat). The Euphrates River will dry up to allow the two-hundred-million-man army to approach from the East. Demons will go forth from the satanic trinity (Satan, the Antichrist, and the False Prophet) and gather other armies from all over the world.

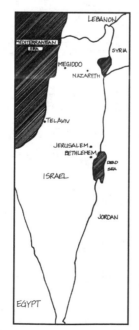

Illustration #10
Megiddo—Modern-day map showing location of the city of Megiddo. It has become a symbol for the final battle of good and evil because Armageddon translated is "Mount of Megiddo."

The Last Judgment

> REVELATION 16:17 *Then the seventh angel poured out his bowl into the air, and a loud voice came out of the temple of heaven, from the throne, saying, "It is done!"* (NKJV)

The seventh bowl judgment will be the last. It will be poured out into the air, and then a voice from the throne of God will say, "It is done!" Just before Jesus died on the cross he said, "It is finished!" (John 19:30 NKJV). Just before Jesus returns to earth he will say, "It is done!" The remaining events will bring an end to Satan's reign.

Off the Richter Scale

> REVELATION 16:18 *And there were noises and thunderings and lightnings; and there was a great earthquake, such a mighty and great earthquake as had not occurred since men were on the earth.* (NKJV)

When the seventh bowl is poured into the air something will happen to the atmosphere. Great flashes of lightning will explode to the ground, and thunder will rattle the earth. Fires will break out, and a tremendous earthquake will shatter the land.

Major Earthquakes of the Last 100 Years
(USGS Reports of 50,000 or More Deaths)

Date	Location	Deaths
December 28, 1908	Messina, Italy	70,000–100,000
December 16, 1920	Gansu, China	200,000
September 1, 1923	Kanto, Japan	143,000
May 22, 1927	Near Xining, China	200,000
December 25, 1932	Gansu, China	70,000
May 30, 1935	Quetta, Pakistan	30,000–60,000
October 5, 1948	Ashgabat, Turkmenistan	110,000
May 31, 1970	Peru	66,000
July 27, 1976	Tangshan, China	255,000
June 20, 1990	Northwest Iran	50,000
December 26, 2004	Sumatra	283,106
October 7, 2005	Pakistan	79,000 (unofficial)

Note: Includes deaths from tsunamis, landslides, floods, fires, etc., caused by earthquakes.

Remembered Again

prophets
Isaiah 13:4–6,
19–20;
Jeremiah 51:7,
25–26

drunkard
Isaiah 24:19–23

> REVELATION 16:19 *Now the great city was divided into three parts, and the cities of the nations fell. And great Babylon was remembered before God, to give her the cup of the wine of the fierceness of His wrath.* (NKJV)

This great earthquake will split the great city of Babylon into three parts, but it will still stand. This cannot be said for other cities because they will be leveled. Every city on earth, except Babylon, will be in ruins as the end of the Tribulation Period approaches. With Babylon still standing, it will come into remembrance before God. One of the three angels (Revelation 14:8) predicted Babylon's doom just a short time before this. The Old Testament prophets predicted her doom long before that. It will be time for those prophecies to be fulfilled. She will get the cup filled with the wine of the fury of his wrath.

Creation Backward

> REVELATION 16:20 *Then every island fled away, and the mountains were not found.* (NKJV)

The surface of the whole earth will be changed. Every island will sink beneath the water. Every mountain will be leveled. The prophet Isaiah said the floodgates of heaven will be opened. The earth will reel to and fro like a drunkard.

This seems hard to believe, but the 2004 Sumatra earthquake and tsunami that killed more than 280,000 people moved islands and caused the earth to tilt on its axis. Some islands temporarily disappeared under a thirty-foot-high wall of water.

According to the U.N. and the International Red Cross, natural disasters are increasing in frequency and intensity, but are earthquakes increasing? Some experts say yes; others say no. The United States Geological Service (USGS) says, "No! More earthquakes are reported, but it's because there are more stations with better equipment, not more earthquakes." Some say earthquakes are not increasing, but the number and severity of aftershocks are. The answer to this question seems to depend on the data used (over 6.0, over 6.5, etc.) and how it's broken down (7.0 in the 1990s vs. 7.0 in the 1980s; total in 2000 vs. total in 2004, etc.). The following charts speak for themselves.

Number of Magnitude 7.0 and Greater Earthquakes per Decade, Since 1900
(USGS Records)

seventh plague
Exodus 9:18–25

Decade	Number
1900–1909	196
1910–1919	226
1920–1929	171
1930–1939	202
1940–1949	298
1950–1959	209
1960–1969	204
1970–1979	204
1980–1989	112
1990–1999	153
2000–2004	74

Total 1900–2004 = 2,049 earthquakes magnitude 7.0 and greater
Average: 19.5 magnitude 7.0 and greater earthquakes per year (195 per decade)

Total Number of Earthquakes Worldwide 2000–2005
(USGS RECORDS)

Year	Total
2000	22,256
2001	23,534
2002	27,454
2003	31,419
2004	31,194
2005	30,458

Hail Bigger Than Bowling Balls

REVELATION 16:21 *And great hail from heaven fell upon men, each hailstone about the weight of a talent. Men blasphemed God because of the plague of the hail, since that plague was exceedingly great. (NKJV)*

The seventh plague in Egypt during the days of Moses was hail mixed with fire. It was directed against Isis, the cow-headed goddess of the air. Giant hail killed the cattle in the fields and broke down all the trees.

This plague will be much worse. These hailstones will weigh more than one hundred pounds apiece and will beat the earth with a fury. What effect will this have on mankind? Will people finally repent of their sins and avoid hell? No. They will still blaspheme God.

Chapter Wrap-Up

- When the seven bowls of God's wrath are poured out his judgments will come to an end.
- After the third bowl is emptied, the angel in charge of the waters and the Tribulation Saints will proclaim these judgments to be just and true. (Revelation 16:5–7)
- The Euphrates River will dry up to make way for the coming of the kings from the East. (Revelation 16:12)
- Three spirits will come out of the mouths of Satan, the Antichrist, and the False Prophet to summon the kings of the earth together for the Battle of Armageddon. (Revelation 16:13–16)
- After the seventh bowl is poured out a great earthquake will rock the planet, destroying all cities except Babylon, which will split in three parts. (Revelation 16:18–19)

Study Questions

1. Who tells the angels to pour out the bowls of wrath?

2. Why will people have to drink blood during the Tribulation Period?

3. What will happen to the kingdom of the Antichrist and how will it affect people?

4. Who will the blessed be during the Tribulation Period?

5. What will the evil spirits do to gather men for the Battle of Armageddon?

Revelation 17

Chapter Highlights:
- Mother of Harlots
- From the Bottomless Pit
- An Eighth King
- Babylon, the Mother, Destroyed

Let's Get Started

Chapter 17 may be beyond our comprehension, but it helps to be aware of the contrasts in the book of Revelation. The coming one-world leader is the Antichrist, but the true world Leader is the Christ. The coming one-world bride of Antichrist is Mystery Babylon the Great the Mother of Harlots, but the Bride of Christ is the Church. The reign of Antichrist will produce the Tribulation Period, but the reign of Christ will produce the Millennium. The Antichrist will establish his headquarters in Babylon, but the Jews will get Jerusalem and the Church will get the New Jerusalem.

Mystery Babylon is a woman. In chapter 12 Israel is portrayed as a woman clothed in the sun who will give birth to Jesus. In chapter 19 the Church is portrayed as a woman clothed in linen, clean and bright, who will marry Jesus. In chapter 17 Mystery Babylon the Great is portrayed as a woman clothed in purple and scarlet, and adorned with gold and precious stones and pearls. Mystery Babylon is a harlot, but Israel and the Church are good women.

Mystery Babylon has a double identity. She is a bad woman who adorns herself with riches, but she is also a city who makes others rich. Jerusalem and the New Jerusalem are good women who use their riches to help others and they are holy cities.

Chapter 17 describes the woman and her fall at the hands of the Antichrist and his ten puppet kings shortly after the Tribulation mid-point. Chapter 18 describes the city and its fall by the hands of God near the end of the Tribulation Period. The fall of Babylon was announced in Revelation 14:8 and Revelation 16:19. The next two chapters fill in the details of both destructions.

As a mother, the great Babylon is a failure. She is a harlot and the Mother of Harlots. The Bible tells us that a harlot is more than just a woman who physically commits sexual sins. A <u>harlot</u> is also a person who spiritually has stopped following the true God and has turned to idol worship. The great Babylon abandoned the true God

harlot
Exodus 34:15–16;
2 Chronicles
21:11–13

wife of Christ
Revelation 19:7

wife of God
Jeremiah 31:32

adulterous
spiritual prostitutes
(people who take up
false religions)

and has raised her daughters (false religions) to do the same. She is the mother of false religions who wants all her daughters to grow up in her one-world harlot religion. The names of some of her daughters are New Age, Satan Worship, Mother Earth Worship, Globalism, Hinduism, and Islamism. Her daughters talk about love and peace, but none of them love Jesus, and none of them talk about peace with God through Jesus. Her daughters' followers are a collection of religious people who will be left behind when the true Church is raptured.

As a city, the great Babylon is also a failure. She is the birthplace of the Mother of Harlots and many of her daughters. During the Tribulation Period, Babylon (the city) will be filled with **adulterous** kings. She will open her doors to one-world government, one-world religion, and global trade. People intoxicated with big government, big money, global commerce, and a lust for pleasure will flock to her. She will even entice these adulterous leaders to marry her daughters, which will represent a merger of one-world harlot religions with one-world government.

Shortly after the Tribulation Period midpoint, the harlot's sons-in-law (the kings of the earth) will become "wife abusers." They will kill the harlot (one-world religious system) and her daughters (the individual false religions). Near the end of the Tribulation Period, God will pour out his wrath on Babylon where many of the sons-in-law live. Jesus will return and destroy Babylon the mother and Babylon the city.

Obviously, kings cannot marry a religion. Think of it spiritually. Just as you and I are the wife of Christ, and Israel is the wife of God, these adulterous kings will marry false religions in the sense that they will espouse the doctrines of the false religions. They will cooperate with the False Prophet and the Antichrist in pushing a false religion on the world.

People of a sound mind don't have to lose it to believe this. Those who founded the United States government believed in the God of Abraham, Isaac, and Jacob. They allowed prayer, Bible teaching, and preaching to permeate the American culture. But in America today, many leaders seem to keep trying to erase God from America's memory, history books, and society. In some cases, world and national Church leaders have risen and aligned themselves with unbelievers who say that the true gospel is divisive and unloving, and they are willing to unite all religions, even at the cost of abandoning the only God and Savior of the Church. It's much the same in Europe where the Antichrist will come from. EU leaders have drafted a Constitution that ignores God. They say Europeans are too pluralistic, sophisticated, and worldly to include anything about Christian values or God in such an important document. And it's no different in the U.N. with its call for a one-world secular society with a global ethic that contradicts many Bible teachings. Following the Rapture, every political and religious leader left behind will be lost. They will tickle the ears of the Antichrist and work to get rid of the true God. Everything else including satanism will be welcome.

Mystery Babylon

Church	Harlot
Union of Jesus and Church is a Mystery (Ephesians 5:32)	Harlot is Mystery Babylon
Bride of Christ	Bride of Antichrist
A good or faithful woman	A bad or unfaithful woman
Honors Christ	Blasphemes Christ
Sits on thrones (24 elders in Revelation 4:4)	Sits on Antichrist
Reigns with Christ	Reigns with Antichrist
Reigns during Tribulation Period and Millennium	Reigns during Tribulation Period
Sealed by Holy Spirit	Sealed by mark of the Beast
Clothed in linen clean and bright	Clothed in purple and scarlet
Drinks fruit of vine (takes Communion = blood)	Drinks blood of saints
Offspring are children of God	Offspring are harlots
Will live forever with Christ	Will be destroyed by Antichrist
Will dwell in New Jerusalem	Will dwell in Babylon
Uses her riches to help others	Adorns herself with riches of others
Joint heir with Jesus	Will be robbed by Antichrist
Is loved by Jesus, King of kings	Will be hated by Antichrist and ten kings
Married to Jesus, who descends out of heaven and goes to New Jerusalem	Married to Antichrist, who ascends out of bottomless pit and goes to perdition

waters
Revelation 17:15

sea
Revelation 4:6

fire
Revelation 15:2

masses
Revelation 17:1

ecumenism
the effort to merge
all the world's reli-
gions into one giant
world religion

harlot
unfaithful religious
people

She Sits on the Masses

> REVELATION 17:1 *Then one of the seven angels who had the seven bowls came and talked with me, saying to me, "Come, I will show you the judgment of the great harlot who sits on many waters, (NKJV)*

John will be invited to look at the punishment of Babylon the mother, the great religious harlot who sits on many waters. This is a revelation of what God plans to do with this harlot religious system.

In the Bible, seas and <u>waters</u> represent great masses of people. They represent people, nations, and tongues. The fact that this wicked woman is pictured as sitting upon these great masses is an indication that she will be supported by them, and she will exercise control over them during the Tribulation Period.

what others say

Arno Froese

The political roots of **ecumenism**, the united world church, are in Rome; the spiritual roots go back to Babylon.[1]

Hal Lindsey

I expect to see more and more mergers between Christian denominations and more emphasis on ecumenism.[2]

The Church in heaven looked like a <u>sea</u> of glass.

The Tribulation Saints in heaven looked like a sea of glass mixed with <u>fire</u>.

Babylon the Great (the mother) will sit on the <u>masses</u> of the world.

No More Separation of Church and State

> REVELATION 17:2 *with whom the kings of the earth committed fornication, and the inhabitants of the earth were made drunk with the wine of her fornication." (NKJV)*

The **harlot** religious system will commit adultery with the kings of the earth. She will conspire with world leaders to produce a merger of religion and government. Here it finally is! A religious system united with a political system to manipulate the people of the earth into a false government-approved religion.

"The wine of her fornication" is a reference to demon <u>possession</u>. This wicked woman will cause people to be led astray by **<u>deceiving spirits</u>**.

possession
Luke 8:26–36

deceiving spirits
1 Timothy 4:1

> ### what others say
>
> ### Jack Van Impe
>
> Teachings of **non-monotheistic** Eastern religions have infected even the Church itself, driving it increasingly toward **apostasy** and a **laissez-faire** interpretation of God's Word. With widespread religious deception so out of control, it is easy to understand how worldwide ecclesiastical trends are leading to the dawn of a one-world church controlled by the spirits of Satan.[3]
>
> ### Ed Hindson
>
> In summary . . .
>
> 1. The spirit of the Antichrist and the mystery of iniquity were already at work in apostolic times.
>
> 2. Apostasy has progressed throughout church history, pre-dating the modern church.
>
> 3. A large segment of modern Christendom is already apostate. Unbelief is rampant in liberal circles.
>
> 4. After the rapture of true believers, all professing "Christians" who are left behind will be apostate believers regardless of their denomination.
>
> 5. The False Prophet will arise to lead apostate Christendom in its acceptance of the Antichrist.[4]

deceiving spirits
demons

non-monotheistic religions
religions that believe in many gods

apostasy
to completely forsake one's faith or religion

laissez-faire
letting people do as they please

Some experts take a very anti-Catholic stance on Revelation. This should be avoided. The one-world religion will have a lot of Catholics in it, but it will also have a lot of Protestants and other religions too. The saved, regardless of religion or denomination, will be raptured, and the lost, regardless of their religious beliefs, will be left behind.

The Woman Rides the Beast

REVELATION 17:3 *So he carried me away in the Spirit into the wilderness. And I saw a woman sitting on a scarlet beast which was full of names of blasphemy, having seven heads and ten horns.* (NKJV)

Antichrist
Revelation 13:1

great city
Revelation 17:18

Holy Grail
a legendary golden
cup that some say
was used to catch
the blood of Jesus
when he was dying
on the cross

Communion
the ritual of taking
bread (his body) and
wine (his blood) to
commemorate the
death of Jesus

John was taken in the Spirit to a desert where he saw something strange—a woman sitting on a scarlet beast. We already know the beast with seven heads and ten horns is the <u>Antichrist</u>. Since the woman will be sitting on the Beast, we must assume that her harlot religion and the Antichrist will exist on earth at the same time.

At first the Antichrist will support her one-world religion and be under her authority, but things will eventually turn sour between the two. Their relationship will be hindered by the woman's double identity. Remember, she is both the mother, the false religious system, and the <u>great city</u>, Babylon. We see from this that all three— the false religious system, the city of Babylon, and the Antichrist— will exist during the first half of the Tribulation Period.

The Holy Grail?

REVELATION 17:4 *The woman was arrayed in purple and scarlet, and adorned with gold and precious stones and pearls, having in her hand a golden cup full of abominations and the filthiness of her fornication.* (NKJV)

Psalm 22 has been called the Psalm of the Cross because it is an accurate prophecy of the crucifixion of Christ. As Jesus was hanging on the cross he said, "I am a worm" (v. 6 NKJV). Many commentators say the Hebrew is *coccus worm.* The Jews used the coccus worm to make scarlet red dye, the color of our sins. The Lord said, "Though your sins are like scarlet, they shall be as white as snow; though they are red like crimson, they shall be as wool" (Isaiah 1:18 NKJV). Jesus was like a coccus worm on the cross because he bore our sins in his own body. The scarlet beast in verse 3 (the Antichrist), and this woman dressed in purple and scarlet are full of sin.

Obviously, it took a great number of tiny coccus worms to accumulate enough dye to make purple clothing. This made purple clothing so expensive it was often called the color of royalty. So this woman dressed in purple and scarlet is a rich harlot of royal stature. She will be adorned in the trappings of her political cronies steadily enticing a bewildered world.

Look at the golden cup she will be holding. Will it be the **Holy Grail**? Will she take **Communion** with it? She may want the world to think that, but she will really be holding a cup filled with abominable things and the filth of her fornication. When the false religions drink from this cup, they will drink the <u>wine</u> of fornication—symbolic of deceiving spirits and demons.

Today, many people think our modern society is too enlightened to believe in the existence of demons. More conservative Christians disagree. Those who accept the authority of the Scriptures accept the existence of demons. They are no less dangerous than Satan, for they are his cohorts doing his will. All who have not accepted Christ are subject to their evil influence. It is unfortunate, but this includes many of the world's religious and political leaders.

In the United States the CIA has secretly used psychics and many police departments have hired them to solve crimes. In *It Takes a Village*, Hillary Clinton wrote that she holds conversations with the deceased former First Lady Eleanor Roosevelt. Officials in China hire sorcerers to ward off diseases. Some communities in England have more Satanists than Christians. Reports have persisted for years that top Russian leaders are involved in the occult. Satan is the unseen force behind this.

wine
Jeremiah 51:7–8

what others say

Billy Graham

> Satan and his demons are known by the discord they promote, the wars they start, the hatred they engender, the murders they initiate, the opposition to God and His commandments . . . He [Satan] works to bring about the downfall of nations, to corrupt moral standards, and to waste human resources. Corrupting society's order, he wants to prevent the attainment of order, and to shake the kingdoms of our God. He uses his destructive power to create havoc, fire, flood, earthquake, storm, pestilence, disease, and the devastation of peoples and nations.[5]

Hal Lindsey

> I have found this about religion. The more false a religion is, usually the more wealth it has. And the more true a religion is, usually the less material things it has. And it doesn't seem to care about it. And I've seen the Christian church become poverty stricken spiritually as they have become wealthy materially.[6]

Birthplace of Abominations

nihilism
all existence is senseless and there is no possibility of an objective basis for truth

Nirvana
the final heaven of Buddhists; a state of perfection

REVELATION 17:5 *And on her forehead a name was written:*
MYSTERY,
BABYLON THE GREAT,
THE MOTHER OF HARLOTS
AND OF THE
ABOMINATIONS OF THE
EARTH. (NKJV)

Mystery Babylon reminds us of Jerusalem in Ezekiel's day. Unfaithful Jerusalem was a harlot and the daughter of a harlot who committed abominations (Ezekiel 16:35–36, 44–45). This harlot's title reveals where she came from and what she will do. She came from Babylon, and she will go back to Babylon during the Tribulation Period. She will be known as the Mother of Harlots and the Mother of Abominations.

Mystery Babylon also reminds us of Babel (predecessor of ancient Babylon) and the Tower of Babel in Nimrod's day. Nimrod, whose name means "let us revolt," attempted to establish a one-world religion based upon astrology, sorcery, and the mysteries or legends of Semiramis and Tammuz. John seems to be saying the roots of the coming one-world harlot religion go back to Babylon. Its heresies will be an outgrowth of that and will be shrouded in secret religious rites and murky rituals with dark or mysterious satanic doctrines.

what others say

Arno Froese

In order to have fellowship with them, she (the prostitute) drinks the wisdom of many religions. Whether this is Buddhism, Hinduism, or Islam, all are welcomed by the "harlot Babylon." It makes no difference that the Lord Jesus is merely one of a thousand gods for the Hindus, nor does it mean anything that for Buddhists only works and **nihilism** count in **Nirvana**. It is said that they all (many waters) lead to the one God. . . . What difference does it make? We can still have fellowship with one another, can't we?[7]

The harlot, which is the one-world religious system, originated at the Tower of Babel, which is located at Old Testament Babylon (see Illustration #9, page 211). Babylon was destroyed, but it is being rebuilt along with the Tower of Babel in Iraq. The prostitute is going full circle. She was born in Babylon, and she will go back there before she dies.

Drunk with the Blood of Her Victims

REVELATION 17:6 *I saw the woman, drunk with the blood of the saints and with the blood of the martyrs of Jesus. And when I saw her, I marveled with great amazement. (NKJV)*

drunk
Revelation 17:2

The harlot will not only make others <u>drunk</u>, but she, too, will be drunk on the blood of the Tribulation Saints. This great ecumenical religious system will be actively involved in the persecution and death of God's people. She will be so determined to establish her one-world religion that she will actually be filled with the blood of the saints.

> **what others say**
>
> **Grant R. Jeffrey**
>
> Obviously, Mystery Babylon, the apostate pagan church of the last days, will not develop overnight. Such an ecumenical organization, involving many diverse religious groups, will be created by negotiation and conferences over a number of years leading up to the beginning of the seven-year tribulation period. It is therefore quite probable that we will witness the initial steps toward this one-world church of the last days before the Rapture takes the Christians home to heaven.[8]

Confusion

REVELATION 17:7 *But the angel said to me, "Why did you marvel? I will tell you the mystery of the woman and of the beast that carries her, which has the seven heads and the ten horns. (NKJV)*

God's angel perceived that John was astonished and maybe even confused, so he told John he would explain two things: the mystery of the woman, and the mystery of the beast with the seven heads and ten horns. The remaining verses of chapter 17 are about this—the meaning of the beast and identity of the woman.

> **what others say**
>
> **F. Kenton Beshore**
>
> It is important to keep in mind that at the Rapture all believers will be caught up to the Lord from the earth—leaving no believers on the earth. All churches, therefore, will be without born-again leaders or members whether Baptist, Lutheran, Presbyterian or Catholic, etc. Thus as we discuss the world church after the Rapture it would obviously be apostate.[9]

Out of the Bottomless Pit

go to

bottomless pit
Revelation 9:1–11

Lake of Fire
Revelation 19:20

mountains
Jeremiah 51:24–25;
Daniel 2:35–45

bottomless pit
the place where God
is holding the worst
of the demonic
spirits

subterranean abode
their prison beneath
the earth's surface

REVELATION 17:8 *The beast that you saw was, and is not, and will ascend out of the **bottomless pit** and go to perdition. And those who dwell on the earth will marvel, whose names are not written in the Book of Life from the foundation of the world, when they see the beast that was, and is not, and yet is. (NKJV)*

The beast existed prior to John's lifetime—once was, did not exist when John received this revelation, now is not, but will reappear at some unspecified time in the future. The beast will have satanic ties to the **subterranean abode** of demonic spirits since he will come out of the Abyss. He will eventually go to his destruction since God will cast him into the Lake of Fire. And he will take his followers, the inhabitants of the earth whose names have not been written in the Book of Life from the creation of the world, with him.

> **what others say**
>
> **Ed Hindson**
>
> A world leader will quickly arise on the international scene promising to bring peace and economic stability. He will receive the support of the European Community and eventually control the whole world.[10]

When the fifth trumpet sounds, Satan will open the bottomless pit and release the demonic spirits being held there.

Put on Your Spiritual Wisdom Cap

REVELATION 17:9 *Here is the mind which has wisdom: The seven heads are seven mountains on which the woman sits. (NKJV)*

Interpreting this verse requires spiritual understanding of the Scriptures (not of world geography). The seven heads on the beast are seven mountains on which the woman sits. This seems simple enough, but it is not as it appears. Revelation 17:10 tells us these seven mountains are not seven actual mountains, but are seven kings (kingdoms or world governments). Herein lies the problem. Is this: (1) a religious system/city that sits on seven mountains, (2) seven kings, or (3) both? The Bible tells us that hills or mountains are a symbol of kingdoms. Therefore, the seven mountains must be seven kings or kingdoms.

Still, some experts say the "seven mountains" is a reference to Rome (the city on seven hills). Even if right, this is only saying the prostitute will control, and be supported by, Rome.

> **what others say**
>
> **Charles H. Dyer**
>
> Identifying the prostitute as Rome because of the seven hills has some serious flaws. The first flaw is the assumed relationship between the woman and the hills. The seven heads are attached to the beast, not the woman. . . . The seven heads do not identify the location of the prostitute because she is not part of the beast. . . . The woman sits on the whole beast, not just on the heads. . . . It is far more consistent to view the harlot's "sitting" as describing her control over the seven mountains instead of pointing to her physical location.[11]

Seven Kingdoms

REVELATION 17:10 *There are also seven kings. Five have fallen, one is, and the other has not yet come. And when he comes, he must continue a short time. (NKJV)*

The seven heads are seven mountains, and they are also seven kings. The word "kings" can also be translated "kingdoms." It makes more sense in this case to say the seven heads are seven kingdoms, because history and Scripture reveal that there have been seven Gentile world kingdoms.

The "five [who] have fallen" are the five Gentile world kingdoms (Assyrian, Medo-Persian, Greek, Egyptian, and Babylonian) that existed before John's lifetime. "One is" refers to the sixth kingdom (Roman) that existed during John's lifetime, and "the other has not yet come" refers to a seventh future kingdom (the Revived Roman Empire), which will exist after John's lifetime. This seventh kingdom will remain ("he must continue a short time") for the duration of the seven-year Tribulation Period.

> **what others say**
>
> **Hal Lindsey**
>
> Here (John) is referring to those great world empires from the time of the original Babylon of Nimrod's day which have been dominated by the false occultic religion of Babylon.[12]

length
Daniel 9:27

beast
Revelation 17:8

The seven Gentile world kingdoms are the Assyrian, Medo-Persian, Greek, Egyptian, Babylonian, Roman, and Revived Roman Empire (Revelation 12:3).

The seventh future kingdom, the Revived Roman Empire, will last for seven years (one week of years) from the day the Antichrist signs a seven-year covenant to protect Israel. Seven years will be the <u>length</u> of the Tribulation Period.

An Eighth King

REVELATION 17:11 *The beast that was, and is not, is himself also the eighth, and is of the seven, and is going to perdition.* (NKJV)

"The beast that was, and is not" is the Antichrist. He is an eighth king (or kingdom). "Is of the seven" means he will be one of the seven already mentioned. Since he is yet to come, he must come out of the seventh Gentile world kingdom, which will be the Revived Roman Empire.

As an eighth king, he will take over the seventh Gentile world kingdom and establish his own brand of world government—a New World Order. The Antichrist will rise to power in that government, take it over, and transform it into a satanic state.

"The <u>beast</u> that was, and is not," is the beast that will come out of the bottomless pit—the Antichrist.

An Hour of Trial

REVELATION 17:12 *The ten horns which you saw are ten kings who have received no kingdom as yet, but they receive authority for one hour as kings with the beast.* (NKJV)

The ten horns are ten kings that will rule with the Antichrist. This presents a picture of what the end-time world government will be like. The Antichrist will rule the world, which will be divided into ten divisions. In charge of each division will be a separate leader who will answer to the Antichrist.

Another significant point: The ten kings will receive authority for one hour. "One hour" is a biblical term that means a short time. In this case, it means the ten kings will reign with the Antichrist for the duration of the Tribulation Period. The significance of this is the fact that Jesus promised to keep faithful believers from the **hour of trial** that is coming upon the world. Obviously there will be a pre-Tribulation Rapture (Revelation 3:10). The Church will not be on earth during the one-hour reign of the ten kings with the Antichrist.

called
2 Timothy 1:9

hour of trial
Tribulation Period

> ### what others say
>
> **Jim Combs**
>
> These are not ten kingdoms which are formed out of the western half of the Roman Empire in the 5th and 6th centuries, as some have taught, but rather ten countries united under Antichrist at a specific time or "hour" in the future, a definite time of short duration, during the 7-year Tribulation.[13]

"Because you have kept My command to persevere, I also will keep you from the hour of trial which shall come upon the whole world, to test those who dwell on the earth" (Revelation 3:10 NKJV).

Puppet Kings

REVELATION 17:13 *These are of one mind, and they will give their power and authority to the beast. (NKJV)*

The ten rulers will be under the Antichrist. They will be nothing more than puppet kings who submit to him.

Dictators usually come to power by using one or more of these tactics: violence, force, or political trickery. After coming to power, they usually have to continue to use force to stay in power. Because of that they usually outlaw basic freedoms such as the freedom of assembly, freedom of speech, and freedom of worship. According to the Bible, the Antichrist will do these things too, but he will be worse than any previous dictator.

Called, Chosen, and Faithful

REVELATION 17:14 *These will make war with the Lamb, and the Lamb will overcome them, for He is Lord of lords and King of kings; and those who are with Him are called, chosen, and faithful." (NKJV)*

At the end of the Tribulation Period, the Antichrist and his ten puppet kings will make war against the Lamb and his <u>called</u>,

go to

chosen
Ephesians 1:4

faithful
Matthew 25:21–23

**declare himself
to be God**
2 Thessalonians 2:4

chosen, and <u>faithful</u> followers. Unfortunately for them, the outcome was determined long ago. The Lamb will defeat them in the Battle of Armageddon because he is the Lord of lords and King of kings. Only those who are called, chosen, and faithful will be with Jesus.

Worldwide Deception

REVELATION 17:15 *Then he said to me, "The waters which you saw, where the harlot sits, are peoples, multitudes, nations, and tongues. (NKJV)*

The waters that the harlot sits on in Revelation 17:1 are peoples, multitudes, nations, and tongues. This base of power and support will give the harlot religious system tremendous control. She will ensnare and deceive people on a worldwide scale.

Babylon, the Mother, No More

REVELATION 17:16 *And the ten horns which you saw on the beast, these will hate the harlot, make her desolate and naked, eat her flesh and burn her with fire. (NKJV)*

During the first half of the Tribulation Period, the Antichrist (the Beast) will be submissive to Babylon (the mother and her false religious system, and the city and its one-world government). Now John tells us that the Antichrist and his ten puppet kings (the ten horns) will rise up against Babylon at the midpoint of the Tribulation Period.

The Antichrist will enter the Jewish temple in Jerusalem and <u>declare himself to be God</u>. Obviously there is no more room for Babylon and her one-world religion and one-world government. The Antichrist cannot be God and subject to those who worship him at the same time. So someone must go! The Antichrist and his allies will destroy the harlot's religious system. They will confiscate her expensive clothing, gold, and precious stones, and they will persecute and kill her poor deceived people. The fact that they will eat her flesh and burn her with fire is indicative of the intensity and totality of the harlot's end. Nothing will remain.

John Hagee

But what the Antichrist does not realize is that God has sovereignly moved to give him the ability to overthrow the Babylonian system—and that soon it will be the Antichrist's turn to experience a judgment that is swift, total, and dreadful.[14]

J. Dwight Pentecost

The Beast, who was dominated by the harlot system (Rev. 17:3), rises against her and destroys her and her system completely. Without doubt the harlot system was in competition with the religious worship of the Beast, promoted by the False Prophet, and her destruction is brought about so that the Beast may be the sole object of false worship as he claims to be God.[15]

This wicked woman, Babylon, has two identities. In addition to being a harlot, she is also an actual city. This verse is about the destruction of the harlot. The destruction of the city will come later.

Antichrist, the Puppet

REVELATION 17:17 *For God has put it into their hearts to fulfill His purpose, to be of one mind, and to give their kingdom to the beast, until the words of God are fulfilled.* (NKJV)

This is an interesting verse. The Antichrist doesn't know it, but he really is a puppet king just like the ten under him. God will plant the idea of destroying the false religious system into his heart and the hearts of his ten puppet kings. Destruction of the harlot religious system is the reason God will agree to give them power. They will be instruments in his hand to accomplish his purpose and fulfill his words.

Babylon, the City, Rebuilt

REVELATION 17:18 *And the woman whom you saw is that great city which reigns over the kings of the earth."* (NKJV)

This verse identifies the woman. She is the great city that rules over the earth. Unfortunately, this is not clear enough for some

spiritualize
not taking anything
literally

experts because they want to **spiritualize** everything in Revelation. Depending upon who the expert is this city could be Rome, Jerusalem, New York, the United States, part of the European group of nations, or a nation in control of those nations.

Babylon is called "that/this great city" in Revelation 14:8; 18:10, 16, 18–19, and 21. It would be inconsistent, if John is referring to any city other than literal Babylon here. All the other cities John writes about in the book of Revelation are literal cities, so why should commentators not think he is talking about a literal city here? Furthermore, chapter 18 talks about Babylon burning in one hour. That fits Isaiah's prophecy that the literal city will be destroyed like Sodom and Gomorrah (Isaiah 13:19–20), and Jeremiah's prediction that God will make the ancient city a burnt mountain (Jeremiah 51:25). The idea that the city will be rapidly rebuilt should not be discounted. Some say Saddam Hussein started rebuilding it in the 1980s. Some predict it will be rebuilt, but located closer to the Persian Gulf. Some predict it will be rebuilt and that the United Nations will move there from New York City. Some say America's presence in Iraq could be the Lord's way of laying the groundwork for some of these things. It's still a mystery, but the literal fulfillment of God's Word happens more than most people realize.

what others say

Charles H. Dyer

Babylon will claw its way to the heights of power and influence one last time. . . . The Bible's prophecies will be fulfilled when someone announces that Babylon will become their capital. . . . Babylon will again become the capital of an empire in the Middle East.[16]

Stanley E. Price

The ecumenical movements under the pope's leadership are leading to religious Babylon (Revelation 17); the world trade movement to commercial Babylon (Revelation 13:11–18; 18); and the New World Order to political Babylon (Revelation 13:1–10). After the Rapture, the whore of religious Babylon will rule the revived empire for three and one-half years, be overthrown, and the Beast of political Babylon will become ruler on planet earth (Revelation 17:16–17).[17]

Chapter Wrap-Up

- An angel will show John the punishment of the harlot who sits on the scarlet beast. She is the one whom the people of the earth will commit adultery with. (Revelation 17:1–5)

- The woman who sits on the beast is the great Babylon. She, the Mother of Harlots, will kill so many of the saints who follow Jesus that she will be drunk on their blood. (Revelation 17:5–6)

- The beast who will come out of the bottomless pit and go to his destruction will astonish many because he was, wasn't, and yet will come. His seven heads represent seven kingdoms—the beast is the eighth kingdom that will come out of the seventh. (Revelation 17:8–11)

- The ten horns are ten kings who will rule with the Antichrist during the Tribulation. Their only purpose is to give their power to the eighth king (the beast). (Revelation 17:11–14)

- God will accomplish his purpose by planting the idea of destroying Babylon, the mother, into the minds of the beast and his ten puppet kings. (Revelation 17:16–17)

Study Questions

1. Who is "Mystery, Babylon the Great"?

2. What was the condition of John when he saw this vision? What does his condition mean?

3. What is the significance of the harlot's clothing and the golden cup in her hand?

4. What is the "mind which has wisdom," and how can it be obtained?

5. Who will cause the beast and the ten horns (kings) to hate and destroy the harlot?

Chapter Highlights:
• A Resplendent Angel
• A Heavenly Voice
• Fall of Babylon
• Heavens Rejoice
• Millstone-Sized Boulder

Revelation 18

Let's Get Started

Chapter 17 is about MYSTERY BABYLON THE GREAT, THE MOTHER OF HARLOTS, AND THE ABOMINATIONS OF THE EARTH. But chapter 18 drops the word "mystery" and picks up the word "city." So it's time to shift our focus from the "mystery" to the city, from the coming one-world harlot religious system to the home of the coming one-world political and economic system, from the bride of Antichrist to the city of Antichrist.

Satan will be cast down to this earth at the middle of the Tribulation Period (12:7–9). He tries to copy everything Jesus does. The ancient city of Babylon and the coming rebuilt version appear to be that old serpent's pathetic effort to have wicked men build him a capital city on earth that will rival the Holy City, New Jerusalem, that Jesus and God will occupy on the new earth (chapters 21–22).

what others say

Andy Woods and Tim LaHaye

Of Revelation's 404 verses, 278 allude to the Old Testament. When the Old Testament uses the word "Babylon," the reference is always to literal Babylon. The same is likely true for Revelation. Human history will eventually cycle back to where it all began. In the same region where the first world emperor led mankind in a universal political and religious revolt against God, the future Antichrist will also lead the last collective revolt before Christ returns.[1]

An Illuminating Angel

REVELATION 18:1 *After these things I saw another angel coming down from heaven, having great authority, and the earth was illuminated with his glory.* (NKJV)

After witnessing the coming destruction of the one-world harlot religious system, John received a new revelation. He saw another angel coming down from heaven that will tackle the powerful and

presence of God
Ezekiel 43:2

prophets
Isaiah 13:19–22;
Jeremiah 50:38–40

wealthy one-world political and economic system. When this angel arrives it will not be the sun, moon, or stars that light the earth but the angel's glory. This suggests that he will come directly from the presence of God.

The Angel's Prophecy

REVELATION 18:2 *And he cried mightily with a loud voice, saying, "Babylon the great is fallen, is fallen, and has become a dwelling place of demons, a prison for every foul spirit, and a cage for every unclean and hated bird!* (NKJV)

The angel will prophesy about the future of Babylon the great. It will fall and become the "dwelling place of demons, a prison for every foul spirit, and a cage for every unclean and hated bird." The great and beautiful city will become a dark and loathsome place. This fulfills what the Old Testament prophets said.

"Babylon is fallen, is fallen, that great city" (Revelation 14:8 NKJV).

Certain scholars suggest the great city described in this chapter cannot be the literal Babylon. They seem to think the current city of Babylon is too small, too remote, and more of a tourist attraction. They overlook what the Antichrist could do if several dozen nations flew in work crews and materials from around the world. A hundred nations with unlimited financing, hundreds of engineers, modern equipment, and thousands of workers could turn Babylon into a great city virtually overnight.

what others say

Joseph Chambers

The prophecy world is filled with ministers and Bible teachers that refuse to take Revelation chapter 18 literally. That is why I stress this point, because this will soon be a great frontier in fresh Bible prophecy fulfillment and hopefully new understanding.[2]

Facts About Babylon

Fact	Scripture
The first city mentioned in the Bible after the Flood	Genesis 11
The city where one-world religion and one-world government originated	Genesis 11

Facts About Babylon (cont'd)

Fact	Scripture
The city that began the "Times of the Gentiles"	Mentioned more than 275 times in the Bible, second only to Jerusalem
More than 10 percent of the book of Revelation is about Babylon	Daniel 1:1–2
The Antichrist is called the King of Babylon	Isaiah 14:4
"It will never be inhabited" requires a future destruction of what is there today	Isaiah 13:19–20
Its final destruction will occur during the Day of the Lord	Isaiah 13–14; Jeremiah 50–51

Drunkard Nations

REVELATION 18:3 *For all the nations have drunk of the wine of the wrath of her fornication, the kings of the earth have committed fornication with her, and the merchants of the earth have become rich through the abundance of her luxury." (NKJV)*

This is a picture of government and business becoming obsessed with, and controlled by, a concept. Every nation on earth has delved into the idea of world government and world trade. By the time the Tribulation Period arrives, they will be intoxicated with it. The idea will receive their full support, and the businessmen involved will become extremely wealthy.

what others say

Ed Hindson

The fall of communism has paved the way for a world economy and a world government. The global web is tightening around us every day.[3]

Many people ask what prophecy says about the United States. Some students of prophecy think the United States is mentioned in a general way (not by name), but that is mostly speculation and cannot be proved. Others think the United States will collapse or be destroyed because it is not specifically mentioned, but that is also impossible to prove. The United States would be wise to support Israel during the Tribulation Period, but with the Church gone it seems reasonable to conclude that it will be closely aligned with Europe and its Antichrist.

go to

Tower of Babel
Genesis 11:1–9

Tower of Babel
a tower built to
reach to God

Don't Fall into the Same Fate

REVELATION 18:4 *And I heard another voice from heaven say-ing, "Come out of her, my people, lest you share in her sins, and lest you receive of her plagues. (NKJV)*

A voice from heaven will urge God's people to leave Babylon for two reasons: so they will not become involved in Babylon's sin, and so they will not fall victim to the plagues God will inflict on Babylon. Even during this terrible time of God's wrath being poured out, it's obvious that God still cares about his people. The Church has been raptured, so these are Tribulation Saints not the Church. But it's clear that God will have people living on earth at the close of the Tribulation Period. How they will survive in Babylon without taking the mark of the Beast is a mystery, but they will, and some will even make it into the Millennium.

> **what others say**
>
> **Leon Morris**
>
> Persecuted and harried as they were, the people of God must have been sorely tempted to come to terms with the city. Then not only would their persecution cease, but the city would make them rich and comfortable. But it is important that they see the issues for what they really are and have noth-ing to do with unclean things.[4]

No Skipping Town

REVELATION 18:5 *For her sins have reached to heaven, and God has remembered her iniquities. (NKJV)*

In the Old Testament, God did not overlook what Babylon was doing when she tried to build a tower to heaven, and he will not overlook this. To stop construction on the **Tower of Babel**, he con-fused their language and scattered them around the world. In the future, to stop their sins from piling any higher, he will burn her to the ground.

> **what others say**
>
> **Mal Couch and Joseph Chambers**
>
> Some strongly argue that though a long time has passed since the early wickedness of Babylon, it only seems as if God has

forgotten her sins. But the Lord will recall them to mind. The last Babylon is but the final outgrowth of the same principles that animated the first. Old offenses will help flame the final vengeance (Seiss).[5]

mercy
Galatians 6:7

cup
Revelation 17:4

Belshazzar
Daniel 5:17–31

Double Jeopardy

REVELATION 18:6 *Render to her just as she rendered to you, and repay her double according to her works; in the cup which she has mixed, mix double for her. (NKJV)*

Life in Babylon will be like a boomerang. God's law of sowing and reaping will come into effect. Those who offer no <u>mercy</u> will receive no mercy. Farmers must decide what kind of crop they want to harvest. Then, they must sow the kind of seed that will produce that crop. Babylon's citizens should consider how they want God to treat them and then treat others accordingly. Someone once said, "What goes around comes around."

It is predicted that in thirty years there will be no Christians in the Palestinian-controlled areas of Israel. Palestinian persecution is driving them out of the land where Christ was born.

Babylon's <u>cup</u> will be filled with abominable things.

The Taller They Are . . .

REVELATION 18:7 *In the measure that she glorified herself and lived luxuriously, in the same measure give her torment and sorrow; for she says in her heart, 'I sit as queen, and am no widow, and will not see sorrow.' (NKJV)*

This godless city will be filled with the proud and haughty. Her residents will declare her beauty, greatness, glory, and her reign over all the earth. They will think she is a queen, and that she is married to the kings of the earth. As such, she is not a widow but a wealthy queen who has nothing to mourn about. They will be self-deceived and will extol her around the world. Never mind the fact that God brought her down in one day during the reign of <u>Belshazzar</u>.

The voice from heaven will say, "In the measure that she glorified herself and lived luxuriously, in the same measure give her torment and sorrow." This will be one of God's standards of judgment when he remembers Babylon: the great grief of the godly will be turned into glory, and the glory of the godless will be turned into great grief.

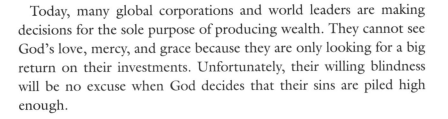

what others say

J. H. Melton

When nations become wealthy, they become independent, and no longer sense the need of God. The history of the great nations in the past reveals wealth and prosperity to be responsible for their fall.[6]

Today, many global corporations and world leaders are making decisions for the sole purpose of producing wealth. They cannot see God's love, mercy, and grace because they are only looking for a big return on their investments. Unfortunately, their willing blindness will be no excuse when God decides that their sins are piled high enough.

Quick and Painful

REVELATION 18:8 *Therefore her plagues will come in one day— death and mourning and famine. And she will be utterly burned with fire, for strong is the Lord God who judges her. (NKJV)*

As the home of one-world government and global trade, Babylon will think she is very powerful. She will control powerful weapons and great armies. But compared to the Lord God, who will judge her, this highly touted strength will be like a dart gun.

What no earthly army can do, God will accomplish in one day. First, the angel of death will pass over Babylon. Second, this city that just finished saying, "[I]will not see sorrow," will grieve bitterly. Third, this rich city will suddenly run out of food. Last, it will be burned to the ground.

what others say

Jack Van Impe

The treasures of the Tribulation enterprises do not last. Neither will they last for you if this is all you want out of life.[7]

The Smart Guide to the Bible

The head of a Gentile world kingdom in Egypt was a man called Pharaoh. He <u>dreamed</u> about seven fat cows with plenty to eat followed by seven skinny cows with very little to eat. He thought this was very significant and called in his advisers, but they could not interpret the dream. Then he called in Joseph, who told him God is letting Pharaoh know that Egypt will go through seven years of good harvests with plenty to eat followed by seven years of poor harvests with very little to eat. Pharaoh believed Joseph, built storehouses for food, and located them in areas where the food could be easily distributed. The preparations paid off. Seven years of tremendous harvests came followed by seven years of worldwide famine with Egypt being severely affected, but the nation handled it well.

After moving to the Promised Land, Abraham and his nephew Lot decided to separate. Lot eventually moved to the city of Sodom. It was a beautiful city, but it was full of injustice and sordid sins called sodomy (homosexuality). Because of this God decided to destroy Sodom and the equally sinful neighbor city of Gomorrah. He sent angels to tell <u>Lot</u> what was going to happen and to get Lot and his family out of Sodom. Lot barely escaped when fire fell from heaven and burned the cities to the ground.

dreamed
Genesis 41:25–37

Lot
Genesis 19:1–28

Weeping Kings

REVELATION 18:9 *The kings of the earth who committed fornication and lived luxuriously with her will weep and lament for her, when they see the smoke of her burning,* (NKJV)

The destruction of Babylon will be worldwide news. Kings, dictators, politicians, and those who supported her will see the smoke billowing up into the air, causing them to grieve and cry. By sundown they will see a heap of smoldering rubble. It will remind many of what happened to the World Trade Center Towers in New York City. It will be time for the "cradle of civilization" to bury the coming New World Order.

A Quick Fate

REVELATION 18:10 *standing at a distance for fear of her torment, saying, 'Alas, alas, that great city Babylon, that mighty city! For in one hour your judgment has come.'* (NKJV)

The kings, dictators, and politicians will shake in fear. Panic will grip them. Their cry of "Alas, alas" reveals deep anguish and terror because her destruction will come in one hour. A few experts suggest that one hour could mean "a short space of time" or "spread out over a few days," but most think it means suddenly or instantaneously. That will add to the panic and terror.

Notice that Babylon is called that "mighty city." Some translations say "city of power." This will be the power center of Antichrist, the ten kings, the False Prophet, presidents, and prime ministers; the super center of global governance and global trade. In the near future, vigilant Christians may want to focus on the efforts to rebuild Iraq and the struggle for so-called religious freedom in that Islamic hotbed.

No More Deliveries

> REVELATION 18:11 *And the merchants of the earth will weep and mourn over her, for no one buys their merchandise anymore: (NKJV)*

Not only will the heads of state weep but so will the world's big businessmen. However, it will not be over the loss of life, loss of souls to hell, or even their own sins. They will weep and mourn over their loss of customers.

Following the disasters that struck the United States early this century, some oil companies, lumber companies, and others were criticized for making windfall profits. It's not surprising to learn that Babylon will be filled with merchants who enrich themselves during the disasters of the Tribulation Period.

what others say

Warren W. Wiersbe

The wealth of the city provides for many nations and employs many people. It is worth noting that not only do the merchants lament the fall of Babylon (v. 11), but also the kings of the earth (v. 9). Business and government are so intertwined that what affects one affects the other.[8]

Dead Inventory

> REVELATION 18:12 *merchandise of gold and silver, precious stones and pearls, fine linen and purple, silk and scarlet, every*

kind of citron wood, every kind of object of ivory, every kind of object of most precious wood, bronze, iron, and marble; (NKJV)

Purple and scarlet were worn by royalty in John's day. Silk was so scarce at one time it was outlawed. Citron wood was also scarce and highly sought for ornamental purposes. However, during the Tribulation Period, Babylon will import these cargoes frequently. These are the goods of an affluent society. The global traders will pile them up in Babylon, but the apostle James warned about such things when he said, "Come now, you rich, weep and howl for your miseries that are coming upon you! Your riches are corrupted, and your garments are moth-eaten. Your gold and silver are corroded, and their corrosion will be a witness against you and will eat your flesh like fire. You have heaped up treasure in the last days" (James 5:1–3 NKJV). It will be boom time in Babylon when the billionaires head there, but it will be bust when the ball of fire falls. God gives wealth, but he meant for it to benefit society, not to enrich a few.

"The woman was arrayed in purple and scarlet, and adorned with gold and precious stones and pearls" (Revelation 17:4 NKJV).

Even the Souls of Man

REVELATION 18:13 *and cinnamon and incense, fragrant oil and frankincense, wine and oil, fine flour and wheat, cattle and sheep, horses and chariots, and bodies and souls of men. (NKJV)*

Some additional products large corporations of the world will deal in during the Tribulation Period are: expensive perfumes, spices, food, grain, cattle, and even human beings. This is a picture of large corporations that will sell anything for a profit. It is also a picture of businessmen crying because they have lost sales.

It seems almost unthinkable that we would have slavery in this modern world. Nevertheless, slavery is a tragic reality in Sudan, and there is virtually no outcry from global leaders or human rights activists around the world. The jihad (holy war) being waged against Christians and non-Muslims in Sudan has caused the deaths of about three million people. Christian and non-Muslim villages are being burned, the men are being killed, and the women and children are being sold in open slave markets for sometimes as little as $10–$15 apiece.

When the tsunami struck several southeastern nations in 2004, thousands of children were separated from their parents. Some news reports expressed concern that these children would be seized and sold into slavery, but if anything was ever done to stop people who deal in slaves, it didn't get reported. Christians are sold as slaves in some Islamic countries. Women are sold into slavery as prostitutes in some Asian countries, and there are even reports of this happening in the Caribbean and some South American countries.

what others say

The Preacher's Outline and Sermon Bible

The picture will be the same as has been true in every holocaust down through history: the souls of men will mean no more than another piece of merchandise or commodity—all to be used for the benefit of the state and the comfort of the supporters of the state.[9]

From their treasures the wise men gave the baby Jesus gifts of gold, frankincense, and myrrh (see Matthew 2:11).

To Be No More

REVELATION 18:14 *The fruit that your soul longed for has gone from you, and all the things which are rich and splendid have gone from you, and you shall find them no more at all.* (NKJV)

The global traders will acknowledge that the Babylonian dream has been destroyed. All her riches and glory will be gone forever.

what others say

Oliver B. Greene

Heaven is here announcing to this woman that her playhouse is wrecked forever, and she is down, never to rise again.[10]

Babylon has always been associated with wealth. It is appropriately called the Kingdom of Gold in Daniel 2. The most famous gardens the world has ever known are called "The Hanging Gardens of Babylon." They have been designated one of the Seven Wonders of the World. In order to make the mountain princess he married feel at home, King Nebuchadnezzar built terraces for gardens that were four hundred feet square and as high as seventy-five feet. Flowers, shrubs, and trees were planted on those terraces, and slaves worked the gardens day and night.

Shaking in Their Boots

REVELATION 18:15 *The merchants of these things, who became rich by her, will stand at a distance for fear of her torment, weeping and wailing,* (NKJV)

The businessmen who prospered by brokering deals at Babylon will not go near the burned-out ruins. They will cry and grieve at a distance because they are terrified at her judgment. Some may stand in their executive suites halfway around the world watching (on television), weeping, and wailing.

what others say

Ed Hindson

Here is a great society, not unlike our own, which has forgotten God in all her success. Rather than praising Him for His abundant blessings, they have become obsessed with the pursuit of those blessings. And in the process, they have forgotten the divine One from whom all those blessings come. Worse, they have forgotten there is no permanent satisfaction in that which is temporal. They are caught in an endless and mindless pursuit of that which can never satisfy their souls.[11]

Beauty Isn't Everything

REVELATION 18:16 *and saying, 'Alas, alas, that great city that was clothed in fine linen, purple, and scarlet, and adorned with gold and precious stones and pearls!* (NKJV)

We have already learned that the businessmen of the world will cry because Babylon's great power will not protect her. Now we learn that they will cry because her beauty and wealth will also fail to protect her. It matters not how powerful an entity is, how beautiful or how rich, if God decides it should fall, it will surely fall.

what others say

Hal Lindsey

It's not often that you see grown men weeping and wailing, at least not in public, but at this time there will be no pride left

great riches
Matthew 6:19–21

in any man. Everything they have will be lost. The panic will be a hundred times greater than that which followed the U.S. stock market crash of 1929.[12]

Jesus said, "Do not lay up for yourselves treasures on earth, where moth and rust destroy and where thieves break in and steal; but lay up for yourselves treasures in heaven, where neither moth nor rust destroys and where thieves do not break in and steal" (Matthew 6:19–20 NKJV). Good financial planning includes much more than large bank accounts, sound investments, and a diversified portfolio. Everyone needs to think about these things, but the only permanent investments are spiritual. Giving to the Lord's work is truly sound financial planning because it becomes legal tender in heaven. That is the most careful money management of all.

Don't Get Too Close

> REVELATION 18:17 *For in one hour such great riches came to nothing.' Every shipmaster, all who travel by ship, sailors, and as many as trade on the sea, stood at a distance* (NKJV)

The sudden destruction of such <u>great riches</u> in a short time will be catastrophic for multitudes. First, we read that the kings, dictators, and politicians who supported Babylon will cry. Then we read that the global merchants who do business with her will cry. Now we learn that the seamen who transport her goods will cry. Hauling the merchandise of Babylon will be big business, but in one hour her great wealth will be gone. Every sea pilot, every sea traveler to Babylon, all the sailors, and all who will be earning a living on the sea will stand back and mourn the loss of goods, jobs, and business.

This seems unimaginable, but planes crashing into the World Trade Center Towers brought them down in one hour. And when Hurricane Katrina struck the Gulf Coast of the United States in 2005, the city of New Orleans and virtually all the cities and towns near the coasts of Louisiana, Mississippi, and Alabama were damaged or destroyed. Multitudes lost everything they had in a matter of minutes.

Tyre
Ezekiel 27:32

what others say

Life Application Bible Commentary

The dirge of each group—the kings, the merchants, and the seamen—begins with "woe, woe," and then describes the city according to their own relationship with it. For the kings, it is power (18:10); for the merchants, it is the commodities (18:12–13); for the sea captains and sailors, it is their income from the vessels carrying the commodities. All will see the fate of the city and will be stunned by it.[13]

Ed Hindson

This aspect (a world economy) of globalism is already upon us. No developed nation of any kind can survive today without networking with the global economy. There is almost no such thing as an "American" product that is not dependent on parts, trade, or investments from foreign countries.[14]

Smoldering Ashes

REVELATION 18:18 *and cried out when they saw the smoke of her burning, saying, 'What is like this great city?'* (NKJV)

This cry is similar to the lament people heard when the beautiful city of Tyre was destroyed for a second time. Nebuchadnezzar wiped out the original city on the mainland, so the Phoenicians rebuilt it on an island. They made it their capital and turned it into a great trading center. Alexander the Great came along and pushed the ruins of the old city into the sea, making a causeway out to the island. His troops walked out on dry land and destroyed the rebuilt city. People compared that to the sinking of a great ship. They cried and asked, "What city is like Tyre, destroyed in the midst of the sea?" (Ezekiel 27:32 NKJV). When people see the smoke of Babylon rising in the air they will ask, "What is like this great city?"

what others say

N. W. Hutchings

Babylon is one of the two nations that destroyed the [Jewish] temple, so it must be destroyed as Sodom and Gomorrah. This has not yet happened, but it will (Jeremiah 50:28; Isaiah 13:19).[15]

The Captains Cry

one hour
Revelation 18:10, 17

money
1 Timothy 6:10

prophets
Isaiah 13:19–22;
Jeremiah 50:38–40

apostles
James 5:1–6

REVELATION 18:19 *They threw dust on their heads and cried out, weeping and wailing, and saying, 'Alas, alas, that great city, in which all who had ships on the sea became rich by her wealth! For in one hour she is made desolate.' (NKJV)*

This is the third time we are told Babylon will fall in <u>one hour</u>. The sudden nature of her destruction will leave the political, business, and shipping worlds bitterly weeping, reeling, and stunned. This is a clear sign of what the love of <u>money</u> will do to people. When money is god, and God is gone, what is left but godless grief?

Some think the destruction of this great city in just one hour could mean an atomic or nuclear explosion. The fact that people will not go near it is another indication of that.

It's also possible that they are feeling the effects of disaster fatigue or disaster overload, a malady that some physicians started talking about following the many disasters that struck around the world early this century. One-third of the ships sinking, the sea turning to blood, and ports burning are bound to have psychological consequences for those who make their living on the sea.

What a Difference an Hour Makes

Event	Scripture
For in one hour your judgment has come	Revelation 18:10
For in one hour such great riches came to nothing	Revelation 18:17
For in one hour she [Babylon] is made desolate	Revelation 18:19

The Heavens Rejoice

REVELATION 18:20 *Rejoice over her, O heaven, and you holy apostles and prophets, for God has avenged you on her!" (NKJV)*

This is something the Old Testament <u>prophets</u> prophesied, the New Testament <u>apostles</u> predicted, and the Tribulation Period Saints will pray for. We should join the angels in heaven in rejoicing when God's Word is fulfilled and the prayers of God's people are answered.

Here we have a difference between God's people and the godless. One group will rejoice and sing the praises of God. The other will grieve and mourn the loss of their god (money). In the end, Babylon will have brought this judgment on herself by mistreating God's people.

Three Who Mourn and Three Who Dance

Alas, alas	Rejoice
Kings of the earth (Revelation 9–10)	Heaven (saints, angels, etc.)
Merchants of the earth (Revelation 11–15)	Apostles
Shipmasters, travelers, sailors, traders (Revelation 17–19)	Prophets

Never to Rise Again

> REVELATION 18:21 *Then a mighty angel took up a stone like a great millstone and threw it into the sea, saying, "Thus with violence the great city Babylon shall be thrown down, and shall not be found anymore.* (NKJV)

Several times we have read about a mighty angel. Whether these will be different angels or the same angel is not known, but the picture is that of a huge stone being violently hurled down into the sea where it will disappear forever. This symbolizes the sudden, violent, and eternal destruction of future Babylon.

Silenced

> REVELATION 18:22 *The sound of harpists, musicians, flutists, and trumpeters shall not be heard in you anymore. No craftsman of any craft shall be found in you anymore, and the sound of a millstone shall not be heard in you anymore.* (NKJV)

Everything from entertainment to manual labor jobs will cease. There will be no more music in Babylon, no people going to work, and no craftsmen on the job. She will be silenced forever.

Who Turned Out the Lights?

go to

lamb
Revelation 13:11

deceive
Matthew 24:11

REVELATION 18:23 *The light of a lamp shall not shine in you anymore, and the voice of bridegroom and bride shall not be heard in you anymore. For your merchants were the great men of the earth, for by your sorcery all the nations were deceived.* (NKJV)

The street lights; the lights in the malls, shops, and homes will all be dark. Joyous occasions such as marriages will never be heard again. Babylon will be an utter waste. The merchants in Babylon will be great men on earth. They will use black magic, sorcery, and demonic practices to lead people astray. The forces of darkness will reign until God turns their lights off.

> **what others say**
>
> ### Craig S. Keener
>
> By contrast, new Jerusalem will need no earthly lamp, illumined by the glory of God and the Lamb (21:23; 22:5), and that city herself will be a bride (19:7; 21:2, 9; 22:17). That the harpists will no longer be heard in Babylon (18:22) may contrast with the harpists heard in heaven (14:2). God's people struggled to use their harps in captivity (Psalm 137:2–4), but the new temple city will prove a fitting place for harps (cf. 2 Chronicles 9:11; 20:28; 29:25) . . . Babylon who thought herself a queen (Isaiah 47:5–7; Revelation 18:7) and denied her impending widowhood (Isaiah 47:8; Revelation 18:7), vainly thought to protect herself by sorceries (Isaiah 47:9, 12).[17]

Filled with Blood

REVELATION 18:24 *And in her was found the blood of prophets and saints, and of all who were slain on the earth."* (NKJV)

Babylon has a long history as the city of Satan. The False Prophet will make his headquarters there during the last half of the Tribulation Period. He will worship the Antichrist and have no tolerance for the people of God. He will kill all those who lack the mark of the Beast. Babylon's destruction will be well deserved.

The False Prophet came with two horns like a <u>lamb</u>. Lambs do not have horns, so we know he will be a fake in lamb's clothing.

Jesus warned that false prophets will <u>deceive</u> many in the last days. The winds of deceit will reach gale force during the Tribulation

Period. Beware of any religious leader who speaks ill of Jesus and opposes the Scriptures. Any message that contradicts the Bible, no matter how sweet-sounding, is not from God.

Chapter Wrap-Up

- An angel will come from the presence of God and declare the destruction of the great city, Babylon. (Revelation 18:1–3)

- A heavenly voice will call God's people out of Babylon so that they will not share in her crimes and judgment. (Revelation 18:4–7)

- Babylon will be destroyed by God in one hour. Her sudden destruction will leave the world wailing and weeping over the loss of money. (Revelation 18:8–19)

- Those in heaven, who suffered at Babylon's hands, will rejoice over God's judgment of her. (Revelation 18:20)

- A mighty angel will throw a boulder the size of a large millstone into the sea. This will represent the totality of Babylon's destruction; she will never rise again. (Revelation 18:21–24)

Study Questions

1. How many nations have been defiled by Babylon?

2. What will be the extent of Babylon's punishment?

3. What was Babylon's magic spell and does any of it exist today?

4. Whose blood will Babylon be responsible for shedding?

5. What will Babylon use to lead people astray?

Revelation 19

Chapter Highlights:
- Heavenly Rejoicing
- Marriage Supper of the Lamb
- Second Coming
- Battle of Armageddon
- A Second Supper

Let's Get Started

The terrible judgments of the Tribulation Period will be brought to an end. All rebellion will stop. Man's efforts to bring peace on earth without God will cease, and, finally, Jesus will return, bringing days of blessing and bounty for all believers.

The contrasts continue, but this time the focus shifts from the Mother of harlots in Babylon to the Bride of Christ in heaven; from the Antichrist who will destroy the wicked harlot to the Christ who will marry the forgiven Bride; from the weeping of kings, merchants, and sailors on earth to the rejoicing of the inhabitants in heaven; from the temporary value of money and goods to the eternal value of salvation and true worship; from the silence of musicians who will witness the funeral of Babylon to a multitude of noisy musicians at a wedding.

Alleluia
comes from a Hebrew word meaning "praise the Lord"

A Heavenly Roar

> **REVELATION 19:1** *After these things I heard a loud voice of a great multitude in heaven, saying, "**Alleluia**! Salvation and glory and honor and power belong to the Lord our God! (NKJV)*

After the destruction of Babylon and the worldwide reaction that will follow, the roar of a great multitude will be heard in heaven. This multitude will most likely be the Tribulation Saints, but it may include others such as the Old Testament Saints, the Church, and the angels. Praise will be directed to God because salvation, glory, and power belong to him. Salvation speaks of his deliverance. Glory speaks of his judgment. Power refers to his ability to overcome his enemies.

Blood Repaid

> **REVELATION 19:2** *For true and righteous are His judgments, because He has judged the great harlot who corrupted the earth*

avenged
Romans 12:19

with her fornication; and He has avenged on her the blood of His servants shed by her." (NKJV)

Those praising God in heaven will declare his truth and justice because he destroyed the one-world harlot religious system, and <u>avenged</u> the death of his people. The wicked will not get away with their sin forever. God will personally repay those who harm his people. His judgments are true and just, because he gives people what they deserve.

> **what others say**
>
> **Henry M. Morris**
>
> Many and long had been the years when it seemed that God didn't care about the sufferings of His people nor about the blasphemies of Babylon, and many had even claimed that God was dead.[1]

Eternal Fire

REVELATION 19:3 *Again they said, "Alleluia! Her smoke rises up forever and ever!"* (NKJV)

This is the second time in this chapter that we hear a shout of "Alleluia!" in heaven. One Alleluia is for the destruction of Babylon, the mother of harlots, and the other one is for the destruction of Babylon the city. However, this verse refers to more than the destruction on earth. It means they have gone to their everlasting destruction. The only smoke that will go up forever and ever is the smoke of their eternal burning in the Lake of Fire.

However, there won't be rejoicing in heaven because people on earth have perished or property has been destroyed. The rejoicing will occur because God has stopped the carnage of Satan's crew on earth. This is another reason to believe Babylon will be rebuilt. Smoke isn't going up from Babylon today.

> **what others say**
>
> **Tim LaHaye**
>
> No wonder there is rejoicing in heaven at the realization that never again will Satan's religious, commercial, or political systems be permitted to lead men astray.[2]

Worshiping the Father

REVELATION 19:4 *And the twenty-four elders and the four living creatures fell down and worshiped God who sat on the throne, saying, "Amen! Alleluia!"* (NKJV)

elders
Revelation 4:4

worship God
Psalm 106:47–48;
Revelation 5:8, 14;
7:11; 11:16

what others say

David Jeremiah with C. C. Carlson

The angels, the Old Testament Saints, the Church Saints, and the Tribulation Saints will raise their voices in a choir which will reverberate louder than thunder. I've heard great choirs before, but I'm really looking forward to being in this one.[3]

The Church and the four living creatures will fall down and worship the God who sits on the heavenly throne. Here again we see the elders and living creatures falling down as they did before.

- The twenty-four <u>elders</u> represent the entire Church from Pentecost to the Rapture.
- The elders and living creatures fall down to <u>worship God</u>.

All Join In

REVELATION 19:5 *Then a voice came from the throne, saying, "Praise our God, all you His servants and those who fear Him, both small and great!"* (NKJV)

It is impossible to say whose voice this will be. The Father and the Son will both be on the throne, so it could be either one of them. Some who disagree say it is the voice of one of the Four Living Creatures that surround the throne because the voice speaks of God as *our God*. It appears to be directed to the servants of God on earth because the inhabitants of heaven are already praising God. The only certainty is that someone on the throne will approve of the heavenly praise and worship. They will invite everyone who serves God to praise the Lord.

what others say

J. H. Melton

The element of praise is so often missing in the life and service of the average Christian and the average church. . . . The

would have a different image of Christianity if there were more rejoicing and praise on the part of the people of God.[4]

Thunderous Acclamation

REVELATION 19:6 *And I heard, as it were, the voice of a great multitude, as the sound of many waters and as the sound of mighty thunderings, saying, "Alleluia! For the Lord God Omnipotent reigns! (NKJV)*

This will be the response to the invitation found in the last verse. All God's servants on earth will shout praises to him because the Lord God Almighty reigns.

This brings to mind King David's plans to build the first temple of God. He bought the temple site, gathered materials, appointed 24,000 Levites to work on it, 6,000 to oversee the construction, 4,000 to guard the building while it was being built, and 4,000 to play instruments and sing praises to God. Think of it—4,000 people to play music and praise the Lord!

what others say

J. Vernon McGee

It takes us all the way back to that covenant which God made with David in which he promised to raise one upon David's throne who would rule the world.[5]

J. Ramsey Michaels

This is the visible realization of what was announced seven chapters earlier in connection with the seventh trumpet: "The kingdom of the world has become the kingdom of our Lord and of his Christ, and he will reign for ever and ever" (11:15).[6]

The Bride of Christ

REVELATION 19:7 *Let us be glad and rejoice and give Him glory, for the marriage of the Lamb has come, and His wife has made herself ready." (NKJV)*

This will be a great day in heaven because it will be time for the Lamb's (Christ's) marriage to the Church, the Bride of Christ. God's servants will rejoice and give him glory in anticipation of this event. With regard to timing, this event will take place after the destruction of Babylon near the end of the Tribulation Period. With regard to permanency, this will be "until death do us part," but no one in the wedding party will ever die again.

A special union will exist between Jesus and the Church similar to the union that exists between a bridegroom and a bride upon their marriage. In both instances, the two <u>become one</u>. <u>Jesus is coming back</u> to earth where he and his bride will reign together as one. Before they can reign together, though, they have to be married. The idea is that the Church will be <u>joined together</u> with Jesus in a special relationship that will equip them to reign with him. He will not come back without his people, and they will not reign without him.

Be ready for the future events of the Church:

1. We'll be taken up in the Rapture—1 Thessalonians 4:13–18.

2. We'll go before the judgment seat of Christ—1 Corinthians 3:12–15; 2 Corinthians 5:10.

3. We'll attend the marriage and the marriage supper—Revelation 19:7–9.

4. We'll return with Christ for his millennial reign—Revelation 20:6.

The Bridal Gown

REVELATION 19:8 *And to her it was granted to be arrayed in fine linen, clean and bright, for the fine linen is the righteous acts of the saints. (NKJV)*

Before its marriage the Church will wear fine linen, which is their own righteous acts. A person's deeds will follow one to heaven where they will be worn like a gown or a robe. Faith in <u>God</u> makes that possible. When the marriage takes place, the Church will lay their righteousness aside. The holiness and righteousness of Jesus imparted to them will form their clothing for eternity.

The Bride's "fine linen, clean and bright," contrasts with the Mother of Harlots, arrayed in "purple and scarlet, and adorned with gold and precious stones and pearls." The Bride's righteousness contrasts with the Mother of Harlots' having in her "hand a golden cup full of abominations and the filthiness of her fornication." The Bride being made "ready" contrasts with the harlot who is "drunk with the blood of the saints and with the blood of the martyrs of Jesus."

become one
Ephesians 5:31

Jesus is coming back
Matthew 22:1–14

joined together
2 Corinthians 11:2

God
Philippians 3:9

go to

ten virgins
Matthew 25:1–13

wedding banquet
Matthew 22:1–14

something to ponder

Supper Time!

REVELATION 19:9 *Then he said to me, "Write: 'Blessed are those who are called to the marriage supper of the Lamb!'" And he said to me, "These are the true sayings of God." (NKJV)*

Again John heard an angel tell him to write. This time he was told to write about the Wedding Supper of the Lamb. All those who are invited to attend this supper are blessed or happy.

Robert Frost said a parable is a story "that means what it says, and something else besides." Some call them "earthly stories with heavenly meanings." The English word "parable" comes from the Greek word *parabole*, which means "to place beside or alongside of." Thus, a parable is a story that says one thing for the purpose of teaching or illustrating something else. Jesus used them often. He took well-known and easily understood truths about earthly things to help people understand difficult truths about spiritual things.

The following two parables help us to better understand the Marriage Supper of the Lamb:

1. The parable of the <u>ten virgins</u>—Just as the ten virgins (people) heard that the bridegroom (Jesus) and his bride (the Church) were coming back for their wedding banquet, so too will Jesus come back to earth with his Church at the end of the Tribulation Period for the marriage supper of the Lamb. Only those who have received the Holy Spirit (those with oil) will be allowed to attend this banquet on earth.

2. The parable of the <u>wedding banquet</u>—This parable tells us about a king (God) who prepared a wedding banquet for his son (Jesus). He sent out invitations, but many of those invited (unbelievers) made excuses for not attending, so he invited others (the Church). One man (an unbeliever) was not wearing the right kind of wedding apparel (fine linen), so he was escorted out. The wedding apparel signifies the kind of righteousness needed to attend the banquet. God provides that apparel to all those who accept Jesus as their Savior. Those who do not have it are not prepared to spend eternity with God. This should not be taken lightly. We cannot go to heaven or attend this feast as we are right now. We must be properly dressed, or we will be cast into outer darkness where there will be "weeping and gnashing of teeth" (Matthew 8:12 NKJV).

Another verse that provides insight to understanding the marriage supper concerns the Lord's **Last Supper**. Jesus said he will not drink the <u>fruit</u> of the vine again until he drinks it in his Father's kingdom. His Father's kingdom is his **millennial kingdom** on earth.

"Behold, I stand at the door and knock. If anyone hears My voice and opens the door, I will come in to him and dine with him, and he with Me" (Revelation 3:20 NKJV).

fruit
Matthew 26:29

worship of anyone or anything other than God is forbidden
Exodus 20:3

he would die, be buried, be raised from the dead
1 Corinthians 15:3–4

come again
Matthew 24:27;
John 14:3

> **what others say**
>
> **Hal Lindsey**
>
> While Revelation 19:9 pronounces a blessing on the guests at this supper, it doesn't indicate the time or place of it . . . . It's my feeling that the wedding feast of the Lamb and his bride will take place on earth at the very beginning of the Millennial Kingdom of God.[7]

A Case of Mistaken Identity

REVELATION 19:10 *And I fell at his feet to worship him. But he said to me, "See that you do not do that! I am your fellow servant, and of your brethren who have the testimony of Jesus. Worship God! For the testimony of Jesus is the spirit of prophecy."* *(NKJV)*

After writing what the angel said, John fell at the angel's feet to worship him. That was the wrong thing to do, and the angel stopped John. He called himself a fellow servant of God and told John to "worship God!" During the Tribulation Period multitudes will worship Satan and his Antichrist because the False Prophet will demand it. However, <u>worship of anyone or anything other than God is forbidden</u>.

The testimony of Jesus is an interesting idea. Among other things, Jesus predicted that <u>he would die, be buried, be raised from the dead</u>, and <u>come again</u>. His predictions are his testimony and also prophecy. Everything he predicted is prophecy. Many people do not understand this. They want to throw out or discard prophecy in the Bible, not realizing they would be throwing out many things Jesus said. Those who understand this hold to the testimony of Jesus.

Last Supper
the last meal Jesus ate before he was crucified

millennial kingdom
the one-thousand-year reign of Jesus on earth

go to

prophets
Daniel 2:34–35, 44

Jesus
Matthew 24:30

writers
Titus 2:13;
1 Corinthians 1:17

John went up
Revelation 4:1–2

first rider on a white horse
Revelation 6:2

come back
Matthew 16:27

ripe for judgment
Revelation 14:14–20

fiery eyes
Revelation 1:14;
2:18

The Triumphant Return

REVELATION 19:11 *Now I saw heaven opened, and behold, a white horse. And He who sat on him was called Faithful and True, and in righteousness He judges and makes war. (NKJV)*

This verse is sometimes called the climax of the entire Bible. The Old Testament <u>prophets</u> prophesied this event; <u>Jesus</u> predicted it; and the New Testament <u>writers</u> wrote about it. Everything we have studied in Revelation has been building up to this. It will be a precious sight to the saints who are still alive on earth when it happens, but a terrifying sight to the Antichrist and his followers.

Heaven will open: It opened the first time when <u>John went up</u> to heaven identifying the rapture of the Church. It will open a second time when Jesus comes back with his Church.

A rider on a white horse will appear: The <u>first rider on a white horse</u>, the Antichrist, appeared at the beginning of the Tribulation Period. Now, just as in ancient times when mighty warriors and conquerors rode white horses, a second rider on a white horse will come out of heaven to fight and conquer.

The rider (Jesus) will be called Faithful and True: "Faithful" meaning he has done, and will do, everything God asks him to do. When Jesus walked the earth he did everything God asked of him down to the smallest detail. Now when he comes back the second time, he will again do everything God asks him to do. "True" meaning he does everything he says he will do. He said he will <u>come back</u>, and here he fulfills that promise.

"In righteousness He judges and makes war" is a reference to the purpose of his coming. He will return as a warrior to judge the inhabitants of the earth. He will deal with their sin, settle their eternal destinies, and establish his reign. What he will do will be just and right, because the earth will have been declared <u>ripe for judgment</u>.

Greater Than Our Understanding

REVELATION 19:12 *His eyes were like a flame of fire, and on His head were many crowns. He had a name written that no one knew except Himself. (NKJV)*

Christ's <u>fiery eyes</u> reveal his insight, knowledge, and anger. He will have full knowledge of each individual and their sins. His many crowns reveal his royalty, authority, and majesty. He will have full authority in heaven and on earth.

He has many names that we know: Jesus, Lord, Christ, Wonderful, Son of God, Son of Man, etc. However, when he returns he will wear a special name known only to God. Christians know his name is great, but it is greater than their understanding, since God is the only One who fully understands it.

This contrasts with the Antichrist, whose eyes are "like the eyes of a man" (Daniel 7:8 NKJV), having "seven heads and ten horns, and on his horns ten crowns, and on his heads a blasphemous name" (Revelation 13:1 NKJV).

Concerning his second coming, Jesus said, "Take heed that no one deceives you. For many will come in My name, saying, 'I am the Christ,' and will deceive many" (Matthew 24:4–5 NKJV). The apostle Paul said, "The coming of the lawless one is according to the working of Satan, with all power, signs, and lying wonders, and with all unrighteous deception among those who perish" (2 Thessalonians 2:9–10 NKJV). In Revelation 6:1–2 we saw the Antichrist coming on a white horse. Here we see Jesus coming on a white horse. In Revelation 13:1 we saw the Antichrist rise up with ten crowns on his head. Here we see Jesus coming back with many crowns on his head. It would be wise to remember that Satan is a deceiver who <u>transforms</u> himself into an angel.

transforms
2 Corinthians 11:14

blood
Isaiah 63:1–6

flesh
John 1:14

A Bloody Robe

REVELATION 19:13 *He was clothed with a robe dipped in blood, and His name is called The Word of God. (NKJV)*

The robe dipped in blood is a symbol of what is about to take place. The prophet Isaiah tells us it represents the <u>blood</u> of his enemies. He will be coming back to deal with hundreds of millions of unbelievers at the Battle of Armageddon, and it will be a bloodbath.

His name is the Word of God. This can be explained by looking at one of John's other books, the Gospel of John. In his Gospel, he calls Jesus the Word of God made <u>flesh</u>. It will be Jesus on the white horse, and the judgment at Armageddon will be the work of God. This contrasts with the Antichrist, whose number is known, but whose name cannot be revealed until after the Rapture.

According to the Bible there is

      1. the written Word of God—John 5:39.

      2. the spoken Word of God—John 3:34; 6:63.

      3. the living Word of God—John 1:1, 14; Hebrews 4:12.

The Bible is the written Word of God. The message of the Holy Spirit that filled preachers, evangelists, and others is the spoken Word of God. Jesus is the living Word of God. He is the One who fulfills the written and spoken Word of God.

"Blood came out of the winepress, up to the horses' bridles, for one thousand six hundred furlongs" (Revelation 14:20 NKJV).

What, No Fatigues?

REVELATION 19:14 *And the armies in heaven, clothed in fine linen, white and clean, followed Him on white horses. (NKJV)*

The armies of heaven will follow Jesus. One army will be composed of the entire Church from Pentecost to the Rapture. A second army will consist of the holy angels, while a third army will be all the martyred Tribulation Saints. The Old Testament Saints will comprise the fourth army. These armies will not be dressed in dark colors or camouflage. Not one soldier will have to fight or get bloodied or soiled. The fine linen, white and clean, will prove, when it is over, that his armies will not have to lift a finger. The white horses indicate Christ intends for his followers to share in his glory as a conqueror.

Let's be honest about where the glory really belongs. A famous verse of Scripture says, "We are more than conquerors through Him who loved us" (Romans 8:37 NKJV). This victory will not belong to us. It will belong to Jesus. Were it not for his love, we would be in the wrong army and would be defeated.

Armies of Heaven

Army #1	Church
Army #2	Holy angels
Army #3	Tribulation saints
Army #4	Old Testament saints

Note: White Horses of the armies are symbols that Christ's followers will be victors with him.

go to

Word of God
Ephesians 6:17

spoke it into existence
Genesis 1:1–27

fell to the ground
John 18:3–6

rod of iron
Psalm 2:9;
Revelation 2:27

Sharper Than Any Two-Edged Sword

REVELATION 19:15 *Now out of His mouth goes a sharp sword, that with it He should strike the nations. And He Himself will rule them with a rod of iron. He Himself treads the winepress of the fierceness and wrath of Almighty God.* (NKJV)

Jesus will be the only One in this great heavenly army to carry a weapon. The battle will be his to win or lose. His weapon will be a sharp sword, the Word of God.

When this world was created, God spoke it into existence. When soldiers went to the Garden of Gethsemane to arrest Jesus, he spoke and they fell to the ground. At Armageddon he will simply speak to destroy the opposing nations. He will speak, and they will fall.

Things will change during the Millennium. Jesus will rule them with a rod of iron. He will establish a strong set of standards and require everyone to live by them. Crime and unfaithfulness will not be tolerated. There will be no deception, no lies, no murder, no crime, no war. God's brand of righteousness will prevail for a thousand years. Knowledge of the Lord will fill the earth, and Jesus will finally get the worship he so richly deserves.

This will not come about because man has given up his rebellious ways or because man's efforts to establish world peace have succeeded. This will come about because the Son of God has put down the wicked and established his own reign on earth.

Every Knee Shall Bow

REVELATION 19:16 *And He has on His robe and on His thigh a name written:*
> *KING OF KINGS*
> *AND LORD OF LORDS.* (NKJV)

Lamb
Revelation 17:14

Jesus will return as a King to establish his kingdom. Every earthly king will submit to him. Every individual will call him Lord.

The Antichrist and his ten puppet kings will make war against the <u>Lamb</u>, but the Lamb will overcome them because he is Lord of lords and King of kings.

> **what others say**
>
> **Robert H. Mounce**
>
> The title, as it occurs here and elsewhere in Scripture (Rev 17:14; I Tim 6:15; Dan 2:47), goes back to Moses' declaration to Israel, "For the Lord your God is God of gods and Lord of lords" (Deut 10:17; cf. 1 Enoch 9:4).[9]

The Second Supper

REVELATION 19:17 *Then I saw an angel standing in the sun; and he cried with a loud voice, saying to all the birds that fly in the midst of heaven, "Come and gather together for the supper of the great God,* (NKJV)

This is the second of two great suppers mentioned in chapter 19. An angel will stand in the sun and summon the birds to gather together for a great feast prepared by God.

An angel told John to write, "Blessed are those who are called to the wedding supper of the Lamb!" (Revelation 19:9 NKJV). Those who attend the supper of the Lamb will be at the supper, but those who are at Armageddon will be the supper.

Filled to Overflowing

REVELATION 19:18 *that you may eat the flesh of kings, the flesh of captains, the flesh of mighty men, the flesh of horses and of those who sit on them, and the flesh of all people, free and slave, both small and great."* (NKJV)

This predicts the horrible end of the Antichrist's armies. His foolish rulers, mighty men, horses, riders, and troops will become a feast for the birds.

World War III

REVELATION 19:19 *And I saw the beast, the kings of the earth, and their armies, gathered together to make war against Him who sat on the horse and against His army. (NKJV)*

The Antichrist is named first because he will lead these armies. His ten puppet kings will join him with their troops from all over the world. The kings of the East alone will have two hundred million troops. These armies will have the latest and most powerful weapons known to mankind. Never before have there been so many armies gathered together on one side. Notice why they will gather: to make war against the rider on the horse and his army. These armies will gather to fight the Lord Jesus and those who will come out of heaven with him. This answers those who asked, "Who is like the beast? Who is able to make war with him" (Revelation 13:4 NKJV).

"For they are spirits of demons, performing signs, which go out to the kings of the earth and of the whole world, to gather them to the battle of that great day of God Almighty" (Revelation 16:14 NKJV).

Captured!

REVELATION 19:20 *Then the beast was captured, and with him the false prophet who worked signs in his presence, by which he deceived those who received the mark of the beast and those who worshiped his image. These two were cast alive into the lake of fire burning with brimstone. (NKJV)*

signs
Revelation 13:13–15

Amalekites
1 Samuel 15

Lake of Fire
the final abode of
Satan and his
followers

Out of the hundreds of millions gathered at Armageddon, only two people will be captured: the Antichrist and the False Prophet. They will be seized for using great <u>signs</u> to delude people into taking the mark of the Beast and worshiping his image. They will be judged immediately and cast into the **Lake of Fire**.

Of the multitudes on earth, they will be the first two to suffer this fate. But they will be joined by a great crowd when the unbelievers of the world stand before the Great White Throne more than a thousand years later.

what others say

Henry M. Morris

Initially they will be taken to gehenna [Lake of Fire] by the holy angels, and in their presence and in the presence of the Lamb whom they have despised, they will be "tormented," a word which comes from a root meaning "placed underfoot." Their knees must bow and their tongues confess that Jesus Christ is Lord (Philippians 2:10–11), and then they "shall be punished by his power" 2 Thessalonians 1:9). Following this, in other words, the Lord and His angels will withdraw forever from their presence, leaving them in this unending torment of bitterness and defeat, like "wandering stars, to whom is reserved the blackness of darkness for ever" (Jude 13).[12]

J. R. Church

The Antichrist will be perhaps the greatest intellectual, the greatest politician, the greatest statesman, and the greatest economist who ever lived. But when he usurps the throne of God and gives his allegiance to Satan, he will become the greatest fool.[13]

Not One Remaining

REVELATION 19:21 *And the rest were killed with the sword which proceeded from the mouth of Him who sat on the horse. And all the birds were filled with their flesh. (NKJV)*

Not one of the millions of troops will escape. They will all be killed by the powerful word of God, and the birds will consume their bodies.

When Saul was anointed king over Israel, God told him to kill all the <u>Amalekites</u>, including their women and children, and to destroy everything they had including their animals. But Saul only did part of what God commanded. He disobeyed God, let some of the Amalekites live, and took some of their animals for booty. About five hundred years later, <u>Haman</u> the Agagite (the royal family of the Amalekites) attempted to have all the Jews killed. By not carrying out God's seemingly extreme command, King Saul opened a door that almost wiped out the entire Jewish nation. Those who do not know the future should be careful about questioning the Word of God.

Haman
Esther 3:1–15

Chapter Wrap-Up

- Those in heaven will rejoice and praise God because he has destroyed Babylon and because the wedding of the Lamb has come. (Revelation 19:1–8)

- All those who are invited to the marriage supper of the Lamb will be blessed. (Revelation 19:9)

- The second coming of Jesus will be marked by his return on a white horse with the armies of heaven behind him. He will destroy the nations of the earth with the word of God. (Revelation 19:11–16)

- At the Battle of Armageddon, Christ will destroy the armies of the earth. He will capture the Antichrist and False Prophet and cast them into the Lake of Fire. (Revelation 19:19–21)

- An angel standing in the sun will invite all the birds of the air to God's supper, where they will feast on the dead bodies of those who opposed Christ at Armageddon. (Revelation 19:17–18, 21)

Study Questions

1. Is shouting a proper form of worship?

2. What is the spirit of prophecy?

3. Who are the armies of heaven?

4. How will the False Prophet deceive people? Why will he do it?

5. Who will perish at the Battle of Armageddon?

Part Three
The Millennium and Beyond

Revelation 20

Let's Get Started

This chapter reveals something that is mentioned nowhere else in the Bible: That the length of Jesus' reign on earth will be a thousand years, or as we have already called it, the Millennium. Compared to the Antichrist, who will reign just seven years, Jesus will reign a whopping one thousand years, or more than one hundred and forty years of blessing for each year of Tribulation. That's grace.

Chapter 19 revealed the capture of Antichrist. Chapter 20 reveals the capture of Satan. Chapter 20 also goes on to discuss the future destiny of unbelievers. Later, in chapters 21 and 22, that will be contrasted with the future destiny of believers.

Why Believe in an Earthly Reign?

1. "And the stone [Messiah] that struck the image became a great mountain [kingdom] and filled the whole *earth*" (Daniel 2:35 NKJV).

2. "And the LORD shall be King over all the *earth*" (Zechariah 14:9 NKJV).

3. "Your kingdom come. Your will be done on *earth* as it is in heaven" (Matthew 6:10 NKJV).

4. "When the Son of Man comes in His glory, and all the holy angels with Him, then He will *sit on the throne* of His glory" (Matthew 25:31 NKJV).

5. "We shall reign on the *earth*" (Revelation 5:10 NKJV).

(Also see Isaiah 2:2–4; Ezekiel 37:21; Zechariah 9:9–10)

what others say

Jack Van Impe

In Latin, *mille* means "thousand"; *annus* means "years." The Greeks also had a term for this which they called *chilias*— meaning "one thousand." Whenever we use the terms *millennial*, *millennialism*, or *chiliasm*, the meaning is always "a thousand years."[1]

The Key to the Bottomless Pit

REVELATION 20:1 *Then I saw an angel coming down from heaven, having the key to the bottomless pit and a great chain in his hand.* (NKJV)

messianic
having to do with
the Messiah and his
Millennial reign

An unnamed, but seemingly ordinary, angel will come from heaven to earth. He will have the key to the bottomless pit that will be taken from Satan when the devil is cast out of heaven in Revelation 12:7–9. The angel will also have a great chain in his hand.

what others say

J. Vernon McGee

It is true that the Millennium is mentioned only in one chapter, but God mentions it six times. How many times does he have to say a thing before it becomes true? He mentions it more than he mentions some other things that people emphasize and think are important.[2]

Hal Lindsey

The heart of the Old Testament prophetic message is the coming of the Messiah to set up an earthly Kingdom over which he would rule from the throne of David. The only important detail which Revelation adds concerning this promised **messianic** Kingdom is its duration—one thousand years.[3]

Not Before the Time Is Come

REVELATION 20:2 *He laid hold of the dragon, that serpent of old, who is the Devil and Satan, and bound him for a thousand years;* (NKJV)

Obviously, since God is omnipotent, he could seize Satan anytime he wants. But the Bible says Satan's arrest will come at the end of the Tribulation Period. God will not jump the gun and violate his own Word. When the Tribulation Period is over, he will send one ordinary angel to seize and bind Satan for a thousand years.

On the Brink

REVELATION 20:3 *and he cast him into the bottomless pit, and shut him up, and set a seal on him, so that he should deceive the nations no more till the thousand years were finished. But after these things he must be released for a little while.* (NKJV)

The angel will cast Satan, bound and chained, into the bottomless pit. This will keep Satan from deceiving the nations during the Millennium. Survivors from the Tribulation (the Tribulation Saints and the living Jews) will repopulate the earth, and people from all nations will go to Jerusalem once a year to <u>worship Jesus</u>.

Multitudes will be born during the Millennium. During that time, the offspring from the Tribulation Saints and Jews will not know what <u>temptation</u> is. There will be no real test of their faith. Satan will be released one more time to try them, and unfortunately, many will fall.

Some demons are active in the world today (Revelation 16:12–14). Others are chained in the bottomless pit where the Antichrist, Abaddon, and his demon-possessed locusts came from (Revelation 9:1–11; 11:7; 17–8).

worship Jesus
Zechariah 14:16

temptation
Isaiah 2:4; 11:9

judge the world
1 Corinthians 6:2–3

> **what others say**
>
> ### Jack Van Impe
>
> The Targum (Aramaic paraphrase of the Old Testament), Talmud (a vast compendium of Jewish law and lore), and Midrash (an interpretive method to penetrate the deepest meaning of a Hebrew passage) all have concluded there will be a literal thousand-year period when the Messiah will reign on earth.[4]

Raised at Last

REVELATION 20:4 *And I saw thrones, and they sat on them, and judgment was committed to them. Then I saw the souls of those who had been beheaded for their witness to Jesus and for the word of God, who had not worshiped the beast or his image, and had not received his mark on their foreheads or on their hands. And they lived and reigned with Christ for a thousand years.* (NKJV)

"Judgment was committed to them" refers to the Church and martyred Tribulation Saints. They will sit upon thrones and reign with Jesus during the Millennium. They will even be given the authority to <u>judge the world</u>.

"The souls of those who had been beheaded" refers to the martyred Tribulation Saints. They were beheaded for two reasons: because of their testimony for Jesus, and to fulfill the Word of God. These will be Gentiles and Jews who refused to worship the Antichrist or his image, and refused to take his mark. After Satan is bound and chained, their souls will appear, and they will be raised

resurrection
1 Corinthians
15:20–23

Old Testament saints
Matthew 27:52–53;
Daniel 12:1–3

from the dead in the fourth and final phase of the <u>resurrection</u>. A connection may not exist, but some find it interesting that the Antichrist will use the same terror tactic that militant Muslims have been using for years.

"[You] have made us kings and priests to our God; and we shall reign on the earth" (Revelation 5:10 NKJV).

Resurrection of Life

> REVELATION 20:5 *But the rest of the dead did not live again until the thousand years were finished. This is the first resurrection. (NKJV)*

Jesus said, "Do not marvel at this; for the hour is coming in which all who are in the graves will hear His voice and come forth—those who have done good, to the resurrection of life, and those who have done evil, to the resurrection of condemnation" (John 5:28–29 NKJV). The first resurrection is called the resurrection of life or the resurrection of believers. The second resurrection is called the resurrection of damnation or the resurrection of unbelievers. This verse reveals that there will be a thousand years between the two.

Perhaps some clarification would help. Some people think that the first resurrection means only one resurrection, but that is not the case. The first resurrection is a resurrection that began more than nineteen hundred years ago and occurred in four phases (see Time Line #5, Appendix A):

> Phase 1—the resurrection of Christ and some <u>Old Testament Saints</u>
>
> Phase 2—the resurrection of the Church at the Rapture
>
> Phase 3—the resurrection of the two witnesses
>
> Phase 4—the resurrection of the Tribulation Saints and the remainder of the Old Testament Saints at the end of the Tribulation Period
>
> Second Resurrection—the unbelievers at the end of the Millennium

It's a Bodily Resurrection

The body of Elijah disappeared	2 Kings 2:1–16
The body of Jesus disappeared	Luke 24:1–3
Many bodies of the saints arose	Matthew 27:52

The 144,000 and those believers who survive the Tribulation Period will not be resurrected since they will still be alive at the start of the Millennium.

What Will Our Resurrected Body Be Like?

Description	Scripture
I shall be satisfied when I awake in Your likeness	Psalm 17:15 NKJV
And as we have borne the image of the man of dust, we shall also bear the image of the heavenly Man	1 Corinthians 15:49 NKJV
For our citizenship is in heaven, from which we also eagerly wait for the Savior, the Lord Jesus Christ, who will transform our lowly body that it may be conformed to His glorious body	Philippians 3:20–21 NKJV
We know that when He is revealed, we shall be like Him	1 John 3:2 NKJV

Note: Jesus appeared, disappeared, ate, drank, was recognized, no sin nature, etc.

Will We Know Our Loved Ones in Heaven?

Encounter	Scripture
When Samuel returned from the dead, Saul knew him	1 Samuel 28
When the rich man saw Lazarus in Paradise, he knew him	Luke 16:9–31
When Peter, James, and John saw Moses and Elijah on the Mount of Transfiguration, they knew them	Matthew 17:1–13
When Thomas saw Jesus he knew him	John 20:24–29
We shall know as we are known	1 Corinthians 13:12

Note: The Holy Spirit will reveal things and we will have perfect knowledge.

What Will We Do in Heaven?

Activity	Scripture
Worship	Revelation 4:9–10
Learn	1 Corinthians 13:11–12
Fellowship	Revelation 19:9
Serve Jesus	Revelation 22:3
Judge angels	1 Corinthians 6:3

A Thousand-Year Reign

REVELATION 20:6 *Blessed and holy is he who has part in the first resurrection. Over such the second death has no power, but they shall be priests of God and of Christ, and shall reign with Him a thousand years. (NKJV)*

go to

royal priesthood
Revelation 5:10;
1 Peter 2:9

Lake of Fire
Revelation 19:20;
20:10

hundreds of years
Isaiah 65:18–24

nature of man
Jeremiah 17:9;
Romans 8:7–8

royal priesthood
members of Jesus'
family who will work
as priests during the
Millennium

political priesthood
religious people who
will hold political
positions during the
Millennium

This tells us six things about those who will have a part in the first resurrection:

1. *Blessed*—they will be happy in their eternal state

2. *Holy*—they will be separated or identified as God's special people

3. *Priests*—they will minister to, and serve in the presence of God

4. *Reign*—they will be both a **royal** and a **political priesthood**

5. *A thousand years*—the length of their earthly reign with Jesus

6. *The second death has no power over them*—they will never suffer the consequences of their sin by being cast into the <u>Lake of Fire</u> because they have been redeemed

Not Him Again

REVELATION 20:7 *Now when the thousand years have expired, Satan will be released from his prison (NKJV)*

With Satan bound during the Millennium, people will be shielded from temptation and sin. Sickness and disease will not exist, and people will live to be <u>hundreds of years</u> old. A population explosion will occur. However, God is no respecter of persons. Those born during the Millennium will have to be tested just like everyone else. When the Millennium is over, the Abyss will be opened one more time, and Satan will be released to resume his old ways.

World War IV—One Last Try

REVELATION 20:8 *and will go out to deceive the nations which are in the four corners of the earth, Gog and Magog, to gather them together to battle, whose number is as the sand of the sea. (NKJV)*

When Satan is released he will pick up where he left off. He will go out once again to deceive the nations.

Tempting those who were born during the Millennium will prove that eliminating sin is not as simple as changing our environment. Something is wrong with the very <u>nature of man</u>'s heart. Rebellion is our nature, and unless we are born again, we will never see change.

At the **Battle of Gog and Magog** Satan will repeat what he tried at the Battle of Armageddon. He will try one final time to become <u>greater than God</u> by gathering a great horde of people from all over the world, including those from **Gog and Magog**.

go to

greater than God
Isaiah 14:12–13;
Revelation 12:9

City of God
Psalm 87:2–3

Sodom and Gomorrah
Genesis 19:24

fire
Hebrews 12:29

Battle of Gog and Magog
a great rebellion against God following the Millennium

Gog and Magog
the prince (Gog) and his tribes (Magog)

what others say

J. Vernon McGee

Because the rebellion is labeled "Gog and Magog," many Bible students identify it with the Gog and Magog of Ezekiel 38–39. This is not possible at all, for the conflicts described are not parallel as to time, place, or participants—only the names are the same.[5]

Foiled Once Again

REVELATION 20:9 *They went up on the breadth of the earth and surrounded the camp of the saints and the beloved city. And fire came down from God out of heaven and devoured them. (NKJV)*

Jesus will reign from Jerusalem, the <u>City of God</u> (the camp of the saints), during his millennial reign. Satan's army will march across the earth and surround the city, but just as God destroyed the cities of <u>Sodom and Gomorrah</u>, he will again consume Satan's army with fire from heaven.

"God is love" is one of the great truths of the Bible, but we should also remember that God is a consuming <u>fire</u>. It is interesting that the only thing stopping the attack on Jerusalem is fire from heaven and the destruction of Satan. The message here is to not harm the things God loves.

Gone Forever

REVELATION 20:10 *The devil, who deceived them, was cast into the lake of fire and brimstone where the beast and the false prophet are. And they will be tormented day and night forever and ever. (NKJV)*

Satan will not be allowed to lure people into destruction any longer. His deceptive career will be brought to an end when he is captured and thrown into the Lake of Fire where the Antichrist and False Prophet already reside. Unfortunately for them, they will not be destroyed, but will suffer unending torment.

go to

committed
John 5:22

new earth
Isaiah 66:22

old
Matthew 24:35

new earth
another earth that
will replace the one
that now exists

new heaven
another heaven that
will replace the one
that now exists

what others say

Mark Hitchcock

There's an old saying, "The next time Satan comes along and begins to remind you of your past, remind him of his future." The Bible reveals that Satan's future is very bleak. He is doomed to eternal destruction.[6]

Hal Lindsey

I'm sure this doesn't bring any joy to God's heart. This creature, Satan, was God's most beautiful creation and here he ends in terrible infamy.[7]

The Great White Throne

> REVELATION 20:11 *Then I saw a great white throne and Him who sat on it, from whose face the earth and the heaven fled away. And there was found no place for them.* (NKJV)

This is the judgment seat of Almighty God. The one who will be seated on it is not identified, but we have already seen that all judgment has been <u>committed</u> to Jesus. When preachers say people will have to face the judgment of God, this is the judgment most people think about. However, the only ones who will appear before this judgment seat are those who are lost.

"From whose face the earth and the heaven fled away" is something that little is known about. The consensus seems to be that earth and heaven will be moved to make room for the **new earth** and **new heaven**. "There was found no place for them" appears to indicate the <u>old</u> earth and old heaven will be destroyed after being removed.

what others say

John Hagee

When Scripture tells us that heaven and earth will pass away, you can be sure that this world will definitely end. There will be a last baby born, a last marriage performed, a last kiss, a last song, a last hurrah.[8]

They Get What They Have Coming

> REVELATION 20:12 *And I saw the dead, small and great, standing before God, and books were opened. And another book*

was opened, which is the Book of Life. And the dead were judged according to their works, by the things which were written in the books. (NKJV)

go to

none of them will reach heaven
Galatians 3:10

The dead will stand before Jesus as he sits upon the Great White Throne. They will come from all walks of life: small and great, poor and rich, laborers and managers, peasants and kings. They will all stand before the court's judgment bar to be sentenced. Several books will be opened—each one is a "book of works" or a "book of deeds." These books will contain the thoughts, words, and deeds of each individual, and by these things they will be judged.

Another book will be opened—the *Book of Life.* When a person is born, their name is written in this book. If they never get saved, they will die in a lost condition and their name will be removed. Some will deny Jesus so strongly while they are alive that their name will be removed (for example those who take the mark). Some will add to or take away from the Scriptures, and their name will be removed. If they get saved, their name will be left in the Book of Life when they die. It will also be added to the Lamb's Book of Life at the time they get saved. Ultimately, the list of names in both books will be identical.

When the judgment begins, the dead will get what they knew they had coming. They will be judged by their divine record—their deeds as recorded in God's own books. A surprise will come their way, though, for <u>none of them will reach heaven</u>. Only one thing remains—punishment. No mention will be made of salvation or the names in the Lamb's Book of Life, because these people did not accept Jesus as their Savior.

Since the Book of Works has nothing to do with salvation, the only reason to open it is if there are degrees of punishment in hell. Jesus implied this when he said some cities will be worse off than Sodom and Gomorrah on Judgment Day, and some people will be beaten with few stripes and some with many (Matthew 10:15; 11:20–24; Luke 12:46–48).

The question is often asked, "Will those who haven't heard the gospel go to hell?" They can't go to heaven because they don't have a Savior, but this is where degrees of punishment come in. Their punishment will be less than those who heard the gospel and rejected it. Since everyone has some knowledge of God, how often they sinned and the nature of their sins will be factored in.

go to

Book of Life
Exodus 32:33;
Revelation 3:4–5;
22:19

Lamb's Book of Life
Revelation 21:27

die once
Hebrews 9:27

judgment seat
Romans 14:10;
2 Corinthians 5:10

God's Books

Book	Scripture
A book God has written	Exodus 32:32–33
A book about our wanderings and tears	Psalm 56:8
The book of the living	Psalm 69:28
A book containing the names of faithful Jews	Daniel 12:1
A book of remembrance	Malachi 3:16
A record of our idle words	Matthew 12:36–37
A list of our works	1 Corinthians 3:11–15
A book of life	Philippians 4:3; Revelation 3:5; 17:8; 20:8, 15; 22:19
A book of life of the Lamb/Lamb's Book of Life	Revelation 13:8; 21:27

The Book of Life is the list of all who were born once (every person who ever lived), minus the names of those who were removed for sinning against God, denying Jesus, or adding to or taking away from the Scriptures.

The Lamb's Book of Life is the list of all who were born twice (every person who truly accepts Jesus as their Savior).

All Will Be There

REVELATION 20:13 *The sea gave up the dead who were in it, and Death and Hades delivered up the dead who were in them. And they were judged, each one according to his works.* (NKJV)

Everyone will stand before the judgment seat, even those from the bottom of the sea. No one will escape the judgment of God because he will raise them all from the dead. He will even raise them from Hades, the temporary abode of the souls and spirits of the wicked. All will be judged as individuals according to their deeds.

The Bible teaches that man is destined to die once, and then he will face judgment. But believers and unbelievers will be raised separately and judged separately. Believers will go before the judgment seat of Christ where their works will be judged. The purpose of this is not salvation, or we would not be raised at this time. This is a judgment of works for the purpose of receiving rewards or crowns. Unbelievers will go before the Great White Throne where their works will be judged also. The purpose of this is not salvation, but degrees of punishment.

Two different Hebrew words have been translated "grave" in the Old Testament: (1) *Qeber*, which means burying place, sepulcher, or pit, and (2) *Sheol*, which means underworld, subterranean world, world of the dead, or pit. Because both these words mean "pit" about half the time *Sheol* is translated "grave" and about half the time it's translated "hell." This confuses people, and some have mistakenly concluded that "hell" and the "grave" are the same thing. However, a study of the texts in Hebrew reveals that people dug Qebers (graves), touched Qebers, buried people in Qebers, and put Qebers on the face of the earth. But people never dug, touched, or buried anyone in a Sheol (hell). The texts also reveal that people don't know anything in Qebers (graves), but they are conscious in Sheol (hell, see Deuteronomy 18:11; 1 Samuel 28:11–15; Isaiah 14:9). The point is, there is more than one kind of pit. *Sheol* means hell, not the grave.

go to

cast into hell
Matthew 25:41, 46

end of death
1 Corinthians 15:26

heavenly city
another name for the New Jerusalem (the future home of the Church)

The Abode of Wicked People

	English	Hebrew	Greek
Present (temporary)	Hell	Sheol	Hades
Future (permanent)	Lake of Fire	Valley of Hinnom	Gehenna

Note: The fallen angels will spend eternity in *Tartaros* (Greek)

Death and Hades Destroyed

REVELATION 20:14 *Then Death and Hades were cast into the lake of fire. This is the second death. (NKJV)*

This will be the end of the first death—physical death. This is good news for believers but terrible news for unbelievers. They will want to die physically when they are raised from the dead, and cast into hell, but that will no longer be possible. They will have new bodies that cannot be destroyed in the Lake of Fire, so their suffering will be eternal.

This will also be the end of death. An intermediate abode for the lost will no longer be necessary. When the earth is destroyed people will be in one of two places: the **heavenly city**, or hell.

The Bible speaks of two kinds of life or two kinds of birth: (1) physical and (2) spiritual (born again). Birth means "joined to." In physical birth, a soul and spirit are *joined to* a body. In spiritual birth, a soul and spirit are *joined to* God (called receiving Jesus, receiving

the Holy Spirit, the new birth, etc). The Bible also speaks of two kinds of death: (1) physical and (2) spiritual. Death means "separated from." In physical death, a soul and spirit are *separated from* a body. In spiritual death, a soul and spirit are *separated from* God. The second life is eternal life with God. And the second death is eternal separation from God by being cast into the Lake of Fire.

Don't ask if a person ever ceases to exist. The answer is no! The question to ask is, where will that person spend eternity?

Will Your Name Be There?

REVELATION 20:15 *And anyone not found written in the Book of Life was cast into the lake of fire. (NKJV)*

When the sentence is rendered, one's eternal destiny will not be determined by their deeds, but by what is written in the Book of Life. God will make a careful search of the heavenly list.

The names of those who did not accept Jesus before they died will have been blotted out of the Book of Life. Their names will not be found, and they will join Satan, the Antichrist, and the False Prophet in the Lake of Fire forever.

Chapter Wrap-Up

- An angel, carrying a great chain, will bind Satan and cast him into the bottomless pit for a thousand years to keep him from deceiving the nations. (Revelation 20:1–3)

- Those believers who died during the Tribulation will be raised in the last phase of the first resurrection and will reign with Christ for the Millennium. Those who take part in the first resurrection will be blessed because they will not face the second death. (Revelation 20:4–6)

- After the thousand years, Satan will be released once again to test the faith of the nations. Unfortunately, many will fall and make war against God, but God will destroy them with fire and cast Satan into the Lake of Fire where he will suffer unending torment. (Revelation 20:7–10)

- Christ will sit on the Great White Throne and judge the dead. Those whose names are not found in the Book of Life will be cast into the Lake of Fire to suffer the second death. (Revelation 20:11–15)

Study Questions

1. What will be the crime of those who will be beheaded during the Tribulation Period?

2. What will be the position of those who are raised in the first resurrection?

3. By what will those who stand before the Great White Throne be judged?

4. Is there such a thing as degrees of punishment for unbelievers?

5. Why will individuals be cast into the Lake of Fire?

Chapter Highlights:
• New Heaven and
  New Earth
• The Holy City
• The Second Death
• Gates and Foundations
• No Temple or Sun

Revelation 21

Let's Get Started

After revealing the Church Age, the Tribulation Period, and the Millennium, John focused on one last time period that most commentators call "eternity." God will create a new world that John compares to the original creation. The Almighty will create a new city that John compares to Jerusalem and Babylon. Get ready to see some of these comparisons.

new earth
Isaiah 65:17;
2 Peter 3:13

Everything Made New

> **REVELATION 21:1** *Now I saw a new heaven and a new earth, for the first heaven and the first earth had passed away. Also there was no more sea. (NKJV)*

Isaiah predicted a new earth (Isaiah 65:17; 66:22). Jesus said heaven and earth will pass away (Matthew 24:35). Peter said the heavens will pass away with a great noise, and the earth will be burned up (2 Peter 3:10–13). Here John glimpsed a new heaven and a <u>new earth</u>, but they will be different from the original creation when God divided the waters to create seas and cause the dry land to appear (Genesis 1:9–10). The new earth will not have a sea on it.

Bible experts believe there will no longer be large bodies of water to allow for (1) more room for people, and (2) to change the climate, reduce storms, and eliminate social barriers. The Seal, Trumpet, and Bowl Judgments will cause ships to sink and water to turn to blood, but such disasters can't exist in the new creation. Neither can floods, tsunamis, hurricanes, and mudslides. And there won't be a Lake of Fire for unbelievers.

"Then I saw a great white throne and Him who sat on it, from whose face the earth and the heaven fled away. And there was found no place for them" (Revelation 20:11 NKJV).

go to

Holy City
Hebrews 11:13–16

home
John 14:2–3

what others say

John Hagee

This world will not continue forever. The Second Law of Thermodynamics, otherwise known as the Law of Entropy, declares that all organized systems tend to disorder after time. Like all things, the earth, along with this physical universe, will wear out.[1]

A New Jerusalem

REVELATION 21:2 *Then I, John, saw the holy city, New Jerusalem, coming down out of heaven from God, prepared as a bride adorned for her husband. (NKJV)*

In the original creation, God put Adam in the Garden of Eden (Genesis 2:8), but in the new creation God will put his Church in a special city called New Jerusalem. This city will not be like ancient Jerusalem or Babylon that housed sinners. This will be a <u>Holy City</u>.

This city is not heaven. It will come down out of heaven. This city is not the whole creation or the whole new earth. It's just one part or one city that will come down to the new earth. Just as Babylon was the capital of Babylonia, the New Jerusalem will be the capital of the new earth.

Chapter 19 revealed the wedding of the Lamb (the marriage of Jesus and his Church). Invitations will be given to the marriage supper here on earth when Jesus comes back. The New Jerusalem will be the bride's new <u>home</u> after the Millennium. It will be a real city with physical attributes, but it will also be like a bride in that it will be pure and radiant.

"I will write on him the name of My God and the name of the city of My God, the New Jerusalem, which comes down out of heaven from My God" (Revelation 3:12 NKJV).

With His People

REVELATION 21:3 *And I heard a loud voice from heaven saying, "Behold, the tabernacle of God is with men, and He will dwell with them, and they shall be His people. God Himself will be with them and be their God. (NKJV)*

In the original creation, God came down from heaven to walk and talk with Adam (Genesis 3:8–9). In the wilderness, God dwelled in the ark of the covenant from which he talked to his people (Exodus 25:1–22). In the new creation, God will come down with the Holy City to remain and dwell with his people.

what others say

Craig S. Keener

The promise that God "will live" with his people was a frequent Jewish hope that ultimately points back to a promise of God's covenant for Israel (Exodus 25:8; 29:45–46; Leviticus 26:12; 1 Kings 6:13; Ezekiel 37:27; Zechariah 2:10–11). This promise is spelled out more clearly when the text reveals that new Jerusalem is a temple city (21:22) and is shaped like the Most Holy Place (21:16).[2]

Death and Pain Forgotten

REVELATION 21:4 *And God will wipe away every tear from their eyes; there shall be no more death, nor sorrow, nor crying. There shall be no more pain, for the former things have passed away." (NKJV)*

In the original creation, death came upon Adam and he worked, and experienced sorrow and pain because he sinned. And because Eve sinned, she experienced sorrow and pain in childbirth (Genesis 2:16–17; 3:17–19). Likewise, during the Seal, Trumpet, and Bowl Judgments of the Tribulation Period, many will experience sorrow, pain, and death. But the new creation will be different in that everything that causes these things will be done away with.

A Divine Declaration

REVELATION 21:5 *Then He who sat on the throne said, "Behold, I make all things new." And He said to me, "Write, for these words are true and faithful." (NKJV)*

Following the Millennium, Jesus will not fix or repair this old creation. He will re-create everything. This is more than a verbal promise because he says, "Write, for these words are true and faithful."

Never to Thirst Again

go to

thirst
Matthew 5:6

freely
John 7:37–38

satisfied
John 4:13–14

children
1 John 3:2

heirs
Romans 8:16–17

thirst after God
a longing for God

water of life
living waters, the
Holy Spirit

REVELATION 21:6 *And He said to me, "It is done! I am the Alpha and the Omega, the Beginning and the End. I will give of the fountain of the water of life freely to him who thirsts. (NKJV)*

The new creation is inevitable because it is the spoken Word of Jesus. He proved his power to create when he fashioned all things at the beginning of creation. As the Alpha and Omega, he is the first and last word in all things. All authority is his. What he declares will be done.

In the original creation, a river watered the Garden of Eden and divided into four other rivers (Genesis 2:10–14). The new creation will have a fountain that provides the water of life. All who **thirst after God** will be given the privilege of <u>freely</u> drinking from the **water of life**. Their thirst for God will be abundantly <u>satisfied</u>. Incidentally, one of the four rivers is the Euphrates, which flowed under the walls of ancient Babylon.

"I am the Alpha and the Omega, the Beginning and the End," says the Lord, "who is and who was and who is to come, the Almighty" (Revelation 1:8 NKJV).

Heirs with Jesus

REVELATION 21:7 *He who overcomes shall inherit all things, and I will be his God and he shall be My son. (NKJV)*

In the original creation, Adam was told to till the ground from which he was taken (Genesis 3:23). He was a steward over the creation. But overcomers will inherit the new creation. All true Christians are overcomers. God is their God. They are his <u>children</u> and joint <u>heirs</u> with Jesus.

The List Is Long

REVELATION 21:8 *But the cowardly, unbelieving, abominable, murderers, sexually immoral, sorcerers, idolaters, and all liars shall have their part in the lake which burns with fire and brimstone, which is the second death." (NKJV)*

All unbelievers will be cast into the fiery lake of burning brimstone, which is the second death. The original creation was overcome with sin. Cain murdered Abel; the sons of God bore children by the daughters of men; and the Lord saw that the wickedness of man was great. The earth was filled with violence and was corrupt. And God said he was bringing floodwaters on the earth to destroy the abominable (Genesis 4–6). The rains came, and the fountains of the deep were broken up, and all the high hills under the whole heaven were covered, and all the wicked went to their place of death in a great watery lake (Genesis 7). This will not happen in the new creation because the ungodly will find their place of death in the Lake of Fire. The list of those who will not have a part in the new creation includes:

1. *the cowardly*—those who are too embarrassed, ashamed, or afraid to accept Jesus as Lord

2. *the unbelievers*—those who reject Jesus

3. *the abominable*—those who defile themselves with abominable sins such as stealing, taking the mark of the Beast, taking drugs, and drunkenness

4. *murderers*—those who kill

5. *the sexually immoral*—fornicators, adulterers, homosexuals, and rapists

6. *those who practice sorcery*—astrologers, Satan worshipers, witches, and warlocks

7. *idolaters*—those who worship anyone or anything other than God

8. *liars*—those who deceive the lost, falsely accuse Christians, falsely claim to be a Christian, or add to or take away from the Bible

go to

union
Revelation 19:7

The Bride of Christ

REVELATION 21:9 *Then one of the seven angels who had the seven bowls filled with the seven last plagues came to me and talked with me, saying, "Come, I will show you the bride, the Lamb's wife."* (NKJV)

At this point, the vision moved John's thoughts from the original creation to Mystery Babylon the Great the Mother of Harlots and the rebuilt city of Babylon. Revelation 17:1 reads, "Then one of the seven angels who had the seven bowls came and talked with me, saying to me, 'Come, I will show you the judgment of the great harlot who sits on many waters'" (NKJV). Now, that same angel came to John saying, "Come, I will show you the bride, the Lamb's wife." The first time, John saw the harlot. The second time, John saw the bride. Both of these women represented a great city.

God's nature has more than one characteristic. He loves and judges; saves and condemns. Both of these characteristics are demonstrated here. Imagine, one of the same angels who poured out a bowl of God's wrath is now inviting John to see God's love for his Church.

A special <u>union</u> will exist between Jesus and the Church similar to the union that exists between a bridegroom and bride upon their marriage.

what others say

Ben Witherington III

John wants to imply a direct contrast between the two great cities—harlot versus bride, gaudy versus beautiful, full of disease and death versus full of new life.[4]

Carried Away

REVELATION 21:10 *And he carried me away in the Spirit to a great and high mountain, and showed me the great city, the holy Jerusalem, descending out of heaven from God,* (NKJV)

On both occasions, this angel carried John away in the Spirit. But there is a difference. The first time, the angel took John into the wilderness (17:3). And this time, the angel took John to a great and high mountain. The first time, John saw Babylon hurled down with violence (18:21). This time, John saw the New Jerusalem descending out of heaven. How far it will descend is a matter of debate. Nothing is said about it coming to rest on the new earth.

It may do that, but it also may remain suspended above. One thing is for sure: what goes on in the Holy City will be more important than what takes place on the new earth. The Holy City will be the headquarters of the new creation.

John was in the Spirit (an ecstatic spiritual state), which put him in close touch with God and made him able to see visions.

jasper
Revelation 4:3

names
Revelation 17:3–18

The Glow of Glory

REVELATION 21:11 *having the glory of God. Her light was like a most precious stone, like a jasper stone, clear as crystal.* (NKJV)

When the fifth angel dumps his bowl of God's wrath on the Antichrist's throne, his kingdom will be plunged into darkness (16:10). But the Holy City will descend out of heaven lit with the Shekinah glory of God. His light will burst forth in brilliance like the sparkle of a large and expensive jasper (opal, diamond, or topaz) and be crystal clear. Jasper is the first stone in the breastplate of the High Priest (see Illustration #2). It is opaque and translucent like a diamond, and is a symbol of purity and holiness.

what others say

Ben Witherington III

God's own presence is described in these very terms at Rev. 4:3 when his appearance on the throne is approximated. John is saying that the city partakes of the very character of God, and of God's brilliance.[5]

Twelve Gates

REVELATION 21:12 *Also she had a great and high wall with twelve gates, and twelve angels at the gates, and <u>names</u> written on them, which are the names of the twelve tribes of the children of Israel:* (NKJV)

The Holy City will be surrounded by a thick, high wall with twelve gates. I'm sorry, but Saint Peter won't be standing at the gates; angels will. The name of each of the twelve tribes of Israel will be written on a gate.

The wall will be for security. The same can be said of the angels guarding the gates. The names of the twelve tribes of Israel will be a reminder that the Messiah, the Scriptures, and salvation came through the Jews. Without them the Holy City would not be needed, and the Gentiles would be without hope.

Why does the Holy City need security? No one knows the answer. Some suggest it symbolizes that not everyone will have access to God. But it may be that John has the original creation in mind once again. After the first couple sinned, God removed them from the Garden of Eden and posted Cherubim, and a flaming sword which turned every way, to keep them out (Genesis 3:24). Or it may be that John is thinking about ancient Babylon which was surrounded by two great walls.

Three Gates for Each Compass Point

> REVELATION 21:13 *three gates on the east, three gates on the north, three gates on the south, and three gates on the west. (NKJV)*

The wall will have four sides with three gates on each side providing access to the Holy City from every direction on the new earth.

One Foundation for Each Apostle

> REVELATION 21:14 *Now the wall of the city had twelve foundations, and on them were the names of the twelve apostles of the Lamb. (NKJV)*

The city will have twelve foundations. Some experts say these foundations will be stacked on top of one another and will encompass the base of the city. Others speculate that they will be large columns extending down to the new earth like legs or posts.

Each foundation will have the name of one of the twelve apostles of Jesus on it. This is significant because the Bible tells us that the Church is "built on the foundation of the apostles and prophets, Jesus Christ Himself being the chief cornerstone" (Ephesians 2:20 NKJV). It says Jesus "through the Holy Spirit had given commandments to the apostles whom He had chosen" (Acts 1:2 NKJV). With the help of the Holy Spirit the apostles preached the gospel, won converts, organized congregations, wrote the Scriptures, selected deacons, and taught their followers. They relinquished everything for Jesus and his Church, and were threatened, beaten, imprisoned, and killed. They earned the right to have their names inscribed on the foundations of the Holy City.

A Gold Reed

REVELATION 21:15 *And he who talked with me had a gold reed to measure the city, its gates, and its wall. (NKJV)*

A measuring stick in John's day was approximately ten feet long, and the most common material used in heaven seems to be gold. The same angel who talked with John took a golden measuring stick to measure the city, its gates, and its wall.

A Giant Cube?

REVELATION 21:16 *The city is laid out as a square; its length is as great as its breadth. And he measured the city with the reed: twelve thousand furlongs. Its length, breadth, and height are equal. (NKJV)*

The Holy City will be laid out like a square. Its length will be the same as its width, and its height will equal its length. Some suggest that this will be a pyramid, but others think it will be a cube. Not enough information exists to prove either view, but a cube seems most likely. The Holy of Holies in the tabernacle and the one in the Jerusalem Temple were cubes, so it seems that the shape of God's temporary residence among the Jews will be the shape of God's permanent residence among his people.

However, everyone agrees that the Holy City will be enormous.

many mansions
John 14:2

Twelve thousand furlongs is about fifteen hundred miles (approximately the distance from New York City to Dallas, Texas). A city fifteen hundred miles long and fifteen hundred miles wide will be larger than anything the world has ever seen. A city towering fifteen hundred miles high is almost incomprehensible, but the Carpenter of Israel is building <u>many mansions</u>.

By comparison, the walled city of ancient Babylon was fourteen miles long and fourteen miles wide, making it a tiny city in comparison to New Jerusalem.

> **what others say**
>
> **Hal Lindsey**
>
> This covers a lot of territory, and it implies that millions upon millions of redeemed saints will be there.[7]

A Thick Wall

REVELATION 21:17 *Then he measured its wall: one hundred and forty-four cubits, according to the measure of a man, that is, of an angel. (NKJV)*

The wall around the Holy city will be 144 cubits (216 feet) thick. It does not matter whether one uses God's measurements or man's measurements, the result will be the same. This thick wall will provide plenty of protection. According to Herodotus the wall of ancient Babylon was only 87 feet thick.

The Purest Gold

REVELATION 21:18 *The construction of its wall was of jasper; and the city was pure gold, like clear glass. (NKJV)*

In verse 11, we noted that the jasper could be an opal, diamond, or topaz. Although we don't know which one of these it will be, we do know the wall will be made of a gem that is beautiful, hard, and transparent. People will be able to see through it into the Holy City, and the light of God will beam out of the city. The city itself will be made of gold as pure as glass.

In the original creation, God put gold in the Garden of Eden (Genesis 2:12). Later, Babylon was known as the kingdom of gold or the head of gold on the statue in Nebuchadnezzar's dream

(Daniel 2:31–45). Their gold was insignificant compared to the New Jerusalem.

Walls of Precious Stone

> **REVELATION 21:19** *The foundations of the wall of the city were adorned with all kinds of precious stones: the first foundation was jasper, the second sapphire, the third chalcedony, the fourth emerald, (NKJV)*

Each one of the twelve foundations of the city walls will be different. The first four will be:

1. *jasper*—a crystal clear gem that could be a massive diamond

2. *sapphire*—a clear blue gem similar to a diamond in hardness

3. *chalcedony*—a greenish agate with possibly a few stripes of other colors mixed in

4. *emerald*—a bright green stone

"And He who sat there [on the throne] was like a jasper and a sardius stone" (Revelation 4:3 NKJV).

How Rich Can We Get?

> **REVELATION 21:20** *the fifth sardonyx, the sixth sardius, the seventh chrysolite, the eighth beryl, the ninth topaz, the tenth chrysoprase, the eleventh jacinth, and the twelfth amethyst. (NKJV)*

The next eight foundations will be decorated with:

5. *sardonyx*—a reddish white onyx similar to the color of healthy fingernails

6. *sardius*—a fiery red or blood-colored stone from Sardis

7. *chrysolite*—a transparent golden-yellow stone

8. *beryl*—a sea green emerald lighter in color than the third foundation

9. *topaz*—a transparent greenish-yellow stone

light
1 John 1:5

tabernacle
Exodus 25:9

temple
2 Samuel 7:5, 13

10. *chrysoprase*—a yellowish pale green stone similar to the modern aquamarine color

11. *jacinth*—a violet hyacinth-colored gem

12. *amethyst*—a purple-colored stone

A brilliant rainbow would be just a pale glimmer compared to what these foundation stones will look like. God is <u>light</u>, and his light passing through these many different colored stones will be breathtaking.

The Pearly Gates

> REVELATION 21:21 *The twelve gates were twelve pearls: each individual gate was of one pearl. And the street of the city was pure gold, like transparent glass.* (NKJV)

With only twelve gates to this extensive city, and each gate being more than three hundred miles apart, we know the gates will need to be huge. And each gate will consist of a single gigantic pearl. This emphasizes the great wealth and generosity of God.

The street is a mystery. Will this city, with a circumference of 1,500 miles long, 1,500 miles wide, and 1,500 miles high, have only one street? We don't know, but we do know it will be made of pure gold.

Babylon was home of the famous Ishtar Gate, which was named after Ishtar, the so-called queen of heaven. This gate opened to Procession Street, which some people called Festival Avenue. But Babylon's gate and street pale in comparison to the twelve gates of pearl and a street of pure gold. God knows how to make Satan look like a pauper.

No Temple

> REVELATION 21:22 *But I saw no temple in it, for the Lord God Almighty and the Lamb are its temple.* (NKJV)

Because of sin on earth, God withdrew his presence from mankind. He had Moses and others build a <u>tabernacle</u>, and later he had Solomon build a <u>temple</u> where the people would go to worship.

He separated himself from them by residing in the <u>Holy of Holies</u> (see Illustration #5, page 148), and having priests serve as mediators.

After the Millennium, however, things will be different. A temple will not be needed since sin will not be present in the Holy City. God will have no need to <u>separate himself from his people</u>. Mediators will not be necessary. The glorious presence of the Father and the Son will permeate the entire city.

The Bible is filled with truths that are difficult to understand but wonderful to speculate on. One of them is the fact that when he appears, we (believers) shall be like him (1 John 3:2). We will have great insight, great love, and everything else that Jesus has. Also, we will not have a sin nature that could separate us from him.

Also, this is another difference between ancient Babylon and the new creation. Ancient Babylon had its temple area. The famous Temple of Marduk stood there. But things like this won't be needed in the New Jerusalem.

No Sun

REVELATION 21:23 *The city had no need of the sun or of the moon to shine in it, for the glory of God illuminated it. The Lamb is its light.* (NKJV)

The Father and Son are the source of physical light. They spoke light into existence when they <u>created</u> the sun, the moon, and the stars. But they will do away with these when they create the new heaven and earth because their presence in the Holy City will eliminate the need for other heavenly lights.

Think about this. It means we can be in the Holy City, several hundred miles from God, and not need a light. The light of God will cover an area almost as large as the eastern half of the U.S., and it will even be visible in outer space.

The Fourth Bowl Judgment caused the sun to scorch men with fire. This cannot happen in the New Jerusalem.

World's Brightest Night-Light

REVELATION 21:24 *And the nations of those who are saved shall walk in its light, and the kings of the earth bring their **glory and honor** into it.* (NKJV)

Holy of Holies
Leviticus 16:2

separate himself from his people
1 Thessalonians 4:17

created
Genesis 1

glory and honor
their display of praise, thanksgiving, and worship

shut the gates
Isaiah 60:11

Eden
Genesis 2:8

Satan
Genesis 3:1–6

The new earth will be populated with the children of Israel, and the descendants of those who did not follow Satan in his final rebellion after the Millennium. Nations and leaders already will be on the new earth when the Holy City comes out of heaven. They will walk in the light coming from that city instead of the light of the sun and moon.

The inhabitants of the new earth will travel to the Holy City—not to live but to worship. The Holy City will be the future home of the Church. The new earth will be the future home of Israel and all others who will be saved after the Rapture.

During the Tribulation Period, the kings of the earth will take their wealth to Babylon and commit fornication with the harlot (Revelation 17:9–10). During eternity, the kings of the earth will take glory and honor to the New Jerusalem and worship God.

Always Open

REVELATION 21:25 *Its gates shall not be shut at all by day (there shall be no night there). (NKJV)*

The people of some ancient cities opened their gates during the day and closed them at night. The continuous presence of God in the Holy City will mean the continuous presence of light. Darkness will not be known, thereby eliminating any need to <u>shut the gates</u>.

Gifts of Glory and Honor

REVELATION 21:26 *And they shall bring the glory and the honor of the nations into it. (NKJV)*

Visitors will go to the Holy City to give glory and honor to the Lord.

Only Those in the Lamb's Book of Life

REVELATION 21:27 *But there shall by no means enter it anything that defiles, or causes an abomination or a lie, but only those who are written in the Lamb's Book of Life. (NKJV)*

When God created Adam and Eve he placed them in his perfect creation, the Garden of <u>Eden</u>. Then he allowed <u>Satan</u> to enter and tempt them and they fell. God will never allow this to happen again. He will never allow any impure thing to enter the Holy City. Only those with their names found in the Lamb's Book of Life will be permitted to enter.

Chapter Wrap-Up

- God will create a new heaven and a new earth because the old ones will pass away. (Revelation 21:1)

- God will send the Holy City, New Jerusalem, to the new earth. He will dwell among his people and wipe away every tear from their eyes. (Revelation 21:2–4)

- Everyone who rejected God during their lifetime will be cast into the Lake of Fire, which is the second death. (Revelation 21:8)

- New Jerusalem will be built on twelve foundations and have twelve gates. It will be laid out like a square and be made of pure gold and precious stones. (Revelation 21:9–21)

- New Jerusalem will not have a temple because God and Christ will be the temple. Likewise, the city will not need a sun because the Father and Son will be the light. (Revelation 21:22–25)

Study Questions

1. Why do you think John was told to "write, for these words are true and faithful" (Revelation 21:5 NKJV)?

2. Why do you think Jesus can give the water of life?

3. When will the Holy City with the streets of gold come down to earth, and how far down will it come?

4. What is the significance of having the names of the twelve tribes of Israel on the twelve gates of the Holy City?

5. Why will nothing impure, shameful, or deceitful be allowed to enter the Holy City?

Revelation 22

Chapter Highlights:
- River of Water of Life
- Curse Lifted
- A Final Call
- A Final Warning
- A Final Promise

Let's Get Started

This is the last chapter in the Bible's final book. The first five verses continue the theme of the previous chapter: a comparison of the original creation with the new creation. The final sixteen verses have two main themes: (1) the book of Revelation is a book of prophecy, and (2) the Second Coming of Jesus is imminent.

living water
John 4:13–14

Paradise was lost by Adam and Eve, but Paradise was regained by God. Some say most, if not all, Bible prophecy has been fulfilled including the Book of Revelation. Five times, God says the Book of Revelation is a book of prophecy, not history (Revelation 1:3; 22:7, 10, 18, 19). Some ask, where is the promise of his coming? Six times Jesus says he is coming (Revelation 2:5, 13; 3:11; 22:7, 12, 20).

River of Water of Life

> **REVELATION 22:1** *And he showed me a pure river of water of life, clear as crystal, proceeding from the throne of God and of the Lamb.* (NKJV)

John is still comparing the original creation to the new creation. He is either contrasting the river that flowed in the Garden of Eden and under the walls of Babylon to the river that will flow from the throne of God in New Jerusalem, or he is contrasting the life-giving water that flowed through the famous Hanging Gardens to that which will flow from the throne. Slaves turned screws to lift water from the Euphrates River to be released at the top of terraces to flow down through the trees and flowers in the garden.

Up to this point, the angel has been showing John the city's basic framework: foundations, walls, gates, and a street. The Holy City, however, will also contain other things such as water, trees, and fruit. Here we see that it will have a river called the "river of water of life." In other verses of Scripture, this water of life is called <u>living water</u>, and it is used as a symbol for the Holy Spirit.

life-giving
John 3:1–8

Holy Spirit
John 7:37–39

Eden
Genesis 3:22–24

ate
Luke 24:30–43

God is using a physical substance (water) to help explain a spiritual truth. Living water flows pure, clear, and fresh. It is not murky, stagnant, or polluted. It possesses <u>life-giving</u> qualities that man cannot live without. The river of the water of life is portrayed as a river that will possess life-giving powers; water that will restore and refresh, flow in abundance, and satisfy our thirst.

The source of this river will be the throne of God and of the Lamb. They will supply life-giving water and the <u>Holy Spirit</u> in abundance to the Holy City. The Trinity (the Father, Son, and Holy Spirit) will be present to meet all our needs.

> **what others say**
>
> **Leon Morris**
>
> For the third time in this section John adds *and of the Lamb* to his reference to God. He will not let us miss the supreme significance of the Lamb in the final state of things.[1]

"I will give of the fountain of the water of life freely to him who thirsts" (Revelation 21:6 NKJV).

Tree of Life

REVELATION 22:2 *In the middle of its street, and on either side of the river, was the tree of life, which bore twelve fruits, each tree yielding its fruit every month. The leaves of the tree were for the healing of the nations. (NKJV)*

Those who entered ancient Babylon saw the beautiful hanging gardens of Babylon, one of the seven wonders of the world. Those who enter New Jerusalem will see something more beautiful.

Picture a street of pure gold like transparent glass. It will have mansions of gold on each side and a river of crystal clear water flowing down the middle with rows of trees on each side. This is the magnificent scene John is trying to describe.

The tree of life takes us back to the Garden of <u>Eden</u>. Before they sinned, Adam and Eve could have eaten from it and lived forever. In the New Jerusalem, rows of the tree of life will grow. The trees will produce a different kind of fruit every month, which will provide a continuous supply of food from God. This says something about the heavenly bodies. Just as Jesus <u>ate</u> and drank after being raised from the dead, believers will eat and drink in the Holy City.

Believers will diet on manna and fruit from the tree of life. They will not eat the leaves of the tree because the leaves will be for the healing of those who dwell on the new earth. These leaves will sustain life and add to well-being.

curse
Genesis 3:14–19

> ### what others say
>
> **Henry M. Morris**
>
> Most prominent of all is a mighty river of clear sparkling water, coursing down from the center and apex of the city. Although the text does not say so, we are probably justified in inferring that this river (like the river in Eden which was its typological forerunner) parts "into four heads" (Genesis 2:10), which in turn descend from level to level, providing abundant water for every need (aesthetic as well as physiological) of the residents of the city.[2]

The Tree of Knowledge caused Adam and Eve to know right from wrong. It is how they learned what sin was. It caused their spiritual death (separation of their soul and spirit from God) and their physical death (separation of their soul and spirit from the body). It cost them immortality. The Tree of Life does the opposite. Eating its fruit brings immortality.

"To him who overcomes I will give to eat from the tree of life, which is in the midst of the Paradise of God" (Revelation 2:7 NKJV).

"To him who overcomes I will give some of the hidden manna to eat" (Revelation 2:17 NKJV).

The Curse Lifted

> REVELATION 22:3 *And there shall be no more curse, but the throne of God and of the Lamb shall be in it, and His servants shall serve Him. (NKJV)*

When Adam and Eve sinned, God placed a <u>curse</u> upon creation: Because of it, women experience pain in childbirth, both men and women suffer sickness, both must today work for a living, and physical and spiritual death came upon mankind. Sin has caused great harm in this present creation, but it will not affect the new creation. Once God has cast Satan with all his followers into hell, and raised us with new bodies to dwell in his constant presence, all of the curse will be gone.

Moses
Exodus 33:18–23

Philip
John 14:8–9

see the face of our Father
1 John 3:2

The Holy City will be the new location of God's throne. We will not be floating on clouds with harps in our hands, but instead we will be praising and serving our God.

> **what others say**
>
> **Robert H. Mounce**
>
> God has, through the redemption wrought by his Son, set into motion a new humanity. In the present age he rules the hearts of all who have turned to him in faith: in the age to come that reign will find its full completion. Sin will be forever removed and the design of Eden will be totally realized.[3]

In the New Jerusalem there will be no more:

1. death, mourning, crying, or pain (Revelation 21:4)

2. temple (Revelation 21:22)

3. sun or moon (Revelation 21:23)

4. night (Revelation 21:25)

5. impure, shameful, or deceitful thoughts (Revelation 21:27)

6. curse (Revelation 22:3)

"[You] have made us kings and priests to our God; and we shall reign on the earth" (Revelation 5:10 NKJV).

See God's Face

> REVELATION 22:4 *They shall see His face, and His name shall be on their foreheads. (NKJV)*

In the Old Testament, it was <u>Moses</u> who wanted to see the face of God. In the New Testament, it was <u>Philip</u>. God did not allow them to see his face, because if they did, they would die. However, as residents of the Holy City, we will actually <u>see the face of our Father</u> and his Son. The name of God will be written on believers' foreheads to identify them as God's own.

A name stands for much or little, depending upon whose it is. The name of the Antichrist on the foreheads of his followers will bring them everlasting torment. The name of God on the foreheads of his followers is the greatest name of all. It stands for his character, honor, glory, faithfulness, and much more. It means he is staking his reputation on that person.

"I will write on him the name of My God" (Revelation 3:12 NKJV).

No More Night

REVELATION 22:5 *There shall be no night there: They need no lamp nor light of the sun, for the Lord God gives them light. And they shall reign forever and ever. (NKJV)*

This is the second time we have been told there will be no night in the Holy City. Lamps, lightbulbs, and flashlights will not be needed. We will not need the sun for heat or to grow our crops. God and Jesus will light the entire creation. They will be all that is needed, and believers will have the honor and privilege of reigning with them forever.

what others say

Randall Price

The city qualifies in every sense as a physical reality, with measurable architectural structures, planned design, building materials, rivers, trees, and human inhabitants. What appears to be an incredible description is intended to accommodate our present inability to grasp such heavenly realities. An eternal city designed for an eternal people is not of earth, and as the handiwork of an infinite God, we should not expect it to conform to human convention.[4]

The Truth Is Found Here

REVELATION 22:6 *Then he said to me, "These words are faithful and true." And the Lord God of the holy prophets sent His angel to show His servants the things which must shortly take place. (NKJV)*

This marks a turning point in this final chapter. John now turns from the contrast of the original creation with the new creation to some closing promises and warnings. The angel reminded John of the truthfulness of these words. He is giving his assurance that this prophecy is trustworthy and will be fulfilled.

go to

spiritual understanding
Colossians 1:9

unsaved
unbelievers (those who have not accepted Jesus as their Savior)

The angel also reminded John of how this message was given. The Lord Jesus sent his angel to give the prophets <u>spiritual understanding</u>. In other words, Jesus is the source of this revelation, and because he is, it must be fulfilled.

The things that must soon take place have already started. In fact, the first part of this prophecy (Revelation), the Church Age, is almost over. Everything from the Rapture to the Second Coming is near at hand.

"These things says the Amen, the Faithful and True Witness" (Revelation 3:14 NKJV).

> **what others say**
>
> ### J. Vernon McGee
>
> "These words are faithful and true" means that no man is to trifle with them by spiritualizing them or reducing them to meaningless symbols. Our Lord is talking about reality.[5]

In the Blink of an Eye

REVELATION 22:7 *"Behold, I am coming quickly! Blessed is he who keeps the words of the prophecy of this book." (NKJV)*

"Behold, I am coming quickly" can be interpreted in at least two ways: soon or shortly, or suddenly. Soon or shortly means before long. Suddenly means very fast. This is significant because people get the wrong impression when we say, "Jesus will come very soon." What we should say is, "When he comes, it will happen very fast, in the blink of an eye."

Many people wonder why prophecy is so important. It's importance does not lie in predicting the future, but rather, in the changing of our lives, by giving us a desire and concern for the lost and **unsaved**. The fact is, God means for prophecy to be obeyed, and those who do obey are promised a blessing.

"Blessed is he who reads and those who hear the words of this prophecy, and keep those things which are written in it; for the time is near" (Revelation 1:3 NKJV).

Overcome with Awe

REVELATION 22:8 *Now I, John, saw and heard these things. And when I heard and saw, I fell down to worship before the feet of the angel who showed me these things. (NKJV)*

John is repeating his claim that he is the human author of Revelation, and that he both saw and heard the things he writes about. He was so impressed with the angel that revealed these things to him, that he was overcome with awe, and fell down to worship at the angel's feet.

seal them up
Daniel 12:4

God Alone

> **REVELATION 22:9** *Then he said to me, "See that you do not do that. For I am your fellow servant, and of your brethren the prophets, and of those who keep the words of this book. Worship God." (NKJV)*

This is the second time an angel told John not to worship him. Angels are servants of God, the same as John and the prophets are servants of God. It is a mistake to worship angels. Only God is worthy of worship.

"And I fell at his feet to worship him. But he said to me, 'See that you do not do that! I am your fellow servant, and of your brethren who have the testimony of Jesus. Worship God!'" (Revelation 19:10 NKJV).

Leave It Open

> **REVELATION 22:10** *And he said to me, "Do not seal the words of the prophecy of this book, for the time is at hand. (NKJV)*

When Daniel wrote his prophecy several hundred years before the birth of Christ, he did not understand some of the things God had shown him. He wanted an explanation, but the fulfillment of his prophecies was a long time off, so he was told to <u>seal them up</u> until the end time.

Revelation is different. John's prophecy was already unfolding, and the Church Age was taking hold. For this reason, the message was to be left unsealed. God wants people to hear these things now.

A Great Chasm

> **REVELATION 22:11** *He who is unjust, let him be unjust still; he who is filthy, let him be filthy still; he who is righteous, let him be righteous still; he who is holy, let him be holy still." (NKJV)*

go to

gulf
Luke 16:26

quality of work
1 Corinthians
3:11–15

eternal day
the great day of
one's final judgment

gulf
the great impassable
region that separates
heaven from hell

The time will come when a person's final destiny will be determined and sealed forever. When the **eternal day** dawns, all unbelievers will be condemned and cast into the Lake of Fire. They will be without hope because their eternal condition will never change. On the other hand, all believers will be accepted and given entrance to the Holy City where they will continue to grow and improve. Hope and holiness will always be theirs.

This is a warning regarding the separation of the lost and the saved. A great **gulf** will separate the Lake of Fire from the Holy City that no one can cross. The decisions people make in this life will determine their destiny and seal it forever.

Heaven or Hell

REVELATION 22:12 *"And behold, I am coming quickly, and My reward is with Me, to give to every one according to his work. (NKJV)*

This is a repeat of Christ's personal promise that he will return, and when he does, he will bring rewards with him. He will separate the lost from the saved, and everyone will receive rewards according to the quality of work they have done.

Not much is said in Church about rewards. For the most part it is a neglected message. No one deserves rewards, but we know they will be given because this verse says so. If we would let the goodness of God sink in, most of us would do more to honor him, and follow the advice of the apostle John: "Look to yourselves, that we do not lose those things we worked for, but that we may receive a full reward" (2 John 8 NKJV).

The All in All

REVELATION 22:13 *I am the Alpha and the Omega, the Beginning and the End, the First and the Last." (NKJV)*

Jesus is using three of his titles to identify himself with the Father. He has used them several times <u>before</u>. No one else can use them because they assert his deity. Explain it? No one can. It must be taken by faith.

before
Revelation 1:8, 17;
2:8; 21:6

Sermon on the Mount
Matthew 5–7

Beatitudes
Matthew 5:3–10

Beatitudes
proclamations of
blessing(s)

Heavenly Laundry?

REVELATION 22:14 *Blessed are those who do His commandments, that they may have the right to the tree of life, and may enter through the gates into the city. (NKJV)*

Christ's words here imply a choice between washing our robes or leaving them dirty. Those who choose to wash their robes and therefore accept Christ will be blessed with two rewards: access to the tree of life, and permission to pass through the gates of the Holy City. Those who leave their robes dirty by refusing to accept Christ will be rejecting his rewards.

The <u>Sermon on the Mount</u> is one of the most popular and best-known teachings of Jesus. It begins with several principles Christians call the **Beatitudes**. Revelation also contains some Beatitudes, but very few people are aware of it.

The Beatitudes in Revelation

Beatitude	Scripture
"Blessed is he who reads and those who hear the words of this prophecy, and keep those things which are written it"	Revelation 1:3 NKJV
"Blessed are the dead who die in the Lord from now on"	Revelation 14:13 NKJV
"Blessed is he who watches, and keeps his garments, lest he walk naked and they see his shame"	Revelation 16:15 NKJV
"Blessed are those who are called to the marriage supper of the Lamb!"	Revelation 19:9 NKJV
"Blessed and holy is he who has part in the first resurrection. Over such the second death has no power, but they shall be priests of God and of Christ, and shall reign with Him a thousand years"	Revelation 20:6 NKJV
"Blessed is he who keeps the words of the prophecy of this book"	Revelation 22:7 NKJV
"Blessed are those who do His commandments, that they may have the right to the tree of life, and may enter through the gates into the city"	Revelation 22:14 NKJV

David
Jeremiah 33:15

Star
Numbers 24:17;
Revelation 2:28

Access Denied

REVELATION 22:15 *But outside are dogs and sorcerers and sexually immoral and murderers and idolaters, and whoever loves and practices a lie. (NKJV)*

Jesus is providing his own list of those who will not be blessed with access to the tree of life and the Holy City. Instead of fruit from the tree of life, the dogs (those involved in the occult, sexual immorality, idolatry, and lying) will eat the garbage of hell. Instead of access to the Holy City, these dogs will scavenge in the Lake of Fire.

"But the cowardly, unbelieving, abominable, murderers, sexually immoral, sorcerers, idolaters, and all liars shall have their part in the lake which burns with fire and brimstone" (Revelation 21:8 NKJV).

A Star from David

REVELATION 22:16 *"I, Jesus, have sent My angel to testify to you these things in the churches. I am the Root and the Offspring of David, the Bright and Morning Star." (NKJV)*

Here Jesus reiterates the first two verses of chapter 1 by saying that Revelation is a testimony he gave to an angel for delivery to the churches.

"The Root and the Offspring of <u>David</u>" comes from the Old Testament and is a reference to the Messiah. Jesus is the Messiah.

"The Bright and Morning <u>Star</u>" comes from both the Old and New Testaments. Jesus is identifying himself as the One who will appear near the end of earth's darkest hour (Tribulation Period). He alone will bring a brighter day to the world (Millennium).

> **what others say**
>
> **Henry M. Morris**
> The claim is actually that of being the God/man. There is no other way that one could be both an ancestor and descendant of the same person.[7]

The Seven "I Am's" in Revelation

I Am	Scripture
"I am the Alpha and the Omega, the Beginning and the End," says the Lord, "who is, and who was, and who is to come, the Almighty"	Revelation 1:8 (NKJV)
"I am the Alpha and the Omega, the First and the Last"	Revelation 1:11 (NKJV)
"I am the First and the Last"	Revelation 1:17 (NKJV)
"I am He who lives, and was dead, and behold, I am alive for evermore"	Revelation 1:18 (NKJV)
"I am the Alpha and the Omega, the Beginning and the End"	Revelation 21:6 (NKJV)
"I am the Alpha and the Omega, the Beginning and the End, the First and the Last"	Revelation 22:13 (NKJV)
"I am the Root and the Offspring of David, and the Bright and Morning Star"	Revelation 22:16 (NKJV)

Come!

> REVELATION 22:17 *And the Spirit and the bride say, "Come!" And let him who hears say, "Come!" And let him who thirsts come. Whoever desires, let him take the water of life freely. (NKJV)*

This is God's final call. It is a call for all believers to "come!" and a call for all believers to tell all unbelievers to "come!" The Holy Spirit works in and through the Bride of Christ (the Church), using them to invite all unbelievers to come to Jesus and drink of his salvation, the water of life.

Let him who thirsts come! Those who are tired of living without Jesus should come! God invites all who desire to receive his free gift of salvation through his Son, Jesus, to come!

Nothing New

> REVELATION 22:18 *For I testify to everyone who hears the words of the prophecy of this book: If anyone adds to these things, God will add to him the plagues that are written in this book; (NKJV)*

Revelation was given by God, and it is his word alone. He alone has authority over it. Anyone who adds anything new to the words of Revelation will feel the wrath of God upon him.

There are religious groups today that teach God is love, but refute the message of salvation, the wrath of God, the judgment of God,

Ananias and Sapphira
Acts 5:1–11

the Tribulation Period, and hell. Wouldn't you call this adding and taking away from the Word of God? Here are some examples:

1. Jesus is really the Archangel Michael (Jehovah's Witnesses).

2. Hell is really the grave (Jehovah's Witnesses).

3. God, rather than Jesus, was once a mortal human being (Mormons).

4. Worthy humans are going to become gods and goddesses (Mormons).

5. God is a cosmic force, not a personal being (New Age).

6. Eve's sin was a sexual affair with Satan (Moonies).

If God struck down <u>Ananias and Sapphira</u> for introducing sin into the early Church, what do you think he will do with those who do it today?

<u>Nothing Less</u>

REVELATION 22:19 *and if anyone takes away from the words of the book of this prophecy, God shall take away his part from the Book of Life, from the holy city, and from the things which are written in this book. (NKJV)*

Taking away from this book brings on a second part to God's warning. Anyone who deletes anything from this book risks having his share in the tree of life and Holy City erased. Those who do delete something prove not only that they do not love God or believe in his Word, but that they are destined for the Lake of Fire as well.

A Book of Prophecy, Not History

Prophecy	Scripture
"Blessed is he who reads and those who hear the words of this prophecy, and keep those things which are written in it"	Revelation 1:3 (NKJV)
"Blessed is he who keeps the words of the prophecy of this book"	Revelation 22:7 (NKJV)
"Do not seal the words of the prophecy of this book"	Revelation 22:10 (NKJV)

A Book of Prophecy, Not History (cont'd)

Prophecy	Scripture
"For I testify to everyone who hears the words of the prophecy of this book: If anyone adds to these things, God will add to him the plagues that are written in this book"	Revelation 22:18 (NKJV)
"And if anyone takes away from the words of the book of this prophecy, God shall take away his part from the Book of Life, from the holy city, and from the things which are written in this book"	Revelation 22:19 (NKJV)

go to

grace makes salvation possible
Ephesians 2:8

One Last Promise

REVELATION 22:20 *He who testifies to these things says, "Surely I am coming quickly." Amen. Even so, come, Lord Jesus! (NKJV)*

"I am coming quickly" is his final promise! In answer to this promise of the Lord's return, John responds, "Amen. Even so, come, Lord Jesus!" This is a statement of John's personal belief, and he urges Jesus to come back.

A Final Note of Grace

REVELATION 22:21 *The grace of our Lord Jesus Christ be with you all. Amen. (NKJV)*

These last words of the Bible serve as a reminder that <u>grace makes salvation possible</u>. Grace will keep us out of the Lake of Fire, and let us pass through the gates of the Holy City.

Grace is **G**od's **R**iches **A**t **C**hrist's **E**xpense. "Grace to you and peace from Him who is and who was and who is to come, and from the seven spirits who are before His throne" (Revelation 1:4 NKJV).

Facts about salvation:

- Everyone needs it (Romans 3:23).
- Everyone can have it (John 3:16).
- Only Jesus can give it (John 14:6).
- Only believers receive it (John 3:36).

something to ponder

Chapter Wrap-Up

- The River of Life will flow from the Throne of God through the Holy City. On each side of the river will be the tree of life. (Revelation 22:1–2)

- The curse of the original sin caused by the fall of Adam and Eve will be lifted when God makes everything new. God will once again dwell among his people and be the light for their feet. (Revelation 22:3–5)

- The Spirit and bride call anyone who is thirsty to come and drink freely from the water of life. (Revelation 22:17)

- A final warning goes to anyone who adds to or detracts from Revelation. Those who do not heed this warning face the plagues contained therein. (Revelation 22:18–19)

- Christ has a final promise for all who read Revelation: He is coming soon. (Revelation 22:20)

Study Questions

1. What will believers have on their foreheads in heaven?

2. What can a person do to be blessed by God?

3. How do we know the words of Revelation are true?

4. What was John's mistake that we read about in this chapter?

5. Who will have access to the tree of life and the Holy City?

Appendix A - Time Lines

Time Line #1

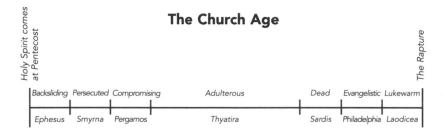

The Church Age

Backsliding	Persecuted	Compromising	Adulterous	Dead	Evangelistic	Lukewarm
Ephesus	Smyrna	Pergamos	Thyatira	Sardis	Philadelphia	Laodicea

Holy Spirit comes at Pentecost ... *The Rapture*

Time Line #2

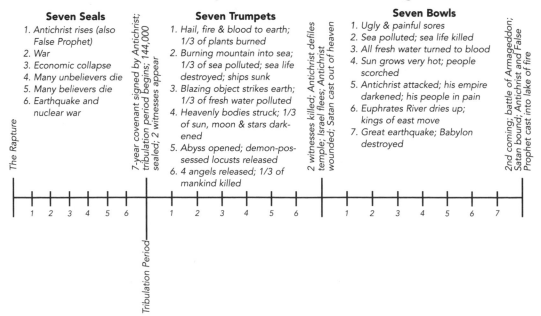

From the Rapture to the Second Coming

Seven Seals
1. Antichrist rises (also False Prophet)
2. War
3. Economic collapse
4. Many unbelievers die
5. Many believers die
6. Earthquake and nuclear war

Seven Trumpets
1. Hail, fire & blood to earth; 1/3 of plants burned
2. Burning mountain into sea; 1/3 of sea polluted; sea life destroyed; ships sunk
3. Blazing object strikes earth; 1/3 of fresh water polluted
4. Heavenly bodies struck; 1/3 of sun, moon & stars darkened
5. Abyss opened; demon-possessed locusts released
6. 4 angels released; 1/3 of mankind killed

Seven Bowls
1. Ugly & painful sores
2. Sea polluted; sea life killed
3. All fresh water turned to blood
4. Sun grows very hot; people scorched
5. Antichrist attacked; his empire darkened; his people in pain
6. Euphrates River dries up; kings of east move
7. Great earthquake; Babylon destroyed

The Rapture

7-year covenant signed by Antichrist; tribulation period begins; 144,000 sealed; 2 witnesses appear

2 witnesses killed; Antichrist defiles temple; Israel flees; Antichrist wounded; Satan cast out of heaven

2nd coming; battle of Armageddon; Satan bound; Antichrist and False Prophet cast into lake of fire

Tribulation Period

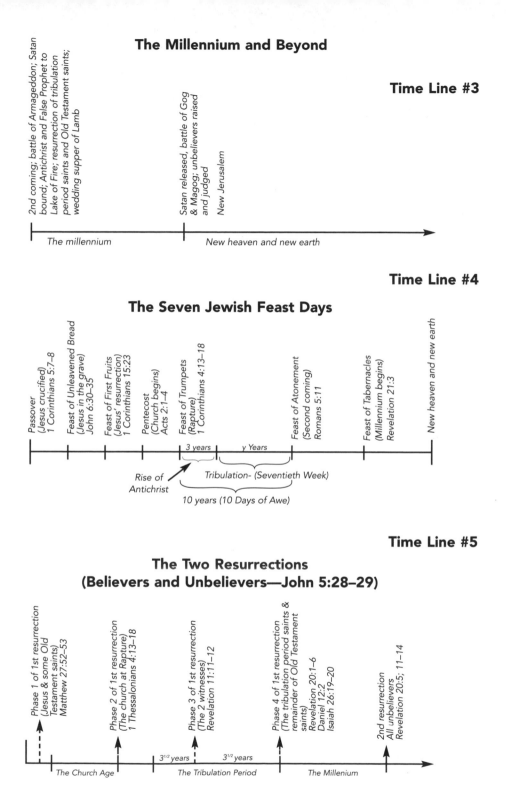

The Millennium and Beyond

2nd coming; battle of Armageddon; Satan bound; Antichrist and False Prophet to Lake of Fire; resurrection of tribulation period saints and Old Testament saints; wedding supper of Lamb

Satan released, battle of Gog & Magog; unbelievers raised and judged

New Jerusalem

The millennium | New heaven and new earth

Time Line #4

The Seven Jewish Feast Days

Passover
(Jesus crucified)
1 Corinthians 5:7–8

Feast of Unleavened Bread
(Jesus in the grave)
John 6:30–35

Feast of First Fruits
(Jesus' resurrection)
1 Corinthians 15:23

Pentecost
(Church begins)
Acts 2:1–4

Feast of Trumpets
(Rapture)
1 Corinthians 4:13–18

Feast of Atonement
(Second coming)
Romans 5:11

Feast of Tabernacles
(Millennium begins)
Revelation 21:3

New heaven and new earth

3 years | y Years

Rise of Antichrist

Tribulation- (Seventieth Week)

10 years (10 Days of Awe)

Time Line #5

The Two Resurrections
(Believers and Unbelievers—John 5:28–29)

Phase 1 of 1st resurrection
(Jesus & some Old Testament saints)
Matthew 27:52–53

Phase 2 of 1st resurrection
(The church at Rapture)
1 Thessalonians 4:13–18

Phase 3 of 1st resurrection
(The 2 witnesses)
Revelation 11:11–12

Phase 4 of 1st resurrection
(The tribulation period saints & remainder of Old Testament saints)
Revelation 20:1–6
Daniel 12:2
Isaiah 26:19–20

2nd resurrection
All unbelievers
Revelation 20:5; 11–14

The Church Age | 3¹/² years | The Tribulation Period | 3¹/² years | The Millenium

Appendix B - The Answers

CHAPTER ONE

1. An angel delivered it to John. (Revelation 1:1)

2. No, because it was given by the one who loves us and died for us. (Revelation 1:5)

3. Everyone alive plus the dead who crucified him. (Revelation 1:7)

4. The good and bad qualities of each church are ideal for instructing all of God's people. (Revelation 1:11)

5. The high priest represents Jesus, who intercedes on our behalf. (Revelation 1:13)

CHAPTER TWO

1. They forsook their first love. (Revelation 2:4)

2. They would be persecuted and tested. (Revelation 2:10)

3. They remained true to the gospel even though they were in a city with many pagan temples. (Revelation 2:13)

4. They tolerated Jezebel, a false prophetess, who led many people into sexual immorality. (Revelation 2:20)

5. Let us hear the call to repent and learn these words so that we don't make these same mistakes. (Revelation 2:29)

CHAPTER THREE

1. They had a reputation for being alive but were really dead. (Revelation 3:1)

2. Several of their church members were not true believers. (Revelation 3:9)

3. They were lukewarm—neither totally for Christ or totally against him. (Revelation 3:16)

4. The letter to the church at Laodicea. (Revelation 3:14–22)

5. Be earnest, repent, and open the door to your heart. (Revelation 3:19–20)

CHAPTER FOUR

1. "Come up here, and I will show you things which must take place after this." (Revelation 4:1 NKJV)

2. Jasper and sardius. (Revelation 4:3)

3. Robes of white and crowns of gold. (Revelation 4:4)

4. The seven spirits of God. (Revelation 4:5)

5. We should lay our crowns of pride, selfishness, and control before the throne as a deliberate act of submission to God's power. (Revelation 4:10)

CHAPTER FIVE

1. The destiny of all mankind will be affected by the scroll. (Revelation 5:1–2)

2. The first time he came as a sacrificial Lamb. The second time he will come as the Lion of the Tribe of Judah. (Revelation 5:5, 12)

3. Up until the Rapture, God has been dealing with man as a lamb because he is giving us every opportunity to repent. After the Rapture he will deal with man as a lion. (Revelation 5:7–8)

4. We have been made a kingdom and priests to serve our God. (Revelation 5:10)

5. There are several reasons: the angels proclaim it along with the living creatures, twenty-four elders, and even the dead. (Revelation 6:11–14)

CHAPTER SIX

1. A bow, but no arrows. (Revelation 6:2)

2. The power to take peace from the earth and to make men slay each other. (Revelation 6:4)

3. The equivalent of a day's wages. (Revelation 6:6)

4. The rider is named Death. He will be followed by Hades. (Revelation 6:8)

CHAPTER SEVEN

1. They will hold back the winds from the four points of the earth. God is still giving people a chance to repent. (Revelation 7:1)

2. They will preach salvation through the blood of the Lamb. The Jews will finally accept Jesus as the Messiah. (Revelation 7:10)

3. Blessing, glory, wisdom, thanksgiving, honor, power, and might. Because God made the sinner's salvation possible. (Revelation 7:12)

4. The twenty-four elders represent Christians of the Church Age. The Tribulation Saints are those saved after the Rapture. (Revelation 7:13–14)

5. Yes, but once in heaven they will never suffer again. (Revelation 7:16)

CHAPTER EIGHT

1. God is a patient God, and he is giving people time to repent. (Revelation 8:1, 4)

2. The death of his Son, who died for the sins of the world. (Revelation 8:3)

3. To avenge the death of the Tribulation Saints and to symbolize God's wrath. (Revelation 8:5)

4. God has rained destruction on Egypt and Sodom and Gomorrah, so there is no reason to believe he won't do it again. (Revelation 8:7)

CHAPTER NINE

1. To show mankind that God is in control of our destinies and to turn some hearts back to him. (Revelation 9:4–6)

2. Their faces will resemble human faces. (Revelation 9:7)

3. The Hebrew and Greek names indicate that the locusts will attack Jews and Gentiles. The double name also indicates a double warning of the pain and suffering the locusts will inflict. (Revelation 9:11)

4. Someone speaking for the martyred saints. (Revelation 9:13)

5. Demon worship, idolatry, murder, sorcery, sexual immorality, and theft. (Revelation 9:20–21)

CHAPTER TEN

1. He has been in the presence of God. (Revelation 10:1)

2. God. (Revelation 10:3)

3. Some of the mysteries include: mystery of lawlessness, the mystery of the Rapture, mystery of Israel's blindness, mystery of God's wisdom, mystery of Christ and the Church, mystery of Christ in us, mystery of the kingdom of heaven, and mystery of godliness. (Revelation 10:7)

4. The two commissions are to assimilate the Word of God into our lives by doing what the Bible says and to spread the Word of God to all peoples, nations, languages, and kings. (Revelation 10:9–11)

CHAPTER ELEVEN

1. Because it has been given to the Gentiles. (Revelation 11:2)

2. An olive tree and a lampstand represent each witness. The olive tree symbolizes that the witnesses are filled with the Holy Spirit, while the lampstand symbolizes that the witnesses will be lights in a dark world. (Revelation 11:4)

3. Because it will be full of wickedness. (Revelation 11:8)

4. The death of the two witnesses. (Revelation 11:10)

5. The death and resurrection of the two witnesses closely parallels the death and resurrection of Jesus. Jesus was crucified but rose from the dead a few days later. The witnesses will be killed, but God will breathe life into them several days later. Another similarity is the ascension of Jesus after his resurrection and the rapture of the witnesses after their resurrection. One last parallel is the earthquake that occurred when Jesus died and the earthquake that will occur when the two witnesses are raptured.

CHAPTER TWELVE

1. A woman and an enormous red dragon. The woman is the nation of Israel at its beginning, and the dragon is Satan. The dragon's seven heads represent the seven Gentile world governments, while the ten horns represent ten kings that will reign during the Tribulation. The seven crowns mean the Antichrist will subdue three of those ten kings. (Revelation 12:1–3)

2. 1,260 days equal 3 and a half years and correspond to the last half of the Tribulation Period when the Jews will flee from Satan to the place God has prepared for them. (Revelation 12:6)

3. Michael. (Revelation 12:7)

4. To the earth. Because he has lost his place in heaven. (Revelation 12:9–10)

5. Believers have three ways to overcome Satan: (1) trust in the blood of the Lamb,

(2) acknowledge faith in Jesus, and (3) not fear death. (Revelation 12:11)

CHAPTER THIRTEEN

1. Yes. (Revelation 13:7)

2. The False Prophet will perform great deeds. (Revelation 13:12, 13)

3. Patience and faith—many will be captured, killed, experience famine, pestilence, etc. (Revelation 13:10)

4. No. It is the mark, number, or name of the Antichrist. (Revelation 13:17)

CHAPTER FOURTEEN

1. He heard something like rushing water and loud peals of thunder. This is actually the heavenly multitude singing a new song for the 144,000 who have been redeemed. (Revelation 14:2)

2. Those who die in the Lord will leave their grief and torment behind, enter heaven, and sit in God's presence. (Revelation 14:13)

3. Jesus will reap the first harvest and angels will do the other one. During these harvests the wicked will be taken and thrown into the Lake of Fire. (Revelation 14:14–18)

4. It implies the wicked will be destroyed beyond recognition. There will be nothing left of their former selves. (Revelation 14:19–20)

CHAPTER FIFTEEN

1. We have a concept of angels doing good deeds, but these angels will do deeds of destruction as they pour out the wrath of God. (Revelation 15:1)

2. No! He would be unjust and unrighteous if he did not punish sin, avenge his people, or avenge his name. (Revelation 15:3–4)

3. Jesus is the only One who lived by all of God's standards, the only sinless person to ever live. (Revelation 15:4)

4. The wrath of God. (Revelation 15:7)

5. To keep everyone out. (Revelation 15:8)

CHAPTER SIXTEEN

1. A voice from the temple—Jesus. (Revelation 16:1)

2. Because they shed the blood of the saints and prophets. (Revelation 16:6)

3. His kingdom will be plunged into darkness, and men will gnaw their tongues in agony. (Revelation 16:10)

4. Those who watch for Jesus and keep their garments. (Revelation 16:15)

5. They will perform miraculous signs. It will be a time of great deception. Not all miracles are good miracles. (Revelation 16:14)

CHAPTER SEVENTEEN

1. She is the mother of harlots and of the abominations of the earth—a great ecumenical religious system. (Revelation 17:5)

2. He was in the Spirit. Capital "S" means he was under the influence of the Holy Spirit when he had this vision. (Revelation 17:3)

3. Her clothing indicates wealth and an alliance with the world leaders. The golden cup indicates an attempt to appear righteous, take Communion, and simulate the true Church. (Revelation 17:4)

4. A "mind which has wisdom" is one that can interpret the things of God and understand the prophecies and symbols. It is obtained by studying the Scriptures. (Revelation 17:9)

5. God. (Revelation 17:17)

CHAPTER EIGHTEEN

1. All of them. (Revelation 18:3)

2. She will be paid double from her own cup, given torture and grief to match the glory and luxury she gives herself. She will reap what she sows. (Revelation 18:6–7)

3. Sorcery, astrology, and cultic practices. These are very prominent today. (Revelation 18:23)

4. The prophets, saints, and all who are killed on earth. Babylon's rich and powerful will promote policies that will cause the death of these people. (Revelation 18:24)

5. Magic. (Revelation 18:23)

CHAPTER NINETEEN

1. Yes. (Revelation 19:6)

2. The testimony of Jesus. His predictions about: future events, his death, burial, resurrection, end-times, plagues, deception, and false Christs. (Revelation 19:10)

3. The Church, angels, Tribulation Period Saints, and Old Testament Saints. (Revelation 19:14)

4. He will deceive people with miraculous signs, and he will do it to get them to receive the mark of the Beast and to worship his image. (Revelation 19:20)

5. All those who take the mark of the Beast and worship his image. (Revelation 19:21)

CHAPTER TWENTY

1. They will refuse to worship the beast or his image and refuse to take his mark on their foreheads or their hands. (Revelation 20:4)

2. They will be priests of God and of Christ and will reign with him for a thousand years. (Revelation 20:6)

3. By what they have done as recorded in the books. (Revelation 20:12)

4. Yes. They will be judged according to what they have done. (Revelation 20:12–13)

5. Because their names cannot be found in the Book of Life. (Revelation 20:15)

CHAPTER TWENTY-ONE

1. Some may doubt the importance or significance of Revelation. Some do not believe in the Rapture, Tribulation Period, Second Coming, or wrath of God. These are the words of one who cannot lie. (Revelation 21:5)

2. All authority is his. He gained the authority and paid the price when he died on the cross. (Revelation 21:6)

3. The Holy City will come down after the new earth is created, but no one knows how far down it will come. (Revelation 21:10)

4. The twelve names will be a reminder to all who enter the city that the Messiah, Scriptures, and salvation came through the Jews. (Revelation 21:12)

5. God allowed Satan to defile the present creation, but he will never let that happen again. (Revelation 21:19–27)

CHAPTER TWENTY-TWO

1. The name of God. (Revelation 22:4)

2. They can keep the words of this book by obeying what it says. (Revelation 22:7)

3. Because John testifies to everything contained in Revelation. (Revelation 22:8)

4. He fell down to worship an angel. (Revelation 22:8)

5. Those who wash their robes. (Revelation 22:14)

Appendix C - The Experts

Breese, David—President of World Prophetic Ministry, and Bible teacher on *The King Is Coming* television program. (World Prophetic Ministry, P.O. Box 907, Colton, CA 92324)

Carlson, Carole C.—Author and coauthor of nineteen books, including the best-selling *The Late Great Planet Earth* with Hal Lindsey.

Church, J. R.—Host of the nationwide television program *Prophecy in the News*. (Prophecy Publications, P.O. Box 7000, Oklahoma City, OK 73153)

Dyer, Charles H.—Professor of Bible exposition at Dallas Theological Seminary.

Froese, Arno—Editor of *Midnight Call* and *News from Israel*. (Midnight Call, Inc., 4694 Platt Springs Road, West Columbia, South Carolina 29170; News from Israel, P.O. Box 4389, West Columbia, SC 29171-4389)

Graham, Billy—World-famous evangelist and author. (Billy Graham Evangelistic Association, 1300 Harmon Place, P.O. Box 779, Minneapolis, MN 55440-0779)

Greene, Oliver B.—Former Director of the Gospel Hour, Inc., author, and radio show host.

Hagee, John—Founder and pastor of Cornerstone Church, and President of Global Evangelism Television.

Halff, Charles—Executive Director of the Christian Jew Foundation, radio host for the *Christian Jew Hour*, and featured writer for *Message of the Christian Jew*. (The Christian Jew Foundation, P.O. Box 345, San Antonio, TX 78292)

Hindson, Ed—Minister of Biblical Studies at Rehoboth Baptist Church in Atlanta, Georgia, Vice President of There's Hope, adjunct professor at Liberty University in Virginia, and an executive board member of the Pre-Trib Research Center in Washington, D.C.

Hocking, David—Pastor, radio host, and Director of Hope for Today Ministries. (P.O. Box 3927, Tustin, CA 92781-3927)

Hutchings, Noah—President of the Southwest Radio Church, one of the oldest and best-known prophetic ministries in the world. (P.O. Box 1144, Oklahoma City, OK 73101)

Jeffrey, Grant R.—Best-selling author of six books. (Frontier Research Publications Inc., Box 129, Station "U," Toronto, Ontario M8Z5M4)

Jeremiah, David—President of Christian Heritage College, Senior Pastor of Scott Memorial Baptist Church in El Cajon, California, and radio host of Turning Point.

LaHaye, Tim—Best-selling author, president, and founder of Family Life Seminars, and husband to Beverly LaHaye, Director of Concerned Women of America.

Lalonde, Peter and Paul—Founders and co-hosts of *This Week in Bible Prophecy*. (This Week in Bible Prophecy, P.O. Box 1440, Niagara Falls, NY 14302-1440)

Lindsey, Hal—Called by many the father of the modern-day prophecy movement, president of Hal Lindsey Ministries, and author of more than a dozen books with combined worldwide sales exceeding thirty-five million copies. (P.O. Box 4000, Palos Verdes, CA 90274)

Malgo, Wim—Former founder of Midnight Call, Inc., and the author of several books. (Midnight Call, Inc., 4694 Platt Springs Road, West Columbia, SC 29170)

McGee, J. Vernon—Former host of the popular *Thru the Bible* radio show. (Thru The Bible Radio, Box 100, Pasadena, CA 91109)

Pollock, Dennis—Pastor with the *Christ in Prophecy* radio program. (Lamb & Lion Ministries, P.O. Box 919, McKinney, TX 75069)

Price, Stanley—Associated with the Southwest Radio Church. He has written articles for one of their many publications, *Bible in the News*. (Southwest Radio Church, P.O. Box 1144, Oklahoma City, OK 73101)

Reagan, David—Host of *Christ in Prophecy*, and

author of the first-ever picture book on prophecy for young children, *Jesus Is Coming Again*.

Tyson, Jerry—Writer for *Bible in the News*, a publication of the Southwest Radio Church. (P.O. Box 1144, Oklahoma City, OK 73101)

Van Impe, Jack—Co-host, along with his wife, Rexella, of a worldwide television ministry that analyzes the news in light of Bible prophecy. (Jack Van Impe Ministries International, P.O. Box 7004, Troy, MI 48007)

White, Vera K.—Christian educator and freelance writer. (Eco-Justice Working Group, National Council of the Churches of Christ, Room 812, 475 Riverside Drive, New York, NY 10115)

Endnotes

Revelation 1

1. David Breese, *The Book of Revelation* (Colton, CA: World Prophetic Ministry) Taped Message #DB111.

2. Todd Strandberg and Terry Jones, *Are You Rapture Ready* (New York, NY: Penguin Group, USA, Inc., 2003), 32.

3. Hal Lindsey, *Revelation: How John Witnessed Our Future* (Palos Verdes, CA: Hal Lindsey Ministries), Taped Message #003B.

4. Hal Lindsey, *Revelation: Keys to Interpreting Revelation* (Palos Verdes, CA: Hal Lindsey Ministries), Taped Message #001A.

5. Breese, *The Book of Revelation*, Taped Message #DB111.

Revelation 2

1. Tim LaHaye, *Revelation Illustrated and Made Plain* (Grand Rapids, MI: Zondervan, 1973), 34–94.

2. Hal Lindsey, *There's a New World Coming* (Eugene, OR: Harvest House Publishers, 1984), 34–56.

3. J. Vernon McGee, *Thru the Bible with J. Vernon McGee, vol. V* (Pasadena, CA: J. Vernon McGee, 1983) 901–15.

4. David Breese, *The Book of Revelation* (Colton, CA: World Prophetic Ministry), Taped Message #DB111.

5. Jack Van Impe, *2001: On the Edge of Eternity* (Dallas, TX: Word Publishing, 1996), 69.

6. Ron Carlson and Ed Decker, *Fast Facts on False Teachings* (Eugene, OR: Harvest House Publishers, 1994), 137.

7. Ed Hindson, *Final Signs* (Eugene, OR: Harvest House Publishers, 1996), 173.

8. McGee, *Thru the Bible with J. Vernon McGee, vol. V*, 909.

9. Lindsey, *There's a New World Coming*, 43.

Revelation 3

1. David Breese, *The Book of Revelation* (Colton, CA: World Prophetic Ministry) Taped Message #DB111.

2. Todd Strandberg and Terry Jones, *Are You Rapture Ready* (New York, NY: Penguin Group, USA, Inc., 2003), 174.

3. *Life Application Bible Commentary: Revelation* (Wheaton, IL: Tyndale House Publishers, Inc., 2000), 39.

4. J. Edwin Orr, *The Rebirth of America*, 63.

5. Jim Combs, *Rainbows from Revelation* (Springfield, MO: Tribune Publishers, 1994), 43.

6. John Hagee, *Beginning of the End* (Nashville, TN: Thomas Nelson Publishers, 1996), 32.

7. Strandberg and James, *Are You Rapture Ready*, 275.

8. Warren W. Wiersbe, *Be Victorious* (Colorado Springs, CO: Cook Communications Ministries, 2004), 36.

9. Hal Lindsey, *Revelation: Laodicea, the Apostle Church* (Palos Verdes, CA: Hal Lindsey Ministries), Taped Message #008A.

10. David Reagan, The Master Plan (Eugene, OR: Harvest House Publishers, 1993), 219.

Revelation 4

1. *The New King James Version Prophecy Bible* (Nashville, TN: Thomas Nelson, Inc., 1985), 1319.

2. David Hocking *The Biola Hour* (La Mirada, CA, Taped Message), #3371.

3. David Reagan, *The Master Plan* (Eugene, OR: Harvest House Publishers, 1993), 90.

4. Grant R. Jeffrey, *Final Warning* (Toronto, Ontario: Grant R. Jeffrey, 1995), 306.

5. David Hocking, *The Coming World Leader*

(Portland, OR: Calvary Communications, Inc., 1988), 112.

6. Bruce Wilkinson with David Kopp, *A Life God Rewards* (Sisters, OR: Multinoma Publishers, Inc., 2002), 62.

Revelation 5

1. Hal Lindsey, *There's a New World Coming* (Eugene, OR: Harvest House Publishers, 1984), 74

2. Leon Morris, *Revelation* (Grand Rapids, MI: Wm. B. Eerdmans Publishing Company, Leon Morris, 1987), 93.

3. Ibid., 96–97.

4. H. Grady Hardin, Joseph D. Quillian Jr., and James F. White, *The Celebration of the Gospel* (Nashville, TN: Abingdon Press, 1964), 13.

5. Mal Couch, *A Pastor's Manual on Doing Church* (Fort Worth, TX, Mal Couch, 2002), 108.

Revelation 6

1. John Hagee, *Beginning of the End* (Nashville, TN: Thomas Nelson Publishers, 1996), 117.

2. David Reagan, *Wrath and Glory* (Green Forest, AR, New Leaf Press, Lamb & Lion Ministries, 2001), 67.

3. Hagee, *Beginning of the End*, 13.

4. Dave Hunt, *The Gathering Storm* (Springfield, MO: 21st Century Press, Mal Couch, Gen. Ed., 2005), 140.

5. Hal Lindsey, *Midnight Call Magazine* (Columbia, SC , Midnight Call, Inc., April 1996), 11.

6. Grant R. Jeffrey, *Final Warning* (Toronto, Ontario: Grant R. Jeffrey, 1995), 228.

7. Ed Hindson, *Final Signs* (Eugene, OR: Harvest House Publishers, 1996), 181.

8. Billy Graham, *Storm Warning* (Minneapolis, MN, Grason, Billy Graham, 1992), 230.

9. Hal Lindsey, *There's a New World Coming* (Eugene, OR: Harvest House Publishers, 1984), 88.

10. Ibid., 93.

11. Graham, *Storm Warning*, 271.

12. David Jeremiah with C. C. Carlson, *Escape the Coming Night* (Dallas: Word Publishing, 1990), 112.

13. Warren W. Wiersbe, *Be Victorious* (Colorado Springs, CO, Cook Communications, Inc., 2004), 66.

14. Graham, *Storm Warning*, 57.

15. Hindson, *Final Signs*, 181.

16. David Breese, *The Book of Revelation* (Colton, CA: World Prophetic Ministry) Taped Message #DB112A.

17. Craig S. Keener, *The NIV Application Commentary* (Grand Rapids, MI, Zondervan, Craig Keener, 2000), 228.

Revelation 7

1. Arnold G. Fruchtenbaum, *The Footsteps of the Messiah* (Tustin, CA: Ariel Ministries, 2003), 177–180.

2. Tim LaHaye, *Revelation Illustrated and Made Plain* (Grand Rapids, MI, Zondervan, 1973), 158.

3. Hal Lindsey, *There's a New World Coming* (Eugene, OR: Harvest House Publishers, 1984), 104.

4. Dennis Pollock, *Lamplighter* (McKinney, TX, Lamb & Lion Ministries, January 1993), 5.

5. David Reagan, *Wrath and Glory* (Green Forest, AR, New Leaf Press, Lamb & Lion Ministries, 2001), 148.

6. Dave Hunt, *Seeking God* (Bend, OR, The Berean Call, Dave Hunt, 2004), 5.

7. Leon Morris, *Revelation* (Grand Rapids, MI: Wm. B. Eerdmans Publishing Company, Leon Morris, 1987), 114.

8. LaHaye, *Revelation Illustrated and Made Plain*, 166.

9. Jack Van Impe, *2001: On the Edge of Eternity* (Dallas, TX: Word Publishing, 2001), 10–11.

10. Jack W. Hayford, *Hayford's Bible Handbook* (Nashville, TN: Thomas Nelson Publishers, 1995), 472.

Revelation 8

1. William Barclay, *The Revelation of John, vol. 2* (Philadelphia, PA, The Westminster Press, 1960), 51.

2. Jack Van Impe, *2001: On the Edge of Eternity* (Dallas, TX: Word Publishing, 2001), 154.

3. Hal Lindsey, *There's a New World Coming* (Eugene, OR: Harvest House Publishers, 1984), 118.

4. Van Impe, *2001: On the Edge of Eternity*, 4.

5. David Hocking, *The Coming World Leader* (Portland, OR: Calvary Communications, Inc, 1988), 156.

6. *The World Book Encyclopedia, vol. 14* (Chicago, IL: World Book, Inc, 1989), 608.

7. J. H. Melton, *52 Lessons in Revelation* (Springfield, OH: Crescendo Publications, old book, no date), 102.

Revelation 9

1. N. W. Hutchings, *Revelation for Today* (Bethany, OK: N. W. Hutchings, 2003), 92.

2. David Jeremiah with C. C. Carlson, *Escape the Coming Night* (Dallas: Word Publishing, 1990), 128–129.

3. *The World Book Encyclopedia, vol. 12* (Chicago, IL: World Book, Inc, 1990), 422–423.

4. David Hocking, *The Coming World Leader* (Portland, OR: Calvary Communications, Inc, 1988), 162–163.

5. J. Vernon McGee, *Thru the Bible with J. Vernon McGee, vol. V* (Pasadena, CA: J. Vernon McGee, 1983) 968.

6. Oliver B. Greene, *The Revelation* (Greenville, SC: The Gospel Hour, Inc., 1963), 256.

7. John F. Walvoord, *Every Prophecy of the Bible* (Colorado Springs, Co., Chariot Victor Publishing, John F. Walvoord, 1999), 567.

8. Jim Combs, *Rainbows from Revelation* (Springfield, MO: Tribune Publishers, 1994), 94.

9. J. H. Melton, *52 Lessons in Revelation* (Springfield, OH: Crescendo Publications, old book, no date), 106.

10. Jack Van Impe, *2001: On the Edge of Eternity* (Dallas, TX: Word Publishing, 2001), 37–38.

11. Tim LaHaye, *Foreshadows of Wrath and Redemption* (Eugene, OR: Harvest House Publishers, William T. James, Gen. Ed., 1997), 175–176.

12. *Life Application Bible Commentary: Revelation*, (Wheaton, IL: Tyndale House Publishers, Inc., 2000), 105.

13. Hal Lindsey, *There's a New World Coming* (Eugene, OR: Harvest House Publishers, 1984), 130.

14. Dave Hunt and T. A. McMahon, *The Seduction of Christianity* (Eugene, OR: Harvest House Publishers, Dave Hunt & T. A. McMahon, 1985), 30.

15. John Hagee, *Day of Deception* (Nashville, TN: Thomas Nelson Publishers, John C. Hagee, 1997), 76.

16. Grant R. Jeffrey, *Final Warning* (Toronto, Ontario: Grant R. Jeffrey, 1995), 180.

17. Van Impe, *2001: On the Edge of Eternity*, 70–71.

Revelation 10

1. David Hocking, *The Coming World Leader* (Portland, OR: Calvary Communications, Inc, 1988), 170.

2. John F. Walvoord, *Every Prophecy of the Bible* (Colorado Springs, Co., Chariot Victor Publishing, John F. Walvoord, 1999), 570.

3. Craig S. Keener, *The NIV Application Commentary* (Grand Rapids, MI, Zondervan, Craig Keener, 2000), 281.

4. David Jeremiah with C. C. Carlson, *Escape the Coming Night* (Dallas: Word Publishing, 1990), 138.

5. Tim LaHaye, *Revelation Illustrated and Made Plain* (Grand Rapids, MI: Zondervan, 1973), 196.

6. Oliver B. Greene, *The Revelation* (Greenville, SC: The Gospel Hour, Inc., 1963), 273.

7. Jim Combs, *Rainbows from Revelation* (Springfield, MO: Tribune Publishers, 1994), 110.

8. N. W. Hutchings, *Revelation for Today* (Bethany, OK: N. W. Hutchings, 2003), 103.

9. David Hocking, *The Coming World Leader* (Portland, OR: Calvary Communications, Inc, 1988), 172.

10. *The Preacher's Outline and Sermon Bible* (Chattanooga, TN: Leadership Ministries Worldwide, Alpha-Omega Ministries, Inc., 1991), 131.

11. John P. Newport, *The Lion and the Lamb* (Nashville, TN: Broadman Press, 1986), 216.

12. Hocking, *The Coming World Leader*, 174.

Revelation 11

1. Thomas Ice and Timothy Demy, *Fast Facts on Bible Prophecy* (Eugene OR: Harvest House Publishers, Pre-Trib Research Center, 1997), 206–207.

2. J. Randall Price, *Dictionary of Premillennial Theology* (Grand Rapids, MI: Kregel Publications, Mal Couch, Gen. Ed., 1996), 404.

3. Arnold G. Fruchtenbaum, *The Footsteps of the Messiah* (Tustin, CA: Ariel Ministries, 2003), 105.

4. Hal Lindsey, *There's a New World Coming* (Eugene, OR: Harvest House Publishers, 1984), 150.

5. Charles H. Dyer, *World News and Bible Prophecy* (Wheaton, IL: Tyndale House Publishers, Charles H. Dyer, 1995), 171.

6. John F. Walvoord, *Every Prophecy of the Bible* (Colorado Springs, Co., Chariot Victor Publishing, John F. Walvoord, 1999), 278.

7. N. W. Hutchings, *Revelation for Today* (Bethany, OK: N. W. Hutchings, 2003), 108.

8. John Hagee, *Beginning of the End* (Nashville, TN: Thomas Nelson Publishers, 1996), 116.

9. David Jeremiah with C. C. Carlson, *Escape the Coming Night* (Dallas: Word Publishing, 1990), 138.

10. *The Preacher's Outline and Sermon Bible* (Chattanooga, TN: Leadership Ministries Worldwide, Alpha-Omega Ministries, Inc., 1991), 140.

11. Hagee, *Beginning of the End*, 95.

12. J. Vernon McGee, *Thru the Bible with J. Vernon McGee, vol. V* (Pasadena, CA: J. Vernon McGee, 1983) 983.

13. *Message of the Christian Jew Newsletter* (San Antonio, TX: The Christian Jew Foundation, November/December 1993), 6.

Revelation 12

1. Jim Combs, *Rainbows from Revelation* (Springfield, MO: Tribune Publishers, 1994), 124.

2. *Harper's Bible Dictionary* (New York, NY: Harper & Row, Publishers, 1973), 299.

3. Charles H. Dyer, *World News and Bible Prophecy* (Wheaton, IL: Tyndale House Publishers, Charles H. Dyer, 1995), 90.

4. N. W. Hutchings, *Revelation for Today* (Bethany, OK: N. W. Hutchings, 2003), 118.

5. Kerby Anderson, *The Gathering Storm* (Springfield, MO, 21st Century Press, Mal Couch, Gen. Ed., 2005), 140.

6. Dyer, *World News and Bible Prophecy*, 90.

7. John P. Newport, *The Lion and the Lamb* (Nashville, TN: Broadman Press, 1986), 233.

8. Dyer, *World News and Bible Prophecy*, 89.

9. John Hagee, *Beginning of the End* (Nashville, TN: Thomas Nelson Publishers, 1996), 171.

10. J. Ramsey Michaels, *Revelation* (Downers Grove, IL: InterVarsity Press, J. Ramsey Michaels, 1997), 152.

11. Noah Hutchings, *Prophetic Observer* (Bethany, OK: Southwest Radio Church, January 1996), 4.

12. David Reagan, *Wrath and Glory* (Green Forest, AR, New Leaf Press, Lamb & Lion Ministries, 2001), 75.

13. Charles Halff, *Message of the Christian Jew* (San Antonio, TX: The Christian Jew Foundation, September/October 1981), 4.

Revelation 13

1. Jack Van Impe, *2001: On the Edge of Eternity* (Dallas, TX: Word Publishing, 2001), 6.

2. Grant R. Jeffrey, *Final Warning* (Toronto, Ontario: Grant R. Jeffrey, 1995), 86.

3. Mal Couch, *The Popular Encyclopedia of Bible Prophecy* (Eugene, OR: Harvest House Publishers, Tim LaHaye and Ed Hindson, 2004), 44.

4. Mark Hitchcock, *The Complete Book of Bible Prophecy* (Wheaton, IL: Tyndale House Publishers, Inc., Mark Hitchcock, 1999), 131.

5. William S. McBirnie, *50 Progressive Messages on Second Coming of Christ* (Norfolk, VA: McBirnie Publications Association, 1944), 158.

6. J. Dwight Pentecost, *Things to Come* (Grand Rapids, MI: Zondervan Publishing House, Dunham Publishing Company, 1976), 335.

7. Van Impe, *2001: On the Edge of Eternity*, 161.

8. David Jeremiah with C. C. Carlson, *Escape the Coming Night* (Dallas: Word Publishing, 1990), 112.

9. Agusta Harting, *Prophecy at Ground Zero* (Lancaster, PA: Starburst Publishers, William T. James, Gen. Ed., 2002), 229.

10. Ed Hindson, *Final Signs* (Eugene, OR: Harvest House Publishers, 1996), 107.

11. Tim LaHaye, *Revelation Illustrated and Made Plain* (Grand Rapids, MI: Zondervan, 1973), 249.

12. Thomas Ice and Timothy Demy, *Fast Facts on Bible Prophecy* (Eugene OR: Harvest House Publishers, Pre-Trib Research Center, 1997), 77.

13. Hitchcock, *The Complete Book of Bible Prophecy*, 134.

14. Harting, *Prophecy at Ground Zero*, 234.

15. Ice and Demy, *Fast Facts on Bible Prophecy*, 78–79.

16. Van Impe, *2001: On the Edge of Eternity*, 78–79.

17. Mark Hitchcock, *The Gathering Storm* (Springfield, MO: 21st Century Press, Mal Couch, Gen. Ed., 2005), 200.

18. John Hagee, *Beginning of the End* (Nashville, TN: Thomas Nelson Publishers, 1996), 135.

Revelation 14

1. *The Preacher's Outline and Sermon Bible* (Chattanooga, TN: Leadership Ministries Worldwide, Alpha-Omega Ministries, Inc., 1991), 180.

2. Jim Combs, *Rainbows from Revelation* (Springfield, MO: Tribune Publishers, 1994), 154.

3. Robert H. Mounce, *The Book of Revelation* (Grand Rapids, MI: William B. Eerdmans Publishing Company, 1997), 264.

4. Ed Hindson, *Revelation: Unlocking the Future* (Chattanooga, TN: AMG Publishers, Tyndale Theological Seminary, 2002), 154.

5. Tim LaHaye, *Revelation Illustrated and Made Plain* (Grand Rapids, MI: Zondervan, 1973), 267.

6. *The Preacher's Outline and Sermon Bible*, 182.

7. J. H. Melton, *52 Lessons in Revelation* (Springfield, OH: Crescendo Publications, old book, no date), 151.

8. John P. Newport, *The Lion and the Lamb* (Nashville, TN: Broadman Press, 1986), 252.

9. Oliver B. Greene, *The Revelation* (Greenville, SC: The Gospel Hour, Inc., 1963), 359.

10. LaHaye, *Revelation Illustrated and Made Plain*, 267.

11. John Hagee, *Beginning of the End* (Nashville, TN: Thomas Nelson Publishers, 1996), 173.

12. David Hocking, *The Coming World Leader* (Portland, OR: Calvary Communications, Inc, 1988), 226.

13. J. R. Church, *Guardians of the Grail* (Oklahoma City, OK: Prophecy Publications, 1989), 316.

14. Hal Lindsey, *There's a New World Coming* (Eugene, OR: Harvest House Publishers, 1984), 194.

15. Homer Ritchie, Omer Ritchie, and Lonnie Shipman, *Secrets of Prophecy Revealed* (Springfield, MO: 21st Century Press, Lonnie Shipman, 2001), 111.

Revelation 15

1. Robert H. Mounce, *The Book of Revelation* (Grand Rapids, MI: William B. Eerdmans Publishing Company, 1997), 285.

2. Hal Lindsey, *There's a New World Coming* (Eugene, OR: Harvest House Publishers, 1984), 197.

3. J. R. Church, *Hidden Prophecies in the Song of Moses* (Oklahoma City, OK, Prophecy Publications, J. R. Church, 1991), 14.

4. Peter and Paul Lalonde, *The Mark of the Beast* (Eugene, OR: Harvest House Publishers, 1994), 189.

5. Jim Combs, *Rainbows from Revelation* (Springfield, MO: Tribune Publishers, 1994), 164.

Revelation 16

1. Peter and Paul Lalonde, *The Mark of the Beast* (Eugene, OR: Harvest House Publishers, 1994), 187–188.

2. J. R. Church, *Hidden Prophecies in the Song of Moses* (Oklahoma City, OK, Prophecy Publications, J. R. Church, 1991), 105.

3. *Life Application Bible Commentary: Revelation* (Wheaton, IL: Tyndale House Publishers, Inc., 2000), 184.

4. Henry M. Morris, *The Revelation Record* (Wheaton, IL: Tyndale House Publishers, Inc., 1983), 298.

5. John F. Walvoord, *Every Prophecy of the Bible* (Colorado Springs, Co., Chariot Victor Publishing, John F. Walvoord, 1999), 597.

6. Wim Malgo, *The Wrath of Heaven on Earth* (West Columbia, SC: Midnight Call, Incorporated, 1985), 116.

7. John Hagee, *Beginning of the End* (Nashville, TN: Thomas Nelson Publishers, 1996), 116.

8. Vera K. White, *It's God's World: Christians, the Environment, and Climate Change*, The Eco-Justice Working Group National Council of the Churches of Christ in the U.S.A., 5.

9. Morris, *The Revelation Record*, 306.

10. J. Dwight Pentecost, *Things to Come* (Grand Rapids, MI: Zondervan Publishing House, Dunham Publishing Company, 1976), 340.

11. David Hocking, *The Coming World Leader* (Portland, OR: Calvary Communications, Inc, 1988), 239–240.

Revelation 17

1. Arno Froese, *News from Israel* (West Columbia, SC: Midnight Call, Inc., January 1996), 8.

2. Hal Lindsey, *Planet Earth—2000 A.D.* (Palos Verdes, CAL: Western Front, Ltd., Hal Lindsey, 1994), 308.

3. Jack Van Impe, *2001: On the Edge of Eternity* (Dallas, TX: Word Publishing, 2001), 11.

4. Ed Hindson, *The Popular Encyclopedia of Bible Prophecy* (Eugene, OR: Harvest House Publishers, Tim LaHaye and Ed Hindson, 2004), 104–105.

5. Billy Graham, *Angels* (Waco, TX: Word Books Publishers, Billy Graham, 1986), 58–60.

6. Hal Lindsey, *Revelation: The Mystery of Babylon* (Palos Verdes, CA: Hal Lindsey Ministries), Taped Message #026A.

7. Arno Froese, *News from Israel* (West Columbia, SC: Midnight Call, Inc., January 1996), 8–9.

8. Grant R. Jeffrey, *Final Warning* (Toronto, Ontario: Grant R. Jeffrey, 1995), 151.

9. F. Kenton Beshore, *The Millennium, the Apocalypse, and Armageddon* (Springfield, MO: 21st Century Press, F. Kenton Beshore, 2001), 393.

10. Ed Hindson, *Final Signs* (Eugene, OR: Harvest House Publishers, 1996), 108.

11. Charles H. Dyer, *World News and Bible Prophecy* (Wheaton, IL: Tyndale House Publishers, Charles H. Dyer, 1993), 149–150.

12. Hal Lindsey, *There's a New World Coming* (Eugene, OR: Harvest House Publishers, 1984), 222.

13. Jim Combs, *Rainbows from Revelation* (Springfield, MO: Tribune Publishers, 1994), 190.

14. John Hagee, *Beginning of the End* (Nashville, TN: Thomas Nelson Publishers, 1996), 165.

15. J. Dwight Pentecost, *Things to Come* (Grand Rapids, MI: Zondervan Publishing House, Dunham Publishing Company, 1976), 368.

16. Dyer, *World News and Bible Prophecy*, 154–55.

17. Stanley E. Price, *Bible in the News* (Bethany, OK, Southwest Radio Church, July 1996), 11.

Revelation 18

1. Andy Woods and Tim LaHaye, *The Popular Encyclopedia of Bible Prophecy* (Eugene, OR: Harvest House Publishers, Tim LaHaye and Ed Hindson, 2004), 104–105.

2. Joseph Chambers, *Revelation Hoofbeats* (Longwood, FL: Xulon Press, Eternal Ministries, Inc., Ron J. Bigalke, Jr., Gen. Ed., 2003), 206.

3. Ed Hindson, *Final Signs* (Eugene, OR: Harvest House Publishers, 1996), 107.

4. Leon Morris, *Revelation* (Grand Rapids, MI: Wm. B. Eerdmans Publishing Company, Leon Morris, 1987), 209.

5. Mal Couch and Joseph Chambers, *Dictionary of Premillennial Theology* (Grand Rapids, MI: Kregel Publications, Mal Couch, Gen. Ed., 1996), 62.

6. J. H. Melton, *52 Lessons in Revelation* (Springfield, OH: Crescendo Publications, old book, no date), 209.

7. Jack Van Impe, *Revelation Revealed* (Nashville, TN: W Publishing Group, Jack Van Impe Ministries, 1982), 214.

8. Warren W. Wiersbe, *Be Victorious* (Colorado Springs, CO: Cook Communications Ministries, 2004), 129.

9. *The Preacher's Outline and Sermon Bible* (Chattanooga, TN: Leadership Ministries Worldwide, Alpha-Omega Ministries, Inc., 1991), 221.

10. Oliver B. Greene, *The Revelation* (Greenville, SC: The Gospel Hour, Inc., 1963), 444.

11. Ed Hindson, *Revelation: Unlocking the Future* (Chattanooga, TN: AMG Publishers, Tyndale Theological Seminary, 2002), 183.

12. Hal Lindsey, *There's a New World Coming* (Eugene, OR: Harvest House Publishers, 1984), 234.

13. *Life Application Bible Commentary: Revelation* (Wheaton, IL: Tyndale House Publishers, Inc., 2000), 218.

14. Hindson, *Final Signs*, 103.

15. N. W. Hutchings, *Revelation for Today* (Bethany, OK: N. W. Hutchings, 2003), 183.

16. Peter and Paul Lalonde, *301 Startling Proofs and Prophecies* (Niagara Falls, Ontario Canada: Prophecy Partners Inc., 1996), 235.

17. Craig S. Keener, *The NIV Application Commentary* (Grand Rapids, MI: Zondervan, 2000), 433.

Revelation 19

1. Henry M. Morris, *The Revelation Record* (Wheaton, IL: Tyndale House Publishers, Inc., Henry M. Morris, 1983), 380.

2. Tim LaHaye, *Revelation Illustrated and Made Plain* (Grand Rapids, MI: Zondervan, 1973), 344.

3. David Jeremiah with C. C. Carlson, *Escape the Coming Night* (Dallas: Word Publishing, 1990), 200.

4. J. H. Melton, *52 Lessons in Revelation* (Springfield, OH: Crescendo Publications, old book, no date), 218.

5. J. Vernon McGee, *Thru the Bible with J.*

Vernon McGee, vol. V (Pasadena, CA: J. Vernon McGee, 1983) 1046.

6. J. Ramsey Michaels, *Revelation* (Downers Grove, IL: InterVarsity Press, J. Ramsey Michaels, 1997), 211.

7. Hal Lindsey, *There's a New World Coming* (Eugene, OR: Harvest House Publishers, 1984), 240–241.

8. Ed Hindson, *Revelation: Unlocking the Future* (Chattanooga, TN: AMG Publishers, Tyndale Theological Seminary, 2002), 195.

9. Robert H. Mounce, *The Book of Revelation* (Grand Rapids, MI: William B. Eerdmans Publishing Company, 1997), 356.

10. Craig S. Keener, *The NIV Application Commentary* (Grand Rapids, MI, Zondervan, Craig Keener, 2000), 455.

11. John Hagee, *Beginning of the End* (Nashville, TN: Thomas Nelson Publishers, 1996), 176.

12. Morris, *The Revelation Record*, 401.

13. J. R. Church, *Guardians of the Grail* (Oklahoma City, OK: Prophecy Publications, 1989), 312.

Revelation 20

1. Jack Van Impe, *2001: On the Edge of Eternity* (Dallas, TX: Word Publishing, 2001), 16.

2. J. Vernon McGee, *Thru the Bible with J. Vernon McGee, vol. V* (Pasadena, CA: J. Vernon McGee, 1983) 1055.

3. Hal Lindsey, *There's a New World Coming* (Eugene, OR: Harvest House Publishers, 1984), 252.

4. Van Impe, *2001: On the Edge of Eternity*, 28.

5. McGee, *Thru the Bible with J. Vernon*, 1058.

6. Mark Hitchcock, *The Complete Book of Bible Prophecy* (Wheaton, IL: Tyndale House Publishers, Inc., Mark Hitchcock, 1999), 183.

7. Lindsey, *There's a New World Coming*, 262.

8. John Hagee, *Beginning of the End* (Nashville, TN: Thomas Nelson Publishers, 1996), 85.

Revelation 21

1. John Hagee, *Beginning of the End* (Nashville, TN: Thomas Nelson Publishers, 1996), 84.

2. Craig S. Keener, *The NIV Application Commentary* (Grand Rapids, MI, Zondervan, Craig Keener, 2000), 486.

3. Ed Hindson, *Revelation: Unlocking the Future* (Chattanooga, TN: AMG Publishers, Tyndale Theological Seminary, 2002), 217.

4. Ben Witherington III, *Revelation* (New York, NY: Cambridge University Press, Ben Witherington III, 2003), 266.

5. Ibid., 269.

6. Randall Price, *The Popular Encyclopedia of Bible Prophecy* (Eugene, OR: Harvest House Publishers, Tim LaHaye and Ed Hindson, 2004), 246.

7. Hal Lindsey, *There's a New World Coming* (Eugene, OR: Harvest House Publishers, 1984), 274.

Revelation 22

1. Leon Morris, *Revelation* (Grand Rapids, MI: Wm. B. Eerdmans Publishing Company, Leon Morris, 1987), 248.

2. Henry M. Morris, *The Revelation Record* (Wheaton, IL: Tyndale House Publishers, Inc., Henry M. Morris, 1983), 464.

3. Robert H. Mounce, *The Book of Revelation* (Grand Rapids, MI: William B. Eerdmans Publishing Company, 1997), 401.

4. Price, Randall *The Popular Encyclopedia of Bible Prophecy* (Eugene, OR: Harvest House Publishers, Tim LaHaye and Ed Hindson, 2004), 246.

5. J. Vernon McGee, *Thru the Bible with J. Vernon McGee, vol. V* (Pasadena, CA: J. Vernon McGee, 1983) 1077.

6. Mounce, *The Book of Revelation*, 406.

7. Henry M. Morris, *The Revelation Record*, 481.

Index

Fruchtenbaum, Arnold G.
   on Tribulation, 100
   on Tribulation Temple, 149
fruit of the Holy Spirit, 30
fullness of the Holy Spirit, 37
futurist, 113

G

Gabriel
   blow that trumpet, 121
   strength of God, 71
Garden of Eden, 21, 314, 320
Gehenna, 294
Gerasenes, 123
global ethic, 183, 184
globalism, 183, 246, 275
glorification, 41
glorified bodies, 91
glory and dominion, 7
glory and honor, 325
go and preach, 141
God has been marking His
      people, 101
God's Riches At Christ's
      Expense, 341
God's wrath, 138, 218
Gog and Magog, 305
golden altar, 111, 128
golden censer, 111, 112
grabbing hold of the horns, 127
grace makes salvation possible,
      341
grace of God, 5
Graham, Billy
   on consequence of
      disobedience, 89
   on humanity, 94
   on martyrs for the Word of
      God, 92
   on Satan's works, 251
Great White Throne Judgment
   definition of, 30
Greene, Oliver, B.
   on Bablyonian dream has been
      destroyed, 272
   on everlasting hell, 213
   on John, 138
   on locusts, 126
gulf, 336

H

Hades, 14
Hagee, John

on Antichrist, 82
on Antichrist's turn for
      judgment, 259
on armies of the world, 293
on identity of the
      Antichrist, 202
on last hurrah, 306
on Law of Entropy, 314
on new age religions, 133
on peace process, 84
on Rapture, 45
on Satan lashes out, 175
on seas turn into blood, 156
on special blessing for saints,
      214
on two witnesses, 158
on uncontrollable fires, 233
Halff, Charles, 179
Haman, 179, 295
Hardin, H. Grady, 76
harlot, 248
Harting, Agusta
   on cults, 191
   on false christs, 196
harvest, 214
Hayford, Jack, 107
heard with one's heart, 5
heathen, 26
heavenly city, 309
heresies, 31
high priest, 10
Hindson, Ed
   on Antichrist, 254
   on apostasy, 249
   on bond-servants of our God,
      208
   on economic disaster, 87
   on global nuclear holocaust, 95
   on global web, 265
   on globalism, 275
   on heavenly army, 291
   on New Age mysticism, 192
   on society's mindless pursuit
      for abundant blessings, 273
   on ultimate crisis in
      education, 27
   on unrepented and
      uncoverted heart, 317
Hinduism, 246, 252
his sheep, 23
Hitchcock, Mark
   on Antichrist's personality,
      187
   on False Prophet, 195

on mark of the beast, 200
on Satan doomed to eternal
      destruction, 306
Hocking, David
   on angels in Revelation, 136
   our coming Judge, 215
   on God cares about what is
      taking place on earth, 140
   on God's judgment and
      wrath, 142
   on miraculous signs, 238
   on Rapture, 57
   on scorpion plague, 124
   on submitting to His authority,
      66
   on third trumpet judgment,
      116
holy
   definition of, 42
Holy City, 153, 263, 314
Holy Grail, 250
Holy of Holies
   definition of, 150
Holy Place
   definition of, 150
Holy Spirit, 5, 17, 25, 64, 73,
      155, 330
hooves of bronze, 12
horses' bridles
   blood will rise as high, 218
   definition of, 218
hour of trial
   definition of, 257
   Jesus promises to keep the
      believers, 44, 257
Hunt, Dave, 132
   on God's judgment on the
      world, 85
   on what lies beyond the grave,
      104
Hutchings, N. W.
   on Babylon's destruction, 275
   on Old Testament prophecies
      of the Messiah, 168
   on Satan and his angels, 122
   on Tribulation, 140
   on Tribulation and the
      Antichrist, 155
Hutchings, Noah, 178

I

Ice, Thomas
   on four temples in
      Jerusalem, 124

on relationship between the
Antichrist and the False
Prophet, 194
on religion and miracles, 198
idolatry, 26
Imperishable Crown, 24
incarnation, 187
incense to mix with the prayers of
the Saints, 112
inclusiveness, 31
iniquity, 75
intercede, 10
in the flesh, 20
iron scepter, 172
Islamism, 246
Island of Patmos, 8
illustration of, 11
Island of Sumatra, 94
It is finished! 240

J

James, Terry
on Jesus Christ, 46
on revealing Jesus Christ in His
full glory, 8
on salvation, 39
Jasper and Sardius, 61
Jebusites, 206
Jeffrey, Grant R.
on economic collapse, 87
on mystery Babylon, 253
on pre-millennial return of
Christ, 60
on social problems and criminal
behaviors, 133
on Ten Regions of the New
World Government, 185
Jeremiah
ate the words of God, 142
Jeremiah, David
on cry for unbelievers, 191
on demons of hell, 122
on fate of believers, 92
on Saints, 283
on thunder, 138
on two witnesses, 156
Jesus Christ
ascended, 136, 141, 160
is coming, 7, 285
Jews rebuild temple, 146
Jezebel, 31, 32
John the Baptist, 72
joined together, 285

joint heir, 69
joint heirs with Jesus, 316
judge the world, 73, 301
justification, 41

K

Keener, Craig S.
on fate worse then death, 293
on God's time, 96
on Most Holy Place, 315
on new Jerusalem, 278
on thunder, 138
keyholder, 42
King of Fierce Countenance, 81
kingdoms, 185, 254
Kopp, David, 66

L

LaHaye, Tim
on apostle John, 138
on celibacy, 208
on China, 130
on greatest revival, 100
on human history cycle, 263
on immortal soul of man, 213
on Lamb's Book of Life, 192
on rejoicing in heaven, 282
on Tribulation Saints, 105
laissez-faire, 249
Lake of Fire
the antichrist and False Prophet
will be judged immediately,
294
the beast will eventually go to
his destruction, 254
better off having a physical
death, 25
definition of, 294
Lalonde, Peter and Paul
on coming Armageddon, 230
on global economy, 277
on where will you spend
eternity, 224
Lamb's Book of Life, 40, 307,
308, 326
lampstands, 10
Last Days False Prophets, 194
Last Supper, 287
laying up their treasures in
heaven, 23
law for redemption of land, 69
lawless one, the, 196, 289

led to the slaughter, 72
life-giving qualities, 330
lights in the world, 28
Lindsey, Hal
on angels, 101
on Babylon, 255
on being an interpreter of
scripture, 10
on ecumenism, 248
on future's ecology, 114
on God's most beautiful
creation, 306
on grown men weeping, 273
on health and wealth gospel,
49
on Jewish Temple being
built, 149
on John describing the future,
12
on judgment of a Christ-
rejecting world, 89
on martyrs of the Tribulation,
222
on occultic mediums, 32
on occultism, 132
on one thousand years, 300
on peace process, 86
on redeemed saints in New
Jerusalem, 322
on religion, 251
on scrolls, 70
on Tribulation judgment, 91
literally fulfilled, 96
on valley of Megiddo, 218
on wedding feast of the
Lamb and His bride, 287
Little Horn, 81
Lord of lords, 46, 172, 215, 258
Lord's Vengeance, 110
Lucifer, 81, 121
See also Satan

M

maddening, 210
Malgo, Wim, 233
Man of Sin, 81
manna from heaven, 29
mark of the beast, 3, 199, 200,
212, 294
martyr
definition of, 26
the number will be more than
any man can count, 103

receive white robes signifying
the righteousness of Jesus, 91
McBirnie, William S., 187
McGee, J. Vernon
on body of Christ, 28
on David's covenant, 284
on Gog and Magog, 305
on life choices, 125
on Millennium, 300
on news on two witnesses, 160
on "these words are faithful
and true," 334
McMahon, T. A., 132
Melton, J. H.
on Christian unity, 212
on elements of praise, 283
on power of the devil, 126
on source of disaster and
trouble (for nonbelievers),
118
on wealth of a nation, 268
mercy, 127, 164, 216
mercy seat, 164, 225
Messiah, 44, 72, 147, 153, 338
See also Jesus Christ
messianic
definition of, 58, 300
expectations are rampant
among Jews in Israel, 58
Michael
angel, 110, 167, 174
Michaels, J. Ramsey
on kingdom of the world,
284
on voice in heaven, 176
Mid-Tribulation Rapture, 56
millennial kingdom, 287
millennium, 15
modern world
definition of, 202
two sets of symbols – the
alphabet and numbers, 202
money, 27, 276
Morris, Henry M.
on being the God/man, 338
on God being dead, 282
on God will finally give them
up, 231
on men love darkness, 234
on mighty river for every
need, 331
on taken to gehenna, 294
Morris, Leon
on angels, 105

on John wailing, 72
on Lamb, 330
on opening the seals, 75
on persecuted people of God,
266
Mosaic Law
definition of, 154
two witnesses to validate
matters, 154
Mother Earth Worship, 246
Mother of All Battles, 153, 218
Mother of Harlots, 245, 252,
285, 318
Mounce, Robert H.
on arrival of the end, 336
on decision of Eden, 332
on Lamb will overcome
because He is Lord of lords,
292
on "their mark declares their
master," 206
on those who emerge
victorious, 222
Mount of Olives, 171
Mount Sinai in a cloud, 136
Muslim
definition of, 151
Muslim, Christian, and Jew, 151,
152, 153
Mystery Babylon, 245, 247, 252,
253, 263, 318
mystery of lawlessness, 140, 348

N

name blotted out, 40
name of God, 46, 332
name of Jesus, 46
New Age, 42
new earth, 306
new heaven, 306
New Jerusalem, 46, 314
Newport, John P.
on God's wrath, 213
on John's two-fold message,
142
on victory of God's anointed
Messiah, 172
Nicodemus, 50
Nicolaitans, 20, 27
nihilism, 252
Ninety-five Theses, 38
Nirvana, 252
no real power, 23

non-monotheistic religion, 249

O

occult
definition of, 31, 189
one-world religion will
dominate this blind and
corrupt world, 189
Olivet Discourse, 150
Omega, 7
omnipotent, 73
omniscient, 73
one thousand six hundred
furlongs, 217
one-world harlot religion, 211
order of Melchizedek, 10
Orr, J. Edwin, 42
one hundred forty-four thousand
(144,000), 101, 205
overcome, 21

P

Pale Horse, 88, 89, 98
paradise, 21
parrot, 186
peace of God, 5
peace treaties, 84
Pentecost, 3, 9, 290
Pentecost, J. Dwight
on Battle of Armageddon,
236
on Beast, 259
on Satan not having the power
to give life, 188
permanent solution, 149
persecution, 22, 91, 175
person of Jesus Christ, 28
Philip, 332
phylacteries, 198
pillar of a cloud, 136
plagues
called the "last plagues," 221
definition of, 156
rider on red horse has four
weapons, 89
seven plagues, 224
political priesthood, 304
Pollock, Dennis, 101
position of power, 34
post-Tribulation rapture, 56
presence of God, 41, 264
pre-Tribulation rapture, 56, 57,
60

on predicted killer
    earthquake, 113
on rejecting the essential truth,
    19
on thousand years, 299
on treasures of the Tribulation,
    268
on war with the saints, 190
on worsening effects of the
    earth, 107
victory, 222

W

Walvoord, John F.
  on Christ's return, 136
  on locusts, 126
  on sea, 231
  on Tribulation, 151
water angel, 232
water into blood, 233
water of life, 316
wedding banquet, 286
wife of Christ, 246
wife of God, 246
White Horse, 83, 288
White, James F., 76
White, Vera K., 234
Wiersbe, Warren W.
  on God is in control, 93
  on Spirit of God, 48
  on wealth of a city, 270
Wilkinson, Bruce, 66
wine of the wrath of God, 212
winning crowns, 8
wisdom, 201
Witherington, Ben, III
  on city partakes of the very
      character of God, 319
  on contrast between the two
      great cities, 318
witness, 8
Woods, Andy
  on human history cycle, 263
Word Made Flesh, 6
works of Jesus, 34
Wormwood, 115, 116
worthiness, 109
wounded head, 188